S0-CPB-908

THE WAITE GROUP'S

Java™ 1.2

How-To

Steve Potts

EARTHWEB
PRESS

SAMS

201 West 103rd Street, Indianapolis, Indiana 46290

The Waite Group's Java 1.2 How-To

Copyright © 1999 by Sams

All rights reserved. No part of this book shall be reproduced, stored in a retrieval system, or transmitted by any means, electronic, mechanical, photocopying, recording, or otherwise, without written permission from the publisher. No patent liability is assumed with respect to the use of the information contained herein. Although every precaution has been taken in the preparation of this book, the publisher and author assume no responsibility for errors or omissions. Neither is any liability assumed for damages resulting from the use of the information contained herein.

International Standard Book Number: 1-57169-157-x

Library of Congress Catalog Card Number: 98-88181

Printed in the United States of America

First Printing: December 1998

00 99 98   4   3   2   1

Trademarks

All terms mentioned in this book that are known to be trademarks or service marks have been appropriately capitalized. The Waite Group cannot attest to the accuracy of this information. Use of a term in this book should not be regarded as affecting the validity of any trademark or service mark.

Warning and Disclaimer

Every effort has been made to make this book as complete and as accurate as possible, but no warranty or fitness is implied. The information provided is on an "as is" basis. The authors and the publisher shall have neither liability or responsibility to any person or entity with respect to any loss or damages arising from the information contained in this book or from the use of the CD or programs accompanying it.

EXECUTIVE EDITOR
Tim Ryan

ACQUISITIONS EDITOR
Steve Anglin

MANAGING EDITOR
Patrick Kanouse

PROJECT EDITOR
Rebecca Mounts

COPY EDITOR
Kitty Jarrett

INDEXER
John Sleeva

PROOFREADER
Kim Cofer

TECHNICAL EDITOR
Alexandre Calsavara

SOFTWARE DEVELOPMENT SPECIALIST
Adam Swetnam

INTERIOR DESIGN
Gary Adair

COVER DESIGN
Karen Ruggles

COVER ILLUSTRATION
Kevin Caddell

LAYOUT TECHNICIANS
Brandon Allen
Heather Moseman
Tim Osborn
Staci Somers
Mark Walchle

EarthWeb Press is a co-publishing partnership between EarthWeb and Macmillan Computer Publishing. Our mission is to serve Web developers, programmers, and IT professionals by giving them the technical information they need to build tomorrow's systems.

EarthWeb Inc. is the leading provider of Internet-based online services to the Information Technology (IT) community worldwide. Through its flagship service, developer.com, and its other integrated business-to-business online services including Datamation and ITKnowledge, EarthWeb addresses the needs of IT professionals for content, community, and commerce.

More than 150,000 technical resources can be found on EarthWeb's online services, including:

- The full text of hundreds of technical books

- 375+ proprietary tutorials

- In-depth explorations of the newest technologies

- Technical discussion boards led by industry experts

- Hard-to-find specialized IT products

- Technical job listings

For more information on EarthWeb, visit the corporate site at `www.earthweb.com`.

Macmillan Computer Publishing (MCP) is the world's largest computer book publisher. The books published in our two leading imprints, QUE and Sams, help computer users and programming professionals deal with the complexities of new technologies. Macmillan Publishing is much more than a print publisher—we are a multimedia content provider. Our information is available not only as bound books, but also as multimedia software products and online interactive Web sites. Our Web site includes:

- BetaBooks (`www.mcp.com/betabooks/`): See cutting-edge books in progress before they publish.

- Resource Center (`www.mcp.com/resources/`): Get code, utilities, Web links, and other support materials for our books and the technologies they cover.

- Personal Bookshelf (`www.mcp.com/personal/`): Register for access to five of our published books at a time for free.

For more information about MCP, please visit our main site at `www.mcp.com`.

CONTENTS AT A GLANCE

TABLE OF CONTENTS

ABOUT THE AUTHOR

Steve Potts is a software engineer at Mobile Security Communications specializing in Internet and Windows development. Steve received his Computer Science degree from Georgia Tech in 1982. He has been programming in C++, Visual Basic, Active Server Pages, and Java for many years. Prior to that he wrote PL/1, Focus, and Fortran programs on mainframe and mid-range computers. Steve has worked in a number of domains, but his deepest experience is in manufacturing. His previous books include *Using Visual C++ 4* and *Killer Borland C++ 4*.

DEDICATION

I would like to dedicate this book to my six children James, Jessica, Jeremy, Julie, Jennifer, and Jacob. They understand why Daddy can't always stop and play "Starcraft" or "Darby the Dragon" with them, even if he would like to. I would also like to thank Suzanne, my wife of 16 years, for the increased burdens she bears when I am "in" the computer, as she calls it.

ACKNOWLEDGMENTS

I would like to thank Tim Ryan, my Acquisitions Editor and his whole staff for their work to polish the book into something really impressive. Somehow my words seem more profound after they lay them into the pages so nicely. I would also like to thank Alexandre Calsavara, my technical editor. He really held my feet to the fire on this book, making sure that every sentence was not only correct, but precise.

TELL US WHAT YOU THINK!

As the reader of this book, *you* are our most important critic and commentator. We value your opinion and want to know what we're doing right, what we could do better, what areas you'd like to see us publish in, and any other words of wisdom you're willing to pass our way.

As the Executive Editor for the Java team at Macmillan Computer Publishing, I welcome your comments. You can fax, email, or write me directly to let me know what you did or didn't like about this book—as well as what we can do to make our books stronger.

Please note that I won't have time to help you with your Java code.

When you write, please be sure to include this book's title and author as well as your name and phone or fax number. I will carefully review your comments and share them with the author and editors who worked on the book.

Fax: 317-817-7070

Email: `java@mcp.com`

Mail: Tim Ryan
           Executive Editor
           Java
           Macmillan Computer Publishing
           201 West 103rd Street
           Indianapolis, IN 46290 USA

INTRODUCTION

As the Java language matures, the need for quality documentation describing its features and syntax increases. Many programmers have made the statement that all they really need is "a good example properly explained." The goal of this book is to give you exactly that. You will not find long, swelling explanations of the history and philosophy of Java and its features. What you will find is example after example covering as broad a range of Java topics as this humble author could create and still get this book to you in a timely fashion. I hope that the explanations will be strong enough for you to understand exactly why each line of code was put there.

I hope that you will find some examples that you can take right off the CD-ROM and place in your programs and then modify them to suit your requirements. You will find that many of the examples in this book are very short. This is intentional; I want you to be able to spend time working on getting your programs to run instead of getting mine to run.

QUESTION-AND-ANSWER FORMAT

The introduction to each example is in the form of a question. This is to make clear what the example is trying to show. A single example may illustrate anywhere between two and a dozen language features. The emphasis of each explanation is on the feature pointed to in the introduction of that example.

WHO THIS BOOK IS WRITTEN FOR

This book is written for programmers. It does not explain basic programming concepts, but assumes that you are familiar with programming in general. Non-Java programmers may be able to follow the text without difficulty if they have a background in object-oriented programming (OOP). Others may need to brush up on their OOP skills in order to derive the maximum benefit from this work.

WHAT YOU NEED TO USE THIS BOOK

In order to run the examples in this book, you will need a copy of the Java Development Kit (JDK) 1.2. You can download the JDK from the JavaSoft Web site at **www.javasoft.com**. The JDK is a command-line facility. You can run all the programs in this book from a UNIX or DOS command line using the `javac` compiler and either the `java` or `appletviewer` commands. It is likely that a number of Java 1.2–compliant development tools will be released about the time this book is released. These tools are nice, but not required.

OTHER RESOURCES

In addition to Sun's main Java site at `java.sun.com`, a great resource is the Gamelan site at `www.gamelan.com`. Gamelan has been around as long as Java, and it is endorsed by Sun Microsystems as the "Official Directory for Java." The site was recently relaunched to meet the new development needs stemming from the release of Java 1.2, and now contains sections covering such topics as e-commerce, security, distributing computing and Y2K, as well as information on progressive Java technologies including Jini, Enterprise JavaBeans, Embedded and Personal Java, Java Plug-in, and Java Cards.

CHAPTER 1

JAVA EXPLAINED

1

JAVA EXPLAINED

1.1 Java Versus C/C++

Java is the greatest buzzword in the history of computing. It is also a great combination of an object-oriented programming language and built-in class library. The developers of Java were trying to develop a powerful language with a small footprint. This small footprint, they reasoned, would enable Java applets to run on very small processors. The evolution of the Internet gave this design a great opportunity to shine. Internet machines are generally large PCs or workstations, but they are normally connected to the Net by "lite" wires, in the form of modems. This causes a bottleneck, and a program with a small footprint downloads quickly when included in an HTML document.

It has been argued that Java is what C++ should have been. Although Java is certainly easier to learn and use than C++, it would be unfair to "armchair quarterback" the fathers of C++ too much. C++ needed to be directly translatable into C, the dominant programming language of the early 1980s. Java had no such need. In addition, the Java designers had a decade of experience with C++ features and were therefore able to choose the best and discard the rest. Going second is always technically easier than being the pioneer.

Java has the familiar look of C and C++. Programmers with experience in C and C++ or related languages experience a short learning curve with Java. The flow control statements and operators function almost identically in Java as in C/C++. In addition, Java implements exception handling in much the same way as C++. Because of its different mission, Java includes a security manager that gives a system administrator control over how powerful a program is allowed to be. Some applets, downloaded from unknown sources, are given no access to the I/O functions, whereas other applications are given free reign.

But Java, unlike C, is object-oriented. And Java gains simplicity by not being bound by some of the dubious features of C and C++. This keeps Java relatively small and reduces much of the burden in programming robust applications. The sum of all the methods in all the classes is large, though, and takes quite a bit of experience to master.

Java is streamlined compared to C and C++. C evolved over many years, and many overlapping features developed. C++ added objects to C, but retained many inherent complexities. One of the major problems with C and C++ is the preprocessor. The C/C++ preprocessor can be used to turn the language into something completely unintelligible. This results in a significant amount of time spent understanding preprocessor macros and directives. Header files containing type information aren't needed in Java because class definitions are compiled into a binary form that retains type information. Java uses constants to serve the same role as a `# define`. It also declares classes instead of using `typedef`s.

In C++, structures and classes exhibit only subtle differences from one another and are, for the most part, redundant. For this reason, Java supports only classes.

Object-oriented programming replaces functional and procedural styles. Anything that can be done with a function can be done by defining a class and creating methods for that class. For this reason functions outside classes are unnecessary and are not present in Java.

C++ supports multiple inheritance, which can yield unpredictable results under pathological conditions. Java does not support multiple inheritance in the same manner as C++. A form of multiple inheritance is implemented by interfaces. An interface is a definition of a set of methods that one or more objects will implement. Interfaces declare only methods and constants, not variables. Interfaces strike a workable balance between full multiple inheritance and single inheritance only.

Although it's a powerful concept, operator overloading is not present in Java. Students of C++ find operator overloading difficult and cumbersome. In fact, many experienced C++ programmers do not use operator overloading effectively.

Although pointers are one of the greatest strengths of C, they are also one of its weaknesses. A misused pointer can yield unpredictable and catastrophic results. Even the most experienced programmer occasionally writes code that may run correctly for years and suddenly fails due to pointer misuse. Java supports pointers in the form of references to objects. References point to the object in much the same way as pointers, but they cannot be modified. All references are checked at compile time/runtime to guarantee that they refer to valid objects, compatible with the declared type. In addition, point math is not legal in Java. When Java no longer needs a piece of memory, automatic garbage collection reclaims it and makes it available for the program to reuse.

Additionally, the Java runtime system checks all array indexing to ensure that indices are within the bounds of an array.

One of the reasons for the popularity of Java is the support of standard class libraries called *packages* and *interfaces*. These packages represent thousands of effort years of coding, debugged and loaded on every platform where Java runs. This fact greatly simplifies cross-platform development. Some of the most important packages and interfaces are

- `java.awt.*`, which is the Abstract Windowing Toolkit. It provides a single way to create graphical applications on all platforms. You will learn how to use this in Chapter 6, "User Interface."

- The runnable interface, which allows you to implement multithreaded applications and applets. We study these in Chapter 4, "Threads."

- The Java Foundation Classes (JFC), which provide a native Java implementation of graphical objects such as buttons and pick lists. We study these in Chapter 8, "The JFC."

- `java.awt.event`, which is the event class. It allows you to detect user actions and respond to them. We study those in Chapter 5, "Events and Parameters."

All programming languages are built with some concept in mind. C was built with the intent to be easy to compile, to run fast, and to be portable between systems. C++ was built with the intent to promote code reusability through the use of class libraries, but with as few basic differences from C as possible. Java was developed with the intent to be similar to C++, so that Java could be learned quickly, but safer than C++, so that Java programmers wouldn't have to spend so much time chasing memory errors.

1.2 Keywords and Operators

Table 1.1 lists the keywords defined in the Java language. Table 1.2 shows the Java operators, listed in order of precedence.

Table 1.1 Java Keywords

abstract	boolean	break	byte	byvalue
case	cast	catch	char	class
const	continue	default	do	double
else	extends	final	finally	float
for	future	generic	goto	if
implements	import	inner	instanceof	int
interface	long	native	new	null
operator	outer	package	private	protected
public	rest	return	short	static
super	switch	synchronized	this	throw
throws	transient	try	var	void
volatile	while strictfp	widefp		

The keywords const and goto are reserved but not used in Java. The goto concept can be implemented using a labeled break. Note that null, true, and false look like keywords but technically are boolean literals. This is in contrast to C++, where boolean is really a typedef, not a part of the language.

Table 1.2 Java Operators

PRECEDENCE	OPERATOR	TYPE(S)	OPERATION PERFORMED
1	++	Arithmetic	Pre- or postincrement
	-	Arithmetic	Pre- or postdecrement
	+, -	Arithmetic	Unary plus, unary minus
	~	Integral	Bitwise complement
	!	Boolean	Logical complement
	(type)	Any	Cast
2	*, /, %	Arithmetic	Multiplication, division, remainder
3	+, -	Arithmetic	Addition, subtraction
	+	String	String concatenation
4	<<	Integral	Left shift
	>>	Integral	Arithmetic right shift
	>>>	Integral	Logical right shift
5	<, <=	Arithmetic	Less than, less than or equal to
	>, >=	Arithmetic	Greater than, greater than or equal to
	instanceof	Object	Type comparison

PRECEDENCE	OPERATOR	TYPE(S)	OPERATION PERFORMED
6	==	Primitive	Equal
	!=	Primitive	Not equal
	==	Object	Equal
	!=	Object	Not equal
7	&	Integral	Bitwise AND
	&	Boolean	Boolean AND
8	^	Integral	Bitwise XOR
	^	Boolean	Boolean XOR
9	¦	Integral	Bitwise OR
	¦	Boolean	Boolean OR
10	&&	Boolean	Conditional AND
11	¦¦	Boolean	Conditional OR
12	?:	Boolean, any, any	Conditional (ternary)
13	=, *=, /=, %=, +=, -=, <<=, >>=, >>>=, &=, ^=, ¦=	Variable, any	Assignment with operator

1.3 Data Types

Java supports all the primitive data types usually found in modern computer languages. For the most part, the Java language is similar to C and C++. The implementation of the data types has been more strictly defined in Java to help simplify the language and allow for platform independence. The size and form of the data types are precisely defined. The primitive data types are summarized in Table 1.3.

Table 1.3 Java Primitive Data Types

TYPE	DESCRIPTION	SIZE	MIN VALUE	MAX VALUE
boolean	True or false	1 bit	NA	NA
char	Unsigned integer	16 bits	\u0000	\uFFFF
byte	Signed integer	8 bits	-128	127
short	Signed integer	16 bits	-32768	32767
int	Signed integer	32 bits	-2147483648	2147483647
long	Signed integer	64 bits	-9223372036854775808	9223372036854775807

continued on next page

continued from previous page

TYPE	DESCRIPTION	SIZE	MIN VALUE	MAX VALUE
float	Signed floating-point	32 bits	+/-3.40282347E+38	+/-1.40239846E-45
double	Signed floating-point	64 bits	+/-1.79769313486231570E+308	+/-4.9406564584124 ➡6544E-324

Java does not allow casting between arbitrary types. Casting between numeric types and between subclasses and superclasses of the same objects is allowed. When lossy casts are done (for example, `int` to `byte`), the conversion is done modulo the length of the smaller type. In addition, Java performs automatic conversion when assigning a numeric value to a "larger" type, but assignment to smaller ones needs explicit casts.

Integer numeric types are 8-bit `byte`, 16-bit `short`, 32-bit `int`, and 64-bit `long`. An integer numeric type is a two's complement signed integer. There are no unsigned data types (except for `char`). The Java language adds the `>>>` operator to perform unsigned (logical) right shift.

Real numeric types are 32-bit `float` and 64-bit `double`. These types and their arithmetic operations are consistent with the IEEE 754 specification.

Character data is slightly different from that of C. Java uses the Unicode character set standard. The Unicode standard `char` is a 16-bit unsigned `char` rather than the 8-bit ASCII `char` used by C.

`boolean` is a data type that may take on the values `True` and `False`. In Java, a `boolean` is a distinct data type and may not be cast into any other type, and no other type may be cast into `boolean`.

Strings in Java are objects that differ from those of C and C++. In Java a string is not a null-terminated array of characters as it is in C. Instead, it is an instance of the `java.lang.String` class.

Java arrays are objects and are single-dimensional. Multidimensional arrays are implemented as arrays of arrays. An array of length n has n components, and the components are referenced by use of integers from 0 to $n-1$.

1.4 Control Statements

Java contains `if`, `else`, `switch`, `for`, `while`, `do`, `break`, `continue`, and `try-catch` statements. These statements are very similar to those in C++. There are only two significant differences. The first is that the Java `boolean` type cannot be cast to other types. The other difference is that the values `0` and `null` are not the same as `False`, and nonzero and `non null` values are not the same as `True`.

1.5 Applets Versus Applications

A Java application is composed of a Java class containing a `main()` method declared `public static void` and accepting a string array argument, plus any other classes that are referenced by the class containing `main()`. It derives its operating environment from the operating system on which it runs. An application can be as simple as a "Hello World" program, or as complicated as a modern word processor, or even a compiler (the `javac` compiler is itself a Java application). The full capabilities of the Java language and class libraries are available to Java applications.

A Java applet is composed of at least one public Java class that must be subclassed from `java.awt.Applet` (or subclassed from a class that subclasses `java.awt.Applet`). It derives its operating environment from a Java-enabled Web browser, such as Netscape Navigator or HotJava.

Applets are limited compared with applications because they are intended to be used across unsecure networks, such as the Internet. Applets aren't usually allowed to read or write to the local file system, and typically are not allowed to open network connections to any system other than the host from which the applet was downloaded.

1.6 Platform Independence

When a Java program is compiled, it is converted to an architecture-neutral byte-code format. This byte-code can then be run on any system, as long as that system implements the Java Virtual Machine (JVM). The JVM is a software layer that implements the portable Java constructs in the facilities available on that machine. Because the Java program is compiled to byte-code, and not native machine code, a Java interpreter is needed to execute the program. Therefore, Java is an interpreted language and currently does not offer the performance of compiled C. The introduction of just-in-time compilers for Java increases the speed closer to that of modern C and C++ compilers. Just-in-time compilers do a last-minute compile immediately before running the application for the first time. In C++, on the other hand, the programmer compiles the program before including it in the installation materials.

A simple Java application can be written just by use of calls to `System.in.readln( )` for input and `System.out.println()` for output. It resembles a simple command-line program such as those typically found in UNIX or MS-DOS. For many applications, this is all that is necessary. On the other hand, most modern operating systems—for example, Macintosh, Windows 98, Windows NT, UNIX—use a graphical user interface (GUI). Application users expect to have windows, icons, and mouse control. GUI environments are different from one operating system to the next, so most programs are written for a specific GUI. The effort necessary to move a program from one environment to another is prohibitive. This is where Java truly shines: If Java code is written once, it can be used in any environment where the JVM has been ported. As of this writing, Java can run under Solaris, IRIX, Linux, Windows 95, Windows 98, Windows NT, Macintosh, OS/2, Windows 3.1, and even palm-top computers. This is the Holy Grail of truly portable code—write it once and it runs everywhere (well, almost).

The key to this unprecedented portability is the Abstract Windowing Toolkit (AWT). The AWT is a set of Java classes that depend on native classes to interact with the native GUI. Each of these classes depends upon the Java virtual machine to translate this behavior to appropriate calls for the native GUI. In addition, the Java Foundation Classes (JFC) provide a 100% Java-built GUI that can imitate the look and feel of Motif or Windows, or display a look and feel that is uniquely Java.

CHAPTER 2
GETTING STARTED

2

GETTING STARTED

How do I...

This chapter covers how to perform many basic operations in Java. These operations include outputting text to the screen, taking input from the keyboard, reading and writing files, using arrays, and manipulating strings and numeric types. The information contained in this chapter is similar to that for C/C++ and should be straightforward to understand for those with C/C++ experience.

Every example in this chapter is an application and does not work as an applet. Some topics covered are specific to applications and would not work in applets. These include command-line arguments (applets have applet parameters), and reading and writing to a file (by default, applets cannot read or write to the local hard drive). However, the fundamental operations, such as converting strings to and from numbers, concatenating strings and numbers, parsing strings, and using arrays and math methods, are applicable in applets and applications.

2.1 Output Text to the Screen

This section shows how to print text. The sample illustrates printing of text and numeric values, but, unlike examples used in most computer books, it does not print `"Hello World"`.

2.2 Accept Input from the Keyboard

This section demonstrates taking input from the keyboard. The example prompts the user to enter a string of characters, and then outputs the string and number of characters in the string.

2.3 Convert Strings to Numbers

It is useful to be able to convert strings to numbers. In Java, input from the keyboard is returned as a string. If the input is needed as a number, the string must be converted to a numeric type. This example demonstrates converting keyboard input to various numeric types.

2.4 Convert Numbers to Strings

This section demonstrates the conversion of numbers to strings. The example computes the current U.S. national debt. Because this number is so large, the application converts the debt to a string and inserts separating commas to make it easier to read. The `Date()` constructor and `getTime()` method are also discussed.

2.5 Access Command-Line Arguments

Command-line arguments are frequently used in programming. This section demonstrates the use of command line arguments in Java. The application takes the month and year as arguments, and outputs them.

2.6 Read from a File

This application demonstrates how to read a file in Java. The filename to be read is taken as a command-line argument. The file is then displayed on the screen, using a process similar to that of the UNIX `more` utility.

2.7 Write to a File

Learning to read from a file would not be complete without learning how to write a file. The application in this section translates text files between DOS,

UNIX, and Macintosh formats. The file is read and the line terminators are changed to the format specified in the command-line argument.

2.8 Concatenate Strings and Numbers

Concatenating strings and numbers allows for easy printing of various values in one print statement. This section concatenates a string with a date.

2.9 Use Arrays

The use of arrays is demonstrated in this section. The data from a file is read into an array and then sorted by using the `quicksort` algorithm.

2.10 Parse a String

This example demonstrates a useful feature, the ability to parse a single string. The string is broken into substrings that are separated by arbitrary characters. The example searches a file of names and phone numbers for a name supplied as a command-line argument.

2.11 Use Math Functions

Java contains many math functions that are required to perform various tasks. This section illustrates the use of several math functions by calculating the monthly payment for a loan.

COMPLEXITY
BEGINNING

2.1 How do I...
Output text to the screen?

Problem

I need to output some common conversion factors on the screen. I need to output both text and double-precision floating-point values. Strict formatting of the numbers is not necessary, but I want each of the factors on a different line. What is the easiest way to output text and numbers?

Technique

The Java runtime provides classes for printing strings and basic numeric types. The methods of interest for this example are `print` and `println`. These methods for printing to the screen (standard output) are contained in the `System.out` stream object. Streams manage the transfer of data from a program to physical devices such as files, printers, and screens.

Steps

1. Create the application source file. Create a new file called `Convert.java` and enter the following source:

```
/*
Convert.class prints a short table of common
➥conversion factors.
*/

class Convert {

/*
 * Note that the main method must be defined as
 * public static void main (String []) to be called from
 * the Java interpreter.
 */

public static void main (String args[]) {

   double mi_to_km = 1.609;
   double gals_to_l = 3.79;
   double kg_to_lbs = 2.2;

   System.out.print ("1 Mile equals\t");
System.out.print (mi_to_km);
   System.out.println ("\tKilometers");

   System.out.print ("1 Gallon equals\t");
   System.out.print (gals_to_l);
   System.out.print ("\tLiters\n");

   System.out.print ("1 Kilogram equals\t");
   System.out.print (kg_to_lbs);
   System.out.println ("\tPounds");
}
}
```

2. Compile and test the application. Compile the source using `javac` or the makefile provided. Test the application by typing

```
java Convert
```

When the application is run, the conversion factors for miles to kilometers, gallons to liters, and pounds to kilograms should be printed on the screen. Figure 2.1 shows an example of the output.

How It Works

The `Convert` class contains only one method, `main`. This is analogous to the `main` function in C and C++. The Java interpreter begins execution of a standalone application by calling the `main` method.

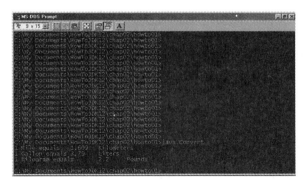

Figure 2.1 Output is sent to the screen using the `System.out.print` method.

Three conversion factors are declared as type **double** and initialized to their respective values. Printing is done by calling the **System.out.print** or **System.out.println** methods. The latter forces a trailing newline, whereas the former does not. Several **print** and **println** methods exist, each accepting different types as arguments. This example uses the methods accepting **String** and **double**.

Many of the escape sequences familiar to the C/C++ programmer are available in Java. Table 2.1 lists the escape sequences and their functions. In this example \t is used for tabbing, and \n is used to force a newline. The Unicode values represent the international character codes. Eastern character sets like Chinese and Japanese are much larger than the ASCII character sets and therefore require a different system of representation.

Table 2.1 Java Escape Sequences

ESCAPE SEQUENCE	UNICODE VALUE	FUNCTION	ASCII NAME
\b	\u0008	Backspace	BS
\t	\u0009	Horizontal tab	HT
\n	\u000a	Line feed	LF
\f	\u000c	Form feed	FF
\r	\u000d	Carriage return	CR
\"	\u0022	Double quote	"
\'	\u0027	Single quote	'
\\	\u005c	Backslash	\

> **NOTE**
>
> The main method must be defined as public static void main
> (String []). If it is not, the Java interpreter will not recognize it as the
> starting point for the application and will print an error message. Also
> note that the program source filename must agree with the name of
> the class containing main under most implementations; for example,
> class myMainClass must be in file myMainClass.java.

Return from **main**, as in C/C++, terminates execution of the program. **main** cannot return values because it is of type **void**. A method analogous to the C function **exit()** provides a mechanism for returning application completion status. It is demonstrated in later examples.

Comments

Java does not provide an equivalent of the C function **printf**. The C **printf** is capable of strict formatting of numeric values and accepts a variable argument list. The Java **print** methods are not as sophisticated; they do not allow the programmer to specify details of numeric formatting and, like all Java methods, accept only a fixed set of arguments and types.

The fact that the arguments to Java methods are always checked for type consistency precludes the possibility of variable arguments and types.

COMPLEXITY
BEGINNING

2.2 How do I...
Accept input from the keyboard?

Problem

I would like to take a string input from the keyboard and display the number of characters typed. How do I accept input from the keyboard?

Technique

The **readLine** method takes input from **BufferedReader** and returns a string. **readLine** is the method needed to accept input from the keyboard. The length of the input string can be determined by use of the **length** method in the **String** class. The string and its length can be printed using **print** or **println**. Each read request made of a **Reader** can cause a corresponding read request to be made of the underlying stream. It is therefore advisable to wrap a **BufferedReader** around any **Reader** whose **read()** operations may be costly, such as a **FileReader** or an **InputStreamReader**.

Steps

1. Create the application source file. Create a new file called `Input.java` and enter the following source:

```java
import java.io.*;

/*
 * Input.class reads a line of text from standard input,
 * determines the length of the line, and prints it.
 */

class Input {
public static void main (String args[]) {
      String input = "";
      boolean error;

/*
 * BufferedReader contains the readLine method.
 * Create a new instance for standard input System.in
 */
BufferedReader in = new BufferedReader
➡(new InputStreamReader(System.in));
/*
 * This loop is used to catch I/O exceptions that may occur
 */
      do {
            error = false;
            System.out.print ("Enter the string > ");

/*
 * We need to flush the output - no newline at the end
 */
            System.out.flush ();

            try {
                  input = in.readLine ();
} catch (IOException e) {
                  System.out.println (e);
System.out.println
➡("An input error was caught");
error = true;
            }
      } while (error);

      System.out.print ("You entered \"");
      System.out.print (input);        /
System.out.println ("\"");
      System.out.print ("The length is ");
      System.out.println (input.length ());
} // end of main ()
}
```

2. Compile and test the application. Compile the source using `javac` or the makefile provided. Test the application by typing

```
java Input
```

3. The application prompts you to enter a string. Type the string and then press Enter. The string and the number of characters in the string are then printed. Figure 2.2 shows sample output.

Figure 2.2 Keyboard input is made available to the program via the BufferedReader class.

How It Works

A new BufferedReader must be created for input from the keyboard. This is accomplished by calling the BufferedReader constructor with System.in (standard input) as the argument. readLine can throw an IOException, so a do-while loop containing a try-catch block is used to accommodate the exception. readLine returns a string that is assigned to the String variable input.

The String input is printed by using print. The length of input is determined by using the length method of the String class.

> **NOTE**
>
> It is necessary to import classes in java.io because that is where BufferedReader is located.

Strings that do not contain newlines at the end may not always be flushed on all systems. To ensure consistent results, System.out is flushed after the user prompt is printed.

Comments

readLine does not include a newline or carriage return at the end of the string it returns. This simplifies code in many cases.

2.3 How do I...
Convert strings to numbers?

Problem

I need a program to calculate the tip for a restaurant bill. The user will enter the bill amount and the percentage of tip in response to a prompt. To make the calculation, I need to convert the input strings to numbers. How do I convert strings to numbers?

Technique

The user will be prompted for the bill amount and tip percentage by use of `print`. The input will be taken by use of `readLine`, as in the previous example. As seen in the previous example, `readLine` takes input from the keyboard and returns a string. The calculation requires the input string to be converted to numbers—`double` and `int`, in this case. The conversions are performed by using the `valueOf` method contained in both the `Double` and `Integer` classes. The `Double` and `Integer` classes wrap a value of the primitive type in an object. An object of type `Double` contains a single field whose type is `double`.

This class provides several methods for converting `integer`s and `double`s to a `String`s.

Steps

1. Create the application source file. Create a new file called `Tip.java` and enter the following source:

```
import java.io.*;

/*
 * Tip.class calculates the tip, given the bill and tip percentage
 */

class Tip {
public static void main (String args[]) {
        String input = "";
        int tip_percent=0;
        double bill=0, tip=0;
        boolean error;

    BufferedReader in = new BufferedReader
➥(new InputStreamReader(System.in));

        do {
                error = false;
```

```
                    System.out.print ("Enter the bill total > ");
                    System.out.flush ();
                    try {
                            input = in.readLine ();
                    } catch (IOException e) {
                            System.out.println (e);
                            System.exit (1);
                    }

 /*
  * Convert input string to double,
  */
                    try {
                            bill = Double.valueOf (input)
➥.doubleValue();
} catch (NumberFormatException e) {
                            System.out.println (e);
                            System.out.println ("Please try again");
                            error = true;
                    }
            } while (error);

            do {
                    error = false;
                    System.out.print ➥
 ("Enter the tip amount in percent > ");
System.out.flush ();
                    try {
                            input = in.readLine ();
                    } catch (IOException e) {
                            System.out.println (e);
                            System.exit (1);
                    }

 /*
  * This time convert to Integer
  */
                    try {
                            tip_percent = Integer.valueOf
➥(input).intValue();
} catch (NumberFormatException e) {
                            System.out.println (e);
                            System.out.println ("Please try again");
                            error = true;
                    }
            } while (error);

        System.out.print ("The total is ");
          tip = bill * ((double) tip_percent)/100.0;
          System.out.println (bill + tip);
} // end of main ()
}
```

2. Compile and test the application. Compile the source using `javac`. Test the application by typing

```
java Tip
```

This application prompts for two values. The first is the amount of the bill, and the second is the percentage of tip you would like to leave. At each prompt, type the value and press Enter. When both values are entered, the total amount of the bill plus tip will be printed. (Please be kind to your servers!) Figure 2.3 shows an example of output from `Tip.java`.

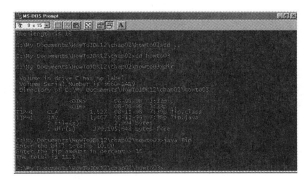

Figure 2.3 The `valueOf()` method performs numeric conversions.

How It Works

The bill is converted to a `double` by use of `Double.valueOf(String)` `.doubleValue ()`. The tip percentage is converted by use of a similar method to convert to an integer—`Integer.valueOf (Integer).intValue()`. The `valueOf` method can throw a `NumberFormatException` if the input string is improperly formatted; for example, if the user were to input `20..30`. This is handled gracefully: The user is asked to enter the value again. The computation and printing of the bill total is straightforward.

Comments

In this example, an `IOException` caught during input causes the program to terminate with exit status 1. This is accomplished by calling `System.exit` with the exit status as an argument.

2.4 How do I...
Convert numbers to strings?

Problem

I have a first-order calculation of the U.S. national debt and the U.S. population. The problem is that the debt is such a large number, it is difficult to read the numbers without delimiting commas. I want to format the numbers with commas every three digits. The print method will not do this. What I need to do is convert the numbers to strings and print them with delimiting commas. How do I convert the numbers to strings?

Technique

The process of converting numbers to strings is similar to converting strings to numbers. The `valueOf` method contained in the `String` class performs exactly this function.

After the numbers are converted to strings, separating commas can be printed by alternately printing three digits and a comma. The three digits are printed by use of the `substring` method in the `String` class.

Steps

1. Create the application source file. Create a new file called `BigNum.java` and enter the following source:

```java
/*
 * BigNum.class converts a very large number to a string
 * and then prints it out
 */
class BigNum {

public static void main (String args[]) {

/*
 * Good thing longs are 64 bits!
 */
    long debt = 3965170506502L;
    long pop = 250410000;

    print ("The 1992 national debt was $", debt);
    print ("The  1992 population was ", pop);
    print ("Each person owed $", debt/pop);
}

/*
 * print method converts a long to a string with commas
```

```
 * for easy reading.  We need it with these big numbers!
 *    String str        preceding label
 *     long n          the long to format and print
 */
public static void print (String str,long n) {
    System.out.print (str);          // print the label
    String buf = String.valueOf (n);     // Integer to String

    int start, end, ncommas, i;
    int buflen = buf.length ();

/*
 * It's a crazy algorithm, It works from left to right
 */
    ncommas = buflen/3;
    if (ncommas * 3 == buflen) ncommas -= 1;
    start = 0;
    end = buflen-(3*ncommas);
    System.out.print (buf.substring (start, end));
    for (i=0; i<ncommas; i+=1) {
        start = end;
        end = start+3;
        System.out.print (",");
        System.out.print (buf.substring (start, end));
    }
    System.out.println ("");    // The final newline
}
}
```

2. Compile and test the application. Compile the source using `javac`. Test the application by typing

```
java BigNum
```

This application prints three lines containing the U.S. national debt, the population, and each personís share of the debt. See Figure 2.4 for an example of the output.

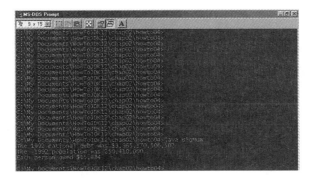

Figure 2.4 The `substring()` method can be used to isolate part of a string.

How It Works

The U.S. national debt and population are calculated to first order by multi-plying the growth rates by the difference in time and adding values at known points in time. This gives the current values of debt and population in 64-bit long integers. A `print` method is defined; it prints a label and then formats and prints long integers with separating commas.

The `print` method takes a long integer and converts it to a string by using the `valueOf` method contained in the `String` class. The number of commas required is calculated. The first digits (up to three digits) are printed by extracting the substring. A `for` loop prints commas and the remaining three-digit groups in pairs.

Comments

`String.valueOf`, unlike `Long.valueOf`, does not throw any exceptions. Therefore, a `try-catch` block should not be used around the conversion.

`Long`s are 64-bit integers. The U.S. national debt and the number of milli-seconds cannot be contained in a 32-bit integer.

COMPLEXITY
BEGINNING

2.5 How do I...
Access command-line arguments?

Problem

I want to write a program and provide the month and year as command-line arguments to the utility. I need to access the command-line arguments. How do I do that?

Technique

The command-line arguments are passed to Java `main` methods as an array of strings. The argument count is determined by the `length` method. The arguments may be converted to numbers by using techniques discussed in previous sections of this chapter.

Steps

1. Create the application source file. Create a new file called `Parms.java` and enter the following source:

```
/* Parms.class prints the month and year, which are passed in
 * as command-line arguments
```

```
 */
class Parms {

public static void main (String args[]) {

/*
 * Java, unlike C/C++, does not need argument count (argc)
 */
        if (args.length < 2) {
                System.out.println ("usage: java Parms <month>
<year>");
System.exit (1);
        }

/*
 * Unlike in C/C++, args[0] is the FIRST argument.
 * The application name is not available as an argument
 */
        int month = Integer.valueOf (args[0]).intValue();
        int year = Integer.valueOf (args[1]).intValue();
        if (month < 1 || month > 12) {
                System.out.println
("Month must be between 1 and 12");
System.exit (1);
        }
        if (year < 1970) {
                System.out.println
("Year must be greater than 1969");
System.exit (1);
        }

        System.out.print ("The month that you entered is  ");
        System.out.println (month);
        System.out.print ("The year that you entered is  ");
        System.out.println (year);
}
}
```

2. Compile and test the application. Compile the source using `javac`. Test the application by typing

```
java Parms <month> <year>
```

3. A response is displayed. Try entering numbers out of range for the arguments (for example, a month equal to 15) or no arguments at all. Figure 2.5 contains sample output.

How It Works

Like all good utilities, **Parms** first checks the number of arguments to make sure that just the month and year have been entered. This is done by applying the **length** method to the command-line argument array **args**. If the number of arguments is not correct, a proper-usage message is printed, and the program exits.

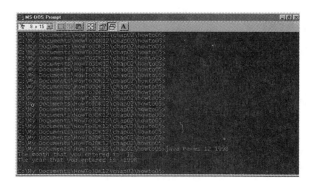

Figure 2.5 Parameters can be placed on the command line.

There are several differences between command-line argument handling in Java and C/C++:

- C/C++ explicitly passes the argument count to `main`; Java does not.

- C/C++ passes an array of characters; Java passes an array of strings.

- The program name is the first argument, `argv[0]`, in C/C++. In Java, the program name is not available; the first argument is the first array element, `args[0]`.

The month and year are converted to integers by means of `Integer.valueOf` and checked to be sure they are within limits. The balance of the code is straightforward.

COMPLEXITY
BEGINNING

2.6   How do I...
Read from a file?

Problem

I want to write a program similar to the UNIX **more** utility. I know how to print strings, but I donít know how to read from a file. How do I open and read from a file?

Technique

You open files by creating a `FileInputStream` with the filename as an argument. `FileInputStream` throws an exception if an error occurs. To read lines from the `FileInputStream`, a `BufferedReader` must be created from `FileInputStream`. This is similar to the procedure outlined in previous examples for keyboard input.

Reading from `BufferedReader` is accomplished by calling `readLine`. `readLine` returns `null` on end of file. A count of lines read and printed is maintained, and the user is prompted to see more when 23 lines are displayed.

Finally, the file is closed by applying the `close` method on the `FileInputStream`.

Steps

1. Create the application source file. Create a new file called `More.java` and enter the following source:

```
import java.io.*;

/*
 * More.class similar to UNIX more utility
 */
class More {

public static void main (String args[])
{
        String buf;
        FileInputStream fs=null;
        int nlines;

        if (args.length != 1) {
                System.out.println ("usage: java More <file>");
                System.exit (1);
         }
/*
 * Try to open the filename specified by args[0]
 */
        try {
                fs = new FileInputStream (args[0]);
        } catch (Exception e) {
                System.out.println (e);
                System.exit (1);
         }

/*
 * Create a BufferedReader associated with FileInputStream fs
 *
 */
        BufferedReader ds = new BufferedReader
➥(new InputStreamReader(fs));
BufferedReader keyboard = new BufferedReader
➥(new InputStreamReader(System.in));
```

```
                        nlines = 0;
                        while (true) {
                                try {
                                        buf = ds.readLine ();          // read 1 line
                                        if (buf == null) break;
                                } catch (IOException e) {
                                        System.out.println (e);
                                        break;
                                }
                                System.out.println (buf);
        nlines += 1;
                                if (nlines % 23 == 0) {  // 23 lines/pages vt100
        System.out.print ("—More—");
                                        System.out.flush ();
                                        try {
                                                keyboard.readLine ();
                                        } catch (IOException e) {
                                        }
                                }
                        }
        /*
         * close can throw an exception also,
         * and catch it for completeness
         */
                try {
                        fs.close ();
                } catch (IOException e) {
                        System.out.println (e);
                }
        }
        }
```

2. Compile and test the application. Compile the source using `javac`. Test the application by typing

```
java More <file>
```

3. The `<file>` specified is displayed, one screen at a time. Use the Enter key to advance to the next screen. An example of the output is shown in Figure 2.6.

How It Works

The name of the file to be viewed is available as the first command-line argument, so this is used to create the **FileInputStream**, **fs**. An exception is thrown if the file does not exist, or if some other error occurs. The exception is caught and printed, and causes immediate program termination.

Two **BufferedReaders** are opened. One is for the file, and the other is for the keyboard. The program continues to read lines from the file until end of file is encountered, which results in a null return from **readLine**. The file is closed when the end of file is encountered. The **close** method throws an **IOException** that is caught and printed.

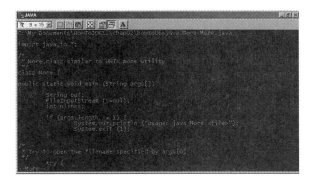

Figure 2.6 Reading from a file can be accomplished by using the `FileInputStream` object.

Comments

Java does not differentiate between text files and binary files because Java does not understand Ctrl+Z as end of file on text files. This is immaterial on UNIX and Macintosh systems, but can be of some consequence on Windows machines. It is safe to assume that the Java runtime treats all files as binary.

As with the keyboard input shown in How-To 2.2, `readLine` from a file does not include the line terminator.

COMPLEXITY
BEGINNING

2.7 How do I...
Write to a file?

Problem

Different systems use different line terminators for text files. DOS uses carriage return and line feed, Macintosh uses only carriage return, and UNIX uses only line feed. I use all these systems and occasionally need to translate text files from one machine to another. I would like to write a utility that could do this kind of translation.

I learned how to read files from the previous example, but now I need to write to files. How do I write to a file?

Technique

As with the previous example, a `FileInputStream` and a `BufferedReader` must be opened for reading a file. To write to a file, you use `FileOutputStream` and `PrintStream`.

The writing is done by applying the **print** and **println** methods to a
PrintStream created from a valid **FileOutputStream**. Each line in the input
file is read into a buffer and written to the output file. Depending on the type of
format translation required, either a carriage return, a line feed, or a carriage
return-line feed is written.

When end of file is encountered, both files are closed, and the program
terminates.

Steps

1. Create the application source file. Create a new file called **Format.java**
and enter the following source:

```java
import java.io.*;

/*
Format.class translates a text file
* to either DOS, Mac, or UNIX
* format.  The differences are in line termination.
 */
class Format {

static final int TO_DOS = 1;
static final int TO_MAC = 2;
static final int TO_UNIX = 3;
static final int TO_UNKNOWN = 0;

static void usage () {
        System.out.print ("usage: java Format -dmu <in-file> ");
        System.out.println ("<out-file>");
        System.out.println ("\t-d converts <in-file> to DOS");
        System.out.println ("\t-m converts <in-file> to MAC");
        System.out.println ("\t-u converts <in-file> to UNIX");
}

public static void main (String args[])
{
        int format=TO_UNKNOWN;
        String buf;
        FileInputStream fsIn = null;
        FileOutputStream fsOut = null;

        if (args.length != 3) { // you must specify format, in, out
usage ();
                System.exit (1);
        }

/*
args[0] is a String, so we can use
 * the equals (String) method for
* comparisons
 */
```

```
            if (args[0].equals ("-d")) format = TO_DOS; else
            if (args[0].equals ("-m")) format = TO_MAC; else
            if (args[0].equals ("-u")) format = TO_UNIX; else {
                    usage ();
                    System.exit (1);
            }

            try {
                    fsIn = new FileInputStream (args[1]);
            } catch (Exception e) {
                    System.out.println (e);
                    System.exit (1);
            }

    /*
     * FileOutputStream is the complement of FileInputStream
     */
            try {
                    fsOut = new FileOutputStream (args[2]);
            } catch (Exception e) {
                    System.out.println (e);
                    System.exit (1);
            }
        BufferedReader dsIn = new BufferedReader
➡(new InputStreamReader(fsIn));

            PrintStream psOut = new PrintStream (fsOut);
            while (true) {
                    try {
                            buf = dsIn.readLine ();
                            if (buf == null) break;          // break on
EOF
                    } catch (IOException e) {
                            System.out.println (e);
                            break;
                    }
                    psOut.print (buf);
                    switch (format) {
                            case TO_DOS:
                            psOut.print ("\r\n");
                            break;

                            case TO_MAC:
                            psOut.print ("\r");
                            break;

                            case TO_UNIX:
                            psOut.print ("\n");
                            break;
                    }
            }

    /*
     */
            try {
                    fsIn.close ();
```

```
                fsOut.close ();
        } catch (IOException e) {
                System.out.println (e);
        }
    }
}
```

2. Compile and test the application. Compile the source using `javac`. Test
the application by typing

```
java Format -<d¦m¦u> <input file> <output file>
```

Use the `-d` option when conversion to DOS is required, the `-m` option for
Macintosh, and the `-u` for UNIX. Figure 2.7 shows output from
`Format.java` when no arguments are supplied and when arguments are
supplied.

Figure 2.7 Data can be written to files using the
`PrintStream` object.

How It Works

Three command-line arguments are expected: the conversion option, the input
filename, and the output filename. If the arguments are not all present, a
proper-usage message is printed and the program terminates immediately. The
conversion option is tested for equality by using the equals method from the
String class to determine which conversion is to be performed.

The input file is opened just as it was in previous examples. The output file
is opened by calling the **FileOutputStream** constructor with the output filename as an argument. Like **FileInputStream**, **FileOutputStream** also throws
an exception if an error occurs.

A **BufferedReader** is created for the input file, and a **PrintStream** is created
for the output file. Lines are read from the input file one at a time and written
to the output file. A **switch** statement determines the type of line termination
required and supplies it.

The files are closed when end of input file is encountered.

Comments

As a point of symmetry, you might ask why `PrintStream` was used for output instead of `DataOutputStream`. Many of the methods contained in `BufferedReader` have counterparts in `DataOutputStream`. Unfortunately, there is no counterpart to `readLine`; that is, there is no `writeLine`. Instead `print` and `println` perform the inverse function to `readLine` and are found in `PrintStream`. Also note that `print` and `println` do not throw any exceptions. Table 2.3 lists the methods available in `PrintStream`.

The final `try-catch` block containing the `close` methods could be done differently. Clearly, an error in the first `close` keeps the second from executing. In this case, there is little consequence because the program immediately exits, and the operating system closes any open files.

Table 2.3 The `PrintStream` Class Constructors and Methods

METHOD	DESCRIPTION
`PrintStream(OutputStream)`	(Constructor) Creates a new `PrintStream`
`PrintStream(OutputStream, boolean)`	Creates a new `PrintStream`, with auto\ (constructor) flushing
`checkError()`	Flushes the print stream and returns whether there was an error on the output stream
`close()`	Closes the stream
`flush()`	Flushes the stream
`print(Object)`	Prints an object
`print(String)`	Prints a string
`print(char[])`	Prints an array of characters
`print(char)`	Prints a character
`print(int)`	Prints an integer
`print(long)`	Prints a `long`
`print(float)`	Prints a `float`
`print(double)`	Prints a double
`print(boolean)`	Prints a boolean
`println()`	Prints a newline
`println(Object)`	Prints an object followed by a newline
`println(String)`	Prints a string followed by a newline
`println(char[])`	Prints an array of characters followed by a newline
`println(char)`	Prints a character followed by a newline

continued on next page

continued from previous page

METHOD	DESCRIPTION
println(int)	Prints an integer followed by a newline
println(long)	Prints a long followed by a newline
println(float)	Prints a float followed by a newline
println(double)	Prints a double followed by a newline
println(boolean)	Prints a boolean followed by a newline
write(int)	Writes a byte
write(byte[], int, int)	Writes a subarray of bytes

COMPLEXITY
INTERMEDIATE

2.8 How do I...
Concatenate strings and numbers?

Problem

I would like to print a date and the day of month, along with some text. I know how to print strings and numbers. I would like to be able to print the text and numbers in a single **print** statement. How do I concatenate strings and numbers?

Technique

In Java the concatenation of strings and numbers is very straightforward. The strings and numbers are concatenated by using the + character.

Steps

1. Create the application source file. Create a new file called Stringcat.java and enter the following source:

```
import java.io.*;

/*
 * Stringcat.class prints integers and strings together.
 */
class Stringcat {

public static void main (String args[]) {
        String today = "";
        int monthday = 15;
```

```
/* The string "Today is " and date are concatenated together and
 * assigned to the String today.
 */
        today = "Today is the " + monthday + "th";

/* The String today is printed with println
 */
        System.out.println (today);

/* Here two text strings are concatenated with the integer
   monthday within the println method.
 */
        System.out.println ("Today is the " + monthday +
        " day of the month");

} // end of main ()
}
```

2. Compile and test the application. Compile the source using `javac`. Test the application by typing

```
java Stringcat
```

Figure 2.8 shows output from `Stringcat.java`.

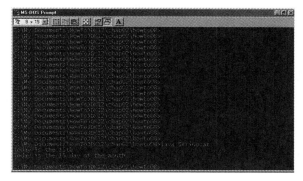

Figure 2.8 Strings can be combined by using the concatenation operator.

How It Works

This example is relatively straightforward. The concatenation of strings and numbers is illustrated in two ways. The first creates the string **today** and assigns it to the date, concatenated with the string of characters **"Today is"** using the concatenation character +. The new string is then printed with `println`. The second example performs the concatenation sequence inside the `println` method. Alternatively, you can concatenate something with a null string (`""+<object>`) as a shortcut to converting any object or primitive type to a string.

2.9 How do I...
Use arrays?

Problem

I have a file of names that I would like to sort. I am told that `quicksort` is an efficient algorithm for sorting data, but the data must reside in an array of some type. I need to read the file into an array, sort it, and print it. How do I use arrays?

Technique

An array needs to be created to hold strings read from the input file. This is done by using the `new` keyword in the same way as is done with other data types. The data in the file is read into the array and sorted by using the `quick-sort` algorithm. `quicksort` is significantly faster than many other sorting methods, such as bubble sort.

Steps

1. Create the application source file. Create a new file called `Sort.java` and enter the following source:

```
import java.io.*;

/*
 * Sort.class reads a text file specified by args[0] and
 * sorts each line for display
 */
class Sort {

static final int NMaxLines = 128;    // an arbitrary limit

public static void main (String args[]) {
/*
 * Allocate new array of strings; this is where the file
 * is read and sorted in place
 */
        String sortArray[] = new String [NMaxLines];
        FileInputStream fs=null;
        int nlines;

        if (args.length != 1) {
                System.out.println ("usage: java Sort <file>");
                System.exit (1);
        }
        try {
                fs = new FileInputStream (args[0]);
```

```
            } catch (Exception e) {
                    System.out.println ("Unable to open "+args[0]);
                    System.exit (1);
            }

        BufferedReader ds = new BufferedReader
➥(new InputStreamReader(fs));

        for (nlines=0; nlines<NMaxLines; nlines += 1) {
                try {
                        sortArray[nlines] = ds.readLine ();
                        if (sortArray[nlines] == null) break;
                } catch (IOException e) {
                        System.out.println
➥ ("Exception caught during read.");
break;
                }
        }
        try {
                fs.close ();
        } catch (IOException e) {
                System.out.println
➥("Exception caught closing file.");
}

/*
 * Sort in place and print
 */
        QSort qsort = new QSort ();
        qsort.sort (sortArray, nlines);
        print (sortArray, nlines);
}

/*
 * print method prints an array of strings of n elements
 *      String a[]    array of strings to print
 *      int n         number of elements
 */
private static void print (String a[], int n) {
        int i;

        for (i=0; i<n; i+=1) System.out.println (a[i]);
        System.out.println ("");
}
}

/*
 * QSort.class uses the standard quicksort algorithm
 * Detailed explanation of the techniques are found in online help
 */
class QSort {

/*
 * This is used internally, so make it private
 */
private void sort (String a[], int lo0, int hi0) {
```

```
                int lo = lo0;
                int hi = hi0;

                if (lo >= hi) return;
                String mid = a[(lo + hi) / 2];
                while (lo < hi) {
                        while (lo<hi && a[lo].compareTo
    ➥ (mid) < 0) lo += 1;
    while (lo<hi && a[hi].compareTo
    ➥ (mid) > 0) hi -= 1;
    if (lo < hi) {
                                String T = a[lo];
                                a[lo] = a[hi];
                                a[hi] = T;
                        }
                }
                if (hi < lo) {
                        int T = hi;
                        hi = lo;
                        lo = T;
                }
                sort(a, lo0, lo);    // Yes, it is recursive
                sort(a, lo == lo0 ? lo+1 : lo, hi0);
        }

        /*
         * The method called to start the sort
         *    String a[]    an array of strings to be sorted in place
         *    int n         the number of elements in the array
         */
        public void sort (String a[], int n) {
                sort (a, 0, n-1);
        }
}
```

2. Compile and test the application. Compile the source using `javac`. Test the application by typing

```
java Sort <input file>
```

A test file, called `PhoneBook.txt`, is supplied on the CD-ROM. Figure 2.9 shows the output from sorting the sample file.

How It Works

An array of `String`s is created by using the new `String` keywords along with array dimensions. In this example a fixed-size array of length 128 is used.

The input file is opened in the same way as in previous examples. The data is read into the array, making sure that array bounds are not exceeded. The file is then closed.

The `QSort` class implements the standard `quicksort` algorithm, in this case comparing `String` variables. `String` comparison is done by using the compareTo method. This method returns an integer less than, equal to, or greater than 0, similarly to the C function strcmp. The sorting is done in place, meaning that no additional arrays are needed.

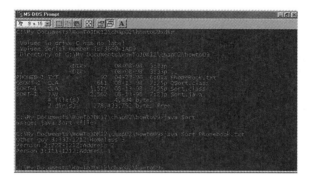

Figure 2.9 Arrays are powerful data structures that simplify certain coding problems.

The sorted array is printed by a special function designed for printing arrays of strings.

Comments

Variable-length arrays cannot be allocated directly in Java. There are mechanisms to implement growable arrays, but this requires the use of the java.util.Vector class, which is discussed in Chapter 8, "The JFC."

COMPLEXITY
INTERMEDIATE

2.10 How do I...
Parse a string?

Problem

I have a file of telephone numbers. Each line in the file contains three fields, separated by tabs or colons. The first field contains a name, the second field has a phone number, and the third field has an address.

I would like to write a program that searches for a record in the file that corresponds to a name given on the command line. I want the name, telephone number, and address printed on separate lines.

This requires some kind of string parsing. How do I parse a string?

Technique

A very useful class found in the `java.util.package` is `StringTokenizer`. `StringTokenizer` can take a string and return substrings that are separated by arbitrary characters. It is functionally similar to the `split` function in Perl.

To use `StringTokenizer`, call the constructor with the target string and an optional set of delimiting characters. Repeated calls to the `nextToken` method return strings delimited in the target string.

Steps

1. Create the application source file. Create a new file called `Phone.java` and enter the following source:

```
import java.io.*;
import java.util.StringTokenizer;

/*
 * Phone.class implements a simple phone book with fuzzy
 * name lookup.  The phone book file could be created with a
 * text editor or a spreadsheet saved as tab-delimited text.
 */
class Phone {

public static void main (String args[])
{
        String buf;
        FileInputStream fs=null;

        if (args.length != 1) {
                System.out.println ("usage: java Phone <name>");
                System.exit (1);
        }

/*
 * PhoneBook.txt is the name of the phone book file.
 */
        try {
                fs = new FileInputStream ("PhoneBook.txt");
        } catch (Exception e) {
                System.out.println
➥ ("Unable to open PhoneBook.txt");
System.exit (1);
        }
     BufferedReader ds = new BufferedReader
➥(new InputStreamReader(fs));
while (true) {
                try {
                        buf = ds.readLine ();
                        if (buf == null) break;
                } catch (IOException e) {
                        System.out.println
➥ ("Exception caught reading file.");
```

```
break;
                }

/*
 * Create a new StringTokenizer for each line read
 * Explicitly specify the delimiters as both colons and tabs
 */
                StringTokenizer st = new StringTokenizer
➡ (buf, ":\t");

                String name = st.nextToken ();
                if (contains (name, args[0])) {
                        System.out.println (name);
                        System.out.println (st.nextToken ());
                        System.out.println (st.nextToken ()
➡ + "\n");
}
        }
        try {
                fs.close ();
        } catch (IOException e) {
                System.out.println ("Exception caught
➡  closing file.");
}
}

/*
 * contains method is a fuzzy string compare that returns true
 * if either string is completely contained in the other one
 *       String s1, s2  two strings to compare
 */
static boolean contains (String s1, String s2) {

        int i;
        int l1 = s1.length ();
        int l2 = s2.length ();

        if (l1 < l2) {
                for (i=0; i<=l2-l1; i+=1)
                        if (s1.regionMatches (true, 0, s2, i, l1))
                                return true;
        }
        for (i=0; i<=l1-l2; i+=1)
                if (s2.regionMatches (true, 0, s1, i, l2))
                        return true;

        return false;
}
}
```

2. Compile and test the application. Compile the source using `javac`. Test the application by typing

```
java Phone <name>
```

The program looks for a file called PhoneBook.txt in the current directory. The file must contain lines with three fields, separated by tabs or colons. Such a file can be created with a text editor or a spreadsheet. A test file is supplied on the CD-ROM. Figure 2.10 shows output from Phone.java.

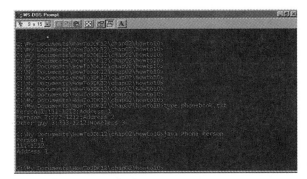

Figure 2.10 The StringTokenizer class facilitates the parsing of strings in Java.

How It Works

The program opens the phone book file (PhoneBook.txt), reads each line and creates a StringTokenizer object, and compares the first field with the given name. A new StringTokenizer object must be created for each line read. So you use a special string-compare function, contains, which ignores case and position. The contains function returns True if either string contains the other.

If a match occurs, the name, phone number, and address are printed on separate lines. Multiple matches may occur.

Comments

StringTokenizer by default uses whitespace (space, tabs, newline, form-feed, and carriage return) as delimiters. The constructor used in this example allows the set of delimiting characters to be specified explicitly. The delimiters may also be changed on a per-token basis. A summary of the constructors and methods available in the StringTokenizer class is presented in Table 2.5.

The contains method uses the regionMatches method, without case-sensitivity, found in the String class. This provides a fuzzy matching mechanism that is more user friendly than the equals or compareTo methods.

Table 2.5 StringTokenizer Class Constructors and Methods

METHOD	DESCRIPTION
StringTokenizer(String, String, boolean)	(Constructor) Constructs StringTokenizer on the specified string, using the specified delimiter set.
StringTokenizer(String, String)	(Constructor) Constructs a StringTokenizer on the specified string, using the specified delimiter set.
StringTokenizer(String)	(Constructor) Constructs a StringTokenizer on the specified string, using the default delimiter set (which is "\t\n\r\f").
countTokens()	Returns the number of tokens remaining hasMoreElements().Returns True if more tokens exist.
hasMoreTokens()	Returns True if more tokens exist.
nextElement()	Returns the next element, nextToken(). Returns the next token of the string.
nextToken(String)	Returns the next token, after switching to the new delimiter set.

COMPLEXITY
BEGINNING

2.11 How do I...
Use math functions?

Problem

I want to write a program to calculate the monthly payment for a loan, given the loan amount and annual interest rate. I have the equation for calculating the payment—it uses both the exponential function and the natural logarithm. How do I access these math functions?

Technique

Like all high-level languages, Java supports many of the math functions programmers require. Exponentiation and natural logarithm, along with many other functions, are contained in the Math class. These functions are declared static, so they may be accessed without creating an instance of the object.

Steps

1. Create the application source file. Create a new file called
`Ammortize.java` and enter the following source:

```java
import java.io.*;

/*
 * Ammortize.class calculates monthly payment given
 * loan amount, interest, and the number of years of the loan
 */
class Ammortize {
public static void main (String args[]) {
        double loanAmount=0, interest=0, years=0;

        BufferedReader in = new BufferedReader
➡(new InputStreamReader(System.in));

        loanAmount = inputDouble
➡("Enter the loan amount in dollars > ", in);

        interest = inputDouble
➡("Enter the interest rate in percent > ", in);

        years = inputDouble
➡("Enter the number of years > ", in);

        System.out.print ("The payment is $");
        System.out.println (payment (loanAmount,
➡interest, years));
} // end of main ()

/*
 * inputDouble method prints a prompt and reads a double
 * BufferedReader
 */
static double inputDouble (String prompt, BufferedReader in) {
        boolean error;
        String input="";
        double value=0;

        do {
                error = false;
                System.out.print (prompt);
                System.out.flush ();
                try {
                        input = in.readLine ();
                } catch (IOException e) {
                        System.out.println
➡("An input error was caught");
System.exit (1);
                }
                try {
                        value = Double.valueOf
➡(input).doubleValue();
} catch (NumberFormatException e) {
```

```
                        System.out.println ("Please try again");
                        error = true;
                }
        } while (error);
        return value;
} // end of inputDouble ()

/*
 * payment method does the magic calculation
 *       double A      loan amount
 *       double I      interest rate, as a percentage
 *       double Y      number of years
 */
static double payment (double A, double I, double Y) {

/*
 * call the exponentiation and natural log functions as
 * static methods in the Math class
 */
        double top = A * I / 1200;
        double bot = 1 - Math.exp (Y*(-12) *
➥ Math.log (1 + I/1200));

        return top / bot;
} // end of payment ()
}
```

2. Compile and test the application. Compile the source using `javac`. Test the application by typing

```
java Ammortize
```

The program prompts you for the loan amount, interest rate, and length of the loan in years. The payment amount is then displayed. Figure 2.11 shows an example of calculating the loan payment for a house.

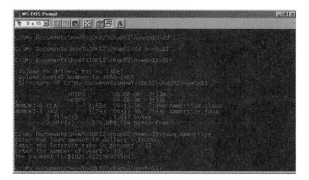

Figure 2.11 The Math object contains a number of calculating methods such as log() and exp().

How It Works

As was done in previous examples, the program creates a `BufferedReader` for taking input from the keyboard. An `inputDouble` method is defined to reduce the amount of code inside the body of `main`. After the values have been typed in, the `payment` method is called to calculate the monthly payment.

The `payment` method performs the standard equation for amortized payments. The derivation of the equation from first principles has been left as an exercise to the reader.

Java math functions are contained in the `Math` class. This example uses exponentiation and natural logarithm (log base e). These functions are declared static, so they may be accessed without creating an instance of the object. Table 2.6 lists the math functions available in the `Math` class.

Table 2.6 Math Class Methods

FUNCTION	DESCRIPTION
IEEEremainder(double, double)	Returns the remainder of f1 divided by f2 as defined by IEEE 754
abs(int a)	Returns the absolute integer value of a
abs(long a)	Returns the absolute long value of a
abs(float a)	Returns the absolute float value of a
abs(double a)	Returns the absolute double value of a
acos(double a)	Returns the arc cosine of a, in the range of 0.0 through pi
asin(double a)	Returns the arc sine of a, in the range of -pi/2 through pi/2
atan(double a)	Returns the arc tangent of a, in the range of -pi/2 through pi/2
atan2(double a, double b)	Converts rectangular coordinates (a, b) to polar (r, theta)
ceil(double a)	Returns the "ceiling," or smallest whole number greater than or equal to a
cos(double)	Returns the trigonometric cosine of an angle
exp(double a)	Returns the exponential number e(2.718...) raised to the power of a
floor(double a)	Returns the "floor," or largest whole number less than or equal to a
log(double a)	Returns the natural logarithm (base e) of a
max(int a, int b)	Takes two int values, a and b, and returns the greater of the two
max(long a, long b)	Takes two long values, a and b, and returns the greater of the two

FUNCTION	DESCRIPTION
max(float a, float b)	Takes two float values, a and b, and returns the greater of the two
max(double a, double b)	Takes two double values, a and b, and returns the greater of the two
min(int a, int b)	Takes two integer values, a and b, and returns the smaller of the two
min(long a, long b)	Takes two long values, a and b, and returns the smaller of the two
min(float a, float b)	Takes two float values, a and b, and returns the smaller of the two
min(double a, double b)	Takes two double values, a and b, and returns the smaller of the two
pow(double a, double b)	Returns the number a raised to the power of b
random()	Generates a random number between 0.0 and 1.0
rint(double)	Returns the closest integer to the argument, but as a floating-point number
round(float)	Rounds off a float value by first adding 0.5 to it and then returning the largest integer that is less than or equal to this new value
round(double)	Rounds off a double value by first adding 0.5 to it and then returning the largest integer that is less than or equal to this new value
sin(double)	Returns the trigonometric sine of an angle
sqrt(double)	Returns the square root of a
tan(double)	Returns the trigonometric tangent of an angle
toDegrees(double)	Translates radians to degrees
toRadians(double)	Translates degrees to radians

CHAPTER 3
BASIC GRAPHICS

3

BASIC GRAPHICS

How do I...

All the examples in Chapter 2, "Getting Started," are text-only applications. In this chapter, basic graphics are demonstrated as applets and applications. Graphics make programs more aesthetically appealing and are almost a requirement in modern end-user software. Applets are small programs that can be downloaded to client machines via popular Web browsers such as Netscape Navigator. Applets are embedded in Web pages through HTML tags. When a Java-enabled browser reaches a page with such a tag, it downloads the applet code and executes it on the client machine. By default, applets are somewhat constrained with respect to access of the client system resources, with the goal that they will not present a security risk. These constraints are modest and allow the programmer enough freedom to explore a variety of interactive ideas. Java graphics require a familiarity with several classes:

- A *frame* is an object that is capable of containing a title bar and a menu bar. A frame cannot be contained by another object.

- A *panel* is a generic container that can hold other graphical controls. A panel can be assigned its own layout manager.

Java supports many different types of graphics objects. Many of the simple ones are included in the Abstract Windowing Toolkit (AWT). Java2D, a new addition in Java 1.2, adds user defined coordinates, gradient fills, and patterns to the list of Java graphics.

3.1 Draw a Line

The first step in creating graphics is drawing lines and points on the screen. In this example a sine curve is plotted on a graph with axes. It demonstrates the use of basic classes contained in the AWT and the basic parts of an applet.

3.2 Add Color

The next step in creating attractive graphics is adding color. This example draws "flying" lines that continuously change color.

3.3 Draw Shapes

The Java API includes methods for drawing rectangles, ovals, arcs, and polygons. You can use variations of these basic shapes to create other shapes such as circles, squares, and triangles. In this example you will read a file containing shape description records and draw them. This example can be used only as an application because it must read files from a local disk.

3.4 Fill Shapes

Java supports drawing of filled shapes. This example shows how to fill several shapes by defining classes for plotting bar charts and pie charts. These classes could be used in other applets and applications.

3.5 Draw Text

Drawing text is fundamental to graphics toolkits. In this example, classes are defined to create scrolling text. This type of animation is currently used in many Web pages.

3.6 Use Fonts

Text in Java programs can be displayed in multiple fonts and styles. This example lists the available fonts and styles and demonstrates their use.

3.7 Handle Screen Updates

Screen updates in Java are handled by the `update()` method. If no `update()` method is declared, the default method is used. The default method sometimes performs an operation that is not desired. This example shows how to create a custom `update()` method to avoid flickering.

3.8 Print Applet Status Messages

You can access the status bar in the Appletviewer, Netscape browser, or another Java-enabled application. Java includes a method that causes a message to be printed in the status bar. This example demonstrates how to print in the status bar.

COMPLEXITY
BEGINNING

3.1 How do I...
Draw a line?

Problem

I'd like to draw lines to the screen and be able to plot a mathematical function like the sine curve. I also want to plot both x and y axes. This can be done by drawing lines only. I know how to access math functions and generate values for plotting, but I don't know how to draw lines. How do I draw lines?

Technique

The Java graphics API, known as the AWT, supports many of the graphics primitives programmers expect, the simplest being `drawLine()`. The `drawLine()` method is contained in the `Graphics` class and takes four integers as arguments. These integers are the x and y values of the starting and the ending points of the line. Figure 3.1 shows an example of the running applet.

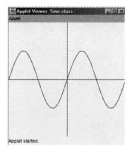

Figure 3.1 The Sine applet demonstrates the use of simple graphics.

Steps

1. Create the applet source file. Create a new file called `Sine.java` and enter the following source:

```java
import java.applet.Applet;
import java.awt.*;

/**
 * Sine curve applet/application
 * Draws one cycle of a sine curve.
 */
public class Sine extends Applet {

/*
 * width and height of the applet panel
 */
int width, height;

/*
 * init() is called when the applet is loaded
 * just get the width and height and save it
 */
public void init () {

        setLayout(null);
        width = 300;
        height = 300;
        setSize(width, height);
}

/**
 * paint() does the drawing of the axes and sine curve
 * @param g - destination graphics object
 */
public void paint (Graphics g) {

        int x, x0;
        double y0, y, A, f, t, offset;

        A = (double) height / 4;
        f = 2;
        offset = (double) height / 2;
        x0 = 0;
        y0 = offset;

        g.drawLine (x0, (int) y0, width, (int) y0);
        g.drawLine (width/2, 0, width/2, height);
        for (x=0; x<width; x+=1) {
                t = (double) x / ((double) width);
                y = offset - A * Math.sin (2 * Math.PI * f * t);
                g.drawLine (x0, (int) y0, x, (int) y);
                x0 = x;
                y0 = y;
        }
}
}
```

2. Create an HTML document that contains the applet. Create a new file called `howto31.html` that contains the following code:

```
<html>
<head>
<title>Sine curve</title>
</head>
<applet code="Sine.class" width=300 height=300>
</applet>
<hr size=4>
</html>
```

3. Compile and test the applet. Compile the source by using `javac` or the makefile provided. Test the applet by using the Appletviewer; enter the following command:

```
APPLETVIEWER howto31.html
```

You can also run `Sine.java` as an application by typing

```
java Sine
```

When Sine is executed, a window will pop up with a sine curve drawn on a set of axes.

How It Works

All classes that are to be used in an applet must be subclasses of the `Applet` class. The Appletviewer, Web browser, or another application that supports applets can load an applet class and execute it. Execution of an applet begins with the `init()` method. After return from `init()`, the applet `start()` method is called. One or both of these methods may be defined (that is, overridden). The `init()` method is called when an applet is first loaded; typically this is used for initialization purposes. The `start()` method is called after the `init()` method and whenever the user returns to a previously visited page in a Web browser. A `stop()` method, which is called when a user leaves a Web browser page, may also be defined. This method is typically used to stop threads and perform cleanup actions. The `destroy()` method is called by the browser or Appletviewer to inform this applet that it is being destroyed. This gives you a chance to clean up your code.

If an applet is executed as a standalone application, as are the examples from Chapter 2, the Java interpreter produces an error noting that a `main()` method was not found. To make an applet run as a standalone application, all that is needed is the addition of a `main()` method, which creates a window for the applet and an instance of the applet. This is what the `main()` method does in the preceding example. When the `main()` method is called, it creates a window frame by calling the `Frame()` constructor with the window title as an argument.

An instance of the applet itself is created by the call to the **Sine()** constructor. The instance of **Sine()** is placed in the center of the window frame by the **add()** method. This can be done because **Applet** is a subclass of **Panel**. This is discussed in greater detail in later chapters.

The **init()** method assigns a width and height. If the program is used as an applet, the size will be the dimensions specified by the width and height attributes of the **<applet>** tag in the associated HTML file.

The **paint()** method is called asynchronously by the Java runtime. It is actually called from the **update()** method, which itself is called in response to update events such as initialization and window expose events. Each time a Java window is created or exposed, all **update()** methods of all panels within that window are called. In this case, a sine curve with axes is plotted.

The x and y axes are plotted first, each with a call to **drawLine()**. The arguments to **drawLine()** are the x and y coordinates of the starting and ending points of the line. The coordinate system is like most other windowing systems; that is, 0,0 is the top left, with increasing values moving down and right. Figure 3.2 shows an example of the Java screen coordinate system.

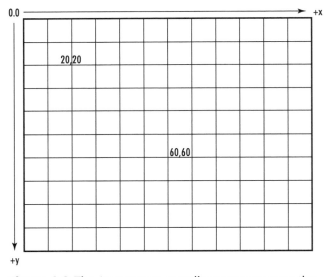

Figure 3.2 The Java screen coordinate system uses the top left as its origin.

The axes are drawn in the center of the window by using the width and height to calculate the coordinates.

The sine curve is plotted by using the **sin()** method, from the **Math** class, and **drawLine()**. The **sin()** and **drawLine()** methods are called within a **for** loop that varies the value of x from **0** to the panel width. The **sin()** method computes the value of y. The `sin()` method returns a **double** between -1.0 and 1.0, which is scaled and translated appropriately to the window coordinates. The call to `drawLine()` in this case draws a line from the previous calculated value to the current calculated value. This in effect draws several small lines that look like a continuous sine curve.

Comments

In many cases, applets may be used as applications by the mechanism described in this example. There are, of course, cases in which both execution environments cannot be supported. These are explored in later examples.

The argument **g** to the **paint()** method is similar to a graphics or device context found in other windowing systems such as X Window, Macintosh, and Windows. It contains all the information you might expect, such as foreground color and font.

In effect, a device context holds a set of current settings for all drawing objects. If you change the stroke width of the device context, all lines drawn will be drawn with that stroke until you change it.

The **main()** method could have been placed in a separate class and could have performed the same function. However, the name of the class containing the **main()** method, rather than the **Applet** class name, would have to be specified to the Java interpreter.

Note that the Appletviewer provided in the Sun JDK is itself written in Java. Based on this example, you can speculate about how some of it works.

COMPLEXITY
BEGINNING

3.2 How do I...
Add color?

Problem

Whenever graphics are displayed or created, adding color is important. In today's world of multimedia and high-impact documents, understanding how to use color is especially important. I want to demonstrate the use of color by drawing "flying" lines that continuously change color similarly to many screen-saver programs that are in use today. I learned how to draw lines in the previous example. How do I add color?

Technique

The `Graphics` class passed to the `paint()` method controls the current color used when drawing to the screen. The foreground color is changed by calling the setColor() method from the **Graphics** class. The argument to setColor() is a **Color** object. The **Color** class has several fixed colors defined, but it also contains methods to allocate arbitrary colors given red, green, and blue component values.

In this example, 24 different colors are allocated. These colors are used to set the foreground color of the flying lines. Figure 3.3 shows an example of the running applet.

Figure 3.3 This applet creates colored lines.

Steps

1. Create the applet source file. Create a new file called **Lines.java** and enter the following source:

```
import java.applet.Applet;
import java.awt.*;

/**
 * class LineColors holds 24 color values
 */
class LineColors {

/**
 * color[] array holds the colors to be used
 */
Color color[];

/**
 * class constructor
 * initializes the color array using an arbitrary algorithm
 */
public LineColors () {

        color = new Color[24];
        int i, rgb;

        rgb = 0xff;
```

```
        for (i=0; i<24; i+=1) {
                color[i] = new Color (rgb);
                rgb <<= 1;
                if ((rgb & 0x1000000) != 0) {
                        rgb |= 1;
                        rgb &= 0xffffff;
                }
        }
}
}

/**
 * class describing one line segment
 */
class Segment {

/*
 * x1, y1 - starting coordinates for this segment
 * x2, y2 - ending coordinates for this segment
 * dx1,...dy2 - velocities for the endpoints
 * whichcolor - the current index into color array
 * width, height - width and height of bounding panel
 * LC - instance of LineColors class
 */
double x1, y1, x2, y2;
double dx1, dy1, dx2, dy2;
int whichcolor, width, height;
LineColors LC;

/**
 * class constructor
 * initialize endpoints and velocities to random values
 * @param w - width of bounding panel
 * @param h - height of bounding panel
 * @param c - starting color index
 * @param lc - instance of LineColors class
 */
public Segment (int w, int h, int c, LineColors lc) {

        whichcolor = c;
        width = w;
        height = h;
        LC = lc;
        x1 = (double) w * Math.random ();
        y1 = (double) h * Math.random ();
        x2 = (double) w * Math.random ();
        y2 = (double) h * Math.random ();

        dx1 = 5 - 10 * Math.random ();
        dy1 = 5 - 10 * Math.random ();
        dx2 = 5 - 10 * Math.random ();
        dy2 = 5 - 10 * Math.random ();
}

/*
 * increment color index
```

```
 * calculate the next endpoint position for this segment
 */
void compute () {

        whichcolor += 1;
        whichcolor %= 24;

        x1 += dx1;
        y1 += dy1;
        x2 += dx2;
        y2 += dy2;

        if (x1 < 0 || x1 > width) dx1 = -dx1;
        if (y1 < 0 || y1 > height) dy1 = -dy1;
        if (x2 < 0 || x2 > width) dx2 = -dx2;
        if (y2 < 0 || y2 > height) dy2 = -dy2;
}

/**
 * draw the line segment using the current color
 * @param g - destination graphics object
 */
void paint (Graphics g) {

        g.setColor (LC.color [whichcolor]);
        g.drawLine ((int) x1, (int) y1, (int) x2, (int) y2);
}
}

/**
 * The applet/application proper
 */
public class Lines extends Applet {

/*
 * Nlines - number of line segments to be displayed
 * lines - array of instances of Segment class
 * LC - instance of LineColors class
 */
int width,height;
final int NLines = 4;
Segment lines[] = new Segment[NLines];
LineColors LC = new LineColors ();

/**
 * init is called when the applet is loaded
 * save the width and height
 * create instances of Segment class
 */
public void init () {

        setLayout(null);
        width = 300;
        height = 300;
        setSize(width, height);
```

```
        int i;
        for (i=0; i<NLines; i+=1)
                lines[i] = new Segment (width,
➥height, (2*i) % 24, LC);
}

/**
 * recompute the next endpoint coordinates for each line
 * invoke paint() method for each line
 * call repaint() to force painting 50ms. later
 * @param g - destination graphics object
 */
public void paint (Graphics g) {

        int i;
        for (i=0; i<NLines; i+=1) {
                lines[i].compute ();
                lines[i].paint (g);
        }
        repaint (50);
}

}
```

2. Create an HTML document that contains the applet. Create a new file called **howto32.html** that contains the following code:

```
<html>
<head>
<title>Flying Lines</title>
</head>
<applet code="Lines.class" width=300 height=300>
</applet>
<hr size=4>
</html>
```

3. Compile and test the applet. Compile the source by using **javac** or the makefile provided. Test the applet by using the Appletviewer; enter the following command:

```
APPLETVIEWER howto32.html
```

When **Lines** is executed, a window pops up with four lines that bounce around while continuously changing color.

How It Works

Two classes are defined in addition to the applet itself: **LineColors** and **Segment**. **LineColors** contains an array of 24 colors. The color values are initialized by the **LineColors** constructor, which uses the **Color()** constructor to allocate new colors. One of the **Color** constructors takes a single-integer argument, which specifies the red, green, and blue (RGB) color components in the lower 24 bits: the red component in bits 16–23, the green component in bits 8–15, and the blue component in bits 0–7 (the least significant byte). The colors allocated in this example blend from blue to green to red in 24 steps. The algorithm rotates a full saturation bit pattern to generate the RGB values.

The `Segment` class describes a single line segment. It contains the endpoints of the segment, their velocities, an instance of `LineColors`, and an index to the current color of the segment. In addition to the constructor, a `compute()` method and a `paint()` method are defined. The constructor initializes the endpoints and velocities to random values using the `Math.random()` method. `Math.random()` returns a positive double between 0 and 1, which is scaled appropriately. The `compute()` method advances the color index and integrates the endpoints of the segment, implementing ideal reflection at the boundary. This gives the effect of bouncing. The `paint()` method sets the foreground color to the current color index using `setColor()` and draws the line.

The applet creates four line segments and stores them in an array. When the applet's `paint()` method is called in response to an update, it calls the `compute()` and `paint()` methods of the respective line segments in the array. In effect, these methods tell each line segment to compute and paint itself.

An applet can force an update by calling `repaint()`. This is what the example does to repeatedly draw the line segments in an animated fashion. `repaint()` queues update requests, which are later serviced by `update()`. Figure 3.4 shows the relationship between `repaint()`, `update()`, and `paint()`. The default `update()` method fills the applet panel with its background color and calls `paint()`. `repaint()` can take an integer argument, which specifies the time in milliseconds when the next update should occur. In this example the value 50 milliseconds is used. The final result is that the applet's `paint()` method is called approximately 20 times per second, producing the illusion of smooth motion.

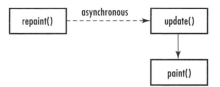

Figure 3.4 repaint(), update(), and paint() work together to display graphics.

Comments

The `Color` class contains several predefined colors. Their types are defined as static final `Color()`, so they can be used without creating an instance of `Color`.

For example, the following code fragment sets the foreground color to magenta:

```
void paint (Graphics g) {

    g.setColor (Color.magenta);
...
}
```

The predefined colors are listed in Table 3.1.

Table 3.1 Java Predefined Colors

PREDEFINED COLOR	RGB VALUES
black	(0,0,0)
blue	(0,0,255)
cyan	(0,255,255)
darkGray	(64,64,64)
gray	(128,128,128)
green	(0,255,0)
lightGray	(192,192,192)
magenta	(255,0,255)
orange	(255,200,0)
pink	(255,175,175)
red	(255,0,0)
white	(255,255,255)
yellow	(255,255,0)

The `Color` class contains several constructors, which take color values in a variety of formats. In addition, useful utility methods are also included. Table 3.2 lists the constructors and methods contained in class `Color`.

Table 3.2 Color Constructors and Methods

METHOD	DESCRIPTION
Color(int, int, int)	(Constructor) Creates a color with the specified red, green, and blue values in the range 0–255
Color(int)	Constructor) Creates a color with the specified combined RGB value consisting of the red component in bits 16–23, the green component in bits 8–15, and the blue component in bits 0–7
Color(float, float, float)	(Constructor) Creates a color with the specified red, green, and blue values in the range 0.0–1.0

continued on next page

continued from previous page

METHOD	DESCRIPTION
HSBtoRGB(float, float, float)	Returns the RGB value, defined by the default RGB ColorModel, of the color corresponding to the given HSB (hue, saturation, brightness) color components
RGBtoHSB(int, int, int, float[])	Returns the HSB values corresponding to the color defined by the red, green, and blue components
brighter()	Returns a brighter version of this color
darker()	Returns a darker version of this color
equals(Object)	Compares this object against the specified object
getBlue()	Gets the blue component
getColor(String)	Gets the specified Color property
getColor(String, Color)	Gets the specified Color property of the specified color
getColor(String, int)	Gets the specified Color property of the color value
GetGreen()	Gets the green component
GetHSBColor(float, float, float)	A static color factory for generating a Color object from HSB values
getRGB()	Gets the RGB value representing the color in the default RGB ColorModel
getRed()	Gets the red component
HashCode()	Computes the hash code
toString()	Returns the String representation of this color's values

Colors allocated in Java are not necessarily exact. The runtime attempts to find a color that is closest to the one requested. This, of course, is platform dependent.

The repeated calls to **paint()** and **repaint()** may appear to be recursive, but they are not. **repaint()** queues update requests and issues them asynchronously. In fact, there may not necessarily be a one-to-one correspondence between calls to **repaint()** and calls to **update()**. **update()** is called at the next convenient time.

3.3 How do I...
Draw shapes?

Problem

I want to write a simple interpreter capable of drawing standard shapes such as rectangles, ovals, and polygons. I want the program to accept input from a text file and interpret the text to draw the objects specified. I know how to read lines from a file and break them up into tokens, but how do I draw shapes?

Technique

This example combines many aspects discussed in Chapter 2, such as reading files and string tokenizing, with an example of how to draw shapes. The Java AWT supports all the graphic primitives mentioned earlier. Similarly to `drawLine()`, (example 3.1), additional graphics primitives are contained in the `Graphics` class. They may be called from an application's `paint()` method as before.

The text file contains one shape definition per line, with parameters separated by spaces. The grammar of a line of the text file is as follows:

```
<color>    <shape>
```

Where `<color>` is one of the following:

```
WHITE ¦ LIGHTGRAY ¦ GRAY ¦ DARKGRAY ¦ BLACK ¦ RED ¦
➡ PINK ¦ ORANGE ¦ YELLOW ¦ GREEN¦ MAGENTA ¦ CYAN ¦ BLUE
```

and `<shape>` is one of the following shapes along with necessary parameters:

```
RECT top-left width height
OVAL top-left width height
ARC top-left width height startangle arcangle
POLY x1 y1 x2 y2 x3 y3 [ x4 y4 ...]
```

Each line in the input file is read and split into tokens by using `StringTokenizer()`, as shown in Chapter 2. Each line is then checked to ensure that it is valid and in proper format. A valid line is used to create a Shape object described by the parameters in that line. An array of shape objects is maintained and painted in response to an update.

Applets cannot directly access disk files, so this example can be run only as an application. Figure 3.5 shows an example of the output.

Figure 3.5 The DrawApp
application shows the use
of predefined shapes in
applets.

Steps

1. Create the application source file. Create a new file called **DrawApp.java**
and enter the following source:

```java
import java.applet.Applet;
import java.awt.*;
import java.awt.event.*;
import java.io.*;
import java.util.StringTokenizer;

/**
 * class describing a shape
 */
class Shape {

/**
 * constants for the shape type
 */
static final int rectType = 1;
static final int ovalType = 2;
static final int arcType = 3;
static final int polyType = 4;

/*
 * the shape type
 */
int type;

/*
 * color for this shape
 */
Color color;
static final int MaxPoints = 10;
```

```
/*
 * arrays of x and y points for this shape
 */
int xp[] = new int[MaxPoints];
int yp[] = new int[MaxPoints];

/*
 * the number of points in this shape
 */
int npoints;

/**
 * shape constructor
 * saves parameters
 * @param tp - shape type
 * @param n - number of points
 * @param pts[] - array of endpoints
 * @param c - color of the shape
 */
public Shape (int tp, int n, int pts[], Color c) {

      int i;
      type = tp;
      color = c;
      npoints = n < MaxPoints ? n : MaxPoints;
      if (type == polyType) {
            npoints >>= 1;
            for (i=0; i<npoints; i+=1) {
                  xp[i] = pts[i << 1];
                  yp[i] = pts[(i << 1) +1];
            }
      } else {
            for (i=0; i<npoints; i+=1)
                  xp[i] = pts[i];
      }
}

/**
 * draw the shape
 * @param g - destination graphics object
 */
void paint (Graphics g) {

      g.setColor (color);
      switch (type) {

      case rectType:
            g.drawRect (xp[0], xp[1], xp[2], xp[3]);
            break;

      case ovalType:
            g.drawOval (xp[0], xp[1], xp[2], xp[3]);
            break;

      case arcType:
            g.drawArc (xp[0], xp[1], xp[2],
➥ xp[3], xp[4], xp[5]);
```

```
            break;

        case polyType:
                g.drawPolygon (xp, yp, npoints);
                break;
        }
}
}

/**
 * application class proper
 */
public class DrawApp extends Panel {

/*
 * the maximum number of shapes allowed
 */
static final int MaxShapes = 25;

/*
 * nshapes - the number of shapes read in
 * nlines - the line number in the input file
 */
static int nshapes, nlines = 0;

/*
 * array of instances of class shape
 */
static Shape shapes[] = new Shape[MaxShapes];

/**
 * invoke paint() method for each shape
 * @param g - destination graphics object
 */
public void paint (Graphics g) {

    int i;
    for (i=0; i<nshapes; i+=1)
            shapes[i].paint (g);
}

/**
 * application entry point
 * @param args - command-line arguments
 */
public static void main (String args[]) {

    String buf;
    FileInputStream fs=null;
    int i, type = 0;

    if (args.length != 1) {
        System.out.println ("usage: java DrawApp <file>");
        System.exit (1);
    }
```

```
/*
 * Try to open the file specified by args[0]
 */
    try {
            fs = new FileInputStream (args[0]);
    } catch (Exception e) {
            System.out.println (e);
            System.exit (1);
    }

/*
 * Create a DataInputStream BufferedReader
 * associated with FileInputStream fs
 */
    BufferedReader ds = new BufferedReader(new
➥ InputStreamReader(fs));
String token;
    Color color = Color.white;
    int pts[] = new int[2 * Shape.MaxPoints];

/*
 * loop until end of file or error
 * read a line and parse it
 */
    while (true) {
            try {
                    buf = ds.readLine ();       // read 1 line
                    if (buf == null) break;
            } catch (IOException e) {
                    System.out.println (e);
break;
            }
            nlines += 1;
            StringTokenizer st = new StringTokenizer (buf);
            token = st.nextToken ();
            if (token.equals ("white")) {
                color = Color.white;
                token = st.nextToken ();
            } else if (token.equals ("lightgray")) {
                color = Color.lightGray;
                token = st.nextToken ();
            } else if (token.equals ("gray")) {
                color = Color.gray;
                token = st.nextToken ();
            } else if (token.equals ("darkgray")) {
                color = Color.darkGray;
                token = st.nextToken ();
            } else if (token.equals ("black")) {
                color = Color.black;
                token = st.nextToken ();
            } else if (token.equals ("red")) {
                color = Color.red;
                token = st.nextToken ();
            } else if (token.equals ("pink")) {
                color = Color.pink;
                token = st.nextToken ();
```

```
              } else if (token.equals ("orange")) {
                  color = Color.orange;
                  token = st.nextToken ();
              } else if (token.equals ("yellow")) {
                  color = Color.yellow;
                  token = st.nextToken ();
              } else if (token.equals ("green")) {
                  color = Color.green;
                  token = st.nextToken ();
              } else if (token.equals ("magenta")) {
                  color = Color.magenta;
                  token = st.nextToken ();
              } else if (token.equals ("cyan")) {
                  color = Color.cyan;
                  token = st.nextToken ();
              } else if (token.equals ("blue")) {
                  color = Color.blue;
                  token = st.nextToken ();
              } else {
                  System.out.println ("Unknown color: "+token);
                  System.out.println ("line "+nlines);
                  System.exit (1);
              }

              int npoints = 0;
              if (token.equals ("rect")) {
                  npoints = getInt (st, pts, 4);
                  type = Shape.rectType;
              } else if (token.equals ("oval")) {
                  npoints = getInt (st, pts, 4);
                  type = Shape.ovalType;
              } else if (token.equals ("arc")) {
                  npoints = getInt (st, pts, 6);
                  type = Shape.arcType;
              } else if (token.equals ("poly")) {
                  npoints = getInt (st, pts, Shape.MaxPoints);
                  type = Shape.polyType;
              } else {
                  System.out.println ("Unknown shape: "+token);
                  System.out.println ("line "+nlines);
                  System.exit (1);
              }
              shapes[nshapes++] = new Shape (type,
    npoints, pts, color);
    }
    /*
     * close can throw an exception also; catch it for completeness
     */
        try {
            fs.close ();
        } catch (IOException e) {
            System.out.println (e);
        }

        Frame f = new Frame ("Drawing shapes");
        DrawApp drawApp = new DrawApp ();
```

```
                f.setSize(410, 430);
                f.addWindowListener(new WindowCloser());
                f.add ("Center", drawApp);
                f.show ();
        }

        /**
         * parse points
         * @param st - StringTokenizer for current line
         * @param pts[] - array of points to be returned
         * @param nmax - maximum number of points to accept
         */
        static int getInt (StringTokenizer st, int pts[], int nmax) {

                int i;
                String token;

                for (i=0; i<nmax; i+=1) {
                        if (st.hasMoreTokens () == false) break;
                        token = st.nextToken ();
                        try {
                                pts[i] = Integer.valueOf (token).intValue ();
                        } catch (NumberFormatException e) {
                                System.out.println (e);
                                System.out.println ("line "+nlines);
                                System.exit (1);
                        }
                }
                return i;
        }
}
class WindowCloser extends WindowAdapter
{
    public void windowClosing(WindowEvent e)
    {
        Window win = e.getWindow();
        win.setVisible(false);
        win.dispose();
        System.exit(0);
    }//windowClosing
}//class WindowCloser
```

2. Create the text file containing the shape definitions. Create a new file called **testfile** and enter the following text:

```
red rect 10 10 100 50
green oval 50 50 50 30
blue arc 75 75 60 70 45 90
cyan poly 100 100 200 200 300 100 100 100
```

3. Compile and test the application. Compile the application with **javac**. **DrawApp.java** is an application and cannot be run as an applet because it must open and read files from local disks. Test the application by typing

```
java DrawApp [filename]
```

When the application is started, a window opens, and a red rectangle, green oval, blue arc, and cyan polygon are drawn.

4. Try editing `testfile` by changing colors, adding new shapes, or moving the shapes around. Then run `DrawApp` again without recompiling. See if you can specify shapes in `testfile` that actually draw a picture.

How It Works

Unlike previous examples, class `DrawApp` extends class `Panel`. As discussed in How-To 3.1, `Applet` is a subclass of `Panel` and is only needed if a program is to be used as an applet. This example is used as an application exclusively; therefore, it is sufficient to create a subclass of `Panel`.

The class `Shape` contains all the information necessary for a given shape. This includes the type of shape, its color, two integer arrays, and the number of points in the arrays. The array `xp` is used to hold the coordinates, width, and height if the shape is a rectangle or oval. If the shape is an arc, two more parameters are used: the arc starting angle in degrees, and the number of degrees in the arc relative to the starting angle. If the shape is a polygon, the `xp` array holds the x coordinates of the polygon vertices, and the `yp` array holds the y coordinates. The number of vertices in a polygon is stored in the variable `npoints`. The `yp` array and variable `npoints` are not used if the shape describes anything other than a polygon.

The `main()` method borrows some techniques used in Chapter 2. It checks command-line arguments for a filename and uses this to open the input file. Upon success, a `BufferedReader` is created in order to read from the input file. The file is read one line at a time. Each line is parsed using `StringTokenizer()` to split a line into tokens. The default delimiters for `StringTokenizer()` (spaces, tabs, and newlines) are sufficient, so they are not explicitly defined.

After a valid color is found, the program looks for one of the four possible shape names in the parameter and then reads the necessary number of points for the given shape. Rectangles and ovals require four points, whereas arcs require six. Polygons can take a variable number of points. All these cases are handled by the `getInt()` method. `getInt()` reads up to `nmax` points and returns the number of points actually found. After this is done, a new shape is created with the information parsed from the input line and then stored in an array of shapes.

The class `Shape` contains the `paint()` method in addition to its constructor. The `Shape.paint()` method is called from the `paint()` method in `DrawApp`, similarly to previous examples. `Shape.paint()` sets the foreground color and draws the shape described in the class.

Comments

Rectangles are described by the top-left corner, width, and height. It is best to use positive values for width and height in order to avoid anomalous behavior that may occur on some platforms. Ovals are described the same way as rectangles; the oval is drawn inside the specified rectangle. Arcs are described by a bounding rectangle along with a starting angle in degrees and the number of degrees in the arc relative to the starting angle. Angles start from the positive x-axis (3 o'clock position), consistent with standard conventions. Positive arc angles indicate counterclockwise rotations; negative arc angles are drawn clockwise. Arcs are actually sections of ovals. The following code fragments draw the same shape:

```
drawOval (10, 10, 75, 90);
...drawArc (10, 10, 75, 90, 0, 360);
...
```

Polygons are defined by an array of x points and y points. They can be drawn open, meaning that the first and last vertices are not connected. (See Table 3.3.)

Table 3.3 Methods for Unfilled Shapes

METHOD	DESCRIPTION
draw3DRect(int, int, int, int, boolean)	Draws a highlighted 3D rectangle
drawOval(int, int, int, int)	Draws an oval inside the specified rectangle using the current color
drawPolygon(int[], int[], int)	Draws a polygon defined by an array of x points and y points
drawRect(int, int, int, int)	Draws the outline of the specified rectangle using the current color
drawRoundRect(int,int,int,int,int,int)	Draws an outlined rounded-corner rectangle using the current color
drawArc(int,int,int,int,int,int)	Draws the outline of an arc covering the specified rectangle, starting at startAngle and extending for arcAngle degrees, using the current color
DrawPolyLine(int[],int[],int)	Draws a sequence of connected lines defined by arrays of x coordinates and y coordinates, using the current color

DrawApp can be easily extended to support all the shapes described earlier. In addition, filled shapes described in the following example can be added along with arbitrary color support. Other features such as nonuniform rational B-splines (NURBS) could be implemented as line segments.

3.4 How do I...
Fill shapes?

Problem

I want to create classes that can draw bar and pie charts. The two types of charts share many similar features, so I want them to share a common superclass. I want to pass an array of values and colors along with coordinates and dimensions to a chart's constructor.

I have a good idea of how to lay out the classes using unfilled shapes, but I want these charts to use filled shapes similarly to the graphing utility in many spreadsheet programs. How do I fill shapes?

Technique

The class `Graphics` contains filled-shape counterparts to the unfilled shapes described in the previous example. They are used to do the drawing (Figure 3.6).

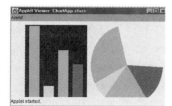

Figure 3.6 Charts can be drawn using Java classes.

Steps

1. Create the applet source file. Create a new file called `ChartApp.java` and enter the following source:

```
import java.applet.Applet;
import java.awt.*;

/**
 * parent class
 */
class Chart {

/*
 * x and y positions of the upper-left of the chart
```

```
 * nvalues - number of values for this chart
 */
int xpos, ypos, nvalues;

/*
 * width and height of this chart
 */
int width, height;

/*
 * maximum number of values allowed
 */
final int MaxValues = 10;

/*
 * data values for this chart
 */
double values[] = new double[MaxValues];

/*
 * color associated with each value
 */
Color colors[] = new Color[MaxValues];

/*
 * sum total of values, used for scaling purposes
 */
double total;

/**
 * class constructor
 * save values and normalizes them so that the max. value is 1.0
 * @param x, y - top-left coordinates
 * @param w, h - width and height
 * @param n - number of points
 * @param val[] - array of values
 * @param c[] - array of colors corresponding to values
 */
public Chart (int x, int y, int w, int h,
➥ int n, double val[], Color c[]) {

    int i;
    double extreme;

    xpos = x;
    ypos = y;
    width = w;
    height = h;
    nvalues = n;
    if (nvalues > MaxValues) nvalues = MaxValues;
    extreme = 0.0;
    for (i=0; i<nvalues; i+=1) {
        if (Math.abs (val[i]) > extreme)
            extreme = Math.abs (val[i]);
        colors[i] = c[i];
    }
```

```
        extreme = 1/extreme;
        total = 0;
        for (i=0; i<nvalues; i+=1) {
                values[i] = extreme * val[i];
                total += values[i];
        }
    }
}

/**
 * class implements a bar chart
 */
class BarChart extends Chart {

/**
 * constructor just calls Chart constructor
 * @param x, y - top left coordinates
 * @param w, h - width and height
 * @param n - number of points
 * @param val[] - array of values
 * @param c[] - array of colors corresponding to values
 */
public BarChart (int x, int y, int w,
➥ int h, int n, double val[], Color c[]) {

        super (x, y, w, h, n, val, c);
}

/**
 * need to add a paint method
 * draws the bar chart using fill3DRect
 * @param g - destination graphics object
 */
void paint (Graphics g) {

        int i;
        int barwidth = 3 * width / (4 * nvalues);
        int bardx = width / nvalues;
        int x, y, h;

        g.setColor (Color.black);
        g.fillRect (xpos, ypos-height, width, height);
        for (i=0; i<nvalues; i+=1) {
                g.setColor (colors[i]);
                x = xpos + bardx*i;
                h = (int) (values[i] * height);
                y = ypos - h;
                g.fill3DRect (x, y, barwidth, h, true);
        }
    }
}

/**
 * class implements a pie chart
 */
class PieChart extends Chart {
```

```
/**
 * class constructor just calls Chart constructor
 * @param x, y - top-left coordinates
 * @param w, h - width and height
 * @param n - number of points
 * @param val[] - array of values
 * @param c[] - array of colors corresponding to values
 */
public PieChart (int x, int y, int w,
➥ int h, int n, double val[], Color c[]) {

     super (x, y, w, h, n, val, c);
}

/**
 * need to add a paint method
 * draws the pie chart using fillArc
 * @param g - destination graphics object
 */
void paint (Graphics g) {

     int i, y;
     int startAngle, arcAngle;

     startAngle = 0;
     y = ypos - height;
     for (i=0; i<nvalues; i+=1) {
          arcAngle = (int) (360.0 * values[i] / total);
          g.setColor (colors[i]);
          g.fillArc (xpos, y, width, height,
➥ startAngle, arcAngle);
startAngle += arcAngle;
     }
}
}

/**
 * the applet/application  proper
 */
public class ChartApp extends Applet {

/*
 * width and height of the bounding panel
 */
int width, height;

/*
 * instances of BarChart and PieChart
 */
BarChart bc1;
PieChart pc1;

/*
 * called when applet is loaded
 * generate random values and plot them
 */
```

```
public void init () {

        int i;
        double values[] = new double[5];
        Color colors[] = new Color[5];

        width = 410;
        height = 230;
        colors[0] = Color.blue;
        colors[1] = Color.orange;
        colors[2] = Color.yellow;
        colors[3] = Color.green;
        colors[4] = Color.magenta;

        for (i=0; i<5; i+=1) values[i] = Math.random () + 0.001;
        int w = (width-40)/2;
        int h = height-20;
        bc1 = new BarChart (10, height-10,
➥ w, h, 5, values, colors);
pc1 = new PieChart (width/2, height-10,
➥ w, h, 5, values, colors);
}

/**
 * invoke the chart paint methods
 * @param g - destination graphics object
 */
public void paint (Graphics g) {

        bc1.paint (g);
        pc1.paint (g);
}

/**
 * application entry point
 * create a window frame and add the applet inside
 * @param args[] - command-line arguments
 */
public static void main (String args[]) {

        Frame f = new Frame ("Charts");
        ChartApp chart = new ChartApp ();

        f.setSize (410, 230);
        f.add ("Center", chart);
        f.show ();
        chart.init ();
        chart.start ();
}
}
```

2. Create an HTML document that contains the applet. Create a new file called howto34.html that contains the following code:

```
<html>
<head>
```

```
<title>Charts</title>
</head>
<applet code="ChartApp.class" width=400 height=230>
</applet>
<hr size=4>

</html>
```

3. Compile and test the applet. Compile the source by using `javac`. Test the applet by using the Appletviewer; enter the following command:

```
APPLETVIEWER howto34.html
```

You can also run `ChartApp.java` as an application by typing

```
java ChartApp
```

When the applet is executed, a window with a bar chart and pie chart drawn inside it opens, as shown in Figure 3.6.

How It Works

The class `Chart` is the superclass for both bar and pie charts. Its constructor stores the array of values along with their corresponding colors. The values are normalized such that the largest value is `1.0`. This makes the code more efficient because the `paint()` method needs only scale the values to the specified width and height. The total value is also computed, as it is needed for the pie chart.

The class `BarChart` extends class `Chart` so that it can inherit the variables and constructor. The constructor for `BarChart` simply passes its arguments to the `Chart` constructor by invoking its `super()` method. The `paint()` method is unique to each type of chart, so it must be defined in `BarChart`. `BarChart.paint()` scales the array of values to the specified height and draws the chart.

The class `PieChart` is similar. Its constructor also calls the `Chart` constructor by invoking `super()`. The `paint()` method draws the pie chart.

Comments

In addition to the filled shapes demonstrated, the AWT supports several others such as arcs, 3D rectangles, and rounded rectangles.

3.5 How do I ...
Draw text?

Problem

In Chapter 2, I printed text to the screen with `println()`. This method will not work to draw text in a graphics window. I would like to create a scrolling text marquee with the capability of moving the text in various directions. How do I draw text in a graphics window?

Technique

The `Graphics` class contains the method `drawString()`. This method is used to draw text in a graphics window. The `drawString()` method takes the string to be drawn and the position of the starting point of the baseline of the string as arguments. Figure 3.7 shows an example of the running applet.

Figure 3.7 Text may be scrolled in many directions.

Steps

1. Create the applet source file. Create a new file called `ScrollApp.java` and enter the following source code:

```java
import java.applet.Applet;
import java.awt.*;

/**
 * a class that handles scrolling text
 */
class Scroll {

/*
 * x and y coordinates of starting point
 */
int xstart, ystart;
```

```
/*
 * width and height of bounding panel
 */
int width, height;

/*
 * text to be scrolled
 */
String text;

/*
 * x and y velocities, respectively
 */
int deltaX, deltaY;

/*
 * current x and y position of the text
 */
int xpos, ypos;

/*
 * the color of the text
 */
Color color;

/**
 * class constructor just saves arguments
 * @param x, y - starting coordinates
 * @param dx, dy - x and y velocities
 * @param w, h - width and height of bounding panel
 * @param t - the text string
 * @param c - color of the text
 */
public Scroll (int x, int y, int dx, int dy,
➥ int w, int h, String t, Color c) {

     xstart = x;
     ystart = y;
     width = w;
     height = h;
     text = t;
     deltaX = dx;
     deltaY = dy;
     color = c;
     xpos = xstart;
     ypos = ystart;
}

/*
 * draw the text at the current position
 * advance the position and reinitialize outside bounding panel
 * @param g - destination graphics object
 */
void paint (Graphics g) {
```

```
        g.setColor (color);
        g.drawString (text, xpos, ypos);
        xpos += deltaX;
        ypos += deltaY;

        FontMetrics fm = g.getFontMetrics ();
        int textw = fm.stringWidth (text);
        int texth = fm.getHeight ();
        if (deltaX < 0 && xpos < -textw) xpos = xstart;
        if (deltaX > 0 && xpos > width) xpos = xstart;
        if (deltaY < 0 && ypos < 0) ypos = ystart;
        if (deltaY > 0 && ypos > height+texth) ypos = ystart;
    }
}

/**
 * the applet/application proper
 */
public class ScrollApp extends Applet {

/*
 * width and height of the bounding panel
 */
int width, height;

/*
 * instances of Scroll for demonstration
 */
Scroll left, right, up, down, diag;

/*
 * called when the applet is loaded
 * create new instances of Scroll
 */
public void init () {


    width = 410;
    height = 230;

    left = new Scroll (400, 50, -5, 0, width, height,
        "Moving left", Color.red);
    right = new Scroll (0, 150, 5, 0, width, height,
        "Moving right", Color.green);
    up = new Scroll (100, 200, 0, -5, width, height,
        "Moving up", Color.blue);
    down = new Scroll (200, 0, 0, 5, width, height,
        "Moving down", Color.cyan);
    diag = new Scroll (0, 0, 7, 3, width, height,
        "Moving diagonally", Color.magenta);
}

/*
 * invoke the paint method of each scrolling text instance
 * force a repaint 50ms later
 */
```

```
public void paint (Graphics g) {

        left.paint (g);
        right.paint (g);
        up.paint (g);
        down.paint (g);
        diag.paint (g);
        repaint (50);
}

/*
 * Application entry point
 * @param args - command-line arguments
 */
public static void main (String args[]) {

        Frame f = new Frame ("Scrolling text");
        ScrollApp scrollApp = new ScrollApp ();

        f.setSize (410, 230);
        f.add ("Center", scrollApp);
        f.show ();
        scrollApp.init ();
}
}
```

2. Create an HTML document that contains the applet. Create a new file called **howto35.html** that contains the following code:

```
<html>
<head>
<title>Scrolling Text </title>
</head>
<applet code="ScrollApp.class" width=410 height=230>
</applet>
<hr size=4>

</html>
```

3. Compile and test the applet. Compile the source by using javac. Test the applet by using the Appletviewer; enter the following command:

```
AppletViewer howto35.html
```

You can also run **ScrollApp** as an application by typing

```
Java ScrollApp
```

When the applet is started, a window opens, with five text strings scrolling in different directions. There is one of each string scrolling left, right, up, down, and diagonally.

How It Works

The class `Scroll` maintains all the information necessary to draw scrolling text. `xpos` and `ypos` are the initial positions of the text. When the text scrolls completely off the screen, it is moved back to the initial position. `deltaX` and `deltaY` are the velocities in the x and y directions. Positive and negative values are allowed, so the text can scroll in any direction. `width` and `height` are the width and height of the bounding panel; these are used to determine whether the text has scrolled off the panel that contains the applet. `text` is the text to be scrolled, and `color` is the color of the text.

You draw the text in this example without specifying a font; therefore, the default font is used. The discussion of using fonts in Java is included in How-To 3.6. The class `FontMetrics` is used to determine the width and height of the text. `stringWidth()` and `getHeight()` perform exactly these functions.

Table 3.4 lists the methods for filled shapes.

Table 3.4 FontMetrics Methods

METHOD	DESCRIPTION
`fill3DRect(int, int, int, int, boolean)`	Paints a highlighted 3D rectangle using the current color.
`fillArc(int, int, int, int, int, int)`	Fills an arc using the current color.
`fillPolygon(int[], int[], int)`	Fills a polygon with the current color using an even-odd fill rule (otherwise known as an alternating rule).
`fillRect(int, int, int, int)`	Fills the specified rectangle with the current color.
`fillOval(int,int,int,int)`	Fills an oval bounded by the specified rectangle with the current color.
`FillRoundRect(int,int,int,int,int,int)`	Fills the specified rounded corner rectangle with the current color.
`FontMetrics(Font)`	Creates a new FontMetrics object with the specified font.
`charWidth(int)`	Returns the width of the specified character in this font.
`charWidth(char)`	Returns the width of the specified character in this font.
`getAscent()`	Gets the font ascent.
`getDescent()`	Gets the font descent.
`getFont()`	Gets the font.
`getHeight()`	Gets the total height of the font.

METHOD	DESCRIPTION
getMaxAdvance()	Gets the maximum advance width of any character in this font.
getMaxAscent()	Gets the maximum ascent of all characters in this font.
getMaxDescent()	Gets the maximum descent of all characters in this font. No character will descend further below the baseline than this distance.
getWidths()	Gets the widths of the first 256 characters in the font.
stringWidth(String)	Returns the width of the specified string in this font.
toString()	Returns the string representation of this FontMetric's values.

When this marquee is running, you may notice a considerable flickering of the text. The flickering can be eliminated with the use of double buffering. This is discussed in Chapter 6, "User Interface."

Comments

The getAscent() method returns the font ascent, which is the distance from the baseline to the top of the characters. The getDescent() method returns the distance from the baseline to the bottom of the characters. Figure 3.7 shows the appearance of this applet.

COMPLEXITY
INTERMEDIATE

3.6 How do I...
Use fonts?

Problem

Programs are more visually interesting when different fonts and text styles are used. I want to write a utility that prints text in all the fonts available in normal, bold, and italic styles. I know how to draw text, but I need to change the font and text style. How do I find out what fonts and styles are available? How do I implement these fonts and styles?

Technique

When text is drawn in a given graphics context, the current font, style, and size are used. To draw text with a different font, the current font must be changed by using `Graphics.setFont()`. `Graphics.setFont()` takes a `Font` object as an argument. The style and size of the font are supplied as parameters to the `Font` constructor.

To determine which fonts are available, the method `getFontList()` is used. It returns an array of strings that are the names of available fonts. To create a font, you invoke the `Font` with the name, style, and size as arguments. Figure 3.8 shows the output of the code.

Figure 3.8
Several fonts and styles are displayed together on the screen.

Steps

1. Create the applet source file. Create a new file called `Fonts.java` and enter the following source:

```
import java.applet.Applet;
import java.awt.*;

/**
 * Class that determines which fonts are available
 */
public class Fonts extends Applet {

/*
 * Maximum number of fonts to display
 */
final int MaxFonts = 10;

/*
 * Width and height of bounding panel
 */
int width, height;
```

```
/*
 * Array of font names
 */
String fontName[];

/*
 * Array of fonts
 * Holds plain, italic, and bold for each font
 */
Font theFonts[] = new Font[3 * MaxFonts];

/*
 * The number of fonts found
 */
int nfonts = 0;

/*
 * Applet entry point
 */
public void init () {

    int i;
    Dimension d = getSize ();

    width = d.width;
    height = d.height;

        theFonts[0] = new Font ("Courier", Font.PLAIN, 12);
        theFonts[1] = new Font ("System", Font.BOLD, 16);
        theFonts[2] = new Font ("Helvetica", Font.BOLD, 18);
    }

/*
 * Draw the font names.
 * @param g - destination graphics object
 */
public void paint (Graphics g) {

    int i;

        g.setFont (theFonts[0]);
        g.drawString ("Courier", 10, 30);
        g.setFont (theFonts[1]);
        g.drawString ("System", 70, 70);
        g.setFont (theFonts[2]);
        g.drawString ("Helvetica", 150, 90);

}

/*
 * Application entry point
 * Creates a window frame and adds the applet inside
 * @param args[] - command-line arguments
 */
public static void main (String args[]) {
```

```
        Frame f = new Frame ("Fonts");
        Fonts fonts = new Fonts ();

        f.setSize (250, 200);
        f.add ("Center", fonts);
        f.show ();
        fonts.init ();
    }
}
```

2. Create an HTML document that contains the applet. Create a new file called howto36.html that contains the following code:

```
<html>
<head>
<title>Fonts</title>
</head>
<applet code="Fonts.class" width=250 height=200>
</applet>
<hr size=4>

</html>
```

3. Compile and test the applet. Compile the source by using javac or the makefile provided. Test the applet by using the Appletviewer; enter the following command:

```
APPLETVIEWER howto36.html
```

You can also run Fonts.java as an application by typing

```
java Fonts
```

When Fonts is executed, a window pops up, with the different font styles printed in plain, bold, and italic. Figure 3.8 shows an example of the running applet.

How It Works

The init() method sets the array of fonts. The paint() method then sets the current font and writes the name of that font in that font, for each of the three fonts.

An array is created that holds each of the fonts in plain, bold, and italic styles. You initialize the array by using the Font constructor with the font name, style, and size as arguments. A fixed size of 12 is used in this example. The font styles are constants defined in class Font; they are summarized in Table 3.5. The style constants can be added to produce combined styles.

The method `paint()` goes through the array of fonts, sets the font using `Graphics.setFont()`, and draws the name of the font and the text **bold** and *italic*, using the appropriate styles.

Table 3.5 The Three Font Styles

CONSTANT	DESCRIPTION
BOLD	The bold style constant
ITALIC	The italicized style constant
PLAIN	The plain style constant

Comments

Methods exist to obtain various properties of the font being used, such as width, height, and line spacing. The methods are contained in the `FontMetrics` class. Figure 3.8 shows the appearance of this applet.

COMPLEXITY
ADVANCED

3.7 How do I...
Handle screen updates?

Problem

I want to create an applet that draws text that jumps around in different colors without erasing the previously drawn text. The previous examples show me how to do most of what I want, but they all erase the panel before drawing. I don't want to do that. I want to give the effect of the text growing on top of itself. How do I handle screen updates, or the lack thereof?

Technique

In all of the previous examples, the `paint()` method is used exclusively to do the drawing. The `paint()` method is called from the `update()` method. The default `update()` method fills the panel with the background color and then calls `paint()`. The result is that any previously drawn graphics and text are erased. To prevent previously drawn graphics and text from being erased, the default `update()` method must be overridden and replaced with a method that does not erase the panel.

The rest of the applet uses many of the techniques described previously (see Figure 3.9).

Figure 3.9 The update() method is overridden to produce a buildup effect.

Steps

1. Create the applet source file. Create a new file called **CrazyText.java** and enter the following source:

```java
import java.applet.Applet;
import java.awt.*;

/*
 * application/applet class
 */
public class CrazyText extends Applet {

String text = "Java";  // string to be displayed
int delta = 5;          // "craziness" factor: max pixel offset
String fontName = "TimesRoman";
int fontSize = 36;

char chars[];           // individual chars in 'text'
int positions[];        // base horizontal position for each char
FontMetrics fm;

/*
 * called when the applet is loaded
 * creates a font and initializes positions of characters
 */
public void init() {

        int fontStyle = Font.BOLD + Font.ITALIC;
        setFont(new Font(fontName, fontStyle, fontSize));
        fm = getFontMetrics(getFont());

        chars = new char[text.length()];
        text.getChars(0, text.length(), chars, 0);

        positions = new int[text.length()];
        for (int i = 0; i < text.length(); i++) {
             positions[i] = fm.charsWidth(chars, 0, i) + 20;
        }
}

/*
 * draws the characters and forces a repaint 100ms later
```

```
 * @param g - destination graphics object
 */
public void paint (Graphics g) {

     int x, y;
     g.setColor (new Color((float) Math.random(),
              (float) Math.random(),
              (float) Math.random()));
     for (int i = 0; i < text.length(); i++) {
          x = (int)(Math.random() * delta * 2) + positions[i];
          y = (int)(Math.random() * delta * 2) +
➡fm.getAscent() - 1;
g.drawChars (chars, i, 1, x, y);
     }
     repaint (100);
}

/*
 * override default update() method to eliminate
 * erasing of the panel
 */
public void update (Graphics g) {
     paint (g);
}

/*
 * application entry point
 * create a window frame and add the applet inside
 * @param args[] - command line arguments
 */
public static void main (String args[]) {

     Frame f = new Frame ("Crazy");
     CrazyText crazy = new CrazyText ();

     f.setSize (130, 80);
     f.add ("Center", crazy);
     f.show ();
     crazy.init ();
}
}
```

2. Create an HTML document that contains the applet. Create a new file called howto37.html that contains the following code:

```html
<html>
<head>
<title>Crazy Text</title>
</head>
<applet code="CrazyText" width=200 height=200>
</applet>
<hr size=2>
</html>
```

3. Compile and test the applet. Compile the source by using javac. Test the applet by using the Appletviewer; enter the following command:

```
Appletviewer howto37.html
```

When CrazyText is executed, a window pops up, with Java printed. As the applet is running, Java is repeatedly printed in different colors, and each character is moved slightly in a direction independent of the other characters. However, each time the characters are printed, the screen is not updated, and the previously printed characters are not erased. This produces an interesting effect, as shown in Figure 3.9.

How It Works

The method paint() sets the foreground color to a random value by using the Math.random() method. The characters are drawn, one at a time, with random variation in position by using the Graphics.drawChars() method. Graphics.drawChars() is similar to Graphics.drawText(), but it takes an array of characters instead of a string as an argument.

Comments

It might occur to you that the code in the paint() method could be moved to the update() method, and the paint() method eliminated entirely. This, however, will not work. When an applet or application is stated, the paint() method, not the update() method, is called. If no paint() method is provided, the default paint() method, which does nothing, is called. The calling of the update() method is platform dependent and therefore not reliable.

COMPLEXITY
INTERMEDIATE

3.8 How do I...
Print applet status messages?

Problem

I liked the line-drawing applet that draws lines in shifting colors. What I want to do is add the necessary code to print the values of the red, green, and blue components of the foreground color as they change. I don't want to put this in the panel where the lines are bouncing. Rather, I want to print the color values in the status bar in the browser or in the Appletviewer. I know how to get the color component values, but how to I print applet status messages?

Technique

The status bar in the Appletviewer or browser can be accessed by the `Applet.showStatus()` method. This method takes as an argument a string that is to be printed in the status bar. In this example, the string comprises hard-coded text concatenated with methods that return integer values. The current foreground red, green, and blue color components can be determined by calling the `Graphics.getColor().getRed()`,`Graphics.getColor().getGreen()`, and `Graphics.getColor().getBlue()` methods, respectively. See Figure 3.10.

Figure 3.10
The
ShowStatus()
method can
provide text
information
to the user.

Steps

1. Create the applet source file. Create a new file called `Status.java` and enter the following source code:

```
import java.applet.Applet;
import java.awt.*;

/*
 * class to hold color values
 */
class LineColors {

/*
 * an array of colors proper
 */
Color color[];

/*
 * the constructor initializes the color array by
 * using an arbitrary algorithm
 */
public LineColors () {
```

```
        color = new Color[24];
        int i, rgb;

        rgb = 0xff;
        for (i=0; i<24; i+=1) {
                color[i] = new Color (rgb);
                rgb <<= 1;
                if ((rgb & 0x1000000) != 0) {
                        rgb |= 1;
                        rgb &= 0xffffff;
                }
        }
}
} // class LineColors

/*
 * class to handle the drawing of one line segment
 */
class Segment {

/*
 * x1, y1 - x and y position of first endpoint
 * x2, y2 - x and y position of second endpoint
 */
double x1, y1, x2, y2;

/*
 * velocities of the endpoints, respectively
 */
double dx1, dy1, dx2, dy2;

/*
 * whichcolor - color index for this segment
 */
int whichcolor;

/*
 * width and height of bounding panel
 */
int width, height;

/*
 * instance of LineColors
 */
LineColors LC;

/*
 * class constructor
 * saves arguments and initializes position and velocities
 * to random values
 * @param w, h - width and height of bounding panel
 * @param c - starting color
 * @param lc - instance of LineColor
 */
public Segment (int w, int h, int c, LineColors lc) {
```

```java
            whichcolor = c;
            width = w;
            height = h;
            LC = lc;
            x1 = (double) w * Math.random ();
            y1 = (double) h * Math.random ();
            x2 = (double) w * Math.random ();
            y2 = (double) h * Math.random ();

            dx1 = 5 - 10 * Math.random ();
            dy1 = 5 - 10 * Math.random ();
            dx2 = 5 - 10 * Math.random ();
            dy2 = 5 - 10 * Math.random ();
    }

    /*
     * increments color index and calculates new endpoint positions
     */
    void compute () {

            whichcolor += 1;
            whichcolor %= 24;

            x1 += dx1;
            y1 += dy1;
            x2 += dx2;
            y2 += dy2;

            if (x1 < 0 || x1 > width) dx1 = -dx1;
            if (y1 < 0 || y1 > height) dy1 = -dy1;
            if (x2 < 0 || x2 > width) dx2 = -dx2;
            if (y2 < 0 || y2 > height) dy2 = -dy2;
    }

    /**
     * prints status message showing the different colors
     * @param g - destination graphics object
     */
    void paint (Graphics g) {

            g.setColor (LC.color [whichcolor]);
            g.drawLine ((int) x1, (int) y1, (int) x2, (int) y2);
    }
} // class Segment

public class Status extends Applet {

    /*
     * width and height of bounding panel
     */
    int width, height;

    /*
     * The number of lines will be set to 1 because the color values
     * displayed will be valid for only one line
     */
```

```
final int NLines = 1;

/*
 * array of instances of Segment
 */
Segment lines[] = new Segment[NLines];

/*
 * instance of LineColor
 */
LineColors LC = new LineColors ();

/*
 * called when applet is loaded
 * save panel dimensions and create instance of Segment
 */
public void init () {


        width = 200;
        height = 200;

        int i;
        for (i=0; i<NLines; i+=1)
                lines[i] = new Segment (width, height, (2*i) % 24,
LC);
}

/**
 * draw the line and print status message
 * @param g - destination graphics object
 */
public void paint (Graphics g) {

        int i;
        for (i=0; i<NLines; i+=1) {
                lines[i].compute ();
                lines[i].paint (g);
        }
        showStatus("red = "+g.getColor().getRed() + "  green = " +
                g.getColor().getGreen() + "  blue = " +
                g.getColor().getBlue());

        repaint (50);
}
}
```

2. Create an HTML document named **howto38.html** that contains the following code:

```
<html>
<head>
<title>Crazy Text</title>
</head>
<applet code="Status" width=200 height=200>
</applet>
```

```
<hr size=2>
</html>
```

3. Compile and test the applet by using `javac`. Test the applet by using the Appletviewer; enter the following:

```
Appletviewer howto38.html
```

`Status.java` cannot be run as an application and does not support the printing of status messages.

When `Status` is executed, a window pops up, with a "flying line" bouncing around while changing colors. This is identical to the example in How-To 3.2, except that only one line is used. One line is used because the multiple lines all had different colors; the color status being printed can indicate only the color of one line. Figure 3.10 shows a snapshot of the running applet. This illustrates the power and usefulness of the `showStatus()` method.

How It Works

Most of the code in this example is identical to that of How-To 3.2. The difference is the addition of calls to `showStatus()` in `Status.paint()`. `ShowStatus()` takes a string as an argument and is straightforward.

CHAPTER 4
THREADS

4

THREADS

How do I...

All the programs shown so far have been sequential programs. A *sequential program* has a beginning, an end, and a sequence, and at any given time during the runtime there is a single point of execution. A thread is a single sequential flow of control within a process. A thread is very similar to a sequential program—it has a beginning, an end, and a sequence, and at any given time the thread has a single point of execution. But a thread itself is not a program and cannot run on its own.

One of Java's greatest strengths is its multithreading capability. Multithreading is the capability to have multiple independent threads that share data and run asynchronously. This must not be confused with multiprocessing. Multiprocessing applications run at the same time on the same machine, but they do not interact with each other. Therefore, there is no need to synchronize these programs.

4.1 Create a Thread

This example demonstrates how to create a single thread within an applet. An analog clock is displayed, and the thread is used to control the clock update.

4.2 Create Multiple Threads

This example demonstrates the use of multiple threads in one program by using the Lines applet/application from Chapter 3, "Basic Graphics." Two independent threads are created and executed to graphically show independent activity.

4.3 Change a Thread's Priority

The Lines applet/application is used again. Several instances of the `Lines` class are defined and executed. The priority of each thread is assigned a different value. The update rate of the graphical display reflects how different priorities affect thread execution.

4.4 Synchronize Methods

Synchronization mechanisms are necessary in any system that contains subsystems that are asynchronous with respect to each other. In this section, synchronization is achieved by specifying the synchronized modifier to critical methods. The goal of a multithreaded application is to allow several threads to work together to solve a problem. Sometimes these threads can go off and work without regard to each other, but at other times, they must coordinate carefully. For example, if one thread fills a buffer and another empties it, the filer may have to wait for the emptier when the buffer is full.

This example shows an animated first-in, first-out (FIFO) structure, often called a *queue*. This type of data structure is commonly used to accommodate variation in data transfer rates in asynchronous systems. Synchronized methods are used to provide controlled access of shared data, avoiding data corruption.

4.5 Synchronize Code Sections

Java provides mechanisms for specifying critical sections at the statement level in addition to the method level. This is generally not recommended, but is demonstrated here for completeness.

The animated FIFO of the previous example is modified to show how code sections can be synchronized.

4.6 Wait for a Thread

There are many instances where one thread must wait for some condition to occur in another thread. One way to do this is to regularly check for the condition. This is known as *polling*. Polling can be inconvenient and slow. Threads can wait for each other by using the built-in thread waiting. The FIFO example is again used to demonstrate this.

4.1 How do I...
Create a thread?

Problem

I want to write a clock applet. It should display a clock face with hands for hours, minutes, and seconds. I know I could continuously get the time, look for a change, and update the clock, but this is inefficient. What I want to do is create a separate thread that sleeps for a tenth of a second or so and then reads the time. I know how to get the current time and how to draw the graphics, but I don't know how to create a thread. How do I create a thread?

Technique

Java supports threads intrinsically. There are two ways to create a thread. In the first way a class must implement the **Runnable** interface. In the second case, the class extends the **Thread** class. The **Thread** class itself implements the **Runnable** interface. If a class extends **Thread**, it automatically implements **Runnable**. This example implements the **Runnable** interface to create a thread.

An instance of class **Thread** must be created with the class containing the thread as an argument. This is necessary only if the class does not subclass **Thread**. If the class containing the thread is creating the instance of **Thread**, the self-reference can be used.

Classes that run as separate threads must also create a **run()** method that accepts no arguments and returns **void**. The **run()** method is called when the thread is started. A thread is started by invoking the **Thread.start()** method. It can be stopped by returning from the **run()** method. Figure 4.1 shows an example of the running applet.

Figure 4.1 The clock applet uses a thread to manage its execution.

Steps

1. Create the applet source file. Create a new file called `Clock.java` and
enter the following source:

```java
import java.awt.*;
import java.applet.*;
import java.util.*;
import java.text.*;

/*
 * class for applet/application
 */
public class Clock extends Applet implements Runnable {

/*
 * the instance of Thread for checking the time periodically
 */
Thread thread = null;
SimpleDateFormat formatter;
Date currentDate;

/*
 * saved values used to draw only when things have changed
 */
int lastxs=0;
int lastys=0;
int lastxm=0;
int lastym=0;
int lastxh=0;
int lastyh=0;

/**
  * sets the background color to light gray
  */
public void init(){
        this.setBackground(Color.lightGray);
}

/**
  * draws the clock face
  * @param g - destination graphics object
  */
public void paint (Graphics g) {

        int xh, yh, xm, ym, xs, ys, s=0,
            ➥m=10, h=10, xcenter, ycenter;
String Today;
    currentDate = new Date();
    SimpleDateFormat formatter = new SimpleDateFormat("s"
                    ➥,Locale.getDefault());
```

```
try{
        s=Integer.parseInt(formatter.format(currentDate));
    }catch(NumberFormatException n){
        s=0;
    }

    formatter.applyPattern("m");
    try{
        m=Integer.parseInt(formatter.format(currentDate));
    }catch(NumberFormatException n){
        m=10;
    }

    formatter.applyPattern("h");
    try{
        h=Integer.parseInt(formatter.format(currentDate));
    }catch(NumberFormatException n){
        h=10;
    }

    xcenter=100;
    ycenter=100;

    xs = (int)(Math.cos(s * 3.14f/30 -
                ➥3.14f/2) * 45 + xcenter);
ys = (int)(Math.sin(s * 3.14f/30 -
                ➥3.14f/2) * 45 + ycenter);
xm = (int)(Math.cos(m * 3.14f/30 -
                ➥3.14f/2) * 40 + xcenter);
ym = (int)(Math.sin(m * 3.14f/30 -
                ➥3.14f/2) * 40 + ycenter);
xh = (int)(Math.cos((h*30 + m/2) *
                ➥ 3.14f/180 - 3.14f/2) * 30
+ xcenter);
    yh = (int)(Math.sin((h*30 + m/2) *
                ➥3.14f/180 - 3.14f/2) * 30
+ ycenter);

// Draw the circle and numbers
    g.setFont(new Font("TimesRoman", Font.PLAIN, 14));
    g.setColor(Color.blue);
    g.drawOval (xcenter-50, ycenter-50, 100, 100);
    g.setColor(Color.darkGray);
    g.drawString("9",xcenter-45,ycenter+3);
    g.drawString("3",xcenter+40,ycenter+3);
    g.drawString("12",xcenter-5,ycenter-37);
    g.drawString("6",xcenter-3,ycenter+45);

// Erase if necessary, and redraw
    g.setColor(Color.lightGray);
    if (xs != lastxs ¦¦ ys != lastys) {
            g.drawLine(xcenter, ycenter, lastxs, lastys);
    }
```

```
        if (xm != lastxm || ym != lastym) {
                g.drawLine(xcenter, ycenter-1, lastxm, lastym);
                g.drawLine(xcenter-1, ycenter, lastxm, lastym);
        }
        if (xh != lastxh || yh != lastyh) {
                g.drawLine(xcenter, ycenter-1, lastxh, lastyh);
                g.drawLine(xcenter-1, ycenter, lastxh, lastyh);
        }

        g.setColor(Color.darkGray);
        g.drawLine(xcenter, ycenter, xs, ys);
        g.setColor(Color.red);
        g.drawLine(xcenter, ycenter-1, xm, ym);
        g.drawLine(xcenter-1, ycenter, xm, ym);
        g.drawLine(xcenter, ycenter-1, xh, yh);
        g.drawLine(xcenter-1, ycenter, xh, yh);
        lastxs=xs; lastys=ys;
        lastxm=xm; lastym=ym;
        lastxh=xh; lastyh=yh;
}

/*
 * called when the applet is started
 * create a new instance of Thread and start it
 */
public void start() {

        if(thread == null) {
                thread = new Thread(this);
                thread.start();
        }
}

/*
 * called when the applet is stopped
 * stops the thread
 */
public void stop() {

        thread = null;
}

/*
 * the thread itself
 * sleeps for 100ms and forces a repaint
 */
public void run() {

        while (thread != null) {
                try {
                        Thread.sleep(100);
                } catch (InterruptedException e) { }
                repaint();
```

```
        }
        thread = null;
}

/**
 * override the default update method to avoid flickering
 * caused by unnecessary erasing of the applet panel
 * @param g - destination graphics object
 */
public void update(Graphics g) {
        paint(g);
}

/**
 * application entry point
 * not used when run as an applet
 * create a new window frame and add the applet inside
 * @param args[] - command-line arguments
 */
public static void main (String args[]) {

        Frame f = new Frame ("Clock");
        Clock clock = new Clock ();

        f.setSize (210, 230);
        f.add ("Center", clock);
        f.show ();
        clock.init ();
        clock.start ();
}
}
```

2. Create an HTML document that contains the applet. Create a new file called howto41.html that contains the following code:

```
<html>
<head>
<title>Clock</title>
</head>
<applet code="Clock.class" width=200 height=200>
</applet>
<hr size=4>

</html>
```

3. Compile and test the applet. Compile the source by using javac or the makefile provided. Test the applet by using the Appletviewer; enter the following command:

```
APPLETVIEWER howto41.html
```

Clock.java may also be run as an application by typing java Clock.

4. When `Clock` is executed, a window opens, with an analog clock running in the center of it.

How It Works

The clock applet contains only one class, the applet itself. The class implements `Runnable` in order to create a separate thread. When the applet is started, the `start()` method is called. The `start()` method creates a new thread instance and starts it by invoking `Thread.start()`. The `stop()` method kills the thread by setting it to `null`.

The `run()` method in the clock applet is called when the thread is started. The `run()` method immediately enters an infinite loop that forces painting by calling `repaint()`. The thread sleeps for 100 milliseconds by calling the `Thread.sleep()` method with the number of milliseconds to sleep as an argument. Figure 4.2 shows the flow of the thread. `Thread.sleep()` throws `InterruptedException` if another thread interrupts it (calling its `Thread.interrupt()` method before the time has passed). No action is taken, in this example, if `InterruptedException` is encountered.

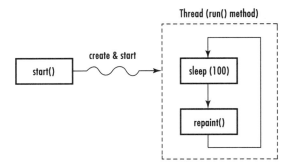

Figure 4.2 The clock applet is based on a thread.

The `update()` method is called asynchronously after a `repaint()`. This method overrides the default `update()` method to avoid flickering caused by erasing in the default `update()`. The new `update()` method simply calls `paint()`.

The `paint()` method does most of the work. Java 1.1 changed the way dates and times were handled in order to better support the internationalization of the language. The `Date` class is still used, but it returns the date and time in milliseconds. Your customers might find a millisecond-based clock acceptable, but most won't. The `SimpleDateFormat` class is used to translate the millisecond version into a version suitable for your customer, based on the locale. The `Local` object contains a method called `getDefault()`. This method returns the default locale for this installation. Simple trigonometry and line drawing are used to paint the clock hands. Drawing is done after comparing the current second with the last second to see if a full second has passed. The maximum error in the reading is 100 milliseconds, which is acceptable for most purposes.

Comments

The `Thread.sleep()` method guarantees only a minimum sleep time. The actual sleep time is dependent on system delays, priorities of other threads, and processes on the system.

COMPLEXITY
BEGINNING

4.2 How do I...
Create multiple threads?

Problem

I like the Lines applet of Chapter 3. I want to create several instances of the `Lines` class, each one running in its own panel. I could use a single thread to initiate drawing in each, but I would rather use multiple threads. I know how to create multiple instances of `LineApp`, but I don't know how to create multiple threads. How do I create multiple threads?

Technique

The `Lines` class is defined with an instance of `Thread`. Each instance of `Lines` creates a separate thread that can run independently. If multiple instances of `Lines` are created, multiple threads execute.

The two instances of `Lines` are added to the main panel. This displays both threads running simultaneously. Figure 4.3 shows an example of the running applet.

Figure 4.3 Java supports multiple threads of execution in the same applet or application.

Steps

1. Create the source file. Create a file called MultiThread.java and enter the following source:

```java
import java.applet.Applet;
import java.awt.*;

/**
 * class LineColors holds 24 color values
 */
class LineColors {

/**
 * color[] array holds the colors to be used
 */
Color color[];

/**
 * class constructor
 * initializes the color array using an arbitrary algorithm
 */
public LineColors () {
        color = new Color[24];
        int i, rgb;

        rgb = 0xff;
        for (i=0; i<24; i+=1) {
                color[i] = new Color (rgb);
                rgb <<= 1;
                if ((rgb & 0x1000000) != 0) {
                        rgb |= 1;
                        rgb &= 0xffffff;
                }
        }
}
}

/**
 * class describing one line segment
 */
class Segment {

/*
 * x1, y1 - starting coordinates for this segment
 * x2, y2 - ending coordinates for this segment
 * dx1,...dy2 - velocities for the endpoints
 * whichcolor - the current index into color array
 * width, height - width and height of bounding panel
 * LC - instance of LineColors class
 */
```

```
double x1, y1, x2, y2;
double dx1, dy1, dx2, dy2;
int whichcolor, width, height;
LineColors LC;

/**
 * class constructor
 * initialize endpoints and velocities to random values
 * @param w - width of bounding panel
 * @param h - height of bounding panel
 * @param c - starting color index
 * @param lc - instance of LineColors class
 */
public Segment (int w, int h, int c, LineColors lc) {

        whichcolor = c;
        width = w;
        height = h;
        LC = lc;
        x1 = (double) w * Math.random ();
        y1 = (double) h * Math.random ();
        x2 = (double) w * Math.random ();
        y2 = (double) h * Math.random ();

        dx1 = 5 - 10 * Math.random ();
        dy1 = 5 - 10 * Math.random ();
        dx2 = 5 - 10 * Math.random ();
        dy2 = 5 - 10 * Math.random ();
}

/*
 * increment color index
 * calculate the next endpoint position for this segment
 */
void compute () {

        whichcolor += 1;
        whichcolor %= 24;

        x1 += dx1;
        y1 += dy1;
        x2 += dx2;
        y2 += dy2;

        if (x1 < 0 || x1 > width) dx1 = -dx1;
        if (y1 < 0 || y1 > height) dy1 = -dy1;
        if (x2 < 0 || x2 > width) dx2 = -dx2;
        if (y2 < 0 || y2 > height) dy2 = -dy2;
}

/**
```

```
 * draw the line segment using the current color
 * @param g - destination graphics object
 */
void paint (Graphics g) {

        g.setColor (LC.color [whichcolor]);
        g.drawLine ((int) x1, (int) y1, (int) x2, (int) y2);
}
}

/**
 * The applet/application proper
 */
class Lines extends Panel implements Runnable {

/*
 * width, height - width and height of bounding panel
 * Nlines - number of line segments to be displayed
 * lines - array of instances of Segment class
 * LC - instance of LineColors class
 */
int width, height;
final int NLines = 4;
Segment lines[] = new Segment[NLines];
LineColors LC = new LineColors ();

/*
 * instance of thread for this line
 */
Thread thread;

/**
 * init is called when the applet is loaded
 * save the width and height
 * create instances of Segment class
 */
public void init () {


        width = 200;
        height = 200;

        thread = new Thread (this);
        thread.start ();

        int i;
        for (i=0; i<NLines; i+=1)
                lines[i] = new Segment (width,
                        ➥height, (2*i) % 24, LC);
}

/**
```

```
 * recompute the next endpoint coordinates for each line
 * invoke paint() method for each line
 * @param g - destination graphics object
 */
public void paint (Graphics g)
{

        int i;
        g.setColor (Color.black);
        g.drawRect (0, 0, width-1, height-1);
        for (i=0; i<NLines; i+=1) {
                lines[i].compute ();
                lines[i].paint (g);
        }
}

/*
 * the thread proper
 * calls paint() every 50ms
 */
public void run()
{
        Graphics g = getGraphics();
        while (true) {
                paint (g);
                try {
                        Thread.sleep (50);
                } catch(InterruptedException e) { }
        }
}
}

/*
 * the applet/application proper
 * creates two instances of Lines and starts them
 * as separate threads
 */
public class MultiThread extends Applet {

/*
 * the instances of Lines
 */
Lines lines1;
Lines lines2;

/*
 * called when the applet is loaded
 */
public void init () {

        setLayout (new GridLayout (2, 1, 0, 0));
```

```
        lines1 = new Lines ();
        lines2 = new Lines ();
        add (lines1);
        add (lines2);
        lines1.setSize (200, 100);
        lines2.setSize (200, 100);
        lines1.init ();
        lines2.init ();
}

/**
 * application entry point, unused when run as an applet
 * create window frame and add applet inside
 * @param args[] - command-line arguments
 */
public static void main (String args[]) {

        Frame f = new Frame ("Colored lines");
        f.setLayout (new GridLayout (2, 1, 0, 0));

        f.setSize (200, 200);

        Lines lines1 = new Lines ();
        Lines lines2 = new Lines ();
        f.add (lines1);
        f.add (lines2);
        f.show ();
        lines1.init ();
        lines2.init ();
}
}
```

2. Create an HTML file that contains the applet. Create a file called
howto42.html that contains the following code:

```
<html>
<head>
<title>Multi Thread</title>
</head>
<applet code="MultiThread.class" width=200 height=200>
</applet>
<hr size=4>

</html>
```

3. Compile and test the applet/application. Compile the source by using
javac. Use the Appletviewer with the HTML file as an argument by typing

```
appletviewer howto42.html
```

You can run the program as an application by typing

```
java MultiThread
```

4. When the program starts, a window appears, with two panels inside.
Each panel displays lines of changing color bouncing around inside.

How It Works

The Lines class from Chapter 3 is modified slightly in order to handle multiple threads. The LineColors and Segment classes are unchanged from the example in Chapter 3.

The Lines class extends Panel and implements Runnable. The Runnable interface is necessary so that each instance of Lines can run as a separate thread. An instance of Thread called thread is declared in the Lines class.

A new thread instance is created by calling the Thread() constructor with this as an argument. The thread is started by calling the Thread.start() method. Finally, an array of lines is created by calling the Segment constructor.

The paint() method in the Lines class is changed slightly from Chapter 3. It first draws a black border around the panel so that each panel is more visible. It then computes and paints all the lines for this instance by calling Segment.compute() and Segment.paint().

The run() method is executed when the thread for this instance of Lines is started. The run() method enters an infinite loop that forces repainting and then sleeps for 50 milliseconds. The cycle repeats forever.

The MultiThread class is the applet itself. If MultiThread is run as an applet, the init() method is called. If it is run as an application, the main() method is called. The init() method creates two instances of Lines, adds them to the applet panel, and starts them by calling their respective init() methods. The main() method is similar, but it must first create a window frame to contain the panels.

Comments

Creating multiple threads is no more difficult than creating single threads. An instance of Thread must be created for each class that contains an independent thread.

COMPLEXITY
INTERMEDIATE

4.3 How do I...
Change a thread's priority?

Problem

I want to experiment with multiple threads demonstrated in How-To 4.2. The different threads of How-To 4.2 appear to run at the same speed. I want to modify the program to work with differing priorities. I learned how to create multiple threads, but I don't know how to change a thread's priority. How do I change a thread's priority?

Technique

The `Thread` class contains methods to change a thread's priority. A priority tells the operating system how much resource should be given to each thread. A high-priority thread is scheduled to receive more time on the CPU than a low-priority thread. A method called `Thread.setPriority()` sets the priority of a thread. `Thread` class constants can be used to set these.

Other methods of the `Thread` class are listed in Table 4.1. Figure 4.4 shows an example of the running applet.

Table 4.1 Thread Methods

METHOD	DESCRIPTION
MAX_PRIORITY	The maximum priority that a thread can have
MIN_PRIORITY	The minimum priority that a thread can have
NORM_PRIORITY	The default priority that is assigned to a thread
Thread()	Constructs a new thread
Thread(Runnable)	Constructs a new thread that applies the run() method of the specified target
Thread(String)	Constructs a new thread with the specified name
Thread(Runnable, String)	Constructs a new thread with the specified name and applies the run() method of the specified target
activeCount()	Returns the current number of active threads in this thread group
checkAccess()	Checks whether the current thread is allowed to modify this thread
currentThread()	Returns a reference to the currently executing thread object
destroy()	Destroys a thread, without any cleanup
dumpStack()	A debugging procedure that prints a stack trace for the current thread
enumerate(Thread[])	Copies, into the specified array, references to every active thread in this thread's group
getName()	Gets and returns this thread's name
getPriority()	Gets and returns the thread's priority
interrupt()	Sends an interrupt to a thread
interrupted()	Asks whether you have been interrupted
isAlive()	Returns a boolean indicating whether the thread is active
isDaemon()	Returns the daemon flag of the thread
isInterrupted()	Asks if another thread has been interrupted
join(long)	Waits for this thread to die

METHOD	DESCRIPTION
join(long, int)	Waits for the thread to die, with more precise time
join()	Waits forever for this thread to die
run()	Defines the actual body of this thread; subclasses of thread should override this method
setDaemon(boolean)	Marks this thread as a daemon thread or a user thread
setName(String)	Sets the thread's name
setPriority(int)	Sets the thread's priority
sleep(long)	Causes the currently executing thread to sleep for the specified number of milliseconds
sleep(long, int)	Causes the currently running thread to sleep for the specified number of milliseconds and nanoseconds
start()	Starts this thread
toString()	Returns a string representation of the thread, including the thread's name, priority, and thread group
yield()	Causes the currently executing thread object to yield

Figure 4.4 Each thread can run at a different priority.

Steps

1. Create the source file. Create a file called MultiThread.java and enter the following source:

```java
import java.applet.Applet;
import java.awt.*;

/**
 * class LineColors holds 24 color values
 */
class LineColors {

/**
 * color[] array holds the colors to be used
 */
Color color[];
```

```
/**
 * class constructor
 * initializes the color array by using an arbitrary algorithm
 */
public LineColors () {
        color = new Color[24];
        int i, rgb;

        rgb = 0xff;
        for (i=0; i<24; i+=1) {
                color[i] = new Color (rgb);
                rgb <<= 1;
                if ((rgb & 0x1000000) != 0) {
                        rgb |= 1;
                        rgb &= 0xffffff;
                }
        }
}
}

/**
 * class describing one line segment
 */
class Segment {

/*
 * x1, y1 - starting coordinates for this segment
 * x2, y2 - ending coordinates for this segment
 * dx1,...dy2 - velocities for the endpoints
 * whichcolor - the current index into color array
 * width, height - width and height of bounding panel
 * LC - instance of LineColors class
 */
double x1, y1, x2, y2;
double dx1, dy1, dx2, dy2;
int whichcolor, width, height;
LineColors LC;

/**
 * class constructor
 * initialize endpoints and velocities to random values
 * @param w - width of bounding panel
 * @param h - height of bounding panel
 * @param c - starting color index
 * @param lc - instance of LineColors class
 */
public Segment (int w, int h, int c, LineColors lc) {

        whichcolor = c;
        width = w;
        height = h;
        LC = lc;
```

```
        x1 = (double) w * Math.random ();
        y1 = (double) h * Math.random ();
        x2 = (double) w * Math.random ();
        y2 = (double) h * Math.random ();

        dx1 = 5 - 10 * Math.random ();
        dy1 = 5 - 10 * Math.random ();
        dx2 = 5 - 10 * Math.random ();
        dy2 = 5 - 10 * Math.random ();
}

/*
 * increment color index
 * calculate the next endpoint position for this segment
 */
void compute () {

        whichcolor += 1;
        whichcolor %= 24;

        x1 += dx1;
        y1 += dy1;
        x2 += dx2;
        y2 += dy2;

        if (x1 < 0 || x1 > width) dx1 = -dx1;
        if (y1 < 0 || y1 > height) dy1 = -dy1;
        if (x2 < 0 || x2 > width) dx2 = -dx2;
        if (y2 < 0 || y2 > height) dy2 = -dy2;
}

/**
 * draw the line segment using the current color
 * @param g - destination graphics object
 */
void paint (Graphics g) {

        g.setColor (LC.color [whichcolor]);
        g.drawLine ((int) x1, (int) y1, (int) x2, (int) y2);
}
}

/**
 * The applet/application proper
 */
class Lines extends Panel implements Runnable {

/*
 * width, height - width and height of bounding panel
 * Nlines - number of line segments to be displayed
 * lines - array of instances of Segment class
 * LC - instance of LineColors class
 */
```

```
int width, height;
final int NLines = 4;
Segment lines[] = new Segment[NLines];
LineColors LC = new LineColors ();

/*
 * instance of thread for this line
 */
Thread thread;

/**
 * init is called when the applet is loaded
 * save the width and height
 * create instances of Segment class
 */
public void init (int inPriority) {

        width = 200;
        height = 200;

        thread = new Thread (this);
        thread.start ();
        thread.setPriority(inPriority);

        int i;
        for (i=0; i<NLines; i+=1)
                lines[i] = new Segment (width,
                        ➥height, (2*i) % 24, LC);
}

/**
 * recompute the next endpoint coordinates for each line
 * invoke paint() method for each line
 * @param g - destination graphics object
 */
public void paint (Graphics g)
{

        int i;
        g.setColor (Color.black);
        g.drawRect (0, 0, width-1, height-1);
        for (i=0; i<NLines; i+=1) {
                lines[i].compute ();
                lines[i].paint (g);
        }
}

/*
 * the thread proper
 * calls paint() every 50ms
 */
public void run()
{
```

```
        Graphics g = getGraphics();
        int iterCount = 0;
        while (true) {
                paint(g);
                try {
                        iterCount += 1;
                        if (iterCount == 5) {
                                Thread.sleep(10);
                                iterCount = 0;
                        }
                }
                catch (InterruptedException e) {
                        System.out.println("Caught exception...");
}
        }
}
}

/*
 * the applet/application proper
 * creates two instances of Lines and starts them
 * as separate threads
 */
public class MultiThread extends Applet {

/*
 * the instances of Lines
 */
Lines lines[];

/*
 * the number of threads to be run
 */
public final static int NumThreads = 5;

/*
 * the priority of the first thread
 */
public final static int StartingPriority = Thread.NORM_PRIORITY;

/*
 * called when the applet is loaded
 * creates several instances of Lines and adds them to the
 * applet panel
 * sets the priority of each thread to 1 less than the previous
 * one
 */
public void init () {

        setLayout (new GridLayout (MultiThread.NumThreads, 1, 0,
0));
        lines = new Lines[MultiThread.NumThreads];
```

```
            for (int i = 0; i< MultiThread.NumThreads; i++) {
                    lines[i] = new Lines ();
                    add (lines[i]);
                    lines[i].setSize (200, 200/MultiThread.NumThreads);
                    lines[i].init (StartingPriority-i);
            }
    }

    /**
     * application entry point, unused when run as an applet
     * create window frame and add applet inside
     * @param args[] - command-line arguments
     */
    public static void main (String args[]) {

            Frame f = new Frame ("Colored lines");
            f.setLayout (new GridLayout (MultiThread.NumThreads
                        ➥, 1, 0, 0));

            f.setSize (200, 200);
            Lines lines[] = new Lines[MultiThread.NumThreads];

            for (int i = 0; i< MultiThread.NumThreads; i++) {
                    lines[i] = new Lines ();
                    f.add (lines[i]);
            }

            f.show ();

            for (int i = 0; i< MultiThread.NumThreads; i++) {
                    lines[i].init (StartingPriority-i);
            }
    }
    }
```

2. Create an HTML file that contains the applet. Create a file called howto43.html that contains the following code:

```
<html>
<head>
<title>Multi Thread</title>
</head>
<applet code="MultiThread.class" width=200 height=200>
</applet>
<hr size=4>

</html>
```

3. Compile and test the applet/application. Compile the source by using javac. Use the Appletviewer with the HTML file as an argument by typing

```
appletviewer howto43.html
```

The program as an application by typing

```
java MultiThread
```

4. When the program starts, a window appears, with several panels inside. Each panel displays lines of changing color bouncing around inside at different speeds.

How It Works

The program is largely the same as that of How-To 4.2. The differences are the init() method in the Lines class and the initialization done in the init() and main() methods of the MultiThread class.

The init() method of the Lines class takes an integer argument. This argument is the priority to be assigned for this instance of Lines. The thread for this instance is created as before by calling the Thread constructor with this as an argument. The thread is started by calling Thread.start(). The priority is set by calling Thread.set-Priority() with the given priority as an argument.

The init() method of the MultiThread class creates several instances of Lines. Each instance of Lines is given slightly lower priority than its predecessor. A similar function is performed in the main() method. The result is a demonstration of multiple threads running at differing levels of priority.

Comments

If you've been paying close attention, you've noticed the subtle change to the run() method of the Lines class. The difference is that five iterations of painting are done before Thread.sleep() is invoked. This is done purely for the purpose of producing a presentable demonstration. This addition to the code allows each thread more time before it is preempted. Without the little trick, the highest-priority thread takes almost all the time. This anomaly has to do more with the code in the example than with the Java runtime.

COMPLEXITY

INTERMEDIATE

4.4   How do I...
Synchronize methods?

Problem

I want to write an applet/application that graphically demonstrates a FIFO or queue data structure. I want to create two threads that run asynchronously with respect to each other: The first thread should write data into the FIFO at a regular rate, and the second thread should wait for the FIFO to be half full and then read out all the data, until the FIFO is empty. There must be some synchronizing mechanism between the reading and writing threads in order to avoid corruption of the data in the FIFO. I know how to create multiple threads and how to draw the graphics, but I don't know how to synchronize methods within the FIFO class. How do I synchronize methods?

Technique

All examples so far in this chapter contain independent, asynchronous threads. Each thread contains all the data and methods required for its execution, runs at its own pace, and doesn't require any outside resources or methods. But in some situations, separate simultaneously running threads share data and must consider the state of other threads.

Java supports the synchronization of methods with the use of monitors. A monitor is associated with a specific data item and functions as a lock on that data. When a thread holds the monitor for a data item, it creates a lock on the data such that other threads cannot manipulate that data.

The example in this section implements synchronization via the **synchronized** keyword in the method declaration. This causes the methods to wait for a monitor before execution. When the method returns, the monitor is released. A monitor is always associated with an object. The methods declared with the **synchronized** keyword locks its object. The use of monitors does not prevent accessing an object by code that bypasses the monitor.

Steps

1. Create the applet source file. Create a new file called `SyncMethod.java` and enter the following source:

```
import java.awt.*;
import java.applet.Applet;

/*
 * a class for handling first in, first out data structure
 */
class FIFO {

/*
 * the maximum depth of the FIFO
 */
final int MaxDepth = 200;

/*
 * the real depth of this FIFO
 */
int depth;

/*
```

```
 * write and read indexes into the data array
 */
int writeIndex;
int readIndex;

/*
 * the number of data items currently in the FIFO
 */
int nItems;

/*
 * the data proper
 */
int data[] = new int[MaxDepth];

/*
 * width and height of the FIFO graphical display
 */
int width;
int height;

/*
 * x and y position of the upper-left corner of the FIFO
 * graphical display
 */
int xpos;
int ypos;

/**
 * the constructor
 * @param d - depth of the FIFO
 */
public FIFO (int d) {

        depth = d;
        writeIndex = 0;
        readIndex = 0;
        nItems = 0;

        width = depth + 4;
        height = 50;
        xpos = 50;
        ypos = 75;
}

/**
 * write one integer value into the FIFO
 * @param value - the value to write
 */
```

```java
synchronized void write (int value) {

        if (nItems >= depth) return;

        data[writeIndex] = value;
        writeIndex += 1;
        writeIndex %= depth;
        nItems += 1;
}

/**
 * read 1 integer value from the FIFO
 */
synchronized int read () {

        if (nItems < 1) return 0;

        int value = data[readIndex];
        readIndex += 1;
        readIndex %= depth;
        nItems -= 1;

        return value;
}

/**
 * returns true if the FIFO is empty
 */
synchronized boolean empty () {

        return nItems > 0 ? false : true;
}

/**
 * returns true if the FIFO is half full
 */
synchronized boolean halfFull () {

        return nItems > (depth >> 1) ? true : false;
}

/**
 * returns true if the FIFO is full
 */
synchronized boolean full () {

        return nItems >= (depth) ? true : false;
}

/**
 * draws the FIFO graphical display
 * @param g - destination graphics context
 */
```

```
synchronized void paint (Graphics g) {

        int x, y, w, h;

        g.setColor (Color.white);
        g.fillRect (xpos, ypos, width, height);
        g.setColor (Color.black);
        g.drawRect (xpos, ypos, width, height);

        x = writeIndex + xpos + 2;
        y = ypos - 22;
        g.drawLine (x, y, x, y + 20);
        g.drawString ("Write index "+writeIndex, x+2, y+10);

        x = readIndex + xpos + 2;
        y = ypos + height + 22;
        g.drawLine (x, y-20, x, y);
        g.drawString ("Read index "+readIndex, x+2, y);

        if (nItems < 1) return;

        if (nItems > (depth>>1)) g.setColor (Color.red);
        else g.setColor (Color.green);

        x = xpos + 2 + readIndex;
        y = ypos + 2;
        if (writeIndex > readIndex) w = nItems;
        else w = width - readIndex - 4;
        h = height - 4;
        g.fillRect (x, y, w, h);

        if (writeIndex > readIndex) return;

        x = xpos + 2;
        w = writeIndex;
        g.fillRect (x, y, w, h);
    }
}

/*
 * a class that generates data continuously
 */
class Source extends Thread {

/*
 * the FIFO to write into
 */
FIFO fifo;
int value;

/**
 * constructor
 * saves the FIFO instance and starts the thread
 * @param f - an instance of FIFO
```

```
  */
 public Source (FIFO f) {

        fifo = f;
        value = 0;

        start ();
 }

 /*
  * the thread that writes one word every 100ms
  */
 public void run () {

        while (true) {
                if (fifo.full() == false)
                        fifo.write (value++);

                try {
                        Thread.sleep (100);
                } catch (InterruptedException e) {
                }
        }
 }
 }

 /*
  * a class that reads data from the FIFO
  */
 class Sink extends Thread {

 /*
  * the FIFO to read from
  */
 FIFO fifo;
 int value;

 /**
  * constructor
  * saves the FIFO instance and starts the thread
  * @param f - an instance of FIFO
  */
 public Sink (FIFO f) {

        fifo = f;

        start ();
 }

 /*
  * the thread that reads all data out after the FIFO is half
  * full
  */
 public void run () {
```

```
        while (true) {
                if (fifo.halfFull()) {
                        try {
                                Thread.sleep (1000);
                        } catch (InterruptedException e) {
                        }
                        while (fifo.empty() == false) {
                                value = fifo.read ();
                                try {
                                        Thread.sleep (50);
                                } catch (InterruptedException e) {
                                }
                        }
                }

                try {
                        Thread.sleep (100);
                } catch (InterruptedException e) {
                }
        }
}
}

/*
 * the applet/application class
 */
public class SyncMethod extends Applet implements Runnable {

Source source;
Sink sink;
FIFO fifo;
Thread thread;

/*
 * called when the applet is loaded
 * create instances of FIFO, Source, Sink, and Thread
 */
public void init () {

        fifo = new FIFO (200);
        source = new Source (fifo);
        sink = new Sink (fifo);

        thread = new Thread (this);
}

/*
 * start the graphics update thread
 */
public void start () {

        thread.start ();
}
```

```
/*
 * the graphics update thread
 * call repaint every 100ms
 */
public void run () {

        while (true) {
                repaint ();
                try {
                        Thread.sleep (100);
                } catch (InterruptedException e) {
                }
        }
}

/**
 * called from update() in response to repaint()
 * @param g - destination graphics context
 */
public void paint (Graphics g) {

        fifo.paint (g);
}

/**
 * main() is the application entry point
 * main() is unused when run as an applet
 * create a window frame and add the applet inside
 * @param args[] - command-line arguments
 */
public static void main (String args[]) {

        Frame f = new Frame ("Synchronized methods example");

        SyncMethod syncMethod = new SyncMethod ();
        f.add ("Center", syncMethod);
        f.setSize (400, 200);
        f.show ();

        syncMethod.init ();
        syncMethod.start ();
}
}
```

2. Create an HTML document that contains the applet. Create a new file
called howto44.html that contains the following code:

```
<html>
<head>
<title>Synchronize Code Methods</title>
</head>
<applet code="SyncMethod.class" width=410 height=230>
```

```
</applet>
<hr size=4>

</html>
```

3. Compile and test the applet. Compile the source by using `javac`. Test the applet by using the Appletviewer; enter the following command:

```
APPLETVIEWER howto44.html
```

You can also use `SyncMethod.java` as an application by typing

```
java SyncMethod
```

4. When `SyncMethod` is executed, a window opens, with a display illustrating the status of the FIFO. The reading and writing of the data is illustrated with markers that indicate the index of the data being read or written. The space between the lines, which represents the data, is shown as a colored bar. The colored bar is green when the buffer is less than half full. When the buffer becomes half full, the bar becomes red and the data is read out until no data remains in the buffer. The cycle then repeats. Figure 4.5 shows an example of the running applet.

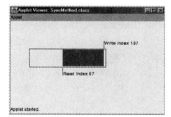

Figure 4.5 Methods can be synchronized.

How It Works

Four classes are defined in the program—FIFO, `Source`, `Sink`, and `SyncMethod`. The `FIFO` class implements the first-in, first-out data structure. The `Source` class is a thread that writes data into the FIFO at a constant rate. The `Sink` class is a thread that reads the data out of the FIFO. The `SyncMethod` class is the applet class proper.

The `FIFO` class contains an array of integers for holding the data. The variables `writeIndex` and `readIndex` are the write and read indices, respectively, for the data array. The variable `nItems` is the number of items in the data array.

Each of the methods in the `FIFO` class is declared `synchronized` so that data and indices cannot be examined or manipulated by more than one thread at a time. The `paint()` method draws a graphical representation of the FIFO in its current state. Markers showing the position of the write and read indices are drawn along with their values. Data within the FIFO is represented by a colored bar. The bar is green when the FIFO buffer is less than half full, red when it is more than half full.

The `Source` method extends `Thread` so that it may run as an independent thread. The constructor simply saves an instance of the FIFO and starts its thread by calling the `start()` method. An infinite loop is entered; this loop writes arbitrary data into the FIFO as long as it is not full. A delay of 100 milliseconds is used to limit the rate of writing into the FIFO. The delay is accomplished by calling `Thread.sleep()` with `100 milliseconds` as an argument.

The `Sink` method also runs as an independent thread by extending `Thread`. The constructor saves an instance of `FIFO` passed to it and starts its thread by calling `Thread.start()`. The `run()` method enters an infinite loop that waits for the FIFO to become half full before the data is read out. A delay of 1 second (1000 milliseconds) is added so that the FIFO display remains red long enough for the observer to notice the change. The data is read out at twice the rate at which it is written in. This guarantees that FIFO overflow will not occur. Data is read out until the FIFO is empty.

The `SyncMethod` class is the applet proper. The `init()` method creates a new instance of `FIFO` in addition to instances of `Source` and `Sink`. A thread for the applet is also created, which is used for regular updating of the graphical FIFO display. The `run()` method forces updating of the display by calling `repaint()`. The update rate is controlled by calling `Thread.sleep()` after each call to `repaint()`. The `paint()` method calls the `FIFO.paint()` method to update the display of the FIFO.

Comments

The `Source` and `Sink` methods do not implement the `Runnable` interface because they extend the `Thread` class. The `Thread` class itself implements the `Runnable` interface, so another implement's `Runnable` would be redundant.

COMPLEXITY
INTERMEDIATE

4.5 How do I...
Synchronize code sections?

Problem

I liked the `synchronized` method example in the previous section. Now I would like to be able to synchronize code sections and not an entire method. I understand that Java supports a mechanism to synchronize code sections only. For the purposes of education, I want to implement the previous example by using synchronized code sections only. How do I synchronize code sections?

Technique

The previous example uses monitors to synchronize methods. In object-oriented design, critical code sections are usually maintained in separate methods. However, it is possible to synchronize critical sections of code in a very similar manner.

Steps

1. Create the applet source file. Create a new file called `SyncCode.java` and enter the following source:

```java
import java.awt.*;
import java.applet.Applet;

/*
 * a class for handling first in, first out data structure
 */
class FIFO {

/*
 * the maximum depth of the FIFO
 */
final int MaxDepth = 200;

/*
 * the real depth of this FIFO
 */
int depth;

/*
 * write and read indexes into the data array
 */
int writeIndex;
int readIndex;

/*
 * the number of data items currently in the FIFO
 */
int nItems;

/*
 * the data proper
 */
int data[] = new int[MaxDepth];

/*
 * width and height of the FIFO graphical display
 */
```

```
int width;
int height;

/*
 * x and y position of the upper-left corner of the FIFO
 * graphical display
 */
int xpos;
int ypos;

/**
 * the constructor
 * @param d - depth of the FIFO
 */
public FIFO (int d) {

        depth = d;
        writeIndex = 0;
        readIndex = 0;
        nItems = 0;

        width = depth + 4;
        height = 50;
        xpos = 50;
        ypos = 75;
}

/**
 * write one integer value into the FIFO
 * @param value - the value to write
 */
void write (int value) {

        if (nItems >= depth) return;

        data[writeIndex] = value;
        writeIndex += 1;
        writeIndex %= depth;
        nItems += 1;
}

/**
 * read one integer value from the FIFO
 */
int read () {

        if (nItems < 1) return 0;

        int value = data[readIndex];
        readIndex += 1;
        readIndex %= depth;
        nItems -= 1;

        return value;
}
```

```java
/**
 * returns true if the FIFO is empty
 */
boolean empty () {

    return nItems > 0 ? false : true;
}

/**
 * returns true if the FIFO is half full
 */
boolean halfFull () {

    return nItems > (depth >> 1) ? true : false;
}

/**
 * returns true if the FIFO is full
 */
boolean full () {

    return nItems >= (depth) ? true : false;
}

/**
 * draws the FIFO graphical display
 * @param g - destination graphics context
 */
void paint (Graphics g) {

    int x, y, w, h;

    g.setColor (Color.white);
    g.fillRect (xpos, ypos, width, height);
    g.setColor (Color.black);
    g.drawRect (xpos, ypos, width, height);

    x = writeIndex + xpos + 2;
    y = ypos - 22;
    g.drawLine (x, y, x, y + 20);
    g.drawString ("Write index "+writeIndex, x+2, y+10);

    x = readIndex + xpos + 2;
    y = ypos + height + 22;
    g.drawLine (x, y-20, x, y);
    g.drawString ("Read index "+readIndex, x+2, y);

    if (nItems < 1) return;

    if (nItems > (depth>>1)) g.setColor (Color.red);
    else g.setColor (Color.green);

    x = xpos + 2 + readIndex;
    y = ypos + 2;
```

```
            if (writeIndex > readIndex) w = nItems;
            else w = width - readIndex - 4;
            h = height - 4;
            g.fillRect (x, y, w, h);

            if (writeIndex > readIndex) return;

            x = xpos + 2;
            w = writeIndex;
            g.fillRect (x, y, w, h);
    }
}

/*
 * a class that generates data continuously
 */
class Source extends Thread {

/*
 * the FIFO to write into
 */
FIFO fifo;
int value;

/**
 * constructor
 * saves the FIFO instance and starts the thread
 * @param f - an instance of FIFO
 */
public Source (FIFO f) {

        fifo = f;
        value = 0;

        start ();
}

/*
 * the thread that writes one word every 100ms
 */
public void run () {

        while (true) {
                synchronized (fifo) {
                        if (fifo.full() == false)
                                fifo.write (value++);
                }
                try {
                        Thread.sleep (100);
                } catch (InterruptedException e) {
                }
        }
}
}
```

```
/*
 * a class that reads data from the FIFO
 */
class Sink extends Thread {

/*
 * the FIFO to read from
 */
FIFO fifo;
int value;

/**
 * constructor
 * saves the FIFO instance and starts the thread
 * @param f - an instance of FIFO
 */
public Sink (FIFO f) {

    fifo = f;

    start ();
}

/*
 * the thread that reads all data out after the FIFO is half
 * full
 */
public void run () {

    boolean empty;
    boolean halfFull;

    while (true) {
        synchronized (fifo) {
            halfFull = fifo.halfFull ();
        }
        if (halfFull) {
            try {
                Thread.sleep (1000);
            } catch (InterruptedException e) {
            }
            do {
                synchronized (fifo) {
                    value = fifo.read ();
                }
                try {
                    Thread.sleep (50);
                } catch (InterruptedException e) {
                }
                synchronized (fifo) {
                    empty = fifo.empty ();
                }
            } while (empty == false);
```

```
            }

            try {
                Thread.sleep (100);
            } catch (InterruptedException e) {
            }
        }
    }
}

/*
 * the applet/application class
 */
public class SyncCode extends Applet implements Runnable {

Source source;
Sink sink;
FIFO fifo;
Thread thread;

/*
 * called when the applet is loaded
 * create instances of FIFO, Source, Sink, and Thread
 */
public void init () {

    fifo = new FIFO (200);
    source = new Source (fifo);
    sink = new Sink (fifo);

    thread = new Thread (this);
}

/*
 * start the graphics update thread
 */
public void start () {

    thread.start ();
}


/*
 * the graphics update thread
 * call repaint every 100ms
 */
public void run () {

    while (true) {
        repaint ();
        try {
            Thread.sleep (100);
        } catch (InterruptedException e) {
        }
```

```
        }
}

/**
 * called from update() in response to repaint()
 * @param g - destination graphics context
 */
public void paint (Graphics g) {

        synchronized (fifo) {
                fifo.paint (g);
        }
}

/**
 * main() is the application entry point
 * main() is unused when run as an applet
 * create a window frame and add the applet inside
 * @param args[] - command-line arguments
 */
public static void main (String args[]) {

        Frame f = new Frame ("Synchronized code example");

        SyncCode syncCode = new SyncCode ();
        f.add ("Center", syncCode);
        f.setSize (400, 200);
        f.show ();

        syncCode.init ();
        syncCode.start ();
}
}
```

2. Create an HTML document that contains the applet. Create a new file called **howto45.html** that contains the following code:

```
<html>
<head>
<title>Synchronize Code Sections</title>
</head>
<applet code="SyncCode.class" width=410 height=230>
</applet>
<hr size=4>

</html>
```

3. Compile and test the applet. Compile the source by using **javac**. Test the applet by using the Appletviewer; enter the following command:

```
APPLETVIEWER howto45.html
```

You can also run **SyncCode.java** as an application by typing

```
java SyncCode
```

4. When `SyncCode` is executed, a window opens, with a display illustrating the status of the `FIFO`. The reading and writing of the data are illustrated with lines that indicate the index of the data being read or written. The space between the lines, which represents the data, is shown as a colored bar. The colored bar is green when the buffer is less than half full. When the buffer becomes half full, the bar becomes red and the data is read out until no data remains in the buffer. The cycle then repeats while the data is being written at a constant rate. Figure 4.6 shows an example of the running applet.

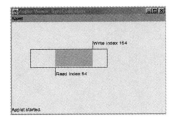

Figure 4.6 Sections, as well as full methods, can be synchronized.

How It Works

Four classes are defined in the program—`FIFO`, `Source`, `Sink`, and `SyncCode`. The `FIFO` class implements the first-in, first-out data structure. The `Source` class is a thread that writes data into the FIFO at a constant rate. The `Sink` class is a thread that reads the data out of the FIFO. The `SyncCode` class is the applet class proper.

This code is very similar to that in the previous example. The difference is that in the previous example the methods in the FIFO class were defined as synchronized. This example uses synchronizing only on the code section of interest.

Comments

Synchronizing code sections is functionally adequate but technically violates strict object-oriented design. The technique of synchronizing methods is preferred.

4.6 How do I...
Wait for a thread?

Problem

In the two previous examples, the `Sink.read()` method polls the FIFO every 100 milliseconds to determine whether data is available. This seems inefficient. There must be a better way to wait for the FIFO to become occupied. How do I wait for a thread?

Technique

The `wait()` and `notify()` methods can be used to wait for a thread. When a method needs to wait for a condition, it may call `wait()`. Execution is suspended until the `notify()` method is called from another thread. The `wait()` and `notify()` methods can be applied on any object; to execute them, a thread must lock the object first; the `wait()` method releases the lock before suspending the thread, and locks it again when resuming it.

Two conditions should cause a thread to block (wait). The first is during a read, when no data is in the FIFO. The second is during a write, when the FIFO is full.

In the first case, the `FIFO.read()` method should call `wait()` if the number of data items in the FIFO is less than one. The `notify()` method should be called after a data item has been written; this releases the thread waiting for a read.

The second case is analogous. `wait()` should be called in the `FIFO.write()` method when the number of items in the FIFO is equal to or greater than the FIFO size (depth). The `notify()` call for this case should be at the end of the `FIFO.read()` method, after an item has been read. Figure 4.7 shows an example of the running applet.

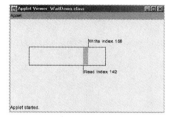

Figure 4.7 One thread waits for the other.

Steps

1. Create the applet source file. Create a new file called `WaitDemo.java` and enter the following source:

```java
import java.awt.*;
import java.applet.Applet;

/*
 * a class for handling first in, first out data structure
 */
class FIFO {

/*
 * the maximum depth of the FIFO
 */
final int MaxDepth = 200;

/*
 * the real depth of this FIFO
 */
int depth;

/*
 * write and read indexes into the data array
 */
int writeIndex;
int readIndex;

/*
 * the number of data items currently in the FIFO
 */
int nItems;

/*
 * the data proper
 */
int data[] = new int[MaxDepth];

/*
 * width and height of the FIFO graphical display
 */
int width;
int height;

/*
 * x and y position of the upper-left corner of the FIFO
 * graphical display
 */
int xpos;
int ypos;

/**
 * the constructor
```

```
 * @param d - depth of the FIFO
 */
public FIFO (int d) {

        depth = d;
        writeIndex = 0;
        readIndex = 0;
        nItems = 0;

        width = depth + 4;
        height = 50;
        xpos = 50;
        ypos = 75;
}

/**
 * write one integer value into the FIFO
 * invoke wait() if the FIFO is full
 * @param value - the value to write
 */
synchronized void write (int value) {

        if (nItems >= depth) {
                try {
                        wait ();
                } catch (InterruptedException e) {
                }
        }

        data[writeIndex] = value;
        writeIndex += 1;
        writeIndex %= depth;
        nItems += 1;
        notify ();
}

/**
 * read one integer value from the FIFO
 * invoke wait() if the FIFO is empty
 */
synchronized int read () {

        if (nItems < 1) {
                try {
                        wait ();
                } catch (InterruptedException e) {
                }
        }

        int value = data[readIndex];
        readIndex += 1;
        readIndex %= depth;
        nItems -= 1;
        notify ();
```

```
        return value;
}

/**
 * returns true if the FIFO is empty
 */
synchronized boolean empty () {

        return nItems > 0 ? false : true;
}

/**
 * returns true if the FIFO is half full
 */
synchronized boolean halfFull () {

        return nItems > (depth >> 1) ? true : false;
}

/**
 * returns true if the FIFO is full
 */
synchronized boolean full () {

        return nItems >= (depth) ? true : false;
}

/**
 * draws the FIFO graphical display
 * @param g - destination graphics context
 */
synchronized void paint (Graphics g) {

        int x, y, w, h;

        g.setColor (Color.white);
        g.fillRect (xpos, ypos, width, height);
        g.setColor (Color.black);
        g.drawRect (xpos, ypos, width, height);

        x = writeIndex + xpos + 2;
        y = ypos - 22;
        g.drawLine (x, y, x, y + 20);
        g.drawString ("Write index "+writeIndex, x+2, y+10);

        x = readIndex + xpos + 2;
        y = ypos + height + 22;
        g.drawLine (x, y-20, x, y);
        g.drawString ("Read index "+readIndex, x+2, y);

        if (nItems < 1) return;

        if (nItems > (depth>>1)) g.setColor (Color.red);
```

```
            else g.setColor (Color.green);

            x = xpos + 2 + readIndex;
            y = ypos + 2;
            if (writeIndex > readIndex) w = nItems;
            else w = width - readIndex - 4;
            h = height - 4;
            g.fillRect (x, y, w, h);

            if (writeIndex > readIndex) return;

            x = xpos + 2;
            w = writeIndex;
            g.fillRect (x, y, w, h);
    }
}

/*
 * a class that generates data continuously
 */
class Source extends Thread {

/*
 * the FIFO to write into
 */
FIFO fifo;
int value;

/**
 * constructor
 * saves the FIFO instance and starts the thread
 * @param f - an instance of FIFO
 */
public Source (FIFO f) {

        fifo = f;
        value = 0;

        start ();
}

/*
 * the thread that writes one word every 50ms on average
 */
public void run () {

        while (true) {
                if (fifo.full() == false)
                        fifo.write (value++);

                try {
                        Thread.sleep ((int) (100 * Math.random ()));
                } catch (InterruptedException e) {
                }
```

```
      }
}
}

/*
 * a class that reads data from the FIFO
 */
class Sink extends Thread {

/*
 * the FIFO to read from
 */
FIFO fifo;
int value;

/**
 * constructor
 * saves the FIFO instance and starts the thread
 * @param f - an instance of FIFO
 */
public Sink (FIFO f) {

      fifo = f;

      start ();
}

/*
 * the thread that tries to read one word every 50ms on average
 */
public void run () {

      while (true) {
            value = fifo.read ();

            try {
                  Thread.sleep ((int) (100 * Math.random ()));
            } catch (InterruptedException e) {
            }
      }
}
}

/*
 * the applet/application class
 */
public class WaitDemo extends Applet implements Runnable {

Source source;
Sink sink;
FIFO fifo;
Thread thread;

      /*
```

```
 * called when the applet is loaded
 * create instances of FIFO, Source, Sink, and Thread
 */
public void init () {

        fifo = new FIFO (200);
        source = new Source (fifo);
        sink = new Sink (fifo);

        thread = new Thread (this);
}

/*
 * start the graphics update thread
 */
public void start () {

        thread.start ();
}


/*
 * the graphics update thread
 * call repaint every 100ms
 */
public void run () {

        while (true) {
                repaint ();
                try {
                        Thread.sleep (100);
                } catch (InterruptedException e) {
                }
        }
}

/**
 * called from update() in response to repaint()
 * @param g - destination graphics context
 */
public void paint (Graphics g) {

        fifo.paint (g);
}

/**
 * main() is the application entry point
 * main() is unused when run as an applet
 * create a window frame and add the applet inside
 * @param args[] - command-line arguments
 */
public static void main (String args[]) {

        Frame f = new Frame ("FIFO Demo");
```

```
            WaitDemo waitDemo = new WaitDemo ();
            f.add ("Center", waitDemo);
            f.setSize (400, 200);
            f.show ();

            waitDemo.init ();
            waitDemo.start ();
    }
}
```

2. Create an HTML document that contains the applet. Create a new file called **howto46.html** that contains the following code:

```
<html>
<head>
<title>Wait for a thread</title>
</head>
<applet code="WaitDemo.class" width=410 height=230>
</applet>
<hr size=4>

</html>
```

3. Compile and test the applet. Compile the source by using **javac**. Test the applet by using the Appletviewer; enter the following command:

```
APPLETVIEWER howto46.html
```

You can also run **WaitDemo.java** as an application by typing

```
java WaitDemo
```

4. When **WaitDemo** is executed, a window opens, showing the running applet/application. This example is slightly different in its behavior. The **Source** class thread writes data at a random rate, and the **Sink** class thread reads data at a random rate. The reading and writing rates are random, but their average rate is the same. This allows the FIFO to be sometimes filled and sometimes empty.

How It Works

As in the examples in How-To 4.4 and How-To 4.5, four classes are defined: **FIFO**, **Source**, **Sink**, and **WaitDemo**. The **FIFO** class implements a first-in, first-out data structure with blocking (waiting) reads and writes. The **Source** class writes data into the FIFO at a random rate that averages to one item every 50 milliseconds. The **Sink** class reads data at a random rate that also averages to 50 milliseconds. Figure 4.8 illustrates this process.

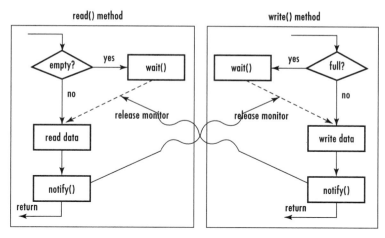

Figure 4.8 The wait() method allows synchronization between threads.

The FIFO constructor initializes the depth, the write index, the read index, and the number of items. It also initializes variables used for graphical display.

The **FIFO.write()** method first checks the number of items stored. If the number of items is equal to or greater than the depth, calling **wait()** blocks the calling thread. The calling thread will be released when **notify()** is called from the **FIFO.read()** method. This logic keeps the FIFO from overflowing, avoiding data loss. After the data is written, **notify()** must be called to release any threads that might be blocked by **FIFO.read()**. Figure 4.8 shows the flow of the **read()** and **write()** methods.

The **FIFO.read()** method checks to make sure that there is data in the FIFO to be read. If not, **wait()** is called, which blocks the calling thread. The calling thread is released when **notify()** is called from the **FIFO.write()** method. After data has been read, **notify()** must be called to release any threads that might be blocked by **FIFO.write()**. It should be noted that the example works for only one **Source** thread and one **Sink** thread; if you have more than one **Source** or **Sink**, one may incorrectly wake up the other.

The remaining routines for determining the FIFO status are identical to those of How-To 4.4 and How-To 4.5. The **FIFO.paint()** method draws the state of the FIFO graphically—this is also unchanged from How-To 4.4 and How-To 4.5.

The **Source** and **Sink** classes appear simpler than in previous examples. This is because the testing and management for FIFO overflow and underflow are handled in the **FIFO** class. The **Source** class creates a thread that writes data into the FIFO at an average rate of one item every 50 milliseconds. The **Sink** class creates a thread that reads data at an average rate of one item every 50 milliseconds. These threads block in order to avoid overflows and underflows.

The WaitDemo class is the applet class proper. It creates instances of FIFO, Source, and Sink. It also creates its own thread for paint updates. The WaitDemo thread forces a repaint every 100 milliseconds by calling repaint(). The main() method creates a window frame and adds an instance of WaitDemo in the event that the program is used as an application.

Comments

The use of wait() and notify() requires some consideration to avoid deadlock conditions which can result if a thread is blocked and cannot be released. This could occur in this example if the FIFO depth were 0, which is, of course, pathological.

Deadlock occurs whenever every thread is waiting on some other thread to release a block. They wait forever unless someone intervenes. It is sort of like a group of people who want to reconcile their differences, but no one is willing to speak first.

Note that all the methods (except for the constructor) are declared synchronized. This is still necessary to avoid data corruption. Synchronized code sections could have been used but would not be as clean. The synchronized methods are necessary to use the wait and notify methods, also.

EVENTS AND PARAMETERS

5

EVENTS AND PARAMETERS

How do I...

Programmers and users have become accustomed to the event-driven approach to application design. Instead of providing users with a limited set of menu choices, we give them an opportunity to interact with applications in a richer way by capturing and handling user events. A user event is an action on the user's part that indicates that he wants to perform some task in the program. If a user clicks the mouse while over a button, he is communicating with the program. Likewise, if he drags, double-clicks, or clicks on the close box, he wants to perform a certain action. As programmers, it is our job to detect this action and respond to it.

Graphical user interface (GUI) environments are composed of an operating system, which detects low-level events such as mouse clicks and keypresses; the Java Virtual Machine (JVM), which translates these actions into messages; and an application layer, which translates these messages into program activities that (hopefully) satisfy the user's wishes. Your job is to tell the JVM which events you want to listen to and to write code to perform a program activity whenever that event occurs.

In a GUI program, the GUI is passive, meaning that it only responds to user actions. The JVM makes the method calls defined in the interfaces. When you implement the interfaces in your classes, you provide the processes for handling these events.

5.1 Handle Action Events

A common event type in the GUI environment is the **Action** event. This high-level event occurs whenever any type of button is clicked. Because so many of the controls on a Java applet are buttons, this event is very important.

5.2 Handle Adjustment Events

Sliders and scrollbars are an integral part of modern applications. The **Adjustment** event is used to communicate between the user and the program.

5.3 Handle Mouse Events

The mouse is an important part of any application that requires user interaction. All computer users have grown to expect programs to accept mouse input. This example shows how to access the mouse position and button presses by creating a simple drawing program that uses the mouse.

5.4 Handle Window Events

Window events are generated whenever the window itself is being manipulated. Examples of this manipulation are activation, closing, deactivation, and opening.

5.5 Access Applet Parameters

Another important part of Java programming is the passing of parameters to the application or applet. Java applets have the capability to receive parameters from the HTML file that called the applet. This is useful when you're creating robust applets that require input to determine the output or function. This example creates a scrolling text marquee that accepts the text string as an applet parameter.

5.6 Parse Applet Parameters

The ability to parse applet parameters is useful when you're passing several parameters to the applet in a single-parameter string. This example creates another text marquee that accepts the text itself, the color, and the direction as a single parameter. The applet can accept up to five different parameters, allowing all five to be scrolling at once.

COMPLEXITY
INTERMEDIATE

5.1 How do I...
Handle action events?

Problem

I would like to create an applet with buttons for the user to click. How do I find out when the user has clicked the button, and where do I place the code to handle that event? In addition, if I have several buttons, how do I know which one was clicked?

Technique

The approach used in this example is to create an applet that contains a button labeled "Say Hello." A special class is created that "listens" for **Action** events. When the button is clicked, this class "hears" the **Action** event and runs some code which proves that the event really heard the click.

This example illustrates the following concepts:

- How to create a listener class

- How to connect the class to a button

- How to tell which button is clicked

- How to connect the event to code that you write

Steps

1. Create a file named **testActionEvents.java** that contains the following code:

```
/*
Example 5.1 This example shows how an action listener
 can be used to coordinate activities among various
components on an applet
 */

import java.awt.*;
import java.awt.event.*;
import java.applet.*;

public class testActionEvents extends Applet
{
    public void init()
    {
        super.init();
```

```
        setLayout(null);
        btnHello = new Button("Say Hello");
        btnHello.setBounds(36,12,108,43);
        add(btnHello);
        Action btnAction = new Action();
        btnHello.addActionListener(btnAction);
        txtField1 = new TextField();
        txtField1.setBounds(36,96,144,31);
        add(txtField1);

    }


    /* Declare Components */
    Button btnHello;
    TextField txtField1;

    class Action implements ActionListener
    {
        public void actionPerformed(ActionEvent event)
        {
            Object object1 = event.getSource();
            if (object1 == btnHello)
                btnHelloAction(event);
        }
    }

    void btnHelloAction(ActionEvent e)
    {
        txtField1.setText("Hi,Mom");
    }
}
```

2. Create an HTML document that contains the applet. Create a new file called howto51.html that contains the following code:

```
<html>
<head>
<title>Test Action Events</title>
</head>
<applet code="testActionEvents.class" width=600 height=460>
</applet>
<hr size=4>

</html>
```

3. Compile and test the applet. Compile the source by using javac. Test the applet by using the Appletviewer; enter the following command:

```
APPLETVIEWER howto51.html
```

4. A window appears on the screen that contains a button and a text box. When the button is clicked, the string "Hi,Mom" (in honor of football season) appears in the text box, thus proving that the button works.

How It Works

In order to listen to any event in Java 1.2, a listener class must be created. This class is normally declared to be an inner class of the applet or application, but it can be the class itself. The code is more readable if implemented as an inner class (a class defined inside another class definition), but it causes the Java compiler to create one more file to download. JAR files can be used to overcome this as you will see in Chapter 11, "Miscellaneous and Advanced Topics."

Listener classes must implement an interface and all the methods that this interface requires. This class definition is fairly simple:

```
class Action implements ActionListener
```

I have named this class **Action** and stated that it implements the **ActionListener** interface. Recall that an interface is like a pure virtual class and therefore cannot be instantiated. In addition, it has no data members. By implementing the class, you are saying that you want your class to inherit the behavior of the **ActionListener** interface. That behavior is that the interface detects the presence of a **Action** event and calls a method called **actionPerformed()**. The name **actionPerformed()** is not arbitrarily chosen, but is a predefined virtual method in the interface. An action event object is passed to this method. You can inquire of this object for details about the event that occurred.

In order to connect this event to the correct button, you have to find out what object fired the event. In order to do that, you create an instance of the **Object** class, as shown here:

```
Object object1 = event.getSource();
```

The **getSource()** method of the event class returns a reference to the object that fired it. You assign this to the object variable. This object can be examined as shown here:

```
if (object1 == btnHello)
    btnHelloAction(event);
```

If you had implemented several buttons in this application, you could use this logic to determine which button was pressed. The connection between the button and the listener class does not happen automatically. An instance of the class must be created, as shown here:

```
Action btnAction = new Action();
```

With this object in memory, a connection between the button and the listener can be made by invoking the **addActionListener()** method of the button class. Any number of listeners can be registered. All registered listeners are called in turn when the corresponding event occurs. This connection is made by calling the addActionListener as shown here:

```
btnHello.addActionListener(btnAction);
```

You create and name the routine **btnHelloAction()**. The event object is passed again to this method in case further information is needed. The event processing method is shown here:

```
void btnHelloAction(ActionEvent e)
{
  txtField1.setText("Hi,Mom");
}
```

This is where you get to practice the art of programming again. The other code has to be "wired" just so in order to ensure that the call to this code happens as expected. An alternative would be to do all the processing in the **actionPerformed()** method itself. Figure 5.1 shows the result of running this code.

Figure 5.1 The ActionListener interface connects buttons to event handler methods.

5.2   How do I...
Handle adjustment events?

Problem

I want to implement a slider on my user interface. When my user wants to order a larger quantity of product, he should move the slider to the right and when he wants less, to the left. I need to be able to detect the event so that I can provide a text box with visual feedback to the user. How do I do this?

Technique

Java contains an `AdjustmentListener` class, which functions sort of like the `ActionListener,` but which is used for continuous events such as the movement of a slider or scrollbar. You declare an inner class that implements the `AdjustmentListener` interface. Each type of listener can be registered only with objects capable of generating the corresponding type of events. Then the adjustment listener object is declared and registered to listen for adjustment events. Finally, a routine is created to do the specific job of updating the text box whenever the slider is moved.

This example illustrates the following concepts:

- How to create a listener class

- How to connect the class to the slider

- How to tell which slider is dragged

- How to connect the event to code that you write

Steps

1. Create a file named **testAdjustEvent.java** and add to it the following code:

```
/*
    A basic extension of the java.applet.Applet class
 */

import java.awt.*;
import java.awt.event.*;
import java.applet.*;

public class testAdjustEvent extends Applet
{
    void ScrollValueChanged( AdjustmentEvent event)
    {
        int intValue = scoreBar.getValue();
        String strValue = String.valueOf(intValue);

        txtScore.setText(strValue);
    }

    public void init()
    {
        super.init();

      setLayout(null);
      label1 = new Label("Score:", Label.RIGHT);
      label1.setBounds(36,36,60,21);
      add(label1);
```

```
        txtScore = new TextField();
        txtScore.setEditable(false);
        txtScore.setBounds(108,36,48,23);
        add(txtScore);
        scoreBar = new Scrollbar(Scrollbar.HORIZONTAL,
        ➥0, 10,0,100);
        scoreBar.setBounds(180,36,137,26);
        add(scoreBar);
        txtScore.setText(String.valueOf(scoreBar.getValue()));

        Adjustment1 lAdjustment = new Adjustment1();
        scoreBar.addAdjustmentListener(lAdjustment);
    }


    Label label1;
    TextField txtScore;
    Scrollbar scoreBar;

    class Adjustment1 implements AdjustmentListener
    {
        public void adjustmentValueChanged(AdjustmentEvent
        ➥event)
        {
        Object object1 = event.getSource();
        if (object1==scoreBar)
            ScrollValueChanged(event);
        }
    }
}
```

2. Create an HTML document that contains the applet. Create a new file called **howto52.html** that contains the following code:

```
<html>
<head>
<title>Test Adjustment Listeners</title>
</head>
<applet code="testAdjustEvent.class" width=600 height=460>
</applet>
<hr size=4>

</html>
```

3. Compile and test the applet. Compile the source by using **javac**. Test the applet by using the Appletviewer; enter the following command:

```
APPLETVIEWER howto52.html
```

4. A window appears on the screen; it contains a slider and a text box. When the slider is dragged, the textbox displays the current value of the slider.

How It Works

In order to listen to the adjustment event in Java 1.2, a class that implements the `AdjustmentListener` interface must be created. This class is normally declared to be an inner class of the applet or application. Listener classes must implement an interface and all the methods that this interface requires. This class definition is fairly simple:

```
class Adjustment1 implements AdjustmentListener
```

I have named this class **Adjustment1** and stated that it implements the `AdjustmentListener` interface. Recall that an interface is like a pure virtual class and therefore cannot be instantiated. By implementing the interface, you are saying that you want your class to inherit the behavior of the `AdjustmentListener` interface: A method called `adjustmentValueChanged()` should be called when an **Adjustment** event occurs. The name `adjustmentValueChanged()` is not arbitrarily chosen, but is a predefined virtual method in the interface. An event object is passed to this method. You can inquire of this object for details about the event that occurred.

In order to connect this event to the correct slider, you have to find out what object fired the event. In order to do that, you create an instance of the **Object** class, as shown here:

```
Object object1 = event.getSource();
```

The **getSource()** method of the event class returns a reference to the object that fired it. You assign this to the object variable. This object has a name that can be examined as shown here:

```
if (object1 == scoreBar)
    ScrollValueChanged(event);
```

If you had implemented several sliders in this application, you could use this logic to determine which one was changed. The connection between the slider and the listener class does not happen automatically. An instance of the class must be created, as shown here:

```
Adjustment1 lAdjustment = new Adjustment1();
```

With this object in memory, a connection between the slider and the listener can be made by invoking the **addAdjustmentListener()** method of the **Scrollbar** class. This connection is shown here:

```
scoreBar.addAdjustmentListener(lAdjustment);
```

You create and name the routine **ScrollValueChanged()**. The event object is passed again to this method in case further information is needed. The event processing method is shown here:

```
void ScrollValueChanged( AdjustmentEvent event)
{
    int intValue = scoreBar.getValue();
    String strValue = String.valueOf(intValue);
```

```
txtScore.setText(strValue);
}
```

This is where you get back to programming again. The other code has to be wired just so in order to ensure that the call to this code happens as expected. Figure 5.2 shows the result of running this code.

Figure 5.2 The
AdjustmentListener inter-
face connects scrollbars and
sliders to event handler
methods.

5.3 How do I...
Access mouse events?

Problem

I would like to create a simple drawing program that uses the mouse. The mouse button should be held down to draw. It would also be nice to have a color bar and use the mouse to select the color to draw in. How do I access mouse events in Java?

Technique

One way to access mouse events using the Abstract Windowing Toolkit (AWT) is to declare a class to implement the MouseListener and MouseMotionListener interfaces. These interfaces declare a set of methods that are called when certain mouse events occur. This application implements mouseDragged() and mousePressed to do the drawing.

Steps

1. Create the applet source file. Create a new file called **Doodle.java** and enter the following source:

```java
import java.applet.Applet;
import java.awt.*;
import java.awt.event.*;

/**
 * The ColorBar class displays a color bar for color selection.
 */
class ColorBar {

/*
 * the top-left coordinate of the color bar
 */
int xpos, ypos;

/*
 * the width and height of the color bar
 */
int width, height;

/*
 * the current color selection index into the colors array
 */
int selectedColor = 3;

/*
 * the array of colors available for selection
 */
static Color colors[] = {
    Color.white, Color.gray, Color.red, Color.pink,
    Color.orange, Color.yellow, Color.green, Color.magenta,
    Color.cyan, Color.blue
};

/**
 * Create the color bar
 */
public ColorBar (int x, int y, int w, int h) {

    xpos = x;
    ypos = y;
    width = w;
    height = h;
}

/**
 * Paint the color bar
 * @param g - destination graphics object
 */
void paint (Graphics g) {

    int x, y;     // position of each color box
```

```
        int w, h;     // size of each color box

        for (int i=0; i<colors.length; i+=1) {
            w = width;
            h = height/colors.length;
            x = xpos;
            y = ypos + (i * h);
            g.setColor (Color.black);
            g.fillRect (x, y, w, h);
            if (i == selectedColor) {
                x += 5;
                y += 5;
                w -= 10;
                h -= 10;
            } else {
                x += 1;
                y += 1;
                w -= 2;
                h -= 2;
            }
            g.setColor (colors[i]);
            g.fillRect (x, y, w, h);
        }
    }

    /**
     * Check to see if the mouse is inside a palette box.
     * If so, set selectedColor and return true,
     *         otherwise return false.
     * @param x, y - x and y position of mouse
     */
    boolean inside (int x, int y) {

        int i, h;

        if (x < xpos || x > xpos+width) return false;
        if (y < ypos || y > ypos+height) return false;

        h = height/colors.length;
        for (i=0; i<colors.length; i+=1) {
            if (y < (i+1)*h+ypos) {
                selectedColor = i;
                return true;
            }
        }
        return false;
    }

}

/**
 * The Doodle applet implements a drawable surface
 * with a limited choice of colors to draw with.
 */
public class Doodle extends Applet
        implements MouseListener, MouseMotionListener
```

```
{

/*
 * the maximum number of points that can be
 * saved in the xpoints, ypoints, and color arrays
 */
static final int MaxPoints = 1000;

/*
 * arrays to hold the points where the user draws
 */
int xpoints[] = new int[MaxPoints];
int ypoints[] = new int[MaxPoints];

/*
 * the color of each point
 */
int color[] = new int[MaxPoints];

/*
 * used to keep track of the previous mouse
 * click to avoid filling arrays with the
 * same point
 */
int lastx;
int lasty;

/*
 * the number of points in the arrays
 */
int npoints = 0;
ColorBar colorBar;
boolean inColorBar;

/**
 * Initialize the drawing space
 */
public void init () {

    setBackground(Color.white);
    colorBar = new ColorBar (10, 10, 30, 200);
    addMouseListener(this);
    addMouseMotionListener(this);
}

/**
 * Redisplay the drawing space
 * @param g - destination graphics object
 */
public void update (Graphics g) {

    int i;

    for (i=0; i<npoints; i+=1) {
        g.setColor (colorBar.colors[color[i]]);
        g.fillOval (xpoints[i]-5, ypoints[i]-5, 10, 10);
```

```
    }
    colorBar.paint (g);
}

/**
 * Repaint the drawing space when required
 * @param g - destination graphics object
 */
public void paint (Graphics g) {

    update (g);
}



public void mouseClicked(MouseEvent e){}
public void mouseEntered(MouseEvent e){}
public void mouseExited(MouseEvent e){}
public void mouseReleased(MouseEvent e){}
public void mouseMoved(MouseEvent e){}

public void mousePressed(MouseEvent e)
{
    int x =e.getX();
    int y =e.getY();

    if (colorBar.inside (x, y)) {
        inColorBar = true;
        repaint ();
    }
    inColorBar = false;
    if (npoints < MaxPoints) {
        lastx = x;
        lasty = y;
        xpoints[npoints] = x;
        ypoints[npoints] = y;
        color[npoints] = colorBar.selectedColor;
        npoints += 1;
        repaint();
        return;
    }
}

public void mouseDragged(MouseEvent e)
{
    if (inColorBar) return;

    int x =e.getX();
    int y =e.getY();

    if ((x != lastx || y != lasty) && npoints < MaxPoints) {
        lastx = x;
        lasty = y;
        xpoints[npoints] = x;
        ypoints[npoints] = y;
        color[npoints] = colorBar.selectedColor;
```

```
            npoints += 1;
            repaint ();
    }

}

/**
 * The main method allows this class to be run as an application
 * in addition to being run as an applet.
 * @param args - command-line arguments
 */

public static void main (String args[]) {

    Frame f = new Frame ("Doodle");
    Doodle doodle = new Doodle ();
        WindowListener l = new WindowAdapter()
        {
            public void windowClosing(WindowEvent e)
            {
                System.exit(0);
            }//windowClosing
        };//WindowListener
        f.addWindowListener(l);


    f.setSize (410, 430);
    f.add ("Center", doodle);
    f.show ();
    doodle.init ();
}
}
```

2. Create an HTML document that contains the applet. Create a new file called howto53.html that contains the following code:

```html
<html>

<head>
<title>Doodle </title>
</head>
<applet code="Doodle.class" width=200 height=200>
</applet>
<hr size=4>

</html>
```

3. Compile and test the applet. Compile the source by using javac. Test the applet by using the Appletviewer; enter the following command:

```
APPLETVIEWER howto53.html
```

You can also run **Doodle.java** as an application by typing

```
java Doodle
```

4. When Doodle is executed, a window opens, containing a drawing area and a color palette on the left. The color palette contains 10 colors. Use the mouse to select a color; then move to the right and hold down the mouse button, and use the mouse to draw. Try changing the color and draw something else. Figure 5.3 shows an example of the running applet.

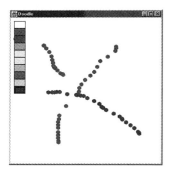

Figure 5.3 The mouseDragged() and mousePressed() methods give you control over the mouse.

How It Works

The Doodle applet/application contains two classes: **Doodle** and **ColorBar**.

The **ColorBar** class draws a color toolbar containing a palette of 10 colors that the user can use to doodle. The constructor for **ColorBar** saves the x and y position, width, and height for the toolbar in the variables **xpos**, **ypos**, **width**, and **height**, respectively.

The **paint()** method in **ColorBar** uses these variables to draw the color toolbar itself. The selected color (the color that the user selects with the mouse) is drawn as a slightly smaller filled rectangle.

The **inside()** method determines which color has been selected by comparing the mouse x and y values passed to it by the **mousePressed()** method in the **Doodle** class. **Inside()** returns **True** if the mouse x and y are inside the color toolbar; it also sets the **selectedColor** variable to the appropriate value.

If the **Doodle** class is run as an application, control is transferred to the **main()** method. The **main()** method creates a window frame to contain the applet, creates an instance of the **Doodle** class, and adds that instance to the **Frame**.

If the mouse coordinates are not within the color toolbar, the mouse coordinates are saved in two arrays, **xpoints** and **ypoints**. The color of the point is also saved in the array **color**. Because these arrays are static, the number of points actually saved (and therefore painted) is limited by the variable **MaxPoints**.

The first time an applet is run, the `paint()` method is called directly. Every subsequent paint is achieved by calling `repaint()`. The `repaint()` method requests an update to occur as soon as it can. The default `update()` method erases the frame by filling the frame with the current background color and then calls `paint()`.

In this example, the `paint()` method calls the `update()` method. The `update()` method actually performs the painting. This `update()` method over-rides the default `update()` method because the default method continuously erases the frame, which is unnecessary and causes an annoying flicker. `update()` in turn calls the `filloval()` method to draw each point. In a production situation, you would want to use double-buffering in order to guarantee that the background will be erased. (Double-buffering is covered in greater detail in Chapter 7, "Advanced Graphics.")

The idea of having `paint()` call `update()` may seem slightly illogical at first. If the flow of the applet is traced, it can be shown that this technique can actually be beneficial. In this example, the first time the applet is run, the `paint()` method is called, which calls `update()`. From that point on, every time a `repaint()` is requested, `update()` is called, which actually performs the painting. The `paint()` method is never called after the first time. The traditional flow has `update()` being called, which in turn calls `paint()` every time a `repaint()` was requested. The technique shown in this example reduces the number of methods being called. For example, if `repaint()` is requested 1,000 times, the default `update()` and `paint()` would each have to be called 1,000 times. By using the new technique, `update()` would be called 1,000 times, and `paint()` would be called only once.

The `Doodle` class tells the object that generates the event that it wants to listen to both mouse events and mouse motion events by declaring that it will implement the `MouseListener` and `MouseMotionListener` interfaces, as shown here:

```
public class Doodle extends Applet
        implements MouseListener, MouseMotionListener
```

The rules governing interfaces is that a class must implement every method of the interface, even if it is not going to do anything when that event occurs. To conform to this requirement, the following stubbed code is added:

```
public void mouseClicked(MouseEvent e){}
public void mouseEntered(MouseEvent e){}
public void mouseExited(MouseEvent e){}
public void mouseReleased(MouseEvent e){}
public void mouseMoved(MouseEvent e){}
```

Finally, the two events that we are interested in are implemented as shown here:

```
public void mousePressed(MouseEvent e)
{
    int x =e.getX();
    int y =e.getY();
```

```
        .
        .
        .
}

public void mouseDragged(MouseEvent e)
{
    if (inColorBar) return;

    int x =e.getX();
    int y =e.getY();
        .
        .
        .
}
```

The `MouseEvent` object contains the x and y coordinates. You obtain them by calling the `getX()` and `getY()` methods of the `MouseEvent` class.

COMPLEXITY
ADVANCED

5.4   How do I...
Handle window events?

Problem

I need to create a very sophisticated application that must control the closing of the application. I need to be able to handle the window closing event and prevent the application from being closed until I am ready. In addition, I need to keep track of whether the application is active, iconified, and so on. How do I trap these window events?

Technique

As you might guess, Java contains a `WindowListener` class. It can be used to listen for window messages. This gives you a chance to change the behavior of the application: You can make it impossible to close the application without getting one last chance to clean up the application.

Steps

1. Create a file named `Windows1.java` and add the following source code:

```
import java.util.*;
import java.awt.*;
import java.awt.event.*;
import javax.swing.*;
import javax.swing.text.*;
```

```
public class Windows1 extends Object implements WindowListener
{
    public void windowOpened(WindowEvent e)
    {
        System.out.println("Window opened.");
    }

    public void windowClosing(WindowEvent e)
    {
        System.out.println("Window closing.");
 System.exit(0);

    }

    public void windowClosed(WindowEvent e)
    {
        System.out.println("Window closed.");
    }

    public void windowIconified(WindowEvent e)
    {
        System.out.println("Window iconified.");
    }

    public void windowDeiconified(WindowEvent e)
    {
        System.out.println("Window deiconified.");
    }

    public void windowActivated(WindowEvent e)
    {

        System.out.println("Window activated.");
    }

    public void windowDeactivated(WindowEvent e)
    {
        System.out.println("Window deactivated");
    }

    public static void main(String s[])
    {
        JFrame frame = new JFrame("Windows1");

        frame.setDefaultCloseOperation(JFrame.DO_NOTHING
➥_ON_CLOSE);
        frame.addWindowListener(new Windows1());


frame.getContentPane().add( new Label("Hello World"), "Center");

        frame.pack();
        frame.setVisible(true);
    }


}
```

> **NOTE**
>
> The class JFrame is part of the Swing classes. You will learn about both these classes in Chapter 8, "JFC."

2. Compile the program by using **javac**.

3. Run the program by typing the following:

```
java Windows1
```

4. You see the tiny window with "Hello World" displayed in it. As you iconify and close and open the application, you see messages appear in the controlling window as shown in Figure 5.4.

Figure 5.4 Window events can be handled by the WindowListener class.

How It Works

In order to listen to window events, you must create a class that implements the WindowListener interface. This is done in the following code segment:

```
public class Windows1 extends Object implements WindowListener
```

All the following methods are required to implement this listener interface:

```
public void windowOpened(WindowEvent e)
public void windowClosing(WindowEvent e)
public void windowClosed(WindowEvent e)
public void windowIconified(WindowEvent e)
public void windowDeiconified(WindowEvent e)
public void windowActivated(WindowEvent e)
public void windowDeactivated(WindowEvent e)
```

Whenever one of the window events occurs, the corresponding method is called. This gives you the opportunity to change the behavior of the application if you so choose.

5.5 How do I...
Access applet parameters?

Problem

I liked the scrolling text marquee in Example 3.5, except that it requires recompilation of the source every time the text is changed. I would like to run the marquee as an applet and be able to pass a parameter that contains the text to be scrolled. How do I access applet parameters?

Technique

In this example you will create a single scrolling text marquee. The text will scroll from left to right. The text that scrolls will be passed to the Java applet from the HTML file by using the <param> tag. Applet parameters are returned from the `Applet.getParameter()` method with the parameter name as an argument. `Applet.getParameter()` returns the value of the applet parameter as a `String` object.

Steps

1. Create the applet source file. Create a new file called `ScrollApp.java` and enter the following source:

```
import java.applet.Applet;
import java.awt.*;

class Scroll {

int xstart, ystart;
int width, height;
String text;
int deltaX, deltaY;
int xpos, ypos;
Color color;

/**
 * Text scrolls in different directions.
 * @param xpos       initial x position
 * @param ypos       initial y position
 * @param deltax     velocity in x direction
 * @param deltay     velocity in y direction
 * @param width      bounding point for window panel width
 * @param height     bounding point for window panel height
 * @param text       text that is scrolled on the window
 * @param color      color of the text
 */
```

```java
public Scroll (int x, int y, int dx, int dy, int w,
➥int h, String t, Color c) {

    xstart = x;
    ystart = y;
    width = w;
    height = h;
    text = t;
    deltaX = dx;
    deltaY = dy;
    color = c;
    xpos = xstart;
    ypos = ystart;
}

/**
 * Called from update() in response to repaint()
 * @param g - destination graphics object
 */
void paint (Graphics g) {

    g.setColor (color);
    g.drawString (text, xpos, ypos);
    xpos += deltaX;
    ypos += deltaY;

    FontMetrics fm = g.getFontMetrics ();
    int textw = fm.stringWidth (text);
    int texth = fm.getHeight ();
    if (deltaX < 0 && xpos < -textw) xpos = xstart;
    if (deltaX > 0 && xpos > width) xpos = xstart;
    if (deltaY < 0 && ypos < 0) ypos = ystart;
    if (deltaY > 0 && ypos > height+texth) ypos = ystart;
}
} // Class Scroll


/*
 * The applet/application class
 */
public class ScrollApp extends Applet implements Runnable{

/*
 * Width and height of the bounding panel
 */
int width, height;

/*
 * Instance of a left-scrolling Scroll object
 */
Scroll left;
String input_text;
Font font = new Font("Helvetica",1,24);
Thread thread;

/*
 * Called when the applet is loaded
```

```
 * Create instances of FIFO, Source, Sink, and Thread.
 */
public void init () {

    input_text=getParameter("text");
    Dimension d = getSize ();

    width = d.width;
    height = d.height;

    left = new Scroll (400, 50, -5, 0, width, height,
        input_text, Color.red);
} // init()

/*
 * Start the graphics update thread.
 */
public void start() {

    thread = new Thread(this);
    thread.start();
} // start()

/*
 * The graphics update thread
 * Call repaint every 100 ms.
 */
public void run() {

    while (true) {
        try {
            Thread.sleep(100);
        } catch (InterruptedException e) { }
        repaint();
    }
} // run()

/*
 * Stop the graphics update thread.
 */
public void stop() {

    if (thread != null)
    thread = null;
} // stop()

/**
 * Called from update() in response to repaint()
 * @param g - destination graphics object
 */
public void paint (Graphics g) {

    g.setFont(font);
    left.paint (g);
} // paint()
} // class ScrollApp
```

2. Create an HTML document that contains the applet. Create a new file called **howto55.html** that contains the following code:

```
<html>
<head>
<title>Marquee</title>
</head>
<applet code="ScrollApp.class" width=400 height=60>
<param name = "text" value = "The Java(tm) How To">
</applet>
<hr size=4>

</html>
```

3. Compile and test the applet. Compile the source by using **javac**. Test the applet by using the Appletviewer; enter the following command:

```
APPLETVIEWER howto55.html
```

ScrollApp can only be run as an applet because it requires applet parameters to be passed to it.

When **ScrollApp** is executed, a window opens, with the words "The Java(tm) How To" scrolling from the left to the right. Try changing the value of the **text** parameter in the **howto55.html** file and run the applet again. The text changes to whatever is specified in the HTML file. **ScrollApp** does not have to be recompiled to effect the change. Figure 5.5 shows an example of the running applet.

Figure 5.5 Applets can accept parameters and use them to control the execution of a program.

How It Works

The ScrollApp applet contains two classes, **ScrollApp** and **Scroll**. **ScrollApp** is the applet itself, and **Scroll** contains the methods for computing and drawing the moving text.

`ScrollApp` extends `Applet` because it is the applet, and implements `Runnable` because it has a separate thread running within it. An instance of the `Scroll` class, called `left`; a `String`, called `input_text`; and a `Thread`, called `thread`, are created. The font is set to 24-point bold Helvetica.

The `init()` method uses the `getParameter()` method to retrieve the parameter from the html file. The `getParameter()` method takes a string value, and `parameter.getparameter()` returns a null value if the parameter is not defined. This string value is the name the parameter is given in the HTML file. The parameter is defined in the HTML file using the `<param>` tag. An example of defining a parameter with the name `myparameter` and a value of `This is what I want to send` in an HTML file is

```
<param name = "myparameter" value = "This is what I want to send" >
```

This must all be within the `<applet>` `</applet>` section of the HTML file. In the next step, the width and height are set to the width and height of the panel. A new scroll is created, with an initial starting location of 400,50; a horizontal velocity of -5; a vertical velocity of 0; a width and height equal to the panel size; a text value to scroll; and the color red.

The `start()` and `run()` methods are used to create a thread that sleeps for a 100 milliseconds and then redraws the marquee.

The `Scroll` class is identical to that used in Example 3.5.

Comments

This applet draws the text to be scrolled directly to the screen. This method may cause the text to flicker slightly. To eliminate this flickering, you use the method known as double-buffering.

COMPLEXITY
INTERMEDIATE

5.6   How do I...
Parse applet parameters?

Problem

I like the text marquee in Example 3.5 with the text moving in all different directions. I would like to be able to control the direction of the moving text and the text itself, without recompiling the source every time. I want to pass the applet the text to be scrolled, the color, and the direction in a single parameter from the HTML file. I know how to access applet parameters, but how do I parse applet parameters?

Technique

The scrolling text, its color, and the direction are passed to the Java applet from the HTML file by using the **<param>** tag. The parameter is parsed in the Java applet by using the **StringTokenizer()** method.

Steps

1. Create the applet source file. Create a new file called **ScrollApp.java** and enter the following source:

```
import java.applet.Applet;
import java.awt.*;
import java.util.*;

class Scroll {

int xstart, ystart;
int width, height;
String text;
int deltaX, deltaY;
int xpos, ypos;
Color color;

/**
 * Text scrolls in different directions.
 * @param xpos          initial x position
 * @param ypos          initial y position
 * @param deltax        velocity in x direction
 * @param deltay        velocity in y direction
 * @param width         bounding point for window panel width
 * @param height        bounding point for window panel height
 * @param text          text that is scrolled on the window
 * @param color         color of the text
 */
public Scroll (int x, int y, int dx, int dy, int w,➡
 int h, String t, Color ?c) {

    xstart = x;
    ystart = y;
    width = w;
    height = h;
    text = t;
    deltaX = dx;
    deltaY = dy;
    color = c;
    xpos = xstart;
    ypos = ystart;
}

/**
 * Called from update() in response to repaint()
 * @param g - destination graphics object
 */
void paint (Graphics g) {
```

```
        g.setColor (color);
        g.drawString (text, xpos, ypos);
        xpos += deltaX;
        ypos += deltaY;

        FontMetrics fm = g.getFontMetrics ();
        int textw = fm.stringWidth (text);
        int texth = fm.getHeight ();
        if (deltaX < 0 && xpos < -textw) xpos = xstart;
        if (deltaX > 0 && xpos > width) xpos = xstart;
        if (deltaY < 0 && ypos < 0) ypos = ystart;
        if (deltaY > 0 && ypos > height+texth) ypos = ystart;
    }
} // Class Scroll

/*
 * The applet class
 */
public class ScrollApp extends Applet implements Runnable {

/*
 * Width and height of the bounding panel
 */
int width, height;

/*
 * The number of scrolling objects
 */
int nscroll = 0;

/*
 * Array of scrolling objects
 */
Scroll scr[] = new Scroll[5];
Font font = new Font("Helvetica",1,24);
Thread thread;

/*
 * Called when the applet is loaded
 * Parses applet parameters
 */
public void init () {

    String scr_text[] = {"test1","test2","test3"
➥,"test4","test5"};
    int scr_xvel[] =   {-5,5,0,0,7};
    int scr_yvel[] =   {0,0,-5,5,3};
    int scr_xpos[] =   {400,0,100,200,0};
    int scr_ypos[] =   {50,150,200,0,0};
    int scr_red[] =    {255,0,0,100,200};
    int scr_green[] =  {0,255,0,200,100};
    int scr_blue[] =   {0,0,255,50,50};
    Color scr_color[] = new Color[5];
    int i;
    Dimension d = getSize ();
```

```
width = d.width;
height = d.height;
for (i=1; i<=5; i+=1) {
    String param, token;
    int j = 0;

    param = getParameter ("Scroll"+i);
    if (param == null) break;

    StringTokenizer st = new StringTokenizer (param, ",");
    token = st.nextToken ();
    scr_text[nscroll] = token;

    token = st.nextToken ();
    try {
        j = Integer.valueOf (token).intValue();
    } catch (NumberFormatException e){
    }

    switch (j) {
        case 0: //Scroll left.
            scr_xvel[nscroll] = -5;
            scr_yvel[nscroll] = 0;
            scr_xpos[nscroll] = 400;
            scr_ypos[nscroll] = 50;
            break;

        case 1: //Scroll right.
            scr_xvel[nscroll] = 5;
            scr_yvel[nscroll] = 0;
            scr_xpos[nscroll] = 0;
            scr_ypos[nscroll] = 150;
            break;

        case 2: //Scroll up.
            scr_xvel[nscroll] = 0;
            scr_yvel[nscroll] = -5;
            scr_xpos[nscroll] = 100;
            scr_ypos[nscroll] = 200;
            break;

        case 3: //Scroll down.
            scr_xvel[nscroll] = 0;
            scr_yvel[nscroll] = 5;
            scr_xpos[nscroll] = 200;
            scr_ypos[nscroll] = 0;
            break;

        case 4: //Scroll diagonally.
            scr_xvel[nscroll] = 7;
            scr_yvel[nscroll] = 3;
            scr_xpos[nscroll] = 0;
            scr_ypos[nscroll] = 0;
            break;
    }
```

```
          token = st.nextToken ();
          try {
              scr_red[nscroll] = Integer.valueOf
➡(token).intValue();
          } catch (NumberFormatException e) {
          }

          token = st.nextToken ();
          try {
              scr_green[nscroll] = Integer.valueOf
➡(token).intValue();
          } catch (NumberFormatException e) {
          }

          token = st.nextToken ();
          try {
              scr_blue[nscroll] = Integer.valueOf
➡(token).intValue();
          } catch (NumberFormatException e) {
          }

          scr_color[nscroll] = new Color(scr_red[nscroll],
              scr_green[nscroll], scr_blue[nscroll]);
          nscroll +=1;
      }
      for (i=0; i<nscroll; i+=1) {
          scr[i] = new Scroll (scr_xpos[i], scr_ypos[i],
              scr_xvel[i], scr_yvel[i], width, height,
              scr_text[i], scr_color[i]);
      }
} // init()

/*
 * Start the graphics update thread.
 */
public void start() {

    thread = new Thread(this);
    thread.start ();
} // start()

/*
 * The graphics update thread
 * Call repaint every 100 ms.
 */
public void run() {

    while (true) {
        try {
            Thread.sleep(100);
        } catch (InterruptedException e) { }
        repaint();
    }
} // run()

/*
```

```
 * Stop the graphics update thread.
 */
public void stop() {

if (thread != null)
   thread = null;


} // stop();

/**
 * Called from update() in response to repaint()
 * @param g - destination graphics object
 */
public void paint (Graphics g) {

    int i;

    g.setFont(font);
    for (i=0; i<nscroll; i+=1) {
        scr[i].paint (g);
    }
} // paint()
} // Class ScrollApp
```

2. Create an HTML document that contains the applet. Create a new file called **howto56.html** that contains the following code:

```
<html>
<head>
<title>Scrolling Marquee</title>
</head>
<applet code="ScrollApp.class" width=400 height=200>
<param name = "Scroll1" value = "The Java(tm),0,255,0,0">
<param name = "Scroll2" value = "How To,4,0,255,255">
</applet>
<hr size=4>

</html>
```

3. Compile and test the applet. Compile the source by using **javac**. Test the applet by using the Appletviewer; enter the following command:

```
APPLETVIEWER howto56.html
```

ScrollApp.java can only be run as an applet because it requires applet parameters.

When ScrollApp is executed, a window opens, with two different marquees scrolling in different directions. The words "The Java(tm)" scroll from left to right and are red. The words "How To" scroll diagonally and are cyan. The text, color, and direction can all be changed from the HTML file. The parameters passed from the HTML file need to have the following format:

text value to scroll, direction, red comp, green comp, blue comp

The direction is an integer that is 0 for left, 1 for right, 2 for up, 3 for down, and 4 for diagonal. Red, green, and blue are the RGB components of the desired color, from 0 to 255. The values must be separated by commas. There can be up to five different parameters in the HTML file, but they must be called **Scroll1**, **Scroll2**, and so on. The parameters must be named sequentially, starting from **Scroll1**; numbers cannot be skipped. Figure 5.6 shows an example of the running applet.

Figure 5.6 Two scrolling marquees in one window.

How It Works

The applet is very similar to that in Example 5.4. ScrollApp contains two classes, **ScrollApp** and **Scroll**. The **ScrollApp** class creates an array of **Scroll** with five elements. The font is set to 24-point bold Helvetica. A **String** array, scr_text, is initialized to contain five elements with values of **test1** to **test5**. Arrays are also created for the x and y velocity and starting position, and the red, green, and blue color components. Each element of each array is initialized to a default value. These values are arbitrary and are used to ensure that a value is set. A **for** loop is used to obtain the parameters from the HTML file. If the parameter returned is equal to null, it is assumed that the end of the parameters has been reached, and the loop is stopped with **break**. **StringTokenizer()** is used to parse the parameter at the commas. The first token is stored in the scr_text array. The next token represents the direction and should be from 0 to 4. The value is converted to an integer, and a **switch** statement is used to set the x and y starting positions and velocities for the various directions. The last three tokens represent the color values. They are converted to integers and stored in the appropriate arrays. The `nscroll` variable keeps track of the number of tokens retrieved. A `for` loop is then used to create the scrolling marquees for the number of parameters retrieved.

The remainder of the code is identical to that in Example 5.4.

Comments

This example uses hard-wired velocities and initial positions for the five different directions. To make the applet more versatile, the exact positions and velocities could be included in the applet parameter.

USER INTERFACE DEVELOPMENT

6

USER INTERFACE DEVELOPMENT

How do I...

Graphical user interfaces are an important part of programming. For your program to be able to interact with users, you need to understand several types of components, or widgets. An example of widgets commonly are those of an average word processor, such as buttons, choice lists, sliders, check boxes, and menus.

This chapter explains how to create many widgets, which are the basis for many interesting and useful applications. With the use of the event handling covered in Chapter 5, "Events and Parameters," and the widgets in this chapter, you could create games, word processors, spreadsheets, and many other applications.

In this chapter you use layout managers. Layout managers arrange controls on a frame or applet automatically based on a set of rules associated with each manager. For a more complete discussion of layout managers, see Chapter 8, "JFC."

6.1 Create Buttons

This example shows how to create buttons for a simple mathematic calculator. The mouse is used to click the buttons of the calculator keypad.

6.2 Create Check Boxes

Check boxes can be implemented in two ways: an individual check box, or grouped check boxes that are usually referred to as *radio buttons*. A digital/analog clock demonstrates the use of both kinds of check boxes.

6.3 Create Menus

Menus allow the user to perform a task from a predefined set. In this example you modify the drawing program from Example 5.2 and add a menu bar.

6.4 Use Choice Lists

Choice lists allow the user to select a choice from a list. Choice lists are commonly used in forms or questionnaires in HTML documents. This example creates a conversion tool that allows for conversion between various English system and metric system lengths.

6.5 Create Text Fields and Text Areas

Text fields and text areas allow the user to enter information. In this example you create a spreadsheet that implements the four basic mathematic functions: addition, subtraction, multiplication, and division.

6.6 Use Sliders

In Java, sliders are implemented with the `Scrollbar` class. Sliders allow the user to select a value within a predetermined range. This example demonstrates the use of sliders with a simple RGB color selection tool.

COMPLEXITY
INTERMEDIATE

6.1 How do I...
Create buttons?

Problem

I want to create a simple calculator applet that implements the four basic mathematic functions: addition, subtraction, multiplication, and division. The calculator should draw the buttons on the screen, and the user should use the mouse to click the buttons. I know how to use math functions and access mouse events, but how do I create buttons?

Technique

The calculator uses the **Button** class to create the buttons of a calculator. The Calc applet is a fully functional mathematic calculator. Figure 6.1 shows the applet in action.

Figure 6.1 The Calc applet is a fully functional calculator.

Steps

1. Create the applet source file. Create a new file called **Calc.java** and enter the following source:

```java
import java.util.*;
import java.awt.*;
import java.awt.event.*;
import java.applet.*;

/**
 * A simple calculator
 */
public class Calc extends Applet
{

    Display  display = new Display();

/**
 *  Initialize the Calc applet
 */
    public void init () {

        setLayout(new BorderLayout());
        Keypad    keypad = new Keypad();

        add ("North", display);
        add ("Center", keypad);
    }

/**
 * This allows the class to be used either as an applet
 * or as a standalone application.
```

```java
    */
public static void main (String args[]) {

        Frame f = new Frame ("Calculator");
        Calc calc = new Calc ();

        calc.init ();

        f.setSize (210, 200);
        f.add ("Center", calc);
        f.show ();
}

class Keypad extends Panel
implements ActionListener
{
        Button b7;
        Button b8;
        Button b9;
        Button bDiv;
        Button b4;
        Button b5;
        Button b6;
        Button bMult;
        Button b1;
        Button b2;
        Button b3;
        Button bMin;
        Button bDec;
        Button b0;
        Button bSign;
        Button bPlus;
        Button bC;
        Button bEqu;

/**
 * Initialize the keypad, add buttons, set colors, etc.
 */
    Keypad (){

        Font    font = new Font ("Times", Font.BOLD, 14);
        Color   functionColor = new Color (255, 255, 0);
        Color   numberColor = new Color (0, 255, 255);
        Color   equalsColor = new Color (0, 255, 0);
        setFont (font);

        b7 = new Button ("7");
        add (b7);
        b7.setBackground (numberColor);
        b7.addActionListener(this);
```

```
b8 = new Button ("8");
add (b8);
b8.setBackground (numberColor);
b8.addActionListener(this);

b9 = new Button ("9");
add (b9);
b9.setBackground (numberColor);
b9.addActionListener(this);

bDiv = new Button ("/");
add (bDiv);
bDiv.setBackground (numberColor);
bDiv.addActionListener(this);

b4 = new Button ("4");
add (b4);
b4.setBackground (numberColor);
b4.addActionListener(this);

b5 = new Button ("5");
add (b5);
b5.setBackground (numberColor);
b5.addActionListener(this);

b6 = new Button ("6");
add (b6);
b6.setBackground (numberColor);
b6.addActionListener(this);

bMult = new Button ("x");
add (bMult);
bMult.setBackground (numberColor);
bMult.addActionListener(this);

b1 = new Button ("1");
add (b1);
b1.setBackground (numberColor);
b1.addActionListener(this);

b2 = new Button ("2");
add (b2);
b2.setBackground (numberColor);
b2.addActionListener(this);

b3 = new Button ("3");
add (b3);
b3.setBackground (numberColor);
b3.addActionListener(this);

bMin = new Button ("-");
add (bMin);
bMin.setBackground (numberColor);
bMin.addActionListener(this);
```

```
    bDec = new Button (".");
    add (bDec);
    bDec.setBackground (numberColor);
    bDec.addActionListener(this);

    b0 = new Button ("0");
    add (b0);
    b0.setBackground (numberColor);
    b0.addActionListener(this);

    bSign = new Button ("+/-");
    add (bSign);
    bSign.setBackground (numberColor);
    bSign.addActionListener(this);

    bPlus = new Button ("+");
    add (bPlus);
    bPlus.setBackground (numberColor);
    bPlus.addActionListener(this);

    bC = new Button ("C");
    add (bC);
    bC.setBackground (functionColor);
    bC.addActionListener(this);

    add (new Label (""));
    add (new Label (""));

    bEqu = new Button ("=");
    add (bEqu);
    bEqu.setBackground (equalsColor);
    bEqu.addActionListener(this);

    setLayout (new GridLayout (5, 4, 4, 4));
}

public void actionPerformed(ActionEvent event)
{
    Object object = event.getSource();

    if(object == bC)
    {
        display.Clear ();
    }

    if(object == bDec)
    {
        display.Dot ();
    }

    if(object == bPlus)
    {
        display.Plus ();
    }
```

```
if(object == bMin)
{
   display.Minus ();
}

if(object == bMult)
{
   display.Mul ();
}

if(object == bDiv)
{
   display.Div ();
}

if(object == bSign)
{
   display.Chs ();
}

if(object == bEqu)
{
   display.Equals ();
}

if(object == b0)
{
   display.Digit ("0");
}

if(object == b1)
{
   display.Digit ("1");
}

if(object == b2)
{
   display.Digit ("2");
}

if(object == b3)
{
   display.Digit ("3");
}

if(object == b4)
{
   display.Digit ("4");
}

if(object == b5)
{
   display.Digit ("5");
}
```

```
                if(object == b6)
                {
                    display.Digit ("6");
                }

                if(object == b7)
                {
                    display.Digit ("7");
                }

                if(object == b8)
                {
                    display.Digit ("8");
                }

                if(object == b9)
                {
                    display.Digit ("9");
                }

        }
    }
}
/* ------------------------------------------------ */

/**
 * The Keypad handles the input for the calculator
 * and writes to the display.
 */

/* ------------------------------------------------ */

/**
 * The Display class manages displaying the calculated result
 * as well as implementing the calculator function keys.
 */
class Display extends Panel{

    double      last = 0;
    int         op = 0;
    boolean     equals = false;
    int         maxlen = 10;
    String      s;
    Label       readout = new Label("");

/**
 * Initialize the display
 */
    Display () {

        setLayout(new BorderLayout());
        setBackground (Color.red);
         setFont (new Font ("Courier", Font.BOLD +
 ➥ Font.ITALIC, 30));
```

```
        readout.setAlignment(1);
        add ("Center",readout);
      repaint();
      Clear ();
  }

/**
 * Handle clicking a digit.
 */
   void Digit (String digit) {
       checkEquals ();

           /*
            *          Strip leading zeros
            */
       if (s.length () == 1 && s.charAt (0) ==
➥'0' && digit.charAt (0) != '.')
                 s = s.substring (1);

       if (s.length () < maxlen)
                 s = s + digit;
       showacc ();
  }

/**
 * Handle a decimal point.
 */
   void Dot () {
       checkEquals ();

           /*
            *          Already have '.'
            */
       if (s.indexOf ('.') != -1)
                 return;

       if (s.length () < maxlen)
                 s = s + ".";
       showacc ();
  }

/**
If the user clicks equals without
 clicking an operator
 * key first (+,-,x,/), zero the display.
 */
   private void checkEquals () {
       if (equals == true) {
                    equals = false;
                 s = "0";
       }
  }

/**
 * Stack the addition operator for later use.
```

```
        */
        void Plus () {
            op = 1;
            operation ();
        }

    /**
     * Stack the subtraction operator for later use.
     */
        void Minus () {
            op = 2;
            operation ();
        }

    /**
     * Stack the multiplication operator for later use.
     */
        void Mul () {
            op = 3;
            operation ();
        }

    /**
     * Stack the division operator for later use.
     */
        void Div () {
            op = 4;
            operation ();
        }

    /**
     * Interpret the display value as a double, and store it
     * for later use (by Equals).
     */
        private void operation () {
            if (s.length () == 0) return;

            Double xyz = Double.valueOf (s);
            last = xyz.doubleValue ();

            equals = false;
            s = "0";
        }
    /**
     * Negate the current value and redisplay.
     */
        void Chs () {
            if (s.length () == 0) return;

            if (s.charAt (0) == '-') s = s.substring (1);
            else s = "-" + s;

            showacc ();
        }
```

```
/**
 * Finish the last calculation and display the result.
 */
    void Equals () {
        double acc;

        if (s.length () == 0)  return;
        Double xyz = Double.valueOf (s);
        switch (op)  {
            case 1:
                    acc = last + xyz.doubleValue ();
                    break;

            case 2:
                    acc = last - xyz.doubleValue ();
                    break;

            case 3:
                    acc = last * xyz.doubleValue ();
                    break;

            case 4:
                    acc = last / xyz.doubleValue ();
                    break;

            default:
                    acc = 0;
                    break;
        }

        s = new Double (acc).toString ();
        showacc ();
        equals = true;
        last = 0;
        op = 0;
    }

/**
 * Clear the display and the internal last value.
 */
    void Clear () {
        last = 0;
        op = 0;
        s = "0";
        equals = false;
        showacc ();
    }

/**
 * Demand that the display be repainted.
 */
    private void showacc () {
        readout.setText(s);
```

```
        repaint ();
   }

}
```

2. Create an HTML document that contains the applet. Create a new file called **howto61.html** that contains the following code:

```
<html>
<head>
<title>Calculator</title>
</head>
<applet code="Calc.class" width=200 height=200>
</applet>
<hr size=4>

</html>
```

3. Compile and test the applet. Compile the source by using **javac**. Test the applet by using the Appletviewer; enter the following command:

```
appletviewer howto61.html
```

You can also run **Calc.java** as an application by typing

```
java Calc
```

4. When Calc is executed, a window will open, containing 18 buttons (numeric from 0 to 9, +, -, *, /, =, +/-, ., and C) with a display bar above the buttons. Use the mouse to click the buttons.

How It Works

The Calc applet/application contains three classes: **Calc**, **Keypad**, and **Display**. The **Calc** class extends **Applet** and is the applet itself. The **Keypad** and **Display** classes extend **Panel** and are used to hold the calculator keypad and display area, respectively.

The **Calc** class creates a new keypad and display, and adds the display to the top (North) of the main panel and the keypad to the center (Center) of the display panel. North, South, East, and West are used here as they are on a map with North being the top of the paper, East being to the right, and so on. The event handler is used to catch all action events that are an instance of a button click. If the button that was clicked is equal to any of the operator buttons (C, ., +, _, x, /, +/-, =), the appropriate method in the **Display** class is called. If the button click was not any of the operator buttons, that is, it was a number button, the **Digit** method in the **Display** class is called, with the button number as a parameter.

The Keypad class initializes the keypad and adds the buttons. The buttons are created by using the constructor for the Button class, with a string as a parameter. This string is the label that will be written on the button when it is displayed. The text color of the button is set to black with the setForeground method in the component class. The button background is set to various colors with the setBackground method, also in the component class. The number buttons are set to blue, the function buttons are set to yellow, and the equal button to green. The button text is set to 14-point bold Times font. The font is not set directly at the button, but at its parent (Keypad); in the absence of a specific font the buttons use the parent's font.

The Display class contains methods for handling all the button clicks. If a number button is clicked, the Digit method is called, with the button number as the argument. There are similar methods for each operator button.

The Button class contains several constructors and methods. Table 6.1 contains a list of the constructors and methods for the Button class.

Table 6.1 Button Class Constructors and Methods

METHOD	DESCRIPTION
Button()	Constructs a button with no label
Button(String)	Constructs a button with a string label
getLabel()	Gets the label of the button
setLabel(String)	Sets the button with the specified label
addActionListener()	Registers an action listener to receive Action events
removeActionListener()	Unregisters an action listener
setActionCommand()	Sets the command name for this Action event

COMPLEXITY
INTERMEDIATE

6.2 How do I...
Create check boxes?

Problem

I would like to add radio buttons and check boxes to my applets. I want to be able to allow the user to choose one item from a limited number of choices. In addition, I would like to allow her to choose more than one item in certain circumstances. How do I accomplish this?

Technique

The Abstract Windowing Toolkit (AWT) provides a class called `Checkbox` to accomplish this. In Chapter 8 you will learn additional ways of accomplishing this.

The `Checkbox` class supports two modes of operation: grouped and ungrouped. When check boxes are created as part of a group, the class enforces a single choice. When ungrouped, check boxes allow any number of the choices to be checked.

The following example demonstrates both the grouped and ungrouped check boxes (shown in Figure 6.2). It contains one group called the `mfGroup` (for male/female). Two check boxes are added to the group: `maleButton` and `femaleButton`. (They look and act like radio buttons, hence the names.) Obviously, you want the users to choose only one or the other.

An ungrouped set of check boxes are then created; they indicate the user's reading interests. These check boxes are independent of each other and therefore allow more than one to be checked at the time. This makes sense for cases in which the user could be interested in several subjects, or wants both catsup and mustard on the same sandwich.

This example illustrates the following concepts:

- How to create check boxes that act like traditional check boxes

- How to create check boxes that act like radio buttons

- How to create a check box group

- How to set the initial state of a check box

- How to detect the state of a check box at runtime

- How to connect the gathering of the check box state to a user event

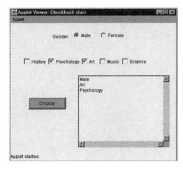

Figure 6.2 The check box can function either as a set of traditional check boxes or as a set of radio buttons.

Steps

1. Create a source file named Checkbox1.java that contains the following applet code:

```java
import java.awt.*;

  import java.applet.*;

 public class Checkbox1 extends Applet
 {

     void displayButton_Clicked(java.awt.event.[ccc]
ActionEvent event)
 {

       // clear the results area

       results.setText("");

      // display the gender

      Checkbox current = genderGroup.getSelectedCheckbox();

      results.append(current.getLabel() + "\r\n");


      // check each of the sports

      if (artCheckbox.getState() == true)

        results.append("Art\r\n");

      if (psychologyCheckbox.getState() == true)

         results.append("Psychology\r\n");

      if (historyCheckbox.getState() == true)

         results.append("History\r\n");

      if (musicCheckbox.getState() == true)

         results.append("Music\r\n");

      if (scienceCheckbox.getState() == true)

         results.append("Science\r\n");

    }

     public void init() {
```

```
// Call parents init method.

super.init();


// This code is automatically generated by Visual Cafe

// when you add components to the visual environment.

// It instantiates and initializes the components. To

// modify the code, use only code syntax that matches

// what Visual Cafe can generate, or Visual Cafe may

// be unable to back parse your Java file into its

// visual environment.

//{{INIT_CONTROLS

setLayout(null);

resize(442,354);

label1 = new java.awt.Label("Gender:",Label.RIGHT);

label1.setBounds(72,24,84,28);

add(label1);

genderGroup = new CheckboxGroup();

maleButton = new java.awt.Checkbox("Male",genderGroup,
      true);

maleButton.setBounds(168,24,58,21);

add(maleButton);

femaleButton = new java.awt.Checkbox("Female",
      genderGroup, false);

femaleButton.setBounds(240,24,71,21);

add(femaleButton);

historyCheckbox = new java.awt.Checkbox("History");

historyCheckbox.setBounds(36,96,60,21);

add(historyCheckbox);
```

```
        psychologyCheckbox = new java.awt.Checkbox("Psychology");

        psychologyCheckbox.setBounds(101,96,85,21);

        add(psychologyCheckbox);

        artCheckbox = new java.awt.Checkbox("Art");

        artCheckbox.setBounds(190,96,40,21);

        add(artCheckbox);

        musicCheckbox = new java.awt.Checkbox("Music");

        musicCheckbox.setBounds(238,96,56,21);

        add(musicCheckbox);

        scienceCheckbox = new java.awt.Checkbox("Science");

        scienceCheckbox.setBounds(298,96,93,21);

        add(scienceCheckbox);

        displayButton = new java.awt.Button("Display");

        displayButton.setBounds(48,204,100,33);

        add(displayButton);

        results = new java.awt.TextArea();

        results.setBounds(180,144,246,198);

        add(results);

        Action lAction = new Action();

        displayButton.addActionListener(lAction);

    }

    java.awt.Label label1;

    java.awt.Checkbox maleButton;

    CheckboxGroup genderGroup;

    java.awt.Checkbox femaleButton;

    java.awt.Label label2;

    java.awt.Checkbox historyCheckbox;
```

```
java.awt.Checkbox psychologyCheckbox;

java.awt.Checkbox artCheckbox;

java.awt.Checkbox musicCheckbox;

java.awt.Checkbox scienceCheckbox;

java.awt.Button displayButton;

java.awt.TextArea results;


class Action implements java.awt.event.ActionListener {

    public void actionPerformed(java.awt.event.ActionEvent

        event) {

      Object object = event.getSource();

      if (object == displayButton)

        displayButton_Clicked(event);

    }

  }

}
```

2. Create an HTML file called **howto62.html** that contains the following code:

```
<html>
<head>
<title>Check boxes using the AWT</title>
</head>
<applet code="Checkbox1.class" width=450 height=375>
</applet>
<hr size=4>

</html>
```

3. Compile the applet file by typing the following:

```
javac Checkbox1.java
```

4. Run the applet by using Appletviewer; type the following:

```
Appletviewer howto62.html
```

5. When the HTML file is run, the window appears, allowing the user to indicate his or her gender. In addition, the user may indicate interest in several areas. After the use clicks the Display button, the current states of the choices are displayed in a text area control.

How It Works

This example is implemented as an applet and therefore does not run from the command line. Traditional check boxes have two states: "Checked" and "Unchecked." The check box was declared, but not created by the statement:

```
Checkbox historyCheckBox;
```

Notice that this object was created outside every method in the class, and is therefore visible to all methods. The actual creation of the object was performed in the addNotify() method. This method creates a *peer*, which is a version of an applet that is created using the native windowing system of the host platform. The Java Foundation Classes (JFC), which is covered in Chapter 8, does not use the native windowing system, but rather creates each object itself. The creation of the check box takes place in the following code:

```
historyCheckBox = new Checkbox("History");
```

The new operator allocates the space for the check box in memory. An internal label called History is defined and is printed beside the check box on the applet when displayed. Whenever a user clicks on the check box, its state toggles between true and false. If you want to find the current state of a check box, you can use the getState() method, as shown here:

```
if (historyCheckBox.getState() == true)
```

In order to get your check boxes to act like radio buttons, all you have to do is create an instance of the CheckboxGroup class and assign the check boxes to it. The following statement creates the group:

```
mfGroup = new CheckboxGroup();
```

Now, when you create a check box, you use a different form of the constructor:

```
maleButton = new Checkbox("Male", mfGroup, true);
```

The label is set by passing a string. The group name mfGroup tells which group this button belongs to. The true at the end tells whether this is the button that will be checked when the applet is initialized. Deciding which check box is checked is easier with a group than with traditional check boxes. All the code has to do is to inquire of the group which of the check boxes is currently checked, as shown here:

```
Checkbox current = mfGroup. getSelectedCheckbox ();
choices.append(current.getLabel() + "\r\n");
```

A check box called current is declared. The method getCurrent() asks the group for a reference to the current check box. The getLabel() method of the Checkbox class is used to inquire as to the label of the current check box.

Finally, the application has to have some event that will allow you to capture and display the states of the check boxes, both within the group and without. You do this with an ActionListener class. As you recall, a listener is created to process a certain type of message. To capture a click on a button, the ActionListener class is the best choice. Now create a class called ButtonAction that implements the ActionListener interface:

```
class ButtonAction implements ActionListener
{
    public void actionPerformed(ActionEvent event)
    {
        Object object1 = event.getSource();
        if (object1 == displayButton)
          displayButton_Clicked(event);
    }
}
```

This class must, by decree from JavaSoft, implement a method called actionPerformed(). This method is called whenever a registered event occurs. The main job of this method is to find out which object caused the event to occur and to call a method to respond to it. In this case, the buttonDisplay_Clicked() method is the choice; it inquires about the state of each button and prints the results in a text field.

COMPLEXITY
INTERMEDIATE

6.3 How do I...
Create menus?

Problem

I would like to learn how to add menu bars to applications. I would like to modify the Doodle example from Chapter 5 to include a menu. How do I create menus?

Technique

Pull-down menus can exist only for a frame and not a panel. Therefore, any program that uses pull-down menus must be run as an application. You create a menu bar by invoking the MenuBar constructor. Menus generate action events. You can handle menu events by attaching an Action listener to the menu itself. This directs the event to the class that you specify as the Action Listener. Figure 6.3 shows an example of the running application.

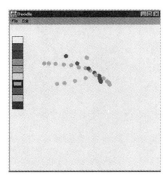

Figure 6.3 Menu choices are managed as Action events, similarly to the way buttons are handled.

Steps

1. Create the applet source file. Create a new file called `Doodle.java` and enter the following source:

```java
import java.applet.Applet;
import java.awt.*;
import java.awt.event.*;

/**
 * The ColorBar class displays a color bar for color selection.
 */
class ColorBar {

/*
 * the top, left coordinate of the color bar
 */
int xpos, ypos;

/*
 * the width and height of the color bar
 */
int width, height;

/*
 * the current color selection index into the colors array
 */
int selectedColor = 3;

/*
 * the array of colors available for selection
 */
static Color colors[] = {
        Color.white, Color.gray, Color.red, Color.pink,
        Color.orange, Color.yellow, Color.green, Color.magenta,
        Color.cyan, Color.blue
};
```

```
/**
 * Create the color bar
 */
public ColorBar (int x, int y, int w, int h) {

        xpos = x;
        ypos = y;
        width = w;
        height = h;
}


/**
 * Paint the color bar
 * @param g - destination graphics object
 */
void paint (Graphics g) {

        int x, y, i;
        int w, h;

        for (i=0; i<colors.length; i+=1) {
                w = width;
                h = height/colors.length;
                x = xpos;
                y = ypos + (i * h);
                g.setColor (Color.black);
                g.fillRect (x, y, w, h);
                if (i == selectedColor) {
                        x += 5;
                        y += 5;
                        w -= 10;
                        h -= 10;
                } else {
                        x += 1;
                        y += 1;
                        w -= 2;
                        h -= 2;
                }
                g.setColor (colors[i]);
                g.fillRect (x, y, w, h);
        }
}

/**
 * Check to see whether the mouse is inside a palette box.
 * If it is, set selectedColor and return true;
 *        otherwise, return false.
 * @param x, y - x and y position of mouse
 */
boolean inside (int x, int y) {

        int i, h;
```

```
            if (x < xpos || x > xpos+width) return false;
            if (y < ypos || y > ypos+height) return false;

            h = height/colors.length;
            for (i=0; i<colors.length; i+=1) {
                    if (y < ((i+1)*h+ypos)) {
                            selectedColor = i;
                            return true;
                    }
            }
            return false;
    }
}

/**
 * The Doodle applet implements a drawable surface
 * with a limited choice of colors to draw with.
 */
public class Doodle extends Frame {

/*
 * the maximum number of points that can be
 * saved in the xpoints, ypoints, and color arrays
 */
static final int MaxPoints = 1000;

/*
 * arrays to hold the points where the user draws
 */
int xpoints[] = new int[MaxPoints];
int ypoints[] = new int[MaxPoints];

/*
 * the color of each point
 */
int color[] = new int[MaxPoints];

/*
 * used to keep track of the previous mouse
 * click to avoid filling arrays with the
 * same point
 */
int lastx;
int lasty;

/*
 * the number of points in the arrays
 */
int npoints = 0;
ColorBar colorBar;
boolean inColorBar;

/**
```

```
       * Set the window title and create the menus
       * Create an instance of ColorBar
       */

           public void New_Action(ActionEvent event)
           {
               Doodle doodle = new Doodle();
           }

           public void Quit_Action(ActionEvent event)
           {
               System.exit(0);
           }

           class ActionListener1 implements ActionListener
           {
               public void actionPerformed(ActionEvent event)
               {
                   String str = event.getActionCommand();
                   if (str.equals("New"))
                       New_Action(event);
                   else if (str.equals("Quit"))
                       Quit_Action(event);
               }
           }

       public Doodle () {

               setTitle ("Doodle");

               setBackground(Color.white);

               MenuBar menuBar = new MenuBar();
               Menu fileMenu = new Menu("File");
               fileMenu.add(new MenuItem("Open"));
               fileMenu.add(new MenuItem("New"));
               fileMenu.add(new MenuItem("Close"));
               fileMenu.add(new MenuItem("-"));
               fileMenu.add(new MenuItem("Quit"));
               menuBar.add (fileMenu);

               Menu editMenu = new Menu("Edit");
               editMenu.add(new MenuItem("Undo"));
               editMenu.add(new MenuItem("Cut"));
               editMenu.add(new MenuItem("Copy"));
               editMenu.add(new MenuItem("Paste"));
               editMenu.add(new MenuItem("-"));
               editMenu.add(new MenuItem("Clear"));
               menuBar.add (editMenu);
               setMenuBar (menuBar);

               colorBar = new ColorBar (10, 75, 30, 200);

           WindowListener1 lWindow = new WindowListener1();
           addWindowListener(lWindow);
```

```java
    MouseListener1 lMouse = new MouseListener1();
    addMouseListener(lMouse);

    MouseMotionListener1 lMouseMotion = new
➡MouseMotionListener1();
    addMouseMotionListener(lMouseMotion);

    ActionListener1 lAction = new ActionListener1();
    fileMenu.addActionListener(lAction);

        setSize (410, 430);
        show ();
}

class WindowListener1 extends WindowAdapter
{
    public void windowClosing(WindowEvent event)
    {
        Window win = event.getWindow();
        win.setVisible(false);
        win.dispose();
        System.exit(0);
    }
}

class MouseMotionListener1 extends MouseMotionAdapter
{
    public void mouseDragged(MouseEvent e)
    {
        int x = e.getX();
        int y = e.getY();
                if (inColorBar) return;
                if ((x != lastx || y != lasty) &&
➡npoints < MaxPoints) {
                        lastx = x;
                        lasty = y;
                        xpoints[npoints] = x;
                        ypoints[npoints] = y;
                        color[npoints] = colorBar.selectedColor;
                        npoints += 1;
                        repaint ();
                }
    }
}

class MouseListener1 extends MouseAdapter
{
    public void mousePressed(MouseEvent e)
    {
        int x = e.getX();
        int y = e.getY();
                if (colorBar.inside (x, y)) {
                        inColorBar = true;
                        repaint ();
                        return;
                }
```

```
                      inColorBar = false;
                      if (npoints < MaxPoints) {
                              lastx = x;
                              lasty = y;
                              xpoints[npoints] = x;
                              ypoints[npoints] = y;
                              color[npoints] = colorBar.selectedColor;
                              npoints += 1;
                      }
                      npoints = 0;
          }
  }

  /**
   * Redisplay the drawing space
   * @param g - destination graphics object
   */
  public void update (Graphics g) {

          int i;

          for (i=0; i<npoints; i+=1) {
                  g.setColor (colorBar.colors[color[i]]);
                  g.fillOval (xpoints[i]-5, ypoints[i]-5, 10, 10);
          }
          colorBar.paint (g);
  }

  /**
   * Repaint the drawing space when required
   * @param g - destination graphics object
   */
  public void paint (Graphics g) {

          update (g);
  }

  /**
   * The main method allows this class to be run as an application
   * @param args - command-line arguments
   */
  public static void main (String args[]) {

          Doodle doodle = new Doodle ();
  }

  }
```

2. Compile and test the application. Compile the source by using `javac`.

3. Test the application by typing

```
java Doodle
```

Doodle can only be run as an application. When Doodle is executed, a window opens, containing a drawing area, a color palette, and a menu bar.

How It Works

This version of the Doodle application includes pull-down menus. Like the earlier version of Doodle, this one contains a `ColorBar` class and a `Doodle` class. The `ColorBar` class is identical to that described earlier. The `Doodle` class is different from that described in many ways. First, this `Doodle` class extends `Frame` instead of extending `Applet` because pull-down menus can exist only for a frame and not a panel (as you recall, `Applet` is a subclass of `Panel`). Second, the `main` method creates an instance of `Doodle`, and does not explicitly create a frame (the default `Frame` method takes care of that). Third, the mouse events are handled using adapter classes, which are similar to listener classes except that they already implement every method in the interface. You only need to override the ones that you want to handle. The window events are handled by an adapter class also.

The `Doodle` constructor sets the title of the frame by invoking the `setTitle()` method, and then sets the background color to white by invoking `setBackground()`. It then creates a menu bar by invoking the `MenuBar` constructor, and creates a new file menu by invoking the `Menu` constructor with the name of the menu (`file`) as an argument. Next, menu items are added to the file menu by invoking the `add()` method with a `MenuItem` constructor as an argument, which in turn is passed the name of that menu item (for example, `Open`). A menu is added to the menu bar by invoking the add method of the `menuBar` instance. The Edit menu is created in the same way. Finally, the menu bar is displayed by invoking the `setMenuBar` method with `menuBar` as an argument.

In order to detect the clicks on the menus, you declare a listener and attach it to the menu, as shown here:

```
ActionListener1 lAction = new ActionListener1();
fileMenu.addActionListener(lAction);
```

Notice that the action listener is attached to `fileMenu` instead of to the frame, as are the window and mouse listeners.

Finally, when your application is aware that a menu click has taken place, it needs to differentiate between the different menu choices. This is done in the `ActionListener` class, as shown here:

```
class ActionListener1 implements ActionListener
{
    public void actionPerformed(ActionEvent event)
    {
        String str = event.getActionCommand();
```

```
        if (str.equals("New"))
            New_Action(event);
        else if (str.equals("Quit"))
            Quit_Action(event);
    }

}
```

By using the **getActionCommand** method on the event, your program can discover which menu choice caused the event to occur and to react according to your wishes. The action command is a string associated with the action event. It can be set manually with a **setActionCommand()** method. By default, the component label is used.

Comments

A number of unimplemented menu choices are created in this application to demonstrate the use of the menu bar and several menus.

COMPLEXITY
ADVANCED

6.4 How do I...
Use choice lists?

Problem

I would like to add choice lists to applications. I want to create a converter application that has dimensions listed in choice lists and that gives the conversion factor between the two selected dimensions. How do I create choice lists?

Technique

In this example you will create two choice lists, each of which contains the following choices: Centimeters, Meters, Kilometers, Inches, Feet, and Miles. The first choice list is used to select the dimension to convert from. The second list is the dimension to convert to. A text field is used to display the conversion factor. Figure 6.4 shows what the application looks like when running.

Figure 6.4 The ItemListener manages events generated by choice lists.

Steps

1. Create the applet source file. Create a new file called `Converter.java` and enter the following source:

```java
import java.awt.*;
import java.awt.event.*;
import java.applet.Applet;

/*
 * the applet class
 */
public class Converter extends Applet {

/*
 * the "from" unit index
 */
int fromindex = 0;

/*
 * the "to" unit index
 */
int toindex = 0;

/*
 * a place to print the conversion factor
 */
TextField textfield = new TextField(12);

/*
 * where the choice lists are displayed
 */
Panel listpanel = new Panel();

/*
```

```
* where the text field is displayed
 */
Panel textpanel = new Panel();
Choice unit1 = new Choice();
Choice unit2 = new Choice();

/*
 * an array of conversion factors
 */
String values[][] = {
        {"1.000", "1.000 E-2", "1.000 E-5", "3.397 E-1", "3.937
➡E-2", "6.214 E-6"},
        {"1.000 E+2", "1.000", "1.000 E-3", "39.37",
➡"3.28", "6.214 E-4"},
        {"1.000 E+5", "1.000 E+3", "1.000", "3.937 E+4",
➡"3.281 E+3", "6.214 E-1"},
        {"2.54", "0.0254", "2.54 E-5", "1.000", "12.0",
➡"1.578 E-5"},
        {"30.48", "0.3048", "3.048 E-4", "12.0", "1.000",
➡"1.894 E-4"},
        {"1.609 E+5", "1.609 E+3", "1609", "6.336 E+4",
➡"5280", "1.000"}
};

/*                       .
 * called when the applet is loaded
 * create the user interface
 */
public void init() {

        textfield.setText(values[fromindex][toindex]);
        textfield.setEditable (false);

        this.setLayout(new BorderLayout());
        listpanel.setLayout(new FlowLayout());
        add("North", listpanel);
        add("South", textpanel);

        Label fromlabel = new Label ("To Convert From  ",1);
        listpanel.add(fromlabel);
        unit1.addItem("Centimeters");
         unit1.addItem("Meters");
         unit1.addItem("Kilometers");
         unit1.addItem("Inches");
         unit1.addItem("Feet");
         unit1.addItem("Miles");
         listpanel.add(unit1);

         Label tolabel = new Label ("  to     ",1);
        listpanel.add(tolabel);
        unit2.addItem("Centimeters");
        unit2.addItem("Meters");
        unit2.addItem("Kilometers");
        unit2.addItem("Inches");
        unit2.addItem("Feet");
        unit2.addItem("Miles");
        listpanel.add(unit2);
```

```java
        Label multlabel = new Label ("Multiply by   ",1);
        textpanel.add(multlabel);
        textpanel.add(textfield);

    ItemListener1 lItem = new ItemListener1();
    unit1.addItemListener(lItem);
    unit2.addItemListener(lItem);

}

/**
 * called when an action event occurs
 * @param evt - the event object
 * @param arg - the target object
 */

class ItemListener1 implements ItemListener
{
    public void itemStateChanged( ItemEvent e)
    {
            fromindex = unit1.getSelectedIndex();
            toindex = unit2.getSelectedIndex();
            textfield.setText(values[fromindex][toindex]);
            repaint();
    }
}

/**
 * application entry point
 * @param args - commandline arguments
 */

public static void main(String args[]) {

        Frame f = new Frame("Converter ");
        Converter converter = new Converter();
        converter.init();
        converter.start();
            f.addWindowListener(new WindowCloser());
        f.add("Center", converter);
        f.setSize(500, 100);
            f.show();
}
}

class WindowCloser extends WindowAdapter
{
    public void windowClosing(WindowEvent e)
    {
        Window win = e.getWindow();
        win.setVisible(false);
        win.dispose();
        System.exit(0);
    }
}
```

2. Create an HTML document that contains the applet. Create a new file called howto64.html that contains the following code:

```
<html>
<head>
<title>Converter</title>
</head>
<applet code="Converter.class" width=500 height=100>
</applet>
<hr size=4>

</html>
```

3. Compile and test the applet. Compile the source by using javac. Test the applet by using the Appletviewer; enter the following command:

```
appletviewer howto64.html
```

You can also run Converter.java as an application by typing

```
java Converter
```

4. When Converter is executed, a window opens, with two choice lists and a text field. The first choice list is the convert-from dimension, and the second choice list is the convert-to dimension. The text field displays the conversion factor. Figure 6.4 shows an example of the running applet.

How It Works

The converter applet/application contains only a single class, the applet itself. The string value is a two-dimensional array that holds the conversion factor for the specified dimensions in the choice lists. The fromindex and toindex values are used to obtain the conversion factor from the values array and are initialized to zero. A text field, textfield, is created with 12 columns; it is used to display the conversion factor. Two panels, listpanel and textpanel, are created to hold the choice lists and text field, respectively. Two choice lists, unit1 and unit2, are created and are the selection tool for the dimensions.

The init() method sets the text field value to the initialized value of the array and sets the text field as uneditable. The layout for the main panel is set to BorderLayout, and listpanel is set to FlowLayout. listpanel is added to the top (North) of the main panel, and textpanel is added to the bottom (South) of the main panel. The selections for the choice lists are added by using the addItem method, and the choice lists are then added to listpanel. A label is added before the unit1 choice lists that says "To Convert From" and a label is added before the unit2 choice list that says "to." A label "Multiply by" and the text field are added to textpanel.

ItemListener is used to detect that the user has interacted with the choice lists. The following code shows the creation of the listener:

```
ItemListener1 lItem = new ItemListener1();
unit1.addItemListener(lItem);
unit2.addItemListener(lItem);
```

The body of itemlistener contains the code to alter what is displayed in the text box:

```
class ItemListener1 implements ItemListener
{
        public void itemStateChanged( ItemEvent e)
        {
            fromindex = unit1.getSelectedIndex();
            toindex = unit2.getSelectedIndex();
            textfield.setText(values[fromindex][toindex]);
            repaint();
    }
}
```

The itemStateChanged() method is called whenever the choice list is changed. Table 6.2 shows the constructors and methods contained in the Choice class.

Table 6.2 Choice Class Constructors and Methods

METHOD	DESCRIPTION
Choice()	Constructs a new choice
addItem(String)	Adds an item to this choice
addNotify()	Creates the choice's peer
getItem(int)	Returns the string at the specified index in the choice
getSelectedIndex()	Returns the index of the currently selected item
getSelectedItem()	Returns a string representation of the current choice
paramString()	Returns the parameter string of this choice
select(int)	Selects the item with the specified position
select(String)	Selects the item with the specified string
add(String)	Adds an item to this choice
addItemListener(ItemListener)	Adds the specified item listener to receive item events from this choice
getItemCount()	Returns the number of items in this choice
getSelectedObjects()	Returns an array (length 1) containing the currently selected item
insert(String, int)	Inserts the item into this choice at the specified position
processEvent(AWTEvent)	Processes events on this choice

continued on next page

continued from previous page

METHOD	DESCRIPTION
processItemEvent(ItemEvent)	Processes item events occurring on this choice by dispatching them to any registered ItemListener objects
remove(int)	Removes an item from the choice menu
remove(String)	Removes the first occurrence of the item from the choice menu
removeAll()	Removes all items from the choice menu
removeItemListener(ItemListener)	Removes the specified item listener so that it no longer receives item events from this choice

COMPLEXITY
INTERMEDIATE

6.5 How do I...
Create text fields and text areas?

Problem

I would like to create a simple spreadsheet program. I know how to access keyboard and mouse events, but how do I create text fields and text areas?

Technique

Text fields and text areas both can be edited and enable selections with the mouse. Text fields are limited in size and don't scroll, and therefore are good for text entry. Text areas can be any given height and width and have scrollbars. Text areas are good for displaying large amounts of data. Figure 6.5 shows an example of the running applet you'll create in this example.

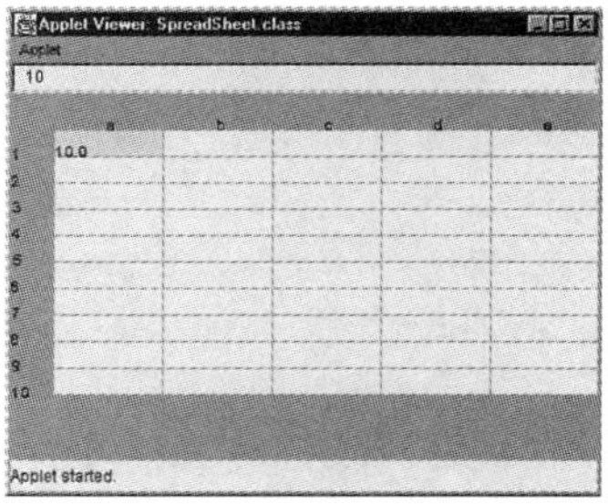

Figure 6.5 Individual keystrokes can be trapped and handled as events.

Steps

1. Create the source file. Create a new file called `SpreadSheet.java` and enter the following source:

```java
import java.io.*;
import java.awt.*;
import java.awt.event.*;
import java.applet.*;
import javax.swing.*;
import javax.swing.text.*;

/*
 * the applet class
 */
public class SpreadSheet extends Applet implements KeyListener{

/*
 * the text entry field
 */
TextField textField;

/*
 * instance of the sheet panel
 */
Sheet sheet;

/*
 * initialize the applet
 */
public void init () {

        setBackground(Color.lightGray);
        setLayout(new BorderLayout());

        textField = new TextField ("", 80);
        sheet = new Sheet (10, 5, 400, 200, textField);
        add ("North", textField);
        add ("Center", sheet);
        textField.addKeyListener(this);
}

/*
 * check for return keypresses
 */
public void keyTyped(KeyEvent e){}
public void keyReleased(KeyEvent e){}
public void keyPressed(KeyEvent e)
{
    char character;
    int x;


    character = e.getKeyChar();
    x=e.getKeyCode();
```

```
            //Check whether the user pressed Return
            if (x == 10)
            {
                    sheet.enter (textField.getText ());
            }
    }
    /*
     * application entry point
     * not used when run as an applet
     * @param args - command-line arguments
     */
    public static void main (String args[]) {

            Frame f = new Frame ("SpreadSheet");
            SpreadSheet spreadSheet = new SpreadSheet ();

            spreadSheet.init ();

            f.addWindowListener(new WindowCloser());
            f.setSize (440, 330);
            f.add ("Center", spreadSheet);
            f.show ();
    }
}

class WindowCloser extends WindowAdapter
{
    public void windowClosing(WindowEvent e)
    {
        Window win = e.getWindow();
        win.setVisible(false);
        win.dispose();
        System.exit(0);
    }
}
```

2. Create the source file. Create a new file called **Sheet.java** and enter the following source:

```
import java.awt.*;
import java.awt.event.*;

/*
 * the panel that holds the cells
 */
public class Sheet extends Panel implements MouseListener
{

/*
 * the number of rows and columns in the spreadsheet
 */
int rows;
int cols;
```

```
/*
 * width and height of the panel
 */
int width;
int height;

/*
 * the array of cells
 */
Cell cells[][];

/*
 * offsets into the panel where the cells are displayed
 */
int xoffset;
int yoffset;

/*
 * the row and column selected by a mouse click
 */
int selectedRow = 0;
int selectedCol = 0;

/*
 * the text entry field
 */
TextField textField;

/*
 * constructor
 * create all the cells and init them
 * @param r - number of rows
 * @param c - number of columns
 * @param w - width of the panel
 * @param h - height of the panel
 * @param t - instance of text entry field
 */
public Sheet (int r, int c, int w, int h, TextField t) {

        int i, j;

        rows = r;
        cols = c;
        width = w;
        height = h;
        xoffset = 30;
        yoffset = 30;
        textField = t;

        cells = new Cell[rows][cols];
        for (i=0; i<rows; i+=1) {
                for (j=0; j<cols; j+=1) {
                        cells[i][j] = new Cell (cells, rows, cols);
```

```
                }
        }
    addMouseListener(this);

}

/*
 * a mapping array for converting column indexes to characters
 */
static String charMap[] = {
        "a", "b", "c", "d", "e", "f", "g", "h", "i", "j",
        "k", "l", "m", "n", "o", "p", "q", "r", "s", "t",
        "u", "v", "w", "x", "y", "z"
};

/*
 * paint each cell
 * @param g - destination graphics object
 */
public void paint (Graphics g) {

        int i, j;
        int x, y;
        int w, h;
        double val;
        String s;

        w = width / cols;
        h = height / rows;

        x = 0;
        g.setColor (Color.black);
        for (i=0; i<rows; i+=1) {
                y = (i * height / rows) + yoffset;
                g.drawString (String.valueOf (i+1), x, y+h);
        }
        y = yoffset-2;
        for (j=0; j<cols; j+=1) {
                x = (j * width / cols) + xoffset+(w/2);
                g.drawString (charMap[j], x, y);
        }
        for (i=0; i<rows; i+=1) {
                for (j=0; j<cols; j+=1) {
                        s = cells[i][j].evalToString ();
                        x = (j * width / cols) + xoffset + 2;
                        y = (i * height / rows) + yoffset - 2;
                        if (i == selectedRow && j == selectedCol) {
                                g.setColor (Color.yellow);
                                g.fillRect (x, y, w-1, h-1);
                        } else {
                                g.setColor (Color.white);
                                g.fillRect (x, y, w-1, h-1);
                        }
```

```
                        g.setColor (Color.black);
                        g.drawString (s, x, y+h);
                }
        }
}

/*
 * called to recalculate the entire spreadsheet
 */
void recalculate () {

        int i, j;

        for (i=0; i<rows; i+=1) {
                for (j=0; j<cols; j+=1) {
                        cells[i][j].evaluate ();
                }
        }
}

/*
 * handle mouse down events
 * @param evt - event object
 * @param x - mouse x position
 * @param y - mouse y position
 */

    public void mouseClicked(MouseEvent e){}
    public void mouseEntered(MouseEvent e){}
    public void mouseExited(MouseEvent e){}
    public void mouseReleased(MouseEvent e){}
    public void mousePressed(MouseEvent e)
    {
        int x = e.getX();
        int y = e.getY();

            int w = width / cols;
            int h = height / rows;

            int sr = (y-yoffset)/h;
            int sc = (x-xoffset)/w;

            if (sr < 0 || sr >= rows || sc < 0 || sc > cols)
            return;


            selectedRow = sr;
            selectedCol = sc;
            repaint ();
            textField.setText (cells[selectedRow]
➥[selectedCol].text);
    }
```

```
/*
 * called to enter a text into a selected cell
 * @param s - the string to enter
 */
void enter (String s) {

        cells[selectedRow][selectedCol].enter (s);
        recalculate ();
        repaint ();
}
}
```

3. Create the source file. Create a new file called **Cell.java** and enter the following source:

```
import java.awt.*;

/*
 * Defines an individual cell
 */
public class Cell {

/*
 * Token types returned by Lex()
 */
static final int NUMBER = 1;
static final int EQUALS = 2;
static final int PLUS = 3;
static final int MINUS = 4;
static final int STAR = 5;
static final int SLASH = 6;
static final int TEXT = 7;
static final int EOT = 8;
static final int LEFT = 9;
static final int RIGHT = 10;
static final int UNKN = 11;
static final int FORMULA = 12;
static final int REFERENCE = 13;

/*
 * What is in this cell
 */
int type;

/*
 * The numeric value, if this cell is numeric
 */
double value;

/*
 * Numeric value for this token
 */
double lexValue;
```

```
/*
 * Index into input string (used for parsing)
 */
int lexIndex;

/*
 * Token value returned from Lex()
 */
int token;

/*
 * The text contents of this cell
 */
String text;
int textLength;
int textIndex;

/*
 * Reference to all cells in spreadsheet
 */
Cell cells[][];

/*
 * Error flag, set if parse error detected
 */
boolean error;

/*
 * Used to force rereading of tokens
 */
boolean lexFlag;

/*
 * Number of rows and columns in the spreadsheet
 * Used for bounds checking
 */
int cols;
int rows;

public Cell (Cell cs[][], int r, int c) {

    cells = cs;
    rows = r;
    cols = c;
    text = "";
    lexFlag = true;
    type = UNKN;
}

/*
 * Called to get the numeric value of this cell
 */
double evaluate () {
```

```
        resetLex ();
        error = false;
        switch (type) {
            case FORMULA:
            Lex ();
            value = Level1 ();
            if (error) return 0;
            return value;

            case NUMBER:
            value = lexValue;
            return value;

            case UNKN:
            return 0;
        }
        error = true;
        return 0;
    }

    /*
     * Returns the string representation of the value
     */
    String evalToString () {

        String s;

        if (type == TEXT || type == UNKN) return text;
        s = String.valueOf (value);
        if (error) return "Error";
        else return s;
    }

    /*
     * Called to enter a string into this cell
     */
    void enter (String s) {

        text = s;
        textLength = text.length ();
        resetLex ();
        error = false;
        switch (Lex ()) {
            case EQUALS:
            type = FORMULA;
            break;

            case NUMBER:
            type = NUMBER;
            value = lexValue;
            break;
```

```
            default:
            type = TEXT;
            break;
    }
}

/*
 * Top level of the recursive descent parser
 * Handle plus and minus.
 */
double Level1 () {

    boolean ok;
    double x1, x2;

    x1 = Level2 ();
    if (error) return 0;

    ok = true;
    while (ok) switch (Lex ()) {
        case PLUS:
        x2 = Level2 ();
        if (error) return 0;
        x1 += x2;
        break;

        case MINUS:
        x2 = Level2 ();
        if (error) return 0;
        x1 -= x2;
        break;

        default:
        Unlex ();
        ok = false;
        break;
    }
    return x1;
}

/*
 * Handle multiply and divide.
 */
double Level2 () {

    boolean ok;
    double x1, x2;

    x1 = Level3 ();
    if (error) return 0;
```

```
        ok = true;
        while (ok) switch (Lex ()) {
            case STAR:
            x2 = Level3 ();
            if (error) return 0;
            x1 *= x2;
            break;

            case SLASH:
            x2 = Level3 ();
            if (error) return 0;
            x1 /= x2;
            break;

            default:
            Unlex ();
            ok = false;
            break;
        }
        return x1;
    }

    /*
    Handle unary minus, parentheses, constants,
    ➥and cell references
     */
    double Level3 () {

        double x1, x2;

        switch (Lex ()) {
            case MINUS:
            x2 = Level1 ();
            if (error) return 0;
            return -x2;

            case LEFT:
            x2 = Level1 ();
            if (error) return 0;
            if (Lex () != RIGHT) {
                error = true;
                return 0;
            }
            return x2;

            case NUMBER:
            case REFERENCE:
            return lexValue;
        }
        error = true;
        return 0;
    }
```

```
/*
 * Reset the lexical analyzer.
 */
void resetLex () {

    lexIndex = 0;
    lexFlag = true;
}

/*
 * Push a token back for rereading.
 */
void Unlex () {

    lexFlag = false;
}

/*
 * Returns the next token
 */
int Lex () {

    if (lexFlag) {
        token = lowlevelLex ();
    }
    lexFlag = true;
    return token;
}

/*
 * Returns the next token in the text string
 */
int lowlevelLex () {

    char c;
    String s;

    do {
        if (lexIndex >= textLength) return EOT;
        c = text.charAt (lexIndex++);
    } while (c == ' ');
    switch (c) {
        case '=':
        return EQUALS;

        case '+':
        return PLUS;

        case '-':
        return MINUS;

        case '*':
        return STAR;
```

```
        case '/':
        return SLASH;

        case '(':
        return LEFT;

        case ')':
        return RIGHT;
    }

    if (c >= '0' && c <= '9') {
        s = "";
        while ((c >= '0' && c <= '9') || c == '.' ||
            c == '-' || c == 'e' || c == 'E') {
            s += c;
            if (lexIndex >= textLength) break;
            c = text.charAt (lexIndex++);
        }
        lexIndex -= 1;
        try {
            lexValue = Double.valueOf (s).doubleValue();
        } catch (NumberFormatException e) {
            System.out.println (e);
            error = true;
            return UNKN;
        }
        return NUMBER;
    }
    if (c >= 'a' && c <= 'z') {
        int col = c - 'a';
        int row;
        s = "";
        if (lexIndex >= textLength) {
            error = true;
            return UNKN;
        }
        c = text.charAt (lexIndex++);
        while (c >= '0' && c <= '9') {
            s += c;
            if (lexIndex >= textLength) break;
            c = text.charAt (lexIndex++);
        }
        lexIndex -= 1;
        try {
            row = Integer.valueOf (s).intValue() - 1;
        } catch (NumberFormatException e) {
            error = true;
            return UNKN;
        }
        if (row >= rows || col >= cols) {
            error = true;
            return REFERENCE;
        }
```

```
            lexValue = cells[row][col].evaluate();
            if (cells[row][col].error) error = true;
            return REFERENCE;
        }
        return TEXT;
    }
}
```

4. Create an HTML document that contains the applet. Create a new file called **howto65.html** that contains the following code:

```
<html>
<head>
<title>SpreadSheet</title>
</head>
<applet code="SpreadSheet.class" width=430 height=300>
</applet>
<hr size=4>

</html>
```

5. Compile and test the applet. Compile the source by using **javac**. SpreadSheet has three source files that must be compiled: **SpreadSheet.java**, **Sheet.java**, and **Cell.java**. Test the applet by using the Appletviewer; enter the following command:

```
appletviewer howto65.html
```

You can also run **SpreadSheet.java** as an application by typing

```
java SpreadSheet
```

6. When SpreadSheet is executed, a window opens and a text area is displayed above a sheet. The sheet contains five columns labeled a to e, and 10 rows labeled 1 to 10. You activate a cell by clicking inside it with the mouse. To enter a value in an active cell, click on the text area, type the desired value, and press Enter. The spreadsheet implements the four basic mathematic functions: addition, subtraction, multiplication, and division.

To evaluate a mathematic expression, an equal sign is entered as the first character in the text area. For example, to add cell a1 and cell b1, select the cell to hold the evaluation and enter the following text in the text area:

```
= a1 + b1
```

If the values in a1 or b1 are changed, the cell containing the expression changes automatically.

How It Works

The SpreadSheet applet/application contains three classes: the **Cell** class, which defines variables and methods for an individual cell; the **Sheet** class, which holds a two-dimensional array of cells and the methods necessary for displaying a cell; and the **SpreadSheet** class, which is the applet itself.

SpreadSheet creates a text field at the top of the frame and also creates an instance of **Sheet**, which it places in the center of the frame. The **TextField** constructor takes the initial string and the number of characters as arguments. The text field is passed as an argument to the **Sheet** constructor for convenience.

The **Sheet** constructor takes the number of rows, number of columns, width, height, and the instance of **TextField** as arguments. The **SpreadSheet** class handles text field events (for example, the pressing of the Enter key) by sending the entered text to the enter method of the **Sheet** class. The **Sheet** constructor simply saves its arguments and creates a two-dimensional array of cells for the given number of columns and rows.

The **keyPressed()** method is used to handle keypress events:

```
public void keyTyped(KeyEvent e){}
public void keyReleased(KeyEvent e){}
public void keyPressed(KeyEvent e)
{
    char character;
    int x;


    character = e.getKeyChar();
    x=e.getKeyCode();

    //Check to see it the user hit Return
    if (x == 10)
    {
        sheet.enter (textField.getText ());
    }
}
```

The interesting occurrence for this application is the pressing of the Enter (Return) key. You listen until you see a keycode of 10, meaning that Enter was pressed. At this point, you use the **getText()** method to find out what the user entered and pass this as a parameter to the **sheet_enter()** method.

The **paint()** method in the **Sheet** class evaluates each cell and prints its contents in the appropriate frame location. It also highlights a cell that has been selected by a previous mouse click. The **recalculate()** method invokes each cell's **evaluate()** method to affect recalculation. The **mousePressed()** method computes the selected row and selected column from the mouse x and y coordinates and also displays the contents of the selected cell in the text field. This is done by using the setText() method of the TextField class.

The enter() method is invoked when the user presses the Enter (or Return) key (which is invoked from KeyListener in the SpreadSheet class). The enter() method invokes the enter() method of the selected cell, passing the text string as an argument. It then forces a recalculation by invoking recalculate() and forces a repaint by invoking repaint(), which then displays all the recalculated values.

The Cell constructor saves its arguments and initializes values. The String text holds the text for this cell. When text is entered in a cell via the enter() method, it is copied into the text variable, and its length is saved for convenience. Next the enter() method determines whether the text is a formula, a numeric constant, or just text, and it sets the type variable accordingly. Text starting with an equal sign is considered a formula; text starting with a digit is assumed to be a numeric constant; otherwise, text is treated as normal text. A single negative number is treated as text. This text parsing is handled by the Lex() method. Next, the recalculate() method invokes evaluate(), which uses the cell type to determine whether it is a formula, and if so, to evaluate the formula. If the cell is a numeric constant or a string, then evaluate() simply returns the cell's contents.

If the cell contains a formula, then the expression is parsed by mutually recursive methods Level1(), Level2(), and Level3(). Level1() handles addition and subtraction. Level2() handles multiplication and division. Level3() handles unary minus, parenthetical expressions, and numeric constants and cell references.

The low-level lexical analysis is handled by the method lowlevelLex(). It uses brute-force techniques to extort tokens from the text.

Comments

This spreadsheet can easily be extended to include mathematic functions, more operators, and more key events (such as arrow keys for navigating cells).

Another design for a Java spreadsheet (and perhaps the most purely object-oriented) is to treat the contents of each cell as Java byte-code to be interpreted by the Java Virtual Machine. In effect, each cell would be its own applet. This exercise is left to the ambitious reader.

COMPLEXITY
INTERMEDIATE

How do I...
Use sliders?

Problem

I would like to make a color selection tool. The tool should have a slider bar for the red, green, and blue components. The color defined by the RGB values should be displayed. How do I use slider bars?

Technique

Java contains a `Scrollbar` class that is used to create scrollbars and sliders (see Figure 6.6). Each color component (red, green, and blue) should have a separate scrollbar and text field to display the scrollbar value. The `Color` class is used to get the color defined by the three color components. This color is then displayed as a panel background color.

Figure 6.6 The `AdjustmentListener` class enables an application to detect changes to scrollbars.

Steps

1. Create the applet source file. Create a new file called `ColorPicker.java` and enter the following source:

```
import java.applet.Applet;
import java.awt.*;
import java.awt.event.*;


/*
 * the Applet class
 */
public class ColorPicker extends Applet
➥implements AdjustmentListener

{
```

```
/*
 * the panel that holds the sliders that
 * control the RGB values
 */
Panel controls = new Panel();

/*
 * the panel that holds the sample color
 */
Panel sample = new Panel();

public void adjustmentValueChanged(AdjustmentEvent evt)
{
        Object object1 = evt.getSource();

        if (object1 ==  (sbRed))
        {
                tfRed.setText(String.valueOf(sbRed.getValue()));
                changecolor();
           }

        if (object1 ==  (sbGreen))
        {
                tfGreen.setText(String.valueOf(
➥sbGreen.getValue()));
                changecolor();
           }

        if (object1 ==  (sbBlue))
        {
                tfBlue.setText(String.valueOf(sbBlue.getValue()));
                changecolor();
           }
}

/*
 *the red scrollbar
 */
Scrollbar sbRed;

/*
 * the green scrollbar
 */
Scrollbar sbGreen;


/*
 * the blue scrollbar
 */
Scrollbar sbBlue;

/*
 * the red component TextField
```

```
 */
TextField tfRed;

/*
 * the green component TextField
 */
TextField tfGreen;

/*
 * the blue component TextField
 */
TextField tfBlue;
int min = 0;
int max = 255;

/*
 * initilaizes the applet
 */
public void init () {

        this.setLayout(new BorderLayout());
        controls.setLayout (new GridLayout(3,3,5,5));
        this.add ("South",controls);
        this.add ("Center",sample);

        tfRed = new TextField (5);
        tfGreen = new TextField (5);
        tfBlue = new TextField (5);
        controls.add (new Label ("Red",1));
        controls.add (new Label ("Green",1));
        controls.add (new Label ("Blue",1));
        controls.add (tfRed);
        controls.add (tfGreen);
        controls.add (tfBlue);

        sbRed = new Scrollbar (Scrollbar.HORIZONTAL,
➥0, 1, min, max);
        //set the values for the scrollbar
        // value, page size, min, max
        controls.add (sbRed);
    sbRed.addAdjustmentListener(this);

        sbGreen = new Scrollbar (Scrollbar.HORIZONTAL,
➥0, 1, min, max);
        //set the values for the scrollbar
        // value, page size, min, max
        controls.add (sbGreen);
    sbGreen.addAdjustmentListener(this);

        sbBlue = new Scrollbar (Scrollbar.HORIZONTAL,
➥0, 1, min, max);
        //set the values for the scrollbar
        // value, page size, min, max
```

```
        controls.add (sbBlue);
      sbBlue.addAdjustmentListener(this);

        // sets the text fields to the slider value
        tfRed.setText(String.valueOf(sbRed.getValue()));
        tfGreen.setText(String.valueOf(sbGreen.getValue()));
        tfBlue.setText(String.valueOf(sbBlue.getValue()));

        changecolor();
}

/** Gets the current value in the text field.
 * That's guaranteed to be the same as the value
 * in the scroller (subject to rounding, of course).
 * @param textField - the textField
 */
double getValue(TextField textField) {

        double f;
        try {
                f = Double.valueOf(textField.getText())
➡doubleValue();
        } catch (java.lang.NumberFormatException e) {
                f = 0.0;
        }
        return f;
}


/*
 * changes the color of the sample to the
 * color defined by the RGB values set by
 * the user
 */
public void changecolor () {

        int i;

        sample.setBackground(new Color((int)getValue(tfRed),
                (int)getValue(tfGreen), (int)getValue(tfBlue)));
        repaint();
}

public void update (Graphics g) {

        paintAll(g);
}

/*
 * application entry point
 * not used when run as an applet
 * @param args - command line arguments
 */
public static void main (String args[]) {
```

```
        Frame f = new Frame ("ColorPicker");
        ColorPicker colorPicker = new ColorPicker ();

        colorPicker.init ();
        f.addWindowListener(new WindowCloser());

    f.setSize (300, 200);
    f.add ("Center", colorPicker);
        f.show ();
}
}

class WindowCloser extends WindowAdapter
{
    public void windowClosing(WindowEvent e)
    {
        Window win = e.getWindow();
        win.setVisible(false);
        win.dispose();
        System.exit(0);
    }
}
```

2. Create an HTML document that contains the applet. Create a new file called **howto66.html** that contains the following:

```
<html>
<head>
<title>Color Picker</title>
</head>
<applet code="ColorPicker.class" width=200 height=200>
</applet>
<hr size=4>

</html>
```

3. Compile and test the applet. Compile the source. Test the applet by using the Appletviewer; enter the following command:

```
appletviewer howto66.html
```

You can also run **ColorPicker.java** as an application by typing

```
java ColorPicker
```

4. When ColorPicker is executed, a window opens, with a colored panel at the top (set to black on startup) and three scrollbars near the bottom. Each scrollbar has a corresponding label and text field. The scrollbar can be moved, and the text field value and the color of the top panel are updated automatically. Figure 6.6 shows an example of the running applet.

How It Works

The ColorPicker applet/application contains only one class, the applet itself. Two panels are created, controls that hold the scrollbars and sample; the sample is an empty panel that is used to display the defined color. Three scrollbars (sbRed, sbGreen, and sbBlue) and three text fields (tfRed, tfGreen, and tfBlue) are created for the selection tool.

The init() method sets the layout for the main panel to BorderLayout. The layout for controls is set to GridLayout with three rows, three columns, and a row and column spacing of five characters. This allows us to add three scrollbars, three text fields, and three labels. Using GridLayout aligns all components in a grid, and each grid cell is of equal size. Chapter 8 discusses layout managers in more detail.

The controls panel is added to the bottom (South), and the sample is added to the center (Center) of the main panel. Each of the three text fields is constructed with five columns. The scrollbars are constructed by using a Scrollbar constructor that takes five integer parameters. The first parameter is orientation, which is either Scrollbar.HORIZONTAL or Scrollbar.VERTICAL. The other four parameters, in order, are the initial value of the scrollbar, the size of the page increment of the scrollbar, the minimum value, and the maximum value. The size of the page increment is sometimes referred to as the *finger size* or the *step increment* of the slider. Table 6.3 lists all the constructors and methods contained in the Scrollbar class.

The scrollbars are then added to the controls panel with the **add** method. You set the text fields to display the value of the corresponding scrollbar by calling the getValue() method for each scrollbar. The value returned from getValue() is converted to a string and set to the text field's displayed string by using the setText() method. The method changeColor() is called, which sets the background of the sample panel to the selected color, as shown in Figure 6.6.

The changeColor() method changes the background color of the sample panel to the color defined by the Scrollbar values. The call to setBackground() uses a new Color constructor with the getValue() method for each text field as the arguments. The getValue() method returns the current value of the TextField as a double. The value must then be cast to an integer for the color constructor. repaint() is then called to update the color.

The handleEvent() method is overridden to capture the scrollbar and text field events. If the event's target is equal to one of the scrollbars, the text field value is set to the scrollbar value with the setText() method, and the changecolor() method is called. If the event was one of the text fields, then the corresponding slider value is set to the entered value with the setSliderValue() method. The text field is then set to the slider value using the setText() method.

Table 6.3 Scrollbar Class Constructors and Methods

METHOD	DESCRIPTION
Scrollbar()	Constructs a new vertical scrollbar
Scrollbar(int)	Constructs a new scrollbar with the specified orientation
Scrollbar(int, int, int, int, int)	Constructs a new scrollbar with the specified orientation, value, page size, and minimum and maximum values
addNotify()	Creates the scrollbar's peer
getMaximum()	Returns the maximum value of this scrollbar
getMinimum()	Returns the minimum value of this scrollbar
getOrientation()	Returns the orientation for this scrollbar
getValue()	Returns the current value of this scrollbar
paramString()	Returns the string parameters for this scrollbar
setValue(int)	Sets the value of this scrollbar to the specified value
setValues(int, int, int, int)	Sets the values for this scrollbar
HORIZONTAL	The horizontal scrollbar variable
VERTICAL	The vertical scrollbar variable
addAdjustmentListener(AdjustmentListener)	Adds the specified adjustment listener to receive adjustment events from this scrollbar
getBlockIncrement()	Gets the block increment for this scrollbar
getUnitIncrement()	Gets the unit increment for this scrollbar
getVisibleAmount()	Returns the visible amount of this scrollbar
paramString()	Returns the string parameters for this scrollbar
processAdjustmentEvent(AdjustmentEvent)	Processes adjustment events occurring on this scrollbar by dispatching them to any registered AdjustmentListener objects

METHOD	DESCRIPTION
processEvent(AWTEvent)	Processes events on this scrollbar
removeAdjustmentListener(AdjustmentListener)	Removes the specified adjustment listener so that it no longer receives adjustment events from this scrollbar
setBlockIncrement(int)	Sets the block increment for this scrollbar
setOrientation(int)	Sets the orientation for this scrollbar
setUnitIncrement(int)	Sets the unit increment for this scrollbar
setVisibleAmount(int)	Sets the visible amount of this scrollbar, which is the range of values represented by the width of the scrollbar's bubble

CHAPTER 7
ADVANCED GRAPHICS

7

ADVANCED GRAPHICS

How do I...

In Chapter 3, "Basic Graphics," the techniques needed to draw basic graphical elements such as lines and polygons are presented. This chapter concentrates on advanced graphics manipulations. Java supports the ability to load images from the server so that they can be presented on the client in a manner that allows far greater control than is available with HTML alone. Java is deterministic, and with experience you can use it to implement interactive games, display real-time data, and animate images for a variety of purposes.

In this chapter image loading, drawing, scaling, and animation are demonstrated.

7.1 Display a Series of Images

This example demonstrates how to load images from a server and cycle through them with a mouse click. The example uses a button that allows the user to skip to the next image.

7.2 Resize an Image

Resizing an image is a feature that allows an image to be displayed at any desired size. This example loads an image and presents buttons for making the image smaller and bigger. The buttons are used to resize the image appropriately.

7.3 Drag an Image with the Mouse

Dragging an image with the mouse is commonly necessary in graphical user interfaces. In this example you load an image and allow it to be dragged with the mouse.

7.4 Implement Double-Buffering

Drawing images on top of each other by using techniques from Example 7.1 is sufficient to effect animation. Unfortunately, the results can be disappointing because unwanted flicker and temporal distortion due to drawing latency can degrade performance. This example demonstrates the use of double-buffering to produce high-quality animation.

7.5 Layer Graphics

This example demonstrates the illusion of depth by layering images on top of each other. Several images are loaded, and you can layer them by using bring to front and send to back buttons.

7.6 Display Part of an Image

There are many instances when only part of an image must be displayed. This example implements several image transition effects such as barn door open and venetian blind. It can be used to save Web page space and draw attention to banner advertisements.

7.7 Create Images from Pixel Values

In addition to loading images from a server, it may be necessary to construct images from pixel values. In this example, the Mandelbrot set is calculated and converted to an image object for display.

7.8 Access Pixels in an Image

Many applications require access to pixel values in an image object. This example extracts pixels from an image for use as the initial conditions in Conway's game of life.

COMPLEXITY
BEGINNING

7.1 How do I...
Display a series of images?

Problem

I want to write an applet that loads a series of images and displays them in sequence when I click a button. This may be used to show the user a series of thumbnail images that are representatives of larger images. I know how to create buttons and handle button events, but I don't know how to display a series of images. How do I display a series of images?

Technique

To display an image, an applet must first load it from the server. This is accomplished by using the `Applet.getImage()` method. `getImage()` takes a URL or server filename as an argument and returns an `Image` object. The image can then be drawn by using one of the `drawImage()` methods available from the `Graphics` class. In this example, six images are loaded in an array of type `Image` and successively drawn in response to a button click. Similar methods to these exist in the `Toolkit` class.

Steps

1. Create the applet source file. Create a new file called `ImageApp.java` and enter the following source:

```
import java.awt.*;
import java.awt.event.*;
import java.applet.Applet;

/*
 * display a series of images
 */
public class ImageApp extends Applet implements ActionListener
{

/*
 * the number of images to load
 */
final int NumImages = 6;
Button button1;


/*
 * an array to hold the images
 */
Image imgs[] = new Image[NumImages];
```

```
/*
 * which image is currently displayed
 */
int which = 0;

/*
 * init method runs when applet is loaded or reloaded
 */
public void init() {

    setLayout(new BorderLayout());

    Panel p = new Panel ();
    add("South", p);
    button1 = new Button("Next Image");
    p.add (button1);
    button1.addActionListener(this);
    for (int i=0; i < NumImages; i+=1) {
        String name = "Globe"+(i+1)+".gif";
        imgs[i] = getImage (getDocumentBase(),name);
    }
}

/**
 * paint method is called by update
 * draw the current image
 * @param g - destination graphics object
 */
public void paint (Graphics g) {

    g.drawImage (imgs[which], 10, 10, this);
}

/**
 * switch to next image when button is pressed
 * @param evt - event object
 * @param arg - target object
 */
public void actionPerformed(ActionEvent evt)
{
        which += 1;
        which %= NumImages;    // wrap around to zero
        repaint ();    // causes update as soon as possible
}
}
```

2. Create an HTML document that contains the applet. Create a new file called howto71.html that contains the following code:

```
<html>
<head>
<title>ImageApp</title>
</head>
<hr size=4>
This is a simple image display applet
<hr size=4>
```

```
<applet code="ImageApp.class" width=200 height=200>
</applet>
<hr size=4>
</html>
```

3. Compile and test the applet. Compile the Java source file `ImageApp.java` by using `javac`. This example loads six images, called `Globe1.gif`, `Globe2.gif`, `Globe3.gif`, and so on. These images can be found on the accompanying CD-ROM in the **Chapter 7** folder. When the applet is executed by using Appletviewer, an image should appear in the upper-left corner, along with a Next Image button at the bottom. Clicking on Next Image should cycle through all six images. Figure 7.1 shows the image as it is displayed by Appletviewer. If the image does not appear, make sure it is in the same directory as the applet class (`ImageApp.class`) and is not corrupted in some way. If the image cannot be loaded, the applet continues without warning.

Figure 7.1
A series of images simulates motion.

How It Works

`Image` is a class used to hold an image. It is contained in `awt.imgs` as an array of type `Image`; six elements are used for this example. The `init()` method creates a new panel at the bottom (South) and adds a button. The `start()` method retrieves each of the four images using the `getImage()` method. Several `getImage()` methods take `URL` as an argument. `GetDocumentBase()` returns the current URL base where the applet resides, so that only the filename of an image relative to the current document base is needed. The `drawImage()` method takes `Image`, `position`, and `ImageObserver` as arguments in order to draw the image. `this` (the applet) is specified as the `ImageObserver` argument.

Comments

It is important to note that the image is not actually loaded with the `getImage()` call. An image is loaded asynchronously when it is needed. Images are loaded only once and kept in memory for future display or use. If you watch carefully when the applet is loaded, you'll notice that the first six image updates are not instantaneous. This is because the Java runtime routines draw the image as it is loaded. After all the images are loaded, the drawing time is not noticeable. The **ImageObserver** interface is used to notify a class as the image is loaded. This image is drawn as soon as it is ready.

COMPLEXITY
BEGINNING

7.2 How do I...
Resize an image?

Problem

Images often need to be scaled to a size different from the way they are stored on disk. For example, two different-sized images need to be displayed as the same size, or I want to simulate in/out motion by making an image smaller or bigger. I know how to load and display images, but I don't know how to scale them. How do I resize an image?

Technique

Example 7.1 uses a **drawImage()** method to display an image. Another **drawImage()** method can scale an image to arbitrary dimensions. The image is retrieved with **getImage()** as in Example 7.1. A version of **drawImage()** that takes **width** and **height** as parameters can be used to scale and display the image.

Steps

1. Create the applet source file. Create a new file called **ImageSize.java** and enter the following source:

```
import java.awt.*;
import java.awt.event.*;
import java.applet.Applet;

/*
 * an applet that allows an image to be resized
 */
public class ImageSize extends Applet implements
➥ ActionListener {

/*
 * the image to draw
 */
Image img;
```

```
Button btnSmaller;
Button btnBigger;

/*
 * the current width and height of the image
 */
double width, height;

/*
 * the image size scale factor
 */
double scale = 1.0;


/*
 * called when the applet is loaded or reloaded
 */
public void init() {

    setLayout(new BorderLayout());
    Panel p = new Panel ();
    add("South", p);
    btnSmaller = new Button("Smaller");
    p.add (btnSmaller);
      btnBigger = new Button("Bigger");
    p.add (btnBigger);
    btnSmaller.addActionListener(this);
        btnBigger.addActionListener(this);

    MediaTracker tracker = new MediaTracker (this);

    img = getImage (getDocumentBase(), "T1.gif");
    tracker.addImage (img, 0);
    showStatus ("Getting image: T1.gif");
    try {
        tracker.waitForID (0);
    } catch (InterruptedException e) { }
    width = img.getWidth (this);
    height = img.getHeight (this);
}

public void paint (Graphics g) {
    double w, h;


    w = scale * width;
    h = scale * height;

    // if we don't have the size yet, we shouldn't draw
    if (w < 0 || h < 0) { w=75; h=75; } //return;

    // explicitly specify width (w) and height (h)
    g.drawImage (img, 10, 10, (int) w, (int) h, this);
}
public void actionPerformed(ActionEvent evt)
{
```

```
            Object object1 = evt.getSource ();
            if (object1 == btnSmaller)
            {
                scale *= 0.9;      // make it 10% smaller
                repaint ();
            }
            if (object1 == btnBigger)
            {
                scale *= 1.1;      // make it 10% bigger
                repaint ();
            }
        }

    }
```

2. Create an HTML document that contains the applet. Create a new file called `howto72.html` that contains the following code:

```
<html>
<head>
<title>ImageSize</title>
</head>
A simple applet that demonstrates image scaling
<hr size=4>
<applet code="ImageSize.class" width=200 height=200>
</applet>
<hr size=4>
</html>
```

3. Compile and test the applet. Compile **ImageSize.java** and test it using the Appletviewer. This example requires an image called **T1.gif** that must reside in the same directory as **ImageSize.class**. This image file can also be found on the CD-ROM. An image should appear in the upper-left corner as before, along with two buttons marked Smaller and Bigger at the bottom. Click either of the buttons to change the size of the image. Figures 7.2 and 7.3 show the applet after and before the image has been resized, respectively.

Figure 7.2
Before the
applet has
been resized.

Figure 7.3
After the
applet has
been resized.

How It Works

A version of `drawImage()` that takes `width` and `height` as parameters is used to scale and display the image. The scale factor is initialized to 1.0. When the user clicks one of the buttons, scale is either increased or decreased by 10%, and an update is forced. When the `paint()` method is called, the width and height are both multiplied by `scale` and supplied as arguments to `drawImage()`.

Comments

Note that `drawImage()` takes only integer types for `width` and `height`. Floating-point values must be typecast appropriately, as shown in the sample code. Large scale factors can be time-consuming, so use them with care. `MediaTracker` monitors the status of the image load and causes the application to wait until an image is loaded to proceed.

COMPLEXITY
INTERMEDIATE

7.3 How do I...
Drag an image with the mouse?

Problem

Drag and drop is a common operation in graphical user interfaces. Mouse control of image placement can also be used in graphical games. How do I drag an image with the mouse?

Technique

The method `drawImage()` requires the x and y screen coordinates of the upper-left corner of the image. The `mousePressed()` and `mouseDrag()` methods both return the x and y positions of the mouse pointer. These are used to specify the drawing coordinates.

Steps

1. Create the applet source file. Create a new file called `ImageMove.java` and enter the following source:

```java
import java.awt.*;
import java.awt.event.*;
import java.applet.Applet;

/*
 * the applet class
 */
public class ImageMove extends Applet implements➡
 MouseListener, MouseMotionListener{

/*
 * the image to be displayed
 */
Image img;

/*
 * the width and height of the image
 */
int width, height;

/*
 * xpos, ypos are the coordinates of the upper left of the image
 */
int xpos=10, ypos=10;

/*
 * dx, dy are the deltas from the mouse point to xpos, ypos
 */
int dx, dy;

/*
 * called when the applet is loaded
 * load the image and use MediaTracker so that
 * the width and height are available immediately
 */
public void init () {

    MediaTracker tracker = new MediaTracker (this);

    img = getImage (getDocumentBase(), "T1.gif");
    tracker.addImage (img, 0);
    showStatus ("Getting image: T1.gif");
    try {
        tracker.waitForID (0);
    } catch (InterruptedException e) { }
    width = img.getWidth (this);
    height = img.getHeight (this);
    addMouseListener(this);
    addMouseMotionListener(this);
}
```

```
/*
 * paint the image in the new location
 * @param g - destination graphics object
 */
public void paint (Graphics g) {

    g.setColor (Color.white);
    g.drawImage (img, xpos, ypos, this);
}


/*
 * adjust the new position and repaint the image
 */

public void mouseClicked(MouseEvent e){}
public void mouseEntered(MouseEvent e){}
public void mouseExited(MouseEvent e){}
public void mouseReleased(MouseEvent e){}
public void mouseMoved(MouseEvent e){}

public void mousePressed(MouseEvent e)
{
    int x =e.getX();
    int y =e.getY();

    dx = x - xpos;
    dy = y - ypos;
}

public void mouseDragged(MouseEvent e)
{
    int x =e.getX();
    int y =e.getY();
    if (dx < width && dx >= 0 && dy < height && dy >= 0)
    {
        xpos = x - dx;
        ypos = y - dy;
        repaint ();
    }
}

}
```

2. Create an HTML document that contains the applet. Create a new file called **howto73.html** that contains the following code:

```
<html>
<head>
<title>ImageMove</title>
</head>
Use the mouse to move the image.
<hr size=4>
<applet code="ImageMove.class" width=200 height=200>
</applet>
<hr size=4>
</html>
```

3. Compile and test the applet. Compile `ImageMove.java` and use the Appletviewer to run the applet. This example requires an image called `T1.gif` that must reside in the same directory as the `ImageMove.class` to run the applet. This image file can be found on the CD-ROM. When the applet is run, an image should appear in the upper left. Use the mouse to move the image around. Figure 7.4 shows the applet after the image has been moved.

Figure 7.4 An image can be dragged by using the mouse events.

How It Works

Only one class is defined, the applet itself. The `init()` method loads the image from the server by invoking `Applet.getImage()` with the document base and filename relative to the applet directory as arguments. The `mousePressed()` method is called in response to a mouse down event. In this case, the relative distance from the mouse down point to the image origin is saved so that the image does not jump when it is moved. The `mouseDrag()` method is called in response to mouse drag events. The new position of the image is calculated and an update is forced by invoking `repaint()`. The `paint()` method draws the image at the new position by calling `Graphics.drawImage()`.

7.4 How do I...
Implement double-buffering?

Problem

I want to write an applet that shows several images bouncing off the edge of the applet panel. I know how to load the images and move them. The problem is that the animation flickers and doesn't appear smooth. I want to use an offscreen object to implement double-buffering. How do I implement double-buffering?

Technique

From the previous examples, animation may appear straightforward. It can be done by using only the methods previously discussed, but may yield unwanted effects, such as visible drawing latency and flicker. This becomes unsatisfactory when there are many images moving simultaneously. A good animation should be smooth and flicker-free.

The drawing latency and flicker problems are solved by maintaining an offscreen image, drawing into it, and copying it to the screen when necessary. This is commonly referred to as *double-buffering*. The screen copy is done very quickly by the Java runtime because rectangular-block transfer routines are highly optimized on all windowing systems. Double-buffering delivers crisp performance even at low frame rates.

Uniform update rates are also needed to give the illusion of smooth motion. This can be accomplished by using the thread mechanisms available to Java applets.

In this example, several balls appear to bounce off the sides of a box. The principles demonstrated here can be used as the basis for games or particle simulations.

Steps

1. Create the applet source file. Create a new file called `Bounce.java` and enter the following source:

```
import java.awt.*;
import java.awt.event.*;
import java.applet.Applet;
import java.awt.image.ImageObserver;

/*
 * a class describing a single ball
 */
```

```
class Ball {

/*
 * the image for this ball
 */
Image img;

/*
 * x position and velocity
 */
double x, dx;

/*
 * y position and velocity
 */
double y, dy;

/*
 * initialize the position and velocity
 * to random values
 */
void random () {

    x = 10 + 380*Math.random ();
    y = 10 + 200*Math.random ();
    dx = 5 - 10*Math.random ();
    dy = 5 - 10*Math.random ();
}

/**
 * calculate the next position of this ball
 * and make sure it bounces off the edge of the panel
 * @param d - dimension of the bounding panel
 */
void compute (Dimension d) {

    if (x <= 0 || x > d.width) dx = -dx;      // bounce horizontal
    if (y <= 0 || y > d.height) dy = -dy;     // bounce vertical
    x += dx;
    y += dy;
}

/**
 * draw the ball image
 * @param g - destination graphics object
 * @param obs - parent image observer
 */
public void paint (Graphics g, ImageObserver obs) {
    g.drawImage (img, (int) x-10, (int) y-10, obs);
}
}

/*
 * the panel containing the bouncing balls
 */
class BouncePanel extends Panel implements Runnable {
```

```
/*
 * the number of balls
 */
final int nballs = 4;

/*
 * the array holding all the balls
 */
Ball balls[] = new Ball[10];

/*
 * offscreen image
 */
Image offimg;

/*
 * size of offscreen image
 */
Dimension offsize;

/*
 * graphics object associated with offscreen image
 */
Graphics offg;

/*
 * thread for periodic updating
 */
Thread thread;

/*
 * the thread recalculates each ball position and
 * redraws them
 */
public void run() {

    offsize = getSize();
    offimg = createImage (offsize.width, offsize.height);
    offg = offimg.getGraphics();
    while (true) {
        for (int i=0; i<nballs; i+=1) {
            balls[i].compute (offsize);
        }
        repaint ();
        try {
            Thread.sleep (25);
        } catch (InterruptedException e) {
            break;
        }
    }
}

/**
 * override update to avoid erase flicker
 * @param g - destination graphics object
 */
```

```
public synchronized void update (Graphics g) {

    offg.setColor (Color.lightGray);
    offg.fillRect (0, 0, offsize.width, offsize.height);

    for (int i = 0 ; i < nballs ; i++)
        balls[i].paint (offg, this);
    offg.setColor (Color.black);
    offg.drawRect (0, 0, offsize.width-1, offsize.height-1);
    g.drawImage(offimg, 0, 0, this);
}

/*
 * start the update thread
 */
public void start() {

    thread = new Thread(this);
    thread.start();
}

/*
 * stop the update thread
 */
public void stop() {

    if (thread != null)
    {
        thread = null;
    }
}
}

/*
 * the applet proper
 */
public class Bounce extends Applet implements ActionListener {

/*
 * instance of BouncePanel
 */
BouncePanel panel;
Button button1;
/*
 * an array containing the images for the balls
 */
Image img[] = new Image[4];

/*
 * called when the applet is loaded
 * create an instance of bounce panel and add the Start button
 * and load images
 */
public void init() {

    setLayout(new BorderLayout());
```

```
        panel = new BouncePanel ();
        add ("Center", panel);
        Panel p = new Panel ();
        add ("South", p);

        button1 = new Button("Start");
        p.add (button1);
        button1.addActionListener(this);

        img[0] = getImage (getDocumentBase(), "whiteball.gif");
        img[1] = getImage (getDocumentBase(), "redball.gif");
        img[2] = getImage (getDocumentBase(), "blueball.gif");
        img[3] = getImage (getDocumentBase(), "greenball.gif");
        for (int i=0; i<panel.nballs; i+=1) {
            panel.balls[i] = new Ball ();
            panel.balls[i].img = img[i & 3];
        }
    }

    /*
     * called when the applet is started
     * just start the bounce panel update thread
     */
    public void start() {

        panel.start();
    }

    /*
     * called when the applet is stopped
     */
    public void stop() {

        panel.stop();
    }

    /*
     * handle Start button press by randomizing balls
     * @param evt - event object
     * @param arg - target object
     */

    public void actionPerformed(ActionEvent evt)
    {
            for (int i=0; i<panel.nballs; i+=1)
                panel.balls[i].random ();
    }

    }
```

2. Create an HTML document that contains the applet. Create a new file called howto74.html that contains the following code:

```
<html>
<head>
<title>Bounce</title>
```

```
</head>
Bouncing balls example.
<hr size=4>
<applet code="Bounce.class" width=400 height=400>
</applet>
<hr size=4>
</html>
```

3. Compile and test the applet. Compile **Bounce.java** and use the Appletviewer to run the applet. Get the images from the CD-ROM from the **Chapter 7** folder. Click the Start button at the bottom of the screen. You should see four balls bouncing off the sides of the box in random directions and rates. The balls are GIF images (**whiteball.gif**, **redball.gif**, **blueball.gif**, and **greenball.gif**) that need to reside in the same directory as the applet. Figure 7.5 shows an example of the running applet.

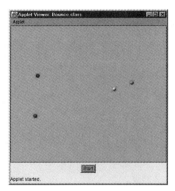

Figure 7.5 Multithreaded applications give the illusion of natural motion.

How It Works

In the spirit of object-oriented programming, a **Ball** class is defined. It contains all the parameters necessary for describing a ball: position (**x**, **y**), velocity (**dx**, **dy**), screen representation (**img**), **compute()** method, **paint()** method, and method to randomize the position and velocity (**random()**).

The **compute()** method increments the x and y positions by **dx** and **dy** each time it is called. If the ball's position exceeds the panel bounds, the corresponding velocity is reversed to give the effect of ideal bouncing.

The **paint()** method draws the ball at its current position into the graphics context given by parameter **g**. The ball's **paint()** method does not know where it is drawing, that is, it may or may not be drawing to the screen.

BouncePanel is a thread that does most of the work. Its **run()** method is called when a thread is started. The **run()** method creates an offscreen image by calling **createImage()** with the screen dimensions as parameters.

This offscreen image has a graphics object associated with it, which can be obtained by calling its **getGraphics()** method. This graphics context is needed to draw into the offscreen image. Drawing into an offscreen graphics object is no different from drawing onscreen; all drawing goes into offscreen memory instead of onscreen. After the offscreen image has been drawn, it can then be displayed on the screen. Figure 7.6 shows an illustration of a screen image and an offscreen image.

The offscreen image is drawn into a buffer without affecting the onscreen image. The offscreen image can then be displayed on the screen. The **run()** method then loops forever. For each iteration, it updates the positions of all the balls by calling their respective **compute()** methods, forces a screen update, and sleeps for 25ms.

When a screen update occurs, the **update()** method is called. The **update()** method erases the offscreen image by filling it with the background color (**lightGray**) using **fillRect()**. It then calls each of the ball's **paint()** methods with the offscreen graphics context as the target context. Finally, the offscreen image is drawn on the screen by using **drawImage()**.

The **Bounce** class does all the initialization and loading of images. It also instructs the balls to randomize themselves when the Start button is clicked.

Figure 7.6
Double-buffering
is used to reduce
flicker.

Comments

This example overrides the **update()** method instead of the **paint()** method. This is done because the default **update()** method fills the panel with the background color first and then calls **paint()**. Because we are drawing over the entire panel from the offscreen image, this is not required. The default **update()** also results in unwanted flicker.

The frame rate for this example is not 25ms, as you might guess from the 25ms sleep time. The frame rate depends somewhat on the performance of the client. Part of this is due to time taken in the **compute()** method of the **BouncePanel**. The time between each redraw is the sum of the sleep time (25ms) and all time that passes before the image is completely drawn. This can be solved, however, by creating another thread whose only function is to provide a strict timing signal, a software interrupt of sorts. The new code might look like this:

```
// Thread to provide a 25ms trigger
class Trigger extends Thread {
    public boolean startFlag= false;

    public void run () {
        while (true) {
            startFlag = true;
            try {
                sleep (25);
            } catch (InterruptedException e) {
                break;
            }
        }
    }
}
```

The **BouncePanel** class should be modified to look like this:

```
Trigger trigger = new Trigger ();

public void run() {
    offsize = size();
    offimg = createImage (offsize.width, offsize.height);
    offg = offimg.getGraphics();
    while (true) {
        if (trigger.startFlag) {
            trigger.startFlag= false;
            for (int i=0; i<nballs; i+=1) {
                balls[i].compute (offsize);
            }
            repaint ();
        }
    }
}
```

The advantage is that the applet will run at the same speed on any platform, assuming that it meets minimum performance requirements. The latter form is more complicated, but must be used if uniform performance is necessary.

You can store a resized image for later use by creating an offscreen image and drawing a scaled image into it. This new image can be used without the performance degradation caused by resizing.

7.5 How do I...
Layer graphics?

Problem

I want to write an image manipulation program. I want to have the ability to select an image with the mouse and either bring it to the front or send it to the back. I learned how to draw images and move them with the mouse in previous examples in this chapter, but now I need to learn how to layer images. How do I layer graphics?

Technique

Images can be drawn on top of each other (as shown in Figure 7.7). The first image drawn appears to be in the back, whereas the last image drawn appears in the front. This gives the illusion of depth.

Figure 7.7 The illusion of depth is created by drawing images in sequence.

Steps

1. Create the applet source file. Create a new file called **LayerApp.java** and enter the following source:

```
import java.awt.*;
import java.awt.event.*;
import java.applet.Applet;
import java.awt.image.*;

/*
```

```
 * class for handling one image
 */
class Picture {

/*
 * position of the image
 */
int xpos, ypos;

/*
 * width and height of the image
 */
int width, height;

/*
 * the image itself
 */
Image image;
ImageObserver obs;

/**
 * constructor saves arguments
 * @param img - the image
 * @param x, y - initial position
 * @param o - imageObserver of parent
 */
public Picture (Image img, int x, int y, ImageObserver o) {

    image = img;
    xpos = x;
    ypos = y;
    obs = o;
    width = image.getWidth (obs);
    height = image.getHeight (obs);
}

/**
 * determine whether the point is inside this image
 * @param x, y - coordinate of point
 */
boolean inside (int x, int y) {

    if (x < xpos || x > (xpos+width)) return false;
    if (y < ypos || y > (ypos+height)) return false;
    return true;
}

/**
 * set the current position of the image
 * @param x, y - position to set
 */
void setPosition (int x, int y) {

    xpos = x;
    ypos = y;
}
```

```
/**
 * draw the image
 * draw a green border around the image if
 * highlight is true
 * @param g - destination graphics object
 * @param highlight - draw border
 */
void paint (Graphics g, boolean highlight) {

    if (highlight) {
        g.setColor (Color.green);
        g.fillRect (xpos-5, ypos-5, width+10, height+10);
    }
    g.drawImage (image, xpos, ypos, obs);
}
}

/*
 * the applet
 */
public class LayerApp extends Applet implements MouseListener,
        MouseMotionListener, ActionListener
{

/*
 * the number of picture objects
 */
final int NPictures = 4;

/*
 * an array containing the picture objects
 */
Picture pictures[] = new Picture[NPictures];

/*
 * the user-selected picture
 */
int selectedPic = -1;

/*
 * offsets from mouse to image origin
 */
int dx, dy;

/*
 * offscreen image for double-buffering
 */
Image offimg;
Button btnBring;
Button btnSend;

/*
 * offscreen graphics context associated with
 * offscreen image
 */
Graphics offg;
```

```
/*
 * dimension of offscreen image
 */
Dimension offsize;

/*
 * called when the applet is loaded
 */
public void init() {

    setLayout(new BorderLayout());

    Panel p = new Panel ();
    add ("South", p);
    btnBring = new Button("Bring to front");
    btnSend = new Button("Send to back");
    p.add(btnBring);
    p.add(btnSend);
    addMouseListener(this);
    addMouseMotionListener(this);
    btnBring.addActionListener(this);
    btnSend.addActionListener(this);

    int i;
    Image img;
    String name;
    MediaTracker tracker = new MediaTracker (this);

    offsize = getSize();
    offimg = createImage (offsize.width, offsize.height);
    offg = offimg.getGraphics();

    for (i=0; i<NPictures; i+=1) {
                if (i < 2) name = "T"+(i+1)+".jpg";
                else name = "T"+(i+1)+".gif";
        img = getImage (getDocumentBase(), name);
        tracker.addImage (img, i);
        showStatus ("Getting image: "+name);
        try {
            tracker.waitForID (i);
        } catch (InterruptedException e) { }
        pictures[i] = new Picture (img, i*10, i*20, this);
    }
}

/**
 * reverse the order of update for efficiency
 * @param g - destination graphics object
 */
public void paint (Graphics g) {

    update (g);
}

/**
 * override update to avoid erase flicker
```

```
 * @param g - destination graphics object
 */
public void update (Graphics g) {

    int i;

    offg.setColor (Color.black);
    offg.fillRect (0, 0, offsize.width, offsize.height);
    for (i=0; i<NPictures; i+=1) {
        if (i == selectedPic) pictures[i].paint (offg, true);
        else pictures[i].paint (offg, false);
    }
    g.drawImage(offimg, 0, 0, this);
}

/**
 * determine which image the user clicked
 * @param evt - event object
 * @param x, y - mouse position
 */
public void mouseClicked(MouseEvent e){}
public void mouseEntered(MouseEvent e){}
public void mouseExited(MouseEvent e){}

public void mouseReleased(MouseEvent e)
{
    repaint ();
}

public void mouseMoved(MouseEvent e){}

public void mousePressed(MouseEvent e)
{
    int x =e.getX();
    int y =e.getY();

    int i;

    selectedPic = -1;
    for (i=NPictures-1; i>=0; i-=1)
    {
        if (pictures[i].inside (x, y))
        {
            selectedPic = i;
            dx = x - pictures[i].xpos;
            dy = y - pictures[i].ypos;
            break;
        }
    }
}

public void mouseDragged(MouseEvent e)
{
    int x =e.getX();
    int y =e.getY();
    int i;
```

```
        if (selectedPic < 0) return;
        /* for (i=NPictures-1; i>=0; i-=1)
        {

            pictures[selectedPic].setPosition (x - dx, y - dy);
            repaint ();
        } */


}
/**
 * reorder the images depending on which button is pressed
 * @param evt - event object
 * @param arg - target object
 */
public void actionPerformed(ActionEvent evt)
{
    Object object1 = evt.getSource();
    int i;
    Picture temp;


    if (object1 == btnBring) {
        if (selectedPic < 0) return;
        temp = pictures[selectedPic];
        for (i=selectedPic; i<NPictures-1; i+=1)
        {
            pictures[i] = pictures[i+1];
        }
        pictures[NPictures-1] = temp;
        selectedPic = NPictures - 1;
        repaint ();
        return;
    }
    if (object1 == btnSend)
    {
        if (selectedPic < 0) return;
        temp = pictures[selectedPic];
        for (i=selectedPic; i>0; i-=1)
        {
            pictures[i] = pictures[i-1];
        }
        pictures[0] = temp;
        selectedPic = 0;
        repaint ();
        return;
    }
}
}
```

2. Create an HTML document that contains the applet. Create a new file called **howto75.html** that contains the following code:

```
<head>
<title>Layer App</title>
</head>
<applet code="LayerApp.class" width=400 height=400>
```

```
</applet>
<hr size=4>
</body>
```

3. Compile and test the applet. Compile the source by using `javac`. Test the applet by using the Appletviewer; enter the following command:

```
appletviewer howto75.html
```

4. When the applet is started, a window opens, with four images displayed. These images are stored on the CD-ROM in the **Chapter 7** folder. Two buttons are labeled Bring to front and Send to back. Each image can be moved with the mouse. You can also send an image to back or bring it to front by selecting the image and then pressing the desired button.

How It Works

The program contains two classes: the **Picture** class and the **LayerApp** class. The **Picture** class contains the information of an image. It contains the position on the screen of the image, its width and height, and the image itself. The **Image** constructor initializes these values and saves them. The **Picture** class contains a method **inside()**. The method **inside()** returns **True** for a given x,y position if it is inside the rectangle containing the image. The **setPosition()** method sets the origin of the image given the position. The **Picture.paint()** method takes two arguments: the **Graphics** context and a Boolean variable **Highlight**. If **Highlight** is **True**, a rectangle slightly larger than the image is drawn first, and then the image itself is drawn.

The **LayerApp** class is the applet itself. It contains an array of pictures and an **int** variable, **selectedPic**, which holds the index of the selected picture. It also contains an offscreen image and an offscreen graphics context maintained to implement double-buffering.

The **init()** method creates a new panel and adds two buttons at the bottom: Bring to front and Send to back. The **init()** method creates the offscreen image and the offscreen graphics context. It then loads the images by using the **getImage()** method and initializes the picture array. **MediaTracker** is used to wait for image loading. The **MediaTracker** class is a utility class that traces the status of media objects, such as images.

The **update()** method is overridden to avoid unnecessary flickering. The **update()** method erases the offscreen image and draws all the pictures into the offscreen image. The offscreen image is then drawn onto the screen.

The **mousePressed()** method determines which picture was selected by using the **Picture.inside()** method. It iterates from the last image drawn and continues to the first. It saves the selected image index in **selectedPic** and returns immediately. The loop runs from the last image to the first because the mouse point may be inside two images. The front image is always selected before the back image.

The `mouseDrag()` method sets the position of the selected image. If no image is selected, `mouseDrag()` returns immediately. After an image has been moved, an update is forced with a call to `repaint()`.

The `mouseReleased()` method forces an `update()`.

The `action()` method handles button clicks. If the Bring to front button is clicked, the array of pictures is shuffled so that the selected picture is at the end of the array. A similar action is performed if the Send to back button is pressed. In this case, the selected image is moved to the beginning of the array. The position of the image in the **images** array determines its position in relation to the others; the array position 0 is the bottom image and the last position is the top.

COMPLEXITY
ADVANCED

7.6 How do I...
Display part of an image?

Problem

I want to write a program to draw images with transition effects, such as barn door open, venetian blind, and checkerboard. This would make advertisements more interesting to the viewer. To do this, I need to draw only parts of an image. How do I draw part of an image?

Technique

The easiest way to draw part of an image is to use clipping (as shown in Figure 7.8). A graphics object can be created with a clipping rectangle specified. This graphics context is created almost identically to the panel's graphics context. The only difference is that all graphics drawn into this context will be clipped. To draw part of an image, the new graphics context must be created with the coordinates and width and height of the section of the image that needs to be drawn.

Figure 7.8
Clipping an image
allows only part
of it to be
displayed.

Steps

1. Create the applet source file. Create a new file called `Advertiser.java` and enter the following source:

```
import java.util.*;
import java.awt.*;
import java.applet.Applet;

/*
 * A class that performs the banner animation
 */
class Banner extends Panel implements Runnable {

/*
 * an instance of the applet for
 * invoking methods from the Advertiser class
 */
Advertiser advertiser;

/*
 * instance of thread used for animation
 */
Thread thread;

/*
 * the next banner image to be displayed
 */
Image theImage;

/*
 * width and height of the new banner image
 */
int img_width, img_height;

/*
 * offscreen image for double-buffering
 */
Image offscreen;

/*
 * offg1 is the graphics object associated with
 * offscreen image. offg2 is the clipped version
 * of offg1
 */
Graphics offg1, offg2;

/*
 * xstart, ystart - x and y coordinate of clipping rectangle
 * width, height - width and height of clipping rectangle
 * effect_type - the effect type applied to the next image
 */
int xstart, ystart, width, height, effect_type;

/**
 * constructor just saves instance of the applet
```

```
 * @param advertiser - instance of advertiser applet
 */
Banner (Advertiser advertiser) {

    this.advertiser = advertiser;
}

/*
 * thread that calls repaint() every 25ms
 * to effect animation
 */
public void run() {

    Dimension d = getSize();
    offscreen = createImage (d.width, d.height);
    offg1 = offscreen.getGraphics ();
    offg1.setFont (getFont ());
    offg1.setColor (Color.gray);
    offg1.fillRect (0, 0, d.width, d.height);
    while (true) {
        repaint ();
        try {
            Thread.sleep (25);
        } catch (InterruptedException e) {
            break;
        }
    }
}

/**
 * override update() method to avoid erase flicker
 * this is where the drawing is done
 * @param g - destination graphics object
 */
public synchronized void update(Graphics g) {

    int i, x, y, w, h;
    switch (effect_type) {
        case 0:
        offg1.drawImage (theImage, 0, 0, null);
        break;

        case 1:          // barn-door open
        if (xstart > 0) {
            xstart -= 5;
            width += 10;
            offg2 = offg1.create (xstart, 0, width, height);
            offg2.drawImage (theImage, -xstart, 0, null);
        } else offg1.drawImage (theImage, 0, 0, null);
        break;

        case 2:          // venetian blind
        if (height < 10) {
            height += 1;
            for (y=0; y<img_height; y+=10) {
                offg2 = offg1.create (0, y, width, height);
```

```
                offg2.drawImage (theImage, 0, -y, null);
            }
        } else offg1.drawImage (theImage, 0, 0, null);
        break;

        case 3:         // checkerboard
        if (width <= 20) {
            if (width <= 10) {
                i = 0;
                for (y=0; y<img_height; y+=10) {
                    for (x=(i&1)*10; x<img_width; x+=20) {
                        offg2 = offg1.create (x, y, width, 10);
                        offg2.drawImage (theImage, -x, -y,➥
null);
                    }
                    i += 1;
                }
            } else {
                i = 1;
                for (y=0; y<img_height; y+=10) {
                    for (x=(i&1)*10; x<img_width; x+=20) {
                        offg2 = offg1.create (x, y,[cc]
width-10, 10);
                        offg2.drawImage (theImage,➥
-x, -y, null);
                    }
                    i += 1;
                }
            }
            width += 5;
        } else offg1.drawImage (theImage, 0, 0, null);
        break;
    }
    g.drawImage (offscreen, 0, 0, null);
}

/**
 * initialize variables for clipping rectangle
 * depending on effect type
 * @param which - the effect type for next image
 * @param img - the next image
 */
public void effect (int which, Image img) {

    img_width = img.getWidth (null);
    img_height = img.getHeight (null);
    theImage = img;
    switch (which) {
        case 0:
        break;

        case 1:         // barn door
        xstart = img_width >> 1;
        width = 0;
        height = img_height;
        break;
```

```
        case 2:
        width = img_width;
        height = 0;
        break;

        case 3:
        width = 0;
        break;
    }
    effect_type = which;
}

/*
 * start the repaint thread
 */
public void start() {

    thread = new Thread(this);
    thread.start();
}

/*
 * stop the repaint thread
 */
public void stop() {

    if (thread != null)
        thread = null;
}
}

/*
 * the Advertiser class proper
 */
public class Advertiser extends Applet implements Runnable {

/*
 * instance of Banner
 */
Banner panel;

/*
 * instance of thread for cycling effects
 * for each new image
 */
Thread thread;

/*
 * the total number of images
 */
int NBanners;

/*
 * the array of images
 */
Image img[] = new Image[10];
```

```
/*
 * the delay (dwell) time in milliseconds for each image
 */
int delay[] = new int[10];

/*
 * the effect type for each image
 */
int effect[] = new int[10];

/*
 * called when applet is loaded
 * add the banner panel, load images, and parse applet
 * parameters
 */
public void init() {

    int i;
    setLayout(new BorderLayout());

    panel = new Banner (this);
    add("Center", panel);
    NBanners = 0;
    MediaTracker tracker = new MediaTracker (this);

    for (i=1; i<=10; i+=1) {
        String param, token;
        int j, next;

        param = getParameter ("T"+i);
        if (param == null) break;

        StringTokenizer st = new StringTokenizer (param, " ,");

        token = st.nextToken ();
        img[NBanners] = getImage (getDocumentBase(), token);
        tracker.addImage (img[NBanners], i);
        showStatus ("Getting image: "+token);
        try {
            tracker.waitForID (i);
        } catch (InterruptedException e) { }

        token = st.nextToken ();
        delay[NBanners] = Integer.parseInt (token);

        token = st.nextToken ();
        effect[NBanners] = Integer.parseInt (token);

        NBanners += 1;
    }
}

/*
 * thread that starts the next image transition
 */
public void run () {
```

```
        int current = 0;

        while (true) {
            panel.effect (effect[current], img[current]);
            try {
                Thread.sleep (delay[current]);
            } catch (InterruptedException e) { }
            current += 1;
            current %= NBanners;
        }
    }

    /*
     * called when applet is started
     * start both threads
     */
    public void start() {

        panel.start();
        thread = new Thread(this);
        thread.start();
    }

    /*
     * called when applet is stopped
     * stops all threads
     */
    public void stop() {

        panel.stop();

        if (panel != null)
            panel = null;

        if (thread != null)
            thread = null;
    }
}
```

2. Create an HTML document that contains the applet. Create a new file called **howto76.html** that contains the following code:

```
<head>
<title>Java Advertiser</title>
</head>
<applet code="Advertiser.class" width=262 height=50>
<param name=T1 value="T1.gif,1000,0">
<param name=T2 value="T2.gif,3000,1">
<param name=T3 value="T3.gif,3000,2">
<param name=T4 value="T4.gif,3000,3">
</applet>
<hr size=4>
</body>
```

3. Compile and test the applet. Compile the source by using **javac**. The applet requires four images to reside in the same directory as the applet class files. Test the applet by using the Appletviewer; enter the following command:

```
APPLETVIEWER howto76.html
```

4. The applet opens, and one image at a time is displayed, for 1,000ms. The transition image can be one of four possibilities: `T1.gif`, `T2.gif`, `T3.gif`, or `T4.gif`. They can be found on the CD-ROM in the `Chapter 7` folder.

How It Works

The Advertiser applet contains two classes, both of which run as independent threads. The first class is `Banner`. `Banner` does the drawing of the images. Its `run()` method creates an offscreen image and a graphic context of `offg1`. It continuously repaints the screen every 25ms.

Clipping is used to display only part of an image: Clipping means displaying a certain area of an image. In Figure 7.9, the large gray rectangle can be thought of as an image. The smaller white rectangle can represent any portion of that image. For example, if you wanted to display only the white rectangle, clipping would be used to display only that area.

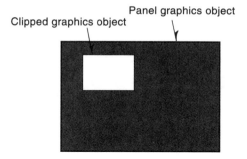

Figure 7.9 Clipping an image.

The `update()` method draws the current image in various ways, depending on the `effect_type`. If no effect is selected, the current image is drawn into the offscreen graphics context. If barn door open is selected, a new graphics context, `Offg2`, is created. The origin of `Offg2` corresponds to the coordinates specified when creating it. This new graphics context is created with a clipping rectangle specified. The clipping rectangle starts in the middle of the image and grows outward with each call.

If the venetian blind effect is selected, offscreen graphics contexts are created repeatedly with different positions and sizes. The positions are fixed, but the sizes grow. This is done in such a way that a venetian blind effect is produced.

The checkerboard effect is created in a similar way. In this case a clipping rectangle is created for each square of the checkerboard. After each iteration of an effect, the offscreen image is drawn on the screen.

The `effect()` method initializes the `effect_type` and the image. Also, the variables `xstart` and `width` are initialized depending on the `effect_type`. The `start()` method creates a thread from `Banner` and starts it. The `stop()` method stops the thread.

The Advertiser applet also runs as a thread. The `Init()` method creates a new panel for `Banner` and adds it to the center. Next, it loads the images into an array, along with information about the transition effect for this image and the time duration. This information is extracted from applet parameters. The applet expects the parameter names to be `T1`, `T2`, ...`T10`. Applet parameters are passed to it from the HTML file that references the application. The value of each parameter contains the name of the image file, the time duration in milliseconds, and `effect_type` as an integer between 0 and 3. More effects such as a barn door close can easily be added.

The `run()` method continuously invokes the `effect()` method with `effect_type` and the current image. It then sleeps for a time, which is determined by the delay array. The `Run()` method cycles through all images forever.

The `start()` method starts the panel and applet's threads. The `stop()` method stops the panel and applet's threads.

Comments

Clipping is a convenient way of drawing parts of an image. In fact, this method can be used to extract individual pixels of an image. This can be very inefficient. There are better ways of extracting pixels of an image; they are discussed in Examples 7.7 and 7.8.

Clipping could also be used to simulate animation, such as the effect of a ball rolling. The traditional method of animating a ball would involve creating several images of a ball that is rolling but not moving. All the images would be loaded into the applet and displayed one at a time. Each image would have to be moved slightly to simulate the motion of the rolling ball. An alternative solution would be to create a larger image that contains images of the ball as it rotates and translates. This larger image could be loaded, and only the appropriate section displayed at a time. The second method is more efficient because it requires only a single file to be loaded into the applet. This saves time opening and closing additional files. It also turns out that the single file is smaller than the sum of all the smaller files. This technique is demonstrated in Example 8.5.

7.7 How do I...
Create images from pixel values?

Problem

I want to write a program to calculate the Mandelbrot set and display it. I know how to calculate the set and create a two-dimensional array of values. To display the set, I need to create an image from these values. How do I create an image from the pixel values?

Technique

Images can be created from pixel values by use of the `createImage()` method in conjunction with `MemoryImageSource` (see Figure 7.10). The pixels are supplied to `MemoryImageSource` as a single-dimensional array of integers. The pixel values contain the red, green, and blue components of the pixel. The dimensions of the image are also given to `MemoryImageSource`. The number of elements in the pixel array is the width times the height of the image to be created.

Figure 7.10
An image can be created mathematically by calculating the value of each pixel.

Steps

1. Create the applet source file. Create a new file called `Mandelbrot.java` and enter the following source:

```
import java.applet.Applet;
import java.awt.*;
import java.awt.event.*;
```

```java
import java.awt.image.*;

/*
 * a class for generating and displaying the
 * Mandelbrot set
 */
public class Mandelbrot extends Applet implements MouseListener,
                        MouseMotionListener, ActionListener
{

/*
 * the maximum number of colors for
 * each pixel
 */
final int MaxColors = 256;

/*
 * the width and height of the image
 */
int mWidth, mHeight;

/*
 * the array of pixel values
 */
int pixels[];

/*
 * the set values
 */
int mandelSet[];

/*
 * the image produce by the set
 */
Image theImage = null;

/*
 * the mapping function from set values to pixel values
 */
int pixMap[] = new int[MaxColors];

/*
 * a flag used for recalculating
 */
boolean startCalculate = false;

/*
 * instance of MandelRect class
 */
MandelRect mandelRect;

/*
 * the control buttons
 */
Button startButton;
Button zoomButton;
```

```
/*
 * called when the applet is loaded
 * initialize the pixmap array and add user interface
 */
public void init () {

    mWidth = 100;
    mHeight = 100;
    pixels = new int [mWidth * mHeight];
    mandelSet = new int [mWidth * mHeight];

    mandelRect = new MandelRect (mWidth, mHeight);

    int red, green, blue;
    int i;

    pixMap[0] = 0xffffffff;
    for (i=1; i<MaxColors-1; i+=1) {
        red = i;
        green = (i<128) ? i << 1 : 255-(i<<1);
        blue = MaxColors-i;
        pixMap[i] = (255 << 24) | (red << 16) |
➥(green << 8) | blue;
    }
    pixMap[MaxColors-1] = 0xff000000;

    setLayout(new BorderLayout());

    startButton = new Button ("Start over");
    zoomButton = new Button ("Zoom in");
    startButton.addActionListener(this);
    zoomButton.addActionListener(this);
    addMouseListener(this);
    addMouseMotionListener(this);

    Panel p = new Panel ();
    p.setLayout (new FlowLayout ());
    p.add (startButton);
    p.add (zoomButton);
    add ("South", p);
}

/*
 * called when the applet is started
 * forces a recalculation of the set
 */
public void start () {

    startCalculate = true;
    repaint ();
}

/*
 * call update for efficiency
 * @param g - destination graphics object
 */
```

```
public void paint (Graphics g) {

    update (g);
}

/**
 * override default update() method to avoid erase flicker
 * @param g - destination graphics object
 */
public void update (Graphics g) {

    if (startCalculate) {
        calculate ();
        startCalculate = false;
    }
    if (theImage != null) g.drawImage (theImage, 0, 0, this);
    else repaint (1000);
    mandelRect.paint (g);
}

/*
 * perform the actual set calculation
 */
void calculate () {

    int i, index;
    double width, height;
    double row, col;
    double zr, zi, cr, ci, tzr, tzi;
    double hFactor, vFactor;
    double x, y;

    theImage = null;

    x = mandelRect.mandelX;
    y = mandelRect.mandelY;
    width = (double) mandelRect.imgWidth;
    height = (double) mandelRect.imgHeight;
    hFactor = mandelRect.mandelWidth/width;
    vFactor = mandelRect.mandelHeight/height;

    index = 0;
    for (row=0; row<height; row+=1) {
        for (col=0; col<width; col+=1) {
            zr = 0;
            zi = 0;
            cr = x + col * hFactor;
            ci = y + row * vFactor;
            for (i=1; i<64; i+=1) {
                tzr = zr*zr - zi*zi + cr;
                tzi = 2*zr*zi + ci;
                zr = tzr;
                zi = tzi;
                if (zr*zr + zi*zi > 4.0) break;
            }
            mandelSet[index++] = (i << 2)-1;
```

```
            }
        }

        for (i=0; i<mWidth*mHeight; i+=1) {
            pixels[i] = pixMap[mandelSet[i]];
        }

        theImage = createImage (
            new MemoryImageSource(mWidth, mHeight, pixels,
    ➥ 0, mWidth));
    }

    public void mouseClicked(MouseEvent e){}
    public void mouseEntered(MouseEvent e){}
    public void mouseExited(MouseEvent e){}

    public void mouseReleased(MouseEvent e)
    {
        int x =e.getX();
        int y =e.getY();

        mandelRect.setWidthHeight (x, y);
        mandelRect.setPaintRect (true);
        repaint ();
    }

    public void mouseMoved(MouseEvent e){}

    public void mousePressed(MouseEvent e)
    {
        int x =e.getX();
        int y =e.getY();

        mandelRect.setXY (x, y);
    }

    public void mouseDragged(MouseEvent e)
    {
        int x =e.getX();
        int y =e.getY();

        mandelRect.setWidthHeight (x, y);
        mandelRect.setPaintRect (true);
        repaint ();

    }
    /**
     * reorder the images, depending on which button is pressed
     * @param evt - event object
     * @param arg - target object
     */
    public void actionPerformed(ActionEvent evt)
    {
        Object object1 = evt.getSource();

        if (object1 == startButton) {
```

```
            mandelRect = new MandelRect (mWidth, mHeight);
            startCalculate = true;
            repaint ();
        }
        if (object1 == zoomButton)
        {
            startCalculate = true;
            mandelRect.setPaintRect (false);
            mandelRect.scaleSet ();
            repaint ();
        }
    }

    /**
     * application entry point
     * create window and new set
     * @param args - command-line arguments
     */
    public static void main (String args[]) {

        Frame f = new Frame ("Mandelbrot set");
        Mandelbrot mandel = new Mandelbrot ();

        mandel.init ();
        f.setSize (210, 275);
        f.add ("Center", mandel);
        f.show ();
        f.addWindowListener(new WindowCloser());

        mandel.start ();
    }
}

class WindowCloser extends WindowAdapter
{
    public void windowClosing(WindowEvent e)
    {
        Window win = e.getWindow();
        win.setVisible(false);
        win.dispose();
        System.exit(0);
    }
}
```

2. Create another file called MandelRect.java that contains the following source:

```
import java.awt.*;

/*
 * a helper class to manage the zoom rectangle
 */
public class MandelRect {

/*
 * the coordinates of the zoom rectangle
```

```
   * in screen space
   */
int x;
int y;
int width;
int height;

/*
 * the final image width and height
 */
int imgWidth;
int imgHeight;

/*
 * the coordinates of the zoom rectangle
 * in set space
 */
double mandelX;
double mandelY;
double mandelWidth;
double mandelHeight;

/*
 * set to true if the zoom rectangle should be painted
 */
boolean paintRect;

/**
 * constructor initializes variables
 * @param iW - final image width
 * @param iH - final image height
 */
public MandelRect (int iW, int iH) {

    imgWidth = iW;
    imgHeight = iH;
    paintRect = false;

    mandelX = -1.75;
    mandelY = -1.125;
    mandelWidth = 2.25;
    mandelHeight = 2.25;
}

/**
 * set the top left of the zoom rectangle in screen space
 * @param ix, iy - top-left corner of zoom rectangle
 */
void setXY (int ix, int iy) {

    x = ix;
    y = iy;
}

/**
 * set the width, height of the zoom rectangle in screen space
```

```
 * @param ix, iy - bottom-right corner of zoom rectangle
 */
void setWidthHeight (int ix, int iy) {

    width = ix - x;
    height = iy - y;
}

/*
 * translate screen coordinates to set coordinates
 */
void scaleSet () {

    int tx, ty, tw, th;

    tx = x;
    ty = y;
    tw = width;
    th = height;
    if (tw < 0) {
        tw = -width;
        tx = x-tw;
    }
    if (th < 0) {
        th = -height;
        ty = y-th;
    }
    mandelX = mandelX + (mandelWidth) * ((double) tx)/
➥((double) imgWidth);
    mandelY = mandelY + (mandelHeight) * ((double) ty)/
➥((double) imgHeight);
    mandelWidth = mandelWidth * ((double) tw)/((double)
➥imgWidth);
    mandelHeight = mandelHeight * ((double) th)/((double)
➥imgHeight);
}

/**
 * set the paintRect flag
 * @param p - true means zoom rectangle should be painted
 */
void setPaintRect (boolean p) {

    paintRect = p;
}

/**
 * paint the zoom rectangle if necessary
 * @param g - destination graphics object
 */
void paint (Graphics g) {

    if (paintRect == false) return;

    int tx, ty, tw, th;
```

```
            tx = x;
            ty = y;
            tw = width;
            th = height;
            if (tw < 0) {
                tw = -width;
                tx = x-tw;
            }
            if (th < 0) {
                th = -height;
                ty = y-th;
            }
            g.setColor (Color.white);
            g.drawRect (tx, ty, tw, th);
    }
}
```

3. Create an HTML document that contains the applet. Create a new file called howto77.html that contains the following code:

```
<html>
<head>
<title>Mandelbrot Set</title>
</head>
<applet code="Mandelbrot.class" width=200 height=200>
</applet>
<hr size=4>

</html>
```

4. Compile and test the applet. Compile the source by using javac. Test the applet by using the Appletviewer; enter the following command:

```
APPLETVIEWER howto77.html
```

How It Works

The Mandelbrot applet contains only one class: Mandelbrot. The init() method creates an array of pixels specified by the width and height. The top, left, bottom, and right are the coordinates in the space of the Mandelbrot set. A pixmap array is created to map values in the set to pixel values. The mapping of set values to pixel values is a subject for study in itself. For purposes of simplicity, an arbitrary algorithm was chosen for assigning pixel values. A button is added at the bottom of the panel; it is used to reset the set coordinates to their original values.

The start() method calculates a new set by invoking the calculate() method. It then draws the set by forcing an update. The update() method draws the image if it exists. If the image does not exist, for example, the calculation is not complete, the image is not drawn, and a repaint() is forced one second later.

The `calculate()` method performs the set calculation based on standard algorithms. Before the calculation is started, the image is set to `null`. This keeps the previous image from being displayed. The inner loop of the iteration is only performed for the number of colors available in `pixmap`. This does not yield a very interesting image, but it is straightforward. After the pixel array is created, the image is created by calling `create image` with `MemoryImageSource()` as an argument. `MemoryImageSource()` takes the width and height of the image, along with the pixel array starting point and format as arguments.

The `mousePressed()` event calculates the top and left coordinates of the new set based on the mouse position. The `mouseReleased()` method calculates the right and the bottom coordinates of the set. Next, it calculates the new set based on the new set coordinates. It then repaints the image.

The `actionPerformed()` method handles button clicks. If the user presses the Start over button, the set coordinates are reset to the original values, and `set` is recalculated and displayed. A `main()` method is also included that creates a frame and an instance of the applet in the event that the program is executed as a standalone application.

Comments

This example is an excellent demonstration of performance. Clearly, Java does not perform as well as an equivalent compiled C or C++ program. The performance is not a limitation of the Java language or the Abstract Windowing Toolkit (AWT); it is due to the implementation of the Java interpreter. Note that `memoryimagesource` is contained in `Java.awt.image`; therefore, `Java.awt.image.*` is imported.

COMPLEXITY
ADVANCED

7.8 How do I...
Access pixels in an image?

Problem

I want to write an applet that simulates life (see Figure 7.11). The simulation shows how an organism might grow under laboratory conditions. Its appearance at any moment depends on what it looked like earlier. I have the algorithm for advancing the generations and plotting the cells. I want to enter the starting conditions as a GIF image. I know how to load images, but I need to extract the pixels in the image. How do I access pixels in an image?

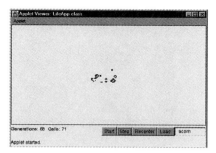

Figure 7.11 Mathematic models can give the illusion of life.

Technique

Pixels can be extracted from an image via the **PixelGrabber** class. **PixelGrabber** delivers some or all of the pixels in an image, given the image, the rectangle containing the pixels to deliver, an integer array to hold the pixel values, offset into the array, and the distance from one row of pixels to the next in the array.

Each pixel in the **integer** array is described by a 24-bit RGB value. The pixels are delivered by the **PixelGrabber.grabPixels()** method. This method throws **InterruptedException**, which must be caught.

Steps

1. Create the source file. Create a file called **LifeApp.java** and enter the following source:

```
import java.util.*;
import java.awt.*;
import java.awt.event.*;
import java.awt.image.ImageObserver;
import java.awt.image.PixelGrabber;

/*
 * class that manages a generation
 */
class LifeGenerator {

/*
 * array containing packed cells
 * n - number of elements in the CellList array
 */
int CellList[], n;
int a[];
int b[];
```

```
int c[];

/*
 * the current generation number
 */
int generations;

/*
 * background and foreground colors
 */
Color background;
Color foreground;

int statusheight;
int displaywidth;
int displayheight;

int originx;
int originy;

int maxcells;

static int countmsk=0x1f;
static int posmsk=0x7fffffe0;
static int maxval=0x7fffffff;

String statusLine;
String loading;

int scroll;

/*
 * the rules of life
 */
static boolean rules[]={
    false, false,
    false, false,
    false, true,
    true,  true,
    false, false,
    false, false,
    false, false,
    false, false,
    false, false
};

/*
 * constructor initializes variables
 */
public LifeGenerator() {

    n=0;
    generations=0;
    maxcells=0;
    background=Color.white;
    foreground=Color.black;
```

```java
        originx=0;
        originy=0;

        loading=null;
        scroll=10;

        statusLine=new String("");
    }

    public void loading(String init_loading) {

        loading=init_loading;
    }

    public void setScroll(int init_scroll) {

        scroll=init_scroll;
    }

    public void setColors(Color init_background,
    ➥Color init_foreground) {

        background=init_background;
        foreground=init_foreground;
    }

    public void setDisplaySize(int width, int height) {

        statusheight=35;

        displaywidth=width;
        displayheight=height-statusheight;
    }

    /**
     * translate the origin
     * @param dx, dy - offsets to translate
     */
    public void translate(int dx, int dy) {

        originx+=dx;
        originy+=dy;
    }

    public void recenter(int x, int y) {

        translate(displaywidth/2-x, displayheight/2-y);
    }

    public void approachcenter(int x, int y) {

        translate((displaywidth/2-x)/scroll,
            (displayheight/2-y)/scroll);
    }

    public void findPattern() {
```

```
        if (n>0) {
            int packed=CellList[n/2];
            int plotx=(((packed>>5)&0x1fff)-(1<<12))*2+originx;
            int ploty=((packed>>18)-(1<<12))*2+originy;
            recenter(plotx, ploty);
        }
    }

    /**
     * print status message
     * @param g - destination graphics object
     */
    public void updateStatusLine(Graphics g) {

        g.setColor(background);
        g.drawString(statusLine,0,displayheight+15);

        if (loading!=null) {
            statusLine="Loading: " + loading;
        } else {
            statusLine="Generations: " + generations +
  ➥ "  Cells: " + n;
        }
        g.setColor(foreground);
        g.drawString(statusLine,0,displayheight+15);
    }

    void resizeIfNeeded(int cellcount) {

        int tmp[];
        int i;

        if (cellcount>maxcells) {

            int newsize=2*cellcount;

            tmp=new int[newsize];
            for (i=0; i<maxcells; i++) tmp[i]=CellList[i];
            CellList=tmp;

            tmp=new int[newsize];
            for (i=0; i<maxcells; i++) tmp[i]=a[i];
            a=tmp;

            tmp=new int[newsize];
            for (i=0; i<maxcells; i++) tmp[i]=b[i];
            b=tmp;

            tmp=new int[newsize];
            for (i=0; i<maxcells; i++) tmp[i]=c[i];
            c=tmp;

            maxcells=newsize;
        }
    }
```

```
static int combineLists(int a[], int na, int b[], int nb,
➥int c[]) {

    int i,j,nc;
    i=0; j=0; nc=0;
    a[na]=maxval;
    b[nb]=maxval;
    while (i<na || j<nb) {
        if ((a[i]^b[j])<=countmsk) {
            c[nc++]=(a[i++]&countmsk)+b[j++];
        } else if (a[i]<b[j]) {
            c[nc++]=a[i++];
        } else {
            c[nc++]=b[j++];
        }
    }
    return nc;
}

static void extractCenterCells(int list[], int n, int
➥counts[]) {

    int i=0, j=0;

    while (i<n) {
        if ((list[i]^counts[j])<=countmsk) {
            counts[j]—;
            i++;
            j++;
        } else j++;
    }
}

static int Cell(int x, int y, int value) {

    return ((y+(1<<12))<<18) +((x+(1<<12))<<5) + value;
}

/**
 * plot an individual cell
 * @param packed - a set of packed cells
 * @param g - destination graphics object
 */
void plotCell(int packed, Graphics g) {

    int plotx=(((packed>>5)&0x1fff)-(1<<12))*2+originx;
    int ploty=((packed>>18)-(1<<12))*2+originy;

    if (plotx > 3 && plotx < displaywidth-5 &&
        ploty > 3 && ploty < displayheight-5 ) {
        g.fillRect(plotx, ploty, 2, 2);
    }
}

/**
 * paint the current generation
```

```
   * @param g - destination graphics object
   */
  public void paintAll(Graphics g) {

      g.clearRect(0,0,displaywidth, displayheight+statusheight);
      g.drawRect(0,0,displaywidth-1, displayheight-1);

      g.setColor(foreground);
      for (int i=0; i<n; i++) {
          plotCell(CellList[i],g);
      }
      updateStatusLine(g);
  }

  int nextGen(int counts[], int ncounts, int list[], Graphics g) {

      int nlist=0;
      for (int i=0; i<ncounts; i++) {
          int count=counts[i]&countmsk;
          if (rules[count]) {
              list[nlist++]=(counts[i]&posmsk)+2;
              if ((count&1)==0) {
                  g.setColor(foreground);
                  plotCell(counts[i],g);
              }
          } else {
              if ((count&1)==1) {
                  g.setColor(background);
                  plotCell(counts[i],g);
              }
          }
      }
      return nlist;
  }

  public void generate(Graphics g) {

      int na, nb, nc;

      for (na=0; na<n; na++) a[na]=CellList[na]-(1<<18);
      resizeIfNeeded(n+na);
      nb=combineLists(CellList,n,a,na,b);

      for (na=0; na<n; na++) a[na]=CellList[na]+(1<<18);
      resizeIfNeeded(na+nb);
      nc=combineLists(a,na,b,nb,c);

      for (na=0; na<nc; na++) a[na]=c[na]-(1<<5);
      resizeIfNeeded(na+nc);
      nb=combineLists(a,na,c,nc,b);

      for (na=0; na<nc; na++) a[na]=c[na]+(1<<5);
      resizeIfNeeded(na+nb);
      nc=combineLists(a,na,b,nb,c);

      extractCenterCells(CellList, n, c);
```

```
    n=nextGen(c, nc, CellList, g);

    generations++;
}

/**
 * load a new initial image
 * @param img - the image to load
 * @param imgobs - the image observer
 */
public boolean loadLifePattern(Image img, ImageObserver
➥imgobs) {

    int w=img.getWidth(imgobs);
    int h=img.getHeight(imgobs);

    if (w<0 ¦¦ h<0) return false;

    originx= (displaywidth-w*2)/2;
    originy= (displayheight-h*2)/2;

    int[] pixels = new int[w * h];

    PixelGrabber pg = new PixelGrabber(img, 0, 0, w, h,
➥pixels, 0, w);

    try {
        pg.grabPixels();
    } catch (InterruptedException e) {
        return false;
    }

    int i,j;

    int pix0= pixels[0];
    int pix1= -1;
    int count1= 0;

    for (i=0; i<h; i++) {
        for (j=0; j<w; j++) {
            if (pixels[i*w+j]!=pix0) {
                pix1= pixels[i*w+j];
                count1++;
            }
        }
    }

    /* figure out which pixel color denotes a live cell */

    if (pix0==0xffffff) {}
    else if (pix1==0xffffff ¦¦ count1 > w*h-count1) {
        pix1=pix0;
        count1=w*h-count1;
    }

    resizeIfNeeded(count1);
```

```
        n=0;
        for (i=0; i<h; i++) {
            for (j=0; j<w; j++) {
                if (pixels[i*w+j]==pix1) {
                    CellList[n++]=Cell(j,i,2);
                }
            }
        }

        return true;
    }
}

/*
 * the applet class
 */
public class LifeApp extends java.applet.Applet
➥implements MouseListener,
                    ActionListener, Runnable {

LifeGenerator LifeList;

/*
 * the thread controlling generations
 */
Thread killme=null;
int speed=50;
boolean neverPainted=true;
int count=0;

/*
 * the image name text field
 */
TextField patfield;
Button pausebutton;
Button stepbutton;
Button recenterbutton;
Button loadbutton;
boolean generating=false;
int stepsleft=0;
int scrollfraction=5;

/*
 * called when applet is loaded
 * create user interface and parse applet parameters
 */
public void init() {

    setLayout(new FlowLayout(FlowLayout.RIGHT, 0,
➥getSize().height-30));
    add(pausebutton=new Button("Start"));
    add(stepbutton = new Button("Step"));
    add(recenterbutton = new Button("Recenter"));
    add(loadbutton = new Button("Load:"));

    pausebutton.addActionListener(this);
```

```java
        stepbutton.addActionListener(this);
        recenterbutton.addActionListener(this);
        loadbutton.addActionListener(this);

        addMouseListener(this);

        String patname=getParameter("pattern");
        if (patname==null) patname="gun30";

        if (getParameter("started")!=null) {
            pausebutton.setLabel("Stop");
            generating=true;
        }

        String pstring;

        if ((pstring=getParameter("speed"))!=null) {
            speed=Integer.valueOf(pstring).intValue();
        }

        if ((pstring=getParameter("scrollfraction"))!=null) {
            scrollfraction=Integer.valueOf(pstring).intValue();
        }

        add(patfield=new TextField(patname,8));

        LifeList=null;
    }

/*
 * called when applet is started
 * start the life thread
 */
public void start() {

    if (killme==null) {
        killme=new Thread(this);
        killme.start();
    }
}

/*
 * called when the applet is stopped
 * stop the life thread
 */
public void stop() {

    killme=null;
}


//*********************************************************
public void mouseClicked(MouseEvent e){}
public void mouseEntered(MouseEvent e){}
public void mouseExited(MouseEvent e){}
```

```
public void mouseReleased(MouseEvent e)
{
}

public void mousePressed(MouseEvent e)
{
    int x =e.getX();
    int y =e.getY();

    LifeList.approachcenter(x,y);
    LifeList.paintAll(getGraphics());
}

/**
 * reorder the images, depending on which button is clicked
 * @param evt - event object
 * @param arg - target object
 */
public void actionPerformed(ActionEvent evt)
{
    boolean acted=true;
    boolean damage=true;

    Object object1 = evt.getSource();

    if (object1 == pausebutton)
    {
        String label= pausebutton.getLabel();
        if (label == "Stop")
        {
            pausebutton.setLabel("Start");
            generating=false;
        } else if (label == "Start")
        {
            pausebutton.setLabel("Stop");
            generating=true;
        }
    }

    if (object1 == stepbutton)
    {
        stepsleft=1;
        if (generating)
        {
            pausebutton.setLabel("Start");
            generating=false;
        }
    }
    if (object1 == recenterbutton)
    {
        LifeList.findPattern();
    }
    if (object1 == loadbutton)
    {
        stop();
        LifeList=null;
```

```
        start();
    }
    if (acted && damage) LifeList.paintAll(getGraphics());

}


//*************************************************************


/**
 * add .gif to the filename
 * @param patname - base filename
 */
static String makeGifName(String patname) {

    int i=patname.indexOf(".");
    String base=(i<0)?patname:patname.substring(0,i);
    return base.concat(".gif");
}

/**
 * load new image file
 * @parame patname - name of image file
 */
void loadNew(String patname) {

    Image img=getImage(getCodeBase(), makeGifName(patname));
    LifeList.loading(patname);
    LifeList.paintAll(getGraphics());

    while(killme!=null && !LifeList.loadLifePattern(img,
➥this)) {
        try {
            Thread.sleep(200);
        } catch (InterruptedException e) {}
    }

    LifeList.loading(null);
    LifeList.paintAll(getGraphics());
}

/*
 * life thread
 * causes new generations to be created
 */
public void run() {

    Graphics g=getGraphics();

    if (LifeList==null) {
        LifeList = new LifeGenerator();
        LifeList.setColors(getBackground(), Color.black);
        LifeList.setScroll(scrollfraction);
        LifeList.setDisplaySize(getSize().width,
➥getSize().height);
```

```
        loadNew(patfield.getText());
    }

    while (killme != null) {
        try {
            Thread.sleep(speed);
        } catch (InterruptedException e) {}
        repaint();
    }
    killme=null;
}

/**
 * paint the current generation
 * @param g - destination graphics object
 */
public void paint(Graphics g) {

    LifeList.paintAll(g);
}

/**
 * override update to avoid erase flicker
 * @param g - destination graphics object
 */
public void update(Graphics g) {

    if (generating || stepsleft- > 0) {
        LifeList.generate(g);
        LifeList.updateStatusLine(g);
    }
}
}
```

2. Create an HTML file that contains the applet. Create a file called
howto78.html that contains the following code:

```
<html>
<head>
<title>Life</title>
</head>
<applet code="LifeApp.class" width=500 height=300>
<param name=pattern value=acorn>
</applet>
<hr size=4>

</html>
```

3. Compile and test the applet. Compile the applet and test it using the
Appletviewer. Several test images are provided on the CD-ROM.

How It Works

LifeApp contains two classes: LifeGenerator and LifeApp. LifeGenerator implements Conway's life algorithm, extracts the image pixels, advances generations, and draws the new generations. LifeApp is the applet itself. LifeApp manages LifeGenerator by loading a starting image, causes LifeGenerator to advance one generation, and handles user events.

The cells are contained by an integer array CellList in the LifeGenerator class. The cells are represented by packed bits for efficiency. Generations are advanced by calling the generate() method, which plots new cells using rules specified by Conway. The method loadLifePattern() takes an image and extracts the pixel by using PixelGrabber. All the pixels are extracted into the array pixels.

The LifeApp() method is the applet itself. It implements Runnable in order to create a separate thread for invoking generations. The init() method creates the buttons and text fields for the user interface and adds them to the applet panel. The start() and stop() methods start and stop the thread, respectively. The action method handles user events.

The loadNew() method loads a new GIF image by calling the Applet.getImage() method. It then loads the image into LifeGenerator.

The run() method first creates an instance of LifeGenerator and enters an infinite loop that forces LifeGenerator to advance and display new generations.

CHAPTER 8
JFC

8

JFC

How do I...

The Java Foundation Classes (JFC), sometimes called by their nickname, Swing, represent an evolutionary step forward for the graphical user interface (GUI) building tools. When Java 1.02 was released in 1995, it included the Abstract Windowing Toolkit (AWT) as its windowing system. The AWT was a rudimentary library for building applications and applets. Although somewhat limited in scope, the AWT provides two important qualities. First, it was portable. Java code that ran on UNIX ran on Windows, Macintosh, and all other supported platforms without code changes. Second, the AWT preserves the look and feel of each operating system's native GUI, again without code changes.

The AWT works by creating a "peer" window in the native GUI for each window in the application. This straightforward "wrapping" approach was good for getting a first release of Java into production, but it suffered from several drawbacks. First, all GUI subsystems are not identical. Even though Windows, Macintosh, and Motif all have windows, buttons, list boxes, check boxes, and so on, their underlying architectures are identical, or even very similar. In reality, differences in the event model and in the management of states begged for a new approach. That new approach is called the JFC.

The JFC design is completely different from that of the AWT. In the JFC, the goal was to create the controls in Java to the maximum practical extent and not rely on high level native windowing routines to create the objects. This approach makes JFC less idiosyncratic than the AWT and produces fewer platform-related differences in behavior than did the AWT. The JFC has not caused the deprecation of the AWT, but it is the direction of all future GUI development from JavaSoft.

The JFC contains a powerful delegation event model, printing, a clipboard, and JavaBeans compliance, all in a lightweight framework. The term *lightweight* here means that these controls were created entirely using the graphics capabilities of Java instead of relying on the host machine's windowing system to draw the controls on the screen. In fact, you could implement controls entirely in Java without using the JFC if you chose. Although the introduction of the JFC did not deprecate the AWT, is not recommended that programmers mix AWT and JFC controls in the same program.

The JFC contains many more controls and layout managers that we have space to demonstrate in this chapter. Table 8.1 lists some of these controls.

Table 8.1 JFC Controls and Layout Managers

COMPONENT	PURPOSE
Box	A lightweight container that uses a BoxLayout object as its layout manager.
BoxLayout	A layout manager that allows multiple components to be laid out either vertically or horizontally.
ButtonGroup	A class used to create a multiple-exclusion scope for a set of buttons.
JButton	An implementation of a pushbutton.
JcheckBox	An implementation of a check box—an item that can be selected or deselected, and that displays its state to the user.
JcheckBoxMenuItem	A menu item that can be selected or deselected.
JcolorChooser	A pane of controls designed to allow a user to manipulate and select a color.

COMPONENT	PURPOSE
JcomboBox	The JFC's implementation of a combo box—a combination of a text field and drop-down list that lets the user either type a value or select it from a list that is displayed when the user asks for it.
JdesktopPane	A container used to create a multiple-document interface or a virtual desktop.
JeditorPane	A text pane to edit various kinds of content, such as HTML and RTF.
JfileChooser	A simple mechanism for the user to choose a file.
Jframe	An extended version of `java.awt`.
Jlabel	A display area for a short text string, an image, or both.
JlayeredPane	A pane that adds depth to a JFC container, allowing components to overlap each other when needed.
JList	A component that allows the user to select one or more objects from a list.
JMenu	An implementation of a menu, which is a pop-up window containing menu items that is displayed when the user selects an item on the menu bar.
JMenuBar	An implementation of a menu bar.
JMenuItem	An implementation of a menu item.
JOptionPane	An option that makes it easy to pop up a standard dialog box to prompt users for a value or inform them of something.
JPanel	A generic lightweight container.
JPasswordField	A lightweight component that allows you to edit a single line of text where the view indicates that something was typed but does not show the original characters.
JPopupMenu	An implementation of a pop-up menu, which is a small window that pops up and displays a series of choices.
JPopupMenu.Separator	A separator in a pop-up menu.
JProgressBar	A component that displays an integer value within a bounded interval.
JRadioButton	An implementation of a radio button, which is an item that can be selected or deselected and that displays its state to the user.
JRadioButtonMenuItem	An implementation of a radio button menu item.
ScrollBar	An implementation of a scrollbar.
JScrollPane	A specialized container that manages a viewport, optional vertical and horizontal scrollbars, and optional row and column heading viewports.

continued on next page

continued from previous page

COMPONENT	PURPOSE
JSeparator	An implementation of a menu separator, which is a divider between menu items that breaks them up into logical groupings.
JSlider	A component that lets the user graphically select a value by sliding a knob within a bounded interval.
JSplitPane	A component that is used to divide two (and only two) components.
JTabbedPane	A component that lets the user switch between a group of components by clicking on a tab with a given title and/or icon.
JTable	A user-interface component that presents data in a two-dimensional table format.
JTextArea	A multiline area that displays plain text.
JTextField	lightweight component that allows the editing of a single line of text.
JTextPane	A text component that can be marked up with attributes that are represented graphically.
JToggleButton	An implementation of a two-state button.
JToolBar	A component that displays commonly used actions or controls.
JToolBar.Separator	A toolbar-specific separator.
JToolTip	A class that is used to display a tip for a component.
JTree	A control that displays a set of hierarchical data as an outline.
JViewport	The viewport, or porthole, through which you see the underlying information.
JWindow	A container that can be displayed anywhere on the user's desktop.
OverlayLayout	A layout manager to arrange components over the top of each other.
ScrollPaneLayout	The layout manager used by JScrollPane.
Timer	An object subclass that causes an action to occur at a predefined rate.
ViewportLayout	The default layout manager for JViewport.

8.1 Program with the JFC

This example shows how to create a program with the Java Foundation Classes. It provides a short example to introduce you to the underlying principles of getting JFC programs to work.

8.2 Create a BorderLayout Program

This example shows how to create a program that uses BorderLayout to manage the placement of controls on the application. BorderLayout allows the programmer to locate controls in any one of five locations: North, South, East, West, or Center.

8.3 Create a FlowLayout Program

This example shows how to create a program that uses FlowLayout to manage the placement of controls on the application. FlowLayout places controls on the application from left to right and then wraps to the next line when it can no longer add more controls on the present line.

8.4 Create a Program with No Layout

This example shows how to place controls on an application manually by specifying exactly where they should go.

8.5 Add ToolTips to Applications

This example shows how to add ToolTips to an application. In addition, it provides an example of how to handle mouse events.

8.6 Create Buttons with Icons on Them

This example shows how to create buttons that contain images instead of just text.

8.7 Create RadioButton Controls

This example shows how to add RadioButton controls to your JFC application. In addition, it shows you how to react to the checking of the box from within your code.

8.8 Create ListBox Controls

This example shows how to populate a list box. In addition, it shows you how to find out which choices the user has made from within your code.

8.9 Add a Menu to My Application

This example shows how to add a menu to your application. It also shows how to trap the event generated by the menu.

COMPLEXITY
BEGINNING

8.1 How do I...
Program with the JFC?

Problem

I have heard a lot and about the JFC. Can you show me how to perform a simple task in the JFC so that I can get a feel for it?

Technique

The JFC provides a lighter, more consistent approach to building GUI applications and applets using Java. By *lighter*, we mean that the applications and applets consume fewer of the native GUI's resources. In this example, we build a simple application that contains a single button. This will help you get a feel for the JFC before we head into more complex applications.

Steps

1. Create the applet source file. Create a new file called OneButton_Applet.java and enter the following source:

```
import javax.swing.*;
import java.awt.event.*;

import java.awt.*;

public class OneButton_Applet extends JApplet
{
    public void init()
    {
        JButton button1 = new JButton("Push Me");

        setBackground(Color.lightGray);
        getContentPane().add(button1,"Center");
    }//init()


}//OneButton_Applet
```

2. Compile and test the applet. Compile the source by using **javac**.

3. Create a file called **Howto81.html** that contains the following code:

```
<head>
<title>One Button only</title>
</head>
<applet code="OneButton_Applet.class" width=262 height=50>
</applet>
<hr size=4>
</body>
```

4. Run the applet by using the appletviewer; enter the following:

```
appletviewer Howto81.html
```

Figure 8.1 shows a snapshot of the running application.

Figure 8.1
Functioning JFC
programs can be
written with very
little code.

How It Works

The first thing you will notice about this program is that the import statement
is a little different from what you may be used to:

```
import javax.swing.*;
```

In Java Version 1.1, the JFC was not a part of the core Application
Programming Interface (API) for the Java language. It was a special-purpose API
that could be downloaded and used if necessary. As a result, the naming
convention `java.xxx.*` was not used.

The very first line of the class definition that follows shows a difference from
what we've seen so far in this book. The applet extends (or inherits from)
`JApplet`, not `Applet`, as we have become accustomed to seeing. Class names
that begin with a `J` are JFC classes. They often contain a superset of the functionality of their AWT predecessors. In other words, they perform the same
functions, but add functionality in some cases.

```
public class OneButton_Applet extends JApplet
{
```

We see that the familiar `init()` method is supported:

```
public void init()
```

The button that we declare is of class `Jbutton`, instead of `Button`. As you
can see, it takes the same format constructor as the `Button` class:

```
JButton button1 = new JButton("Push Me");
```

After setting the background color, we come to a different-looking way of
adding controls to the applet. You make a call to `getContentPane()` to obtain a
reference to the applet's primary pane. This pane is the container for all the
controls in this application. The content pane is contained by an instance of the
`JRootpane` class, which is the base class for the container hierarchy, much as
`JContainer` is for components:

```
setBackground(Color.lightGray);
getContentPane().add(button1,"Center");
```

Upon program initialization, the Java Virtual Machine (JVM) draws the
window on the screen and places the `Jbutton` control on the pane.

8.2 How do I...
Create a BorderLayout program?

Problem

I want to create a program that the user can resize. When this resizing takes place, I want to automatically rearrange the controls on the form to avoid having the application look messy. Do I have to write a series of calculations based on the height and width of the application at any moment, or is there a better way?

Technique

There is a better way. In fact, there are about a dozen different ways to accomplish that exact goal, depending on what you want the resulting window to look like. You achieve the desired effects by declaring a specific layout manager in your application. This layout manager follows a strict set of rules on how to lay out the controls. In this example, we will use **BorderLayout**, which contains five panels that can hold controls:

- North—Occupies the topmost portion of the container.

- South—Occupies the bottommost portion of the container.

- East—Occupies the rightmost portion of the container.

- West—Occupies the leftmost portion of the container.

- Center—Occupies the center portion of the container.

This layout is analogous to that of a map. On the right is East, on the top is North, and so on.

Steps

1. Create the application source file. Create a new file called BorderLayout1.java and enter the following source:

```
import javax.swing.*;
import java.awt.*;
import java.awt.event.*;

public class BorderLayout1 extends JPanel
{

//The constructor initializes the application
```

```java
    public BorderLayout1()
    {
        JButton btnNorth;
        JButton btnSouth;
        JButton btnEast;
        JButton btnWest;
        JButton btnCenter;

        Font font1;

        font1 = new Font("Times-Roman",Font.BOLD,18);

        this.setLayout(new BorderLayout());

        btnNorth = new JButton("North");
        btnNorth.setFont(font1);
        add(btnNorth, "North");

        btnSouth = new JButton("South");
        btnSouth.setFont(font1);
        add(btnSouth, "South");

        btnEast = new JButton("East");
        btnEast.setFont(font1);
        add(btnEast, "East");

        btnWest = new JButton("West");
        btnWest.setFont(font1);
        add( btnWest, "West");

        btnCenter = new JButton("Center");
        btnCenter.setFont(font1);
        add(btnCenter, "Center");

    }//constructor

//main entry point for the application
public static void main(String s[])
    {
        JFrame f = new JFrame("Border Layout");
        BorderLayout1 panel = new BorderLayout1();

        f.setForeground(Color.black);
        f.setBackground(Color.lightGray);
        f.getContentPane().add(panel,"Center");

        f.setSize(400, 150);
        f.setVisible(true);
        f.addWindowListener(new WindowCloser());

    }//main
}//class


//This class handles the closing of the application
class WindowCloser extends WindowAdapter
```

```
    {
        public void windowClosing(WindowEvent e)
        {
            Window win = e.getWindow();
            win.setVisible(false);
            win.dispose();
            System.exit(0);
        }//windowClosing
    }//class WindowCloser
```

2. Compile and test the application. Compile the source by using `javac`.
Figure 8.2 shows a snapshot of the running application.

Figure 8.2 An application
that uses BorderLayout.

How It Works

The package that provides the JFC capabilities is:

```
import javax.swing.*;
```

The application inherits from **JPanel**, which is the JFC version of the AWT
Panel class. It provides a base to host the controls:

```
public class BorderLayout1 extends JPanel
```

The five buttons are declared and named after their locations in the layout
manager:

```
JButton btnNorth;
JButton btnSouth;
JButton btnEast;
JButton btnWest;
JButton btnCenter;

Font font1;
```

A font object is created to control the look of the text on the buttons:

```
font1 = new Font("Times-Roman",Font.BOLD,18);
```

The `setLayout()` method is executed with **BorderLayout()** as its parameter.
This identifies **BorderLayout** as the layout manager for this panel:

```
this.setLayout(new BorderLayout());
```

We place the buttons on the form using the **add** method. By placing the
literal `"North"` as the second parameter, we are telling the layout manager that
we want this button to be located at the top of the window's client area. We
proceed in a similar fashion for each of the buttons:

```
add(btnNorth, "North");

    .
    .
    .
add(btnSouth, "South");

    .
    .
    .
add(btnEast, "East");

    .
    .
    .
add( btnWest, "West");

    .
    .
    .
add(btnCenter, "Center");

    .
    .
    .
```

In the main application, we define an instance of the **BorderLayout1** class:

```
BorderLayout1 panel = new BorderLayout1();
```

BorderLayout is the default layout manager for the primary container. It is declared explicitly for purposes of clarity. Note also that containers can be added to other containers, and each container can have its own layout manager (the same as that of its parent or a different one).

We use the standard Swing **getContentPane()** method call to obtain a reference to the primary container. Next, we add the panel to the center of this container:

```
f.getContentPane().add(panel,"Center");
```

The application is now ready to be run.

COMPLEXITY
INTERMEDIATE

8.3 How do I...
Create a FlowLayout program?

Problem

I want to use a layout manager, but I don't need one as complex as **BorderLayout**. Isn't there one that just puts the controls on the window from left to right?

Technique

You're in luck. The JFC has just the layout manager for you: the **FlowLayout**
manager. This manager gives you a minimum amount of control but still frees
you of the requirement that you program your own layout.

Steps

1. Create the application source file. Create a new file called
FlowLayout1.java and enter the following source:

```
import javax.swing.*;
import java.awt.*;
import java.awt.event.*;


public class FlowLayout1 extends JPanel
{
    public FlowLayout1()
    {
        JButton btnOne;
        JButton btnTwo;
        JButton btnThree;
        JButton btnFour;

        this.setLayout(new FlowLayout(FlowLayout.LEFT));

        btnOne = new JButton("One");
        add(btnOne);

        btnTwo = new JButton("Two");
        add(btnTwo);

        btnThree = new JButton("Three");
        add(btnThree);

        btnFour = new JButton("Four");
        add(btnFour);

    }//constructor


    public static void main(String s[])
    {
        JFrame f = new JFrame("Flow Layout");
        FlowLayout1 panel = new FlowLayout1();

        f.setForeground(Color.black);
        f.setBackground(Color.lightGray);
        f.getContentPane().add(panel, "Center");

        f.setSize(400,100);
        f.setVisible(true);
        f.addWindowListener(new WindowCloser());
```

```
        }//main
}//class


class WindowCloser extends WindowAdapter
{
    public void windowClosing(WindowEvent e)
    {
        Window win = e.getWindow();
        win.setVisible(false);
        win.dispose();
        System.exit(0);
    }//windowClosing
}//class WindowCloser
```

2. Compile and test the application. Compile the source by using `javac`. Figure 8.3 shows a snapshot of the running application.

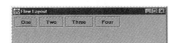

Figure 8.3 The `FlowLayout` manager can right-justify, left-justify, or center the controls on the window.

How It Works

This example is similar to the **BorderLayout** example. The packages are the same and the buttons are declared in much the same way. The first real difference comes in the **setLayout()** method. Not only is **FlowLayout** specified as a parameter; a special value, **FlowLayout.LEFT**, is passed into the constructor. This indicates that you want to left justify the controls in the window:

```
this.setLayout(new FlowLayout(FlowLayout.LEFT));
```

Notice that a different version of the **add()** method is used. Because you have no individual control over where the buttons are placed, you just add them:

```
btnOne = new JButton("One");
add(btnOne);

btnTwo = new JButton("Two");
add(btnTwo);

btnThree = new JButton("Three");
add(btnThree);

btnFour = new JButton("Four");
add(btnFour);
```

8.4 How do I...
Create a program with no layout?

Problem

You know how moody programmers can be. Sometimes I feel like using a layout manager, but sometimes I don't. What can I do to lay out my windows when I am just not in the mood for a layout manager?

Technique

Once again, you have asked the right question. The JFC gives you the option of bypassing a layout manager altogether. Of course, life is full of tradeoffs. If you don't use a layout manager, your program does not automatically adjust to resized windows. If the window is stretched beyond the size that you antici- pated, the controls all appear in one corner. If your user shrinks the window, the controls are hidden also.

Steps

1. Create the application source file. Create a new file called NoLayout1.java and enter the following source:

```java
import javax.swing.*;
import java.awt.*;
import java.awt.event.*;

public class NoLayout1 extends JPanel
{
    public NoLayout1()
    {
        JButton btnOne;
        JButton btnTwo;
        JButton btnThree;
        JButton btnFour;

        this.setLayout(null);

        btnOne = new JButton("One");
        btnOne.setBounds(0,0,100,100);
        add(btnOne);

        btnTwo = new JButton("Two");
        btnTwo.setBounds(100,0,100,50);
        add(btnTwo);

        btnThree = new JButton("Three");
        btnThree.setBounds(0,100,75,100);
```

```
        add(btnThree);

        btnFour = new JButton("Four");
        btnFour.setBounds(115,115,100,100);
        add(btnFour);

    }//constructor


    public static void main(String s[])
    {
        JFrame f = new JFrame("No Layout");
        NoLayout1 panel = new NoLayout1();

        f.setForeground(Color.black);
        f.setBackground(Color.lightGray);
        f.getContentPane().add(panel, "Center");

        f.setSize(250,250);
        f.setVisible(true);
        f.addWindowListener(new WindowCloser());


    }//main
}//class


class WindowCloser extends WindowAdapter
{
    public void windowClosing(WindowEvent e)
    {
        Window win = e.getWindow();
        win.setVisible(false);
        win.dispose();
        System.exit(0);
    }//windowClosing
}//class WindowCloser
```

2. Compile and test the application. Compile the source by using `javac`.
Figure 8.4 shows a snapshot of the running application.

Figure 8.4 A null layout
manager expects you to
specify the exact location of
your controls.

How It Works

The most important statement in this application is the `setLayout()` method. In this case, we specify that the layout manager will be `null`:

```
this.setLayout(null);
```

Now the buttons that we place on the form must be completely specified using the `setBounds()` method. We pass it four parameters, which represent the x location, y location, width, and height of the button:

```
btnOne = new JButton("One");
btnOne.setBounds(0,0,100,100);
add(btnOne);

btnTwo = new JButton("Two");
btnTwo.setBounds(100,0,100,50);
add(btnTwo);

btnThree = new JButton("Three");
btnThree.setBounds(0,100,75,100);
add(btnThree);

btnFour = new JButton("Four");
btnFour.setBounds(115,115,100,100);
add(btnFour);
```

COMPLEXITY
INTERMEDIATE

8.5 How do I...
Add ToolTips to applications?

Problem

Sometimes when I run programs that have been written by really smart programmers, ToolTips appear whenever I rest my cursor over a control for a few seconds. How do they do that? I want to add ToolTips to my programs, too.

Technique

This example uses the built-in ToolTip support to display the location of the mouse. The method `getToolTipText()` is called whenever a ToolTip is about to be displayed.

Steps

1. Create the application source file. Create a new file called `MouseLocation.java` and enter the following source:

```java
import javax.swing.*;
import java.awt.event.*;

import java.awt.*;

public class MouseLocation extends JPanel
{
    public MouseLocation()
    {
       setToolTipText("xxx");
       setBackground(Color.white);
    }//constructor

    public String getToolTipText(MouseEvent event)
    {

       int x = event.getX();
       int y = event.getY();
       String str = "(" + x + "," + y + ")";

       return str;
    }//getToolTipText


    public static void main(String s[])
    {
       JFrame f = new JFrame("MouseLocation Example");
       MouseLocation panel = new MouseLocation();

       f.setDefaultCloseOperation(JFrame.DISPOSE_ON_CLOSE);
       f.setForeground(Color.black);
       f.setBackground(Color.lightGray);
       f.getContentPane().add(panel,"Center");
       f.setSize(300,300);
       f.setVisible(true);
       f.addWindowListener(new WindowCloser());
    }//main

}//class MouseLocation

class WindowCloser extends WindowAdapter
{
    public void windowClosing(WindowEvent e)
    {
       Window win = e.getWindow();
       win.setVisible(false);
       win.dispose();
       System.exit(0);
    }//windowClosing
}//class WindowCloser
```

2. Compile and test the application. Compile the source by using `javac`. Figure 8.5 shows a snapshot of the running application.

Figure 8.5 ToolTip support
is built in to the JFC
controls.

How It Works

We start off by importing the same files that we are used to:

```
import javax.swing.*;
import java.awt.event.*;

import java.awt.*;
import java.lang.*;
```

Next, we create a class to generate the ToolTips:

```
public class MouseLocation extends JPanel
{
    public MouseLocation()
    {
```

In the following constructor we add a call to **setToolTipText** and pass it a dummy string. We will be generating the contents of the ToolTip dynamically in this application, so it doesn't matter what the string is at first. Don't omit it, however, or the ToolTips don't appear.

```
setToolTipText("xxx");
    setBackground(Color.white);
}//constructor
```

Next we override the method **getToolTipText** in order to display our own ToolTip message:

```
public String getToolTipText(MouseEvent event)
```

We want to create a string that contains the x and y coordinates of the mouse whenever it comes to rest. We do that with the **getX()** and **getY()** methods:

```
{
int x = event.getX();
    int y = event.getY();
    String str = "(" + x + "," + y + ")";
```

The value of the string is the return value of this special function.

COMPLEXITY
INTERMEDIATE

8.6 How do I...
Create buttons with icons on them?

Problem

My buttons are so plain. I would like to jazz them up a bit. How do you put icons on buttons? How do you change the icon when the user clicks on it?

Technique

The JButton class was written with programmers like you in mind. Not only can you assign an icon to a button, but you can assign several icons to it, and designate under what conditions they appear.

Steps

1. Create the application source file. Create a new file called IconButtons.java and enter the following source:

```java
import javax.swing.*;
import java.awt.event.*;
import java.awt.*;

public class IconButtons extends JPanel
{
    public IconButtons()
    {
        ImageIcon buttonImage = new ImageIcon("images/T1.gif");
        ImageIcon pressImage = new ImageIcon("images/T2.gif");
        ImageIcon selImage = new ImageIcon("images/T3.gif");
        ImageIcon disabledImage = new ImageIcon("images/T4.gif");
        ImageIcon rolloverImage = new ImageIcon("images/T4.gif");
        ImageIcon selrolloverImage = new ImageIcon("images/
➥T3.gif");
        ImageIcon DOJImage = new ImageIcon("images/T2.gif");
        ImageIcon shapeImage = new ImageIcon("images/T1.gif");
        AbstractButton button1;
        AbstractButton button2;
        AbstractButton button3;
        Font font1;

        font1 = new Font("Serif", Font.PLAIN,16);
        setFont(font1);
        setDoubleBuffered(true);
```

```
        setLayout(new GridLayout(1,3,5,5));

        button1 = new JButton();
        button1.setIcon(buttonImage);
        button1.setPressedIcon(pressImage);
        button1.setRolloverIcon(rolloverImage);
        add(button1);

        button2 = new JButton();
        button2.setIcon(buttonImage);
        button2.setDisabledIcon(disabledImage);
        button2.setEnabled(false);
        add(button2);

        button3 = new JToggleButton();
        button3.setIcon(DOJImage);
        button3.setSelectedIcon(shapeImage);
        button3.setRolloverIcon(shapeImage);
        button3.setRolloverSelectedIcon(selrolloverImage);
        add(button3);

    }//constructor

    public static void main(String s[])
    {
        JFrame f = new JFrame("Icon Buttons ");
        IconButtons panel = new IconButtons();

        f.setForeground(Color.black);
        f.setBackground(Color.lightGray);
        f.getContentPane().add(panel, "Center");

        f.setSize(200,70);
        f.setVisible(true);
        f.addWindowListener(new WindowCloser());


    }//main
}//IconButtons


class WindowCloser extends WindowAdapter
{
    public void windowClosing(WindowEvent e)
    {
        Window win = e.getWindow();
        win.setVisible(false);
        win.dispose();
        System.exit(0);
    }//windowClosing
}//class WindowCloser
```

2. Compile and test the application. Compile the source by using `javac`.
Figure 8.6 shows a snapshot of the running application.

Figure 8.6
Icons on
buttons give
applications
a profes-
sional look.

How It Works

The first thing we do is to create a number of instances of the **ImageIcon** class and assign a bunch of small GIF files to them:

```
ImageIcon buttonImage = new ImageIcon("images/b.gif");
    ImageIcon pressImage = new ImageIcon("images/b.gif");
    ImageIcon selImage = new ImageIcon("images/b.gif");
    ImageIcon disabledImage = new ImageIcon("images/b.gif");
    ImageIcon rolloverImage = new ImageIcon("images/b.gif");
    ImageIcon selrolloverImage = new ImageIcon("images/b.gif");
    ImageIcon DOJImage = new ImageIcon("images/DOJ.gif");
    ImageIcon shapeImage = new ImageIcon("images/shapes.gif");
```

These serve as the icons on the buttons. Next we have to instantiate each of the buttons:

```
button1 = new JButton();
```

Immediately afterward, we assign the main icon to the buttons by using the **setIcon()** command and one of the icons that we set up earlier:

```
button1.setIcon(buttonImage);
```

Next, we tell **setIcon()** which icon to display when the button is being pressed. The method **setPressedIcon()** performs this task:

```
button1.setPressedIcon(pressImage);
```

Similarly, we assign an image for when the mouse is over the button:

```
button1.setRolloverIcon(rolloverImage);
```

Finally, we add the button to the panel:

```
add(button1);
```

We give **button2** a couple of unique features. It has **DisabledIcon** declared, and then the button is disabled as an example:

```
button2.setDisabledIcon(disabledImage);
button2.setEnabled(false);
```

button3 is a toggle button. Toggle buttons have two states: selected and not selected. The icons for them are assigned based on several states:

```
button3 = new JToggleButton();
```

```
button3.setIcon(DOJImage);
button3.setSelectedIcon(shapeImage);
button3.setRolloverIcon(shapeImage);
button3.setRolloverSelectedIcon(selrolloverImage);
```

As you run this application, notice how the buttons behave differently from one another.

COMPLEXITY

INTERMEDIATE

8.7 How do I...
Create RadioButton controls?

Problem

I need to provide my users with a set of choices but allow them to select only one choice at a time. If the users change their mind and choose a different one, the first one should be automatically unselected. Is there a control that behaves this way?

Technique

Yes there is such a control. You have described the functionality of the radio button control. If you are old enough, you may remember when car radios had mechanical buttons that you pushed in to change stations. When one button was pressed, the previously pressed button popped out. This made sense because no one would want to listen to two radio stations at the same time. The JFC version of the radio button is called **JRadioButton**. We place these buttons in groups so that we can have more than one set of buttons on the same pane if we choose.

Steps

1. Create the application source file. Create a new file called **Action1.java** and enter the following source:

```
import java.awt.*;
import java.awt.event.*;
import javax.swing.*;

public class Action1 extends JPanel implements ActionListener
{
    public Action1()
    {
        JButton button1;
        JRadioButton radioButton1;
        JRadioButton radioButton2;
        ButtonGroup grp;
```

```
    //Buffer to reduce flicker
        setDoubleBuffered(true);

        button1 = new JButton("Button");
        button1.addActionListener(this);
        button1.setActionCommand("Button Activated");
        add(button1);

        grp = new ButtonGroup();

        radioButton1 = new JRadioButton("One");
        radioButton1.addActionListener(this);
        radioButton1.setActionCommand("One Activated");
        grp.add(radioButton1);
        add(radioButton1);

        radioButton2 = new JRadioButton("Two");
        radioButton2.addActionListener(this);
        radioButton2.setActionCommand("Two Activated");
        grp.add(radioButton2);
        add(radioButton2);

    }//constructor

    public void actionPerformed(ActionEvent e)
    {
        String cmd;
        Object source;

        source = e.getSource();
        cmd = e.getActionCommand();


        System.out.println("Action: "+cmd+"\n\tperformed
➡by: "+source);
        System.out.println();

    }//actionPerformed

    public static void main(String s[])
     {
        JFrame f = new JFrame("Action1 ");
        Action1 panel = new Action1();

f.getContentPane().add(panel, "Center");

        f.setSize(200,100);
        f.setVisible(true);
        f.addWindowListener(new WindowCloser());


     }//main

}//class Actions
```

```
class WindowCloser extends WindowAdapter
{
    public void windowClosing(WindowEvent e)
    {
        Window win = e.getWindow();
        win.setVisible(false);
        win.dispose();
        System.exit(0);
    }//windowClosing
}//class WindowCloser
```

2. Compile and test the application. Compile the source by using `javac`. Figure 8.7 shows a snapshot of the running application.

Figure 8.7
Radio
buttons are
implemented
in cases
where only
one choice at
the time is
allowed.

How It Works

The first interesting part is the declaration of the buttons. Notice that we have both a **JButton** and a pair of **JRadioButton**s.

Declared:

```
  JButton button1;
      JRadioButton radioButton1;
      JRadioButton radioButton2;
```

The next step is to define a button group for the radio buttons. Radio buttons are unique in that the pressing of one button automatically releases any other radio buttons. The group allows the programmer to release only the radio buttons associated with the one pushed. Otherwise, every radio button in the window, except the one just pressed, would be released:

```
ButtonGroup grp;
```

This application uses the **Action** command strategy to distinguish between action events. When the button is created, a string is assigned to it by using the **setActionCommand()** method. This string is used in the **actionPerformed()** method to differentiate between buttons:

```
button1.setActionCommand("Button Activated");
```

The declaration of radio buttons is similar to that of other types of buttons:

```
grp = new ButtonGroup();

    radioButton1 = new JRadioButton("One");
    radioButton1.addActionListener(this);
    radioButton1.setActionCommand("One Activated");
```

One unique feature of radio buttons is in the assignment of a button to a group:

```
grp.add(radioButton1);
```

The importance of the **Action** command string is clear in the **Action** event handler. **getActionCommand()** allows you to retrieve the string that was stored to identify the buttons. An alternate way of doing the same thing is to inquire with **getSource()**, as we did in Chapter 5, "Events and Parameters":

```
source = e.getSource();
    cmd = e.getActionCommand();
```

COMPLEXITY
INTERMEDIATE

8.8 How do I...
Create ListBox controls?

Problem

I spent many years coding in Visual Basic. I loved to throw multiselect list boxes on the screen for everything. Does the JFC provide a sophisticated multiselect list box?

Technique

The JFC provides a list box that functions very much like the one in Visual Basic. You call methods to populate the items, and then you use a combination of the mouse and the Shift and Ctrl keys to select and deselect items in the list.

Steps

1. Create the application source file. Create a new file called **List1.java** and enter the following source:

```
import java.awt.*;
import java.awt.event.*;
import javax.swing.*;
import javax.swing.event.*;
```

```java
public class List1 extends JPanel
    implements ListSelectionListener
{
    JTextField actField;
    JList list;

    public List1()
    {
        String items[] = { "GA", "AL", "DC","NY",
                            "CA","UT","FL"};

        JPanel footer;
        JPanel tmp;

        setLayout( new BorderLayout());
        setBackground(Color.lightGray);

        //Turn on buffering

        setDoubleBuffered(true);
        list = new JList(items);
        list.addListSelectionListener(this);
        add(new JScrollPane(list), "Center");

        footer = new JPanel();
        footer.setLayout(new GridLayout(3,1,5,5));

        tmp = new JPanel();
        tmp.add(new JLabel("Sel values:"));
        actField = new JTextField(20);
        tmp.add(actField);

        footer.add(tmp);

        add(footer, "South");

    }//constructor

    public void valueChanged(ListSelectionEvent e)
    {
        int first, last;
        int i;
        String newVal = "";
        ListModel listData = list.getModel();
        Object selValues[];


        //Display the selected values

        selValues = list.getSelectedValues();

        if (selValues != null)
            last = selValues.length;
        else
            last = 0;

        newVal = "";
```

```
                    for(i=0;i<last;i++)
                    {
                        if(i!=0) newVal+=" ";
                        newVal += selValues[i].toString();
                    }

                    actField.setText(newVal);
            }

            public static void main(String s[])
            {
                JFrame f = new JFrame("List1");
                List1 panel = new List1();

                f.setForeground(Color.black);
                f.setBackground(Color.lightGray);
                f.getContentPane().add(panel, "Center");

                f.setSize(350,350);
                f.setVisible(true);
                f.addWindowListener(new WindowCloser());


            }//main


    }//class


    class WindowCloser extends WindowAdapter
    {
        public void windowClosing(WindowEvent e)
        {
            Window win = e.getWindow();
            win.setVisible(false);
            win.dispose();
            System.exit(0);
        }//windowClosing
    }//class WindowCloser
```

2. Compile and test the application. Compile the source by using `javac`.
Figure 8.8 shows a snapshot of the running application.

How It Works

Notice that we have a new listener type in this application,
`ListSelectionListener`:

```
public class List1 extends JPanel
    implements ListSelectionListener
{
```

The `JList` class is used to create the list:

```
JList list;
```

Figure 8.8 You can select multiple choices by holding down the Ctrl key or the Shift key while clicking the mouse.

An array is created that holds all the values we want to load into the list:

```
String items[] = { "GA", "AL", "DC","NY",
                    "CA","UT","FL"};
```

A footer panel is created to hold the results:

```
JPanel footer;
JPanel tmp;
```

You populate the list box by passing an array of strings to the constructor:

```
list = new JList(items);
```

As you might expect, a listener is added to this list:

```
list.addListSelectionListener(this);
```

`ListSelectionListener`'s required method is the `valueChanged()` method:

```
public void valueChanged(ListSelectionEvent e)
```

The following code is used to display the selected values in the text field at the bottom of the window:

```
selValues = list.getSelectedValues();

if (selValues != null)
    last = selValues.length;
else
    last = 0;

newVal = "";

for(i=0;i<last;i++)
{
    if(i!=0) newVal+=" ";
    newVal += selValues[i].toString();
}
```

```
actField.setText(newVal);
}
```

Notice that this example creates the viewport view of a **JScrollPane**. This is necessary because **JList** doesn't support scrolling directly:

```
list = new JList(items);
        list.addListSelectionListener(this);
        add(new JScrollPane(list), "Center");
```

COMPLEXITY
INTERMEDIATE

8.9 How do I...
Add a menu to my application?

Problem

My customers have grown accustomed to the Windows look and feel—including menus. How do I place menus on a JFC application?

Technique

Two JFC classes, **JMenuBar** and **JMenuItem**, form the basis for a menu-based user interface. The menu bar holds menu items.

Steps

1. Create the application source file. Create a new file called **Menu1.java** and enter the following source:

```
import java.awt.*;
import java.awt.event.*;
import javax.swing.*;
import javax.swing.event.*;

public class Menu1 extends JPanel
    implements ActionListener, MenuListener
{
    JTextField fldStatus;

    //Create the menu class
    public Menu1(JFrame frm)
    {
        JMenuBar bar = new JMenuBar();
        JMenu menu = new JMenu("Strategy");
        JMenuItem tmp;

        setBackground(Color.lightGray);
        setLayout(new BorderLayout());
```

```
        setDoubleBuffered(true);

        menu.addMenuListener(this);

        tmp = new JMenuItem("Lead");
        tmp.addActionListener(this);
        tmp.setActionCommand("Lead");
        menu.add(tmp);

        tmp = new JMenuItem("Follow");
        tmp.addActionListener(this);
        tmp.setActionCommand("Follow");
        menu.add(tmp);

        tmp = new JMenuItem("Resign");
        tmp.addActionListener(this);
        tmp.setActionCommand("Resign");
        menu.add(tmp);

        tmp = new JMenuItem("Quit");
        tmp.addActionListener(this);
        tmp.setActionCommand("Quit");
        menu.add(tmp);

        bar.add(menu);

        frm.setJMenuBar(bar);

        fldStatus = new JTextField(10);
add(fldStatus,"South");

    }//constructor

    public void actionPerformed(ActionEvent e)
    {
        String cmd;
        cmd = e.getActionCommand();

        if (cmd.equals("Lead"))
        {
            fldStatus.setText("Action: Lead");
        }
        if (cmd.equals("Follow"))
        {
            fldStatus.setText("Action: Follow");
        }
        if (cmd.equals("Resign"))
        {
            fldStatus.setText("Action: Resign");
        }
        if (cmd.equals("Quit"))
        {
            System.exit(0);
        }

    }
```

```
    public void menuSelected(MenuEvent e)
    {
        fldStatus.setText("Menu Selected");
    }

    public void menuDeselected(MenuEvent e)
    {
        fldStatus.setText("Menu Deselected");
    }

    public void menuCanceled(MenuEvent e)
    {
        fldStatus.setText("Menu Cancelled");
    }

public static void main(String s[])
{
    JFrame f = new JFrame("Menu1");
    Menu1 panel = new Menu1(f);

    f.setForeground(Color.black);
    f.setBackground(Color.lightGray);
    f.getContentPane().add(panel, "Center");

    f.setSize(300,200);
    f.setVisible(true);
    f.addWindowListener(new WindowCloser());


}//main


}//class

//close down gracefully
class WindowCloser extends WindowAdapter
{
    public void windowClosing(WindowEvent e)
    {
        Window win = e.getWindow();
        win.setVisible(false);
        win.dispose();
        System.exit(0);
    }//windowClosing
}//class WindowCloser
```

2. Compile and test the application. Compile the source by using `javac`. Figure 8.9 shows a snapshot of the running application.

How It Works

The `MenuListener` interface provides the connection between the menu events and the event-handling code:

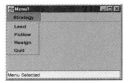

Figure 8.9 The
`MenuListener` class
makes it possible to
add menus to your
applications.

```
public class Menu1 extends JPanel
    implements ActionListener, MenuListener
```

We will create the menu in the constructor for this application. Notice that
the constructor takes `Jframe` as an argument to the constructor:

```
public Menu1(JFrame frm)
    {
```

The menu bar, which holds the menus, is declared first:

```
JMenuBar bar = new JMenuBar();
```

The menu is declared next. An application can have several menus on the
same menu bar:

```
JMenu menu = new JMenu("Strategy");
```

`menuListener` is attached to the menu. This provides a handler for menu-
specific events, not for simple item clicks:

```
menu.addMenuListener(this);
```

Each of the menu items is added to the menu individually. The default
action command is the component label, which is not strictly necessary in
setting the action command when they are equal. They are added explicitly here
for clarity. Notice that each of them adds its own **ActionListener** and
ActionCommand:

```
tmp = new JMenuItem("Lead");
tmp.addActionListener(this);
tmp.setActionCommand("Lead");
menu.add(tmp);

tmp = new JMenuItem("Follow");
tmp.addActionListener(this);
tmp.setActionCommand("Follow");
menu.add(tmp);

tmp = new JMenuItem("Resign");
tmp.addActionListener(this);
tmp.setActionCommand("Resign");
menu.add(tmp);
```

```
tmp = new JMenuItem("Quit");
tmp.addActionListener(this);
tmp.setActionCommand("Quit");
menu.add(tmp);
```

Now that the menu is complete, it can be added to the menu bar:

```
bar.add(menu);
```

Now that the menu bar is complete, it can be added to the frame:

```
frm.setJMenuBar(bar);
```

The menu choices are handled by examining the **ActionCommand** associated with each choice:

```
public void actionPerformed(ActionEvent e)
    {
        String cmd;
        cmd = e.getActionCommand();

        if (cmd.equals("Lead"))
        {
            fldStatus.setText("Action: Lead");
        }
        if (cmd.equals("Follow"))
        {
            fldStatus.setText("Action: Follow");
        }
        if (cmd.equals("Resign"))
        {
            fldStatus.setText("Action: Resign");
        }
        if (cmd.equals("Quit"))
        {
            System.exit(0);
        }

    }
```

The menu events are handled by a set of three event handlers:

```
public void menuSelected(MenuEvent e)
{
    fldStatus.setText("Menu Selected");
}

public void menuDeselected(MenuEvent e)
{
    fldStatus.setText("Menu Deselected");
}

public void menuCanceled(MenuEvent e)
{
    fldStatus.setText("Menu Cancelled");
}
```

Now when the application is run, the menus display and provide the users with a way of communicating their wishes to your program.

MULTIMEDIA

9

MULTIMEDIA

How do I...

Prior to Java 1.2, only 8KHz mono AU files could be played. All sounds had to be translated into this format, with a possible loss of quality. Java 1.2 supports many more formats. AIFF, AU, WAV, and three MIDI-based file formats are supported. As of Java 1.2, applications can load sounds using the `newAudioClip()` method.

In Chapters 3, "Basic Graphics," and 7, "Advanced Graphics," the techniques needed to draw graphical elements were presented. This chapter concentrates on bringing your programs alive with sound. Java supports the ability to load sounds from the server so that they may be presented on the client in a manner that allows far greater control than is available with HTML alone. Sound is a very important aspect when developing high-impact applications.

This chapter addresses audio playing and coordination with animation. How to use image clipping to perform animation is also demonstrated.

9.1 Play Sounds

This example demonstrates how to play sounds in Java. Sounds are important when trying to grab attention or have fun with a game. This example creates a phone dialer application. A button pad similar to the telephone keypad is created. Whenever a button is pressed, the corresponding touch-tone is played.

9.2 Play Sounds in a Loop

Playing sounds in a loop is useful when implementing music to be played in the background. When a sound is played in a loop, a very small file can be played for an arbitrary length of time. This example shows an animation sequence of four balls bouncing around the screen while music is played in the background.

9.3 Play Several Sounds Simultaneously

Audio support in Java uses native sound drivers. On most platforms, several audio clips can be played simultaneously. In this example, a drumbeat plays in the background. Several electric guitar chords can be played over the drums.

9.4 Coordinate Animation and Sound

Coordinating animation and sound is a necessity for games. In this example you will create a game where the user controls the gunship that shoots the invaders. Sound is played when the game starts, when an invader is destroyed, and when the player is shot by an invader.

9.5 Use Clipping to Perform Animation

This example demonstrates an alternative method for performing simple animation that is much quicker than loading many images. A single image that contains several small images is used to animate a ball rolling.

COMPLEXITY
ADVANCED

9.1 How do I...
Play sounds?

Problem

I want to write a program to play the telephone touchtones. I want to create a keypad with telephone buttons on it. When a button is pressed, I want the appropriate tone to be played on the computer speaker. I know how to create buttons and handle button events, but I don't know how to play sounds. How do I play sounds?

Technique

Sound clips are contained in an interface called AudioClip. An AudioClip is loaded by invoking the **getAudioClip()** method with the name of the sound file as an argument. However, the program actually loads the clip if and when the program tries to play it. The AudioClip is played by invoking its **play()** method. Figure 9.1 shows an example of the output.

Figure 9.1
Java applets can load and play audio clips to simulate a telephone keypad.

Steps

1. Create the applet source file. Create a new file called **Dialer.java** and enter the following source:

```java
import java.awt.*;
import java.awt.event.*;
import java.applet.*;

/*
 * the dialer applet
 */
public class Dialer extends Applet implements ActionListener {

AudioClip touchTones[] = new AudioClip[12];

public Button NumberButton1;
public Button NumberButton2;
public Button NumberButton3;
public Button NumberButton4;
public Button NumberButton5;
public Button NumberButton6;
public Button NumberButton7;
public Button NumberButton8;
public Button NumberButton9;
```

```
public Button NumberButton0;
public Button PoundButton;
public Button StarButton;
/*
 * called when the applet is loaded
 * load audio clips and add the keypad panel
 */
public void init () {

    int i;
    String name;

    for (i=0; i<10; i+=1) {
        name = "touchtone."+i+".au";
        showStatus ("Getting "+name);
        touchTones[i] = getAudioClip (getCodeBase(), name);
    }
    name = "touchtone.star.au";
    showStatus ("Getting "+name);
    touchTones[10] = getAudioClip (getCodeBase(), name);

    name = "touchtone.pound.au";
    showStatus ("Getting "+name);
    touchTones[11] = getAudioClip (getCodeBase(), name);

    setLayout(new BorderLayout());

    //add ("Center", keypad = new Keypad (touchTones));

    //Font    font = new Font ("Times", Font.BOLD, 14);

    Color   miscColor = new Color (0, 0, 255);
    //setFont (font);

    NumberButton1 =  new Button ("1");
    add ("South",NumberButton1);
    NumberButton2 = new Button ("2");
    add ("South", NumberButton2 );
    NumberButton3 = new Button ("3");
    add ("South", NumberButton3 );
    NumberButton4 = new Button ("4");
    add ("South", NumberButton4);
    NumberButton5 = new Button ("5");
    add ("South", NumberButton5);
    NumberButton6 = new Button ("6");
    add ("South", NumberButton6 );

    NumberButton7 = new Button ("7");
    add ("South", NumberButton7);
    NumberButton8 = new Button ("8");
    add ("South", NumberButton8 );
    NumberButton9 = new Button ("9");
    add ("South", NumberButton9 );

    PoundButton= new Button ("*");
    add ("South", PoundButton );
```

```
        PoundButton.setBackground (miscColor);

        NumberButton0 =  new Button ("0");
        add ("South", NumberButton0);

        StarButton = new Button ("#");
        add ("South", StarButton);
        StarButton.setBackground (miscColor);

        setLayout (new GridLayout (4, 3, 4, 4));

        NumberButton1.addActionListener(this);
        NumberButton2.addActionListener(this);
        NumberButton3.addActionListener(this);
        NumberButton4.addActionListener(this);
        NumberButton5.addActionListener(this);
        NumberButton6.addActionListener(this);
        NumberButton7.addActionListener(this);
        NumberButton8.addActionListener(this);
        NumberButton9.addActionListener(this);
        NumberButton0.addActionListener(this);
        PoundButton.addActionListener(this);
        StarButton.addActionListener(this);
    }

    public void actionPerformed (ActionEvent ev)
    {
        Object object1 = ev.getSource();
        if (object1 == StarButton)
            touchTones[10].play ();
        else if (object1 == PoundButton)
            touchTones[11].play ();
        else if (object1 == NumberButton0)
            touchTones[0].play ();
        else if (object1 == NumberButton1)
            touchTones[1].play ();
        else if (object1 == NumberButton2)
            touchTones[2].play ();
        else if (object1 == NumberButton3)
            touchTones[3].play ();
        else if (object1 == NumberButton4)
            touchTones[4].play ();
        else if (object1 == NumberButton5)
            touchTones[5].play ();
        else if (object1 ==NumberButton6)
            touchTones[6].play ();
        else if (object1 == NumberButton7)
            touchTones[7].play ();
        else if (object1 ==NumberButton8)
            touchTones[8].play ();
        else if (object1 == NumberButton9)
            touchTones[9].play ();
    }
}
```

CHAPTER 9

2. Create an HTML document that contains the applet. Create a new file called howto91.html that contains the following code:

```
<html>
<head>
<title>Touchtone Dialer</title>
</head>
<applet code="Dialer.class" width=200 height=200>
</applet>
<hr size=4>

</html>
```

3. Compile and test the applet. Compile the source by using javac. Dialer requires several sound files. These files are included on the CD-ROM. Test the applet by using the Appletviewer; enter the following command:

```
appletviewer howto91.html
```

4. The applet creates a number pad similar to that of a telephone. Pressing the buttons causes the corresponding tone to be played.

How It Works

The Dialer applet contains an array of audio clips called **touchTones**. This array contains the tones for the digits, star, and pound sign found on a standard telephone keypad. The **init()** method loads these audio clips into the array by invoking the **getAudioClip()** method.

Table 9.1 lists the AudioClip methods.

Table 9.1 getAudioClip **Methods**

METHOD	DESCRIPTION
loop	Starts playing the audio clip in a loop.
play	Starts playing the audio clip. Each time this method is called, the clip is restarted from the beginning.
stop	Stops playing the audio clip.

Comments

getAudioClip(), like getImage(), is part of the **Applet** class. It can take an absolute URL as an argument, or take a path relative to an absolute URL as arguments. The latter is used in this example.

9.2 How do I...
Play sounds in a loop?

Problem

I would like to play some background noise while an applet is running. I have a small audio file, and it would be nice to just continuously loop through the sound. I know how to play sounds, but how do I play sounds in a loop?

Technique

The Bounce animation example from Example 7.4 is used here with music playing in the background. A small sound file (in AU format) is continuously looped through and played while the applet is running. Sound clips are contained in an interface called AudioClip in the applet package. An AudioClip can be created by invoking the **getAudioClip()** method with the name of the sound file as one of the arguments. The AudioClip is played in a loop by invoking its **loop** method. Figure 9.2 shows an example of the output.

Figure 9.2 Continuous sound provides background music for the bouncing balls.

Steps

1. Create the applet source file. Create a new file called **Bounce.java** and enter the following source:

```
import java.awt.*;
import java.awt.event.*;
import java.applet.*;
import java.awt.image.ImageObserver;
```

```java
/*
 * a class describing a single ball
 */
class Ball {

/*
 * the image for this ball
 */
Image img;

/*
 * x position and velocity
 */
double x, dx;    // x position and velocity

/*
 * y position and velocity
 */
double y, dy;    // y position and velocity

/*
 * initialize the position and velocity
 * to random values
 */
void random () {
    x = 10 + 380*Math.random ();
    y = 10 + 200*Math.random ();
    dx = 5 - 10*Math.random ();
    dy = 5 - 10*Math.random ();
}

/**
 * calculate the next position of this ball
 * and make sure it bounces off the edge of the panel
 * @param d - dimension of the bounding panel
 */
void compute (Dimension d) {
    if (x <= 0 || x > d.width) dx = -dx;    // bounce horizontal
    if (y <= 0 || y > d.height) dy = -dy;    // bounce vertical
    x += dx;
    y += dy;
}

/**
 * draw the ball image
 * @param g - destination graphics object
 * @param obs - parent image observer
 */
public void paint (Graphics g, ImageObserver obs) {

    g.drawImage (img, (int) x-10, (int) y-10, obs);
}
}

/*
 * the panel containing the bouncing balls
```

```
   */
class BouncePanel extends Panel implements Runnable {

/*
 * the number of balls
 */
final int nballs = 4;

/*
 * the array holding all the balls
 */
Ball balls[] = new Ball[10];

/*
 * offscreen image
 */
Image offimg;

/*
 * size of offscreen image
 */
Dimension offsize;

/*
 * graphics object associated with offscreen image
 */
Graphics offg;

/*
 * thread for periodic updating
 */
Thread thread;

/*
 * The thread recalculates each ball position and
 * redraws them
 */
public void run() {

    offsize = getSize();
    offimg = createImage (offsize.width, offsize.height);
    offg = offimg.getGraphics();
    while (true) {
        for (int i=0; i<nballs; i+=1) {
            balls[i].compute (offsize);
        }
        repaint ();
        try {
            Thread.sleep (25);
        } catch (InterruptedException e) {
            break;
        }
    }
}

/**
```

```
 * Override update to avoid erase flicker
 * @param g - destination graphics object
 */
public synchronized void update (Graphics g) {

    offg.setColor (Color.lightGray);
    offg.fillRect (0, 0, offsize.width, offsize.height);

    for (int i = 0 ; i < nballs ; i++)
        balls[i].paint (offg, this);
    offg.setColor (Color.black);
    offg.drawRect (0, 0, offsize.width-1, offsize.height-1);
    g.drawImage(offimg, 0, 0, this);
}

/*
 * Start the update thread
 */
public void start() {

    thread = new Thread(this);
    thread.start();
}

/*
 * Stop the update thread
 */
public void stop()
{

    if (thread != null)
      thread = null;
}

}

/*
 * the applet proper
 */
public class Bounce extends Applet implements ActionListener
{

/*
 * instance of BouncePanel
 */
BouncePanel panel;

/*
 * an array containing the images for the balls
 */
Image img[] = new Image[4];

/*
 * the audio clip to be played in a loop
 */
AudioClip sound;
```

```
Button btnStart;
Button btnStop;
/*
 * Called when the applet is loaded
 * Create an instance of bounce panel and add the start button
 * and load images
 */
public void init() {

    setLayout(new BorderLayout());

    panel = new BouncePanel ();
    add ("Center", panel);
    Panel p = new Panel ();
    add ("South", p);
    btnStart = new Button("Start");
    p.add (btnStart);
    btnStop = new Button("Stop");
    p.add (btnStop);
    btnStart.addActionListener(this);
    btnStop.addActionListener(this);

    sound = getAudioClip(getCodeBase(),  "sound.au");

    img[0] = getImage (getDocumentBase(), "whiteball.gif");
    img[1] = getImage (getDocumentBase(), "redball.gif");
    img[2] = getImage (getDocumentBase(), "blueball.gif");
    img[3] = getImage (getDocumentBase(), "greenball.gif");
    for (int i=0; i<panel.nballs; i+=1) {
        panel.balls[i] = new Ball ();
        panel.balls[i].img = img[i & 3];
    }
}

/*
 * Called when the applet is started
 * Don't do anything
 */
public void start () {

}

/*
 * Called when the applet is stopped
 */
public void stop() {

    panel.stop();
    sound.stop ();
}

/*
 * Handle start button press by randomizing balls
 */
public void actionPerformed(ActionEvent ev)
{
```

```
        Object object1 = ev.getSource();
        if (object1 == btnStart)
        {
            for (int i=0; i<panel.nballs; i+=1)
                panel.balls[i].random ();
            panel.start ();
            sound.loop ();
        }
        if (object1 == btnStop)
        {
            sound.stop ();
        }
    }

}
```

2. Create an HTML document that contains the applet. Create a new file called `howto92.html` that contains the following code:

```
<html>
<head>
<title>Bounce</title>
</head>
Bouncing balls example.
<hr size=4>
<applet code="Bounce.class" width=400 height=400>
</applet>
<hr size=4>
</html>
```

3. Compile and test the applet. Compile the source by using `javac`. Test the applet by using the Appletviewer; enter the following command:

```
appletviewer howto92.html
```

4. When Bounce is executed, a frame opens and has Start and Stop buttons at the bottom. If you press Start, you should see four balls bouncing off the sides of the box in random directions and rates, as in Example 7.4. The difference in this example is that music is being played in the background.

The sound is contained in the `sound.au` file, which must reside in the same directory as the applet. The balls are GIF images (`whiteball.gif`, `redball.gif`, `blueball.gif`, and `greenball.gif`) that need to reside in the same directory as the applet. These files can be found on the accompanying CD-ROM in the folder named `Chap9`.

How It Works

This example is identical to the Bounce applet of Example 7.4, except for the addition of the sound. An AudioClip, `sound`, is declared, and the file `sound.au` is loaded into the class with the `getAudioClip()` method. The `getAudioClip()` method needs a URL and filename as parameters. The URL is supplied with the `getCodeBase()` method, which returns the URL of the applet. The filename `sound.au` is supplied as the file. To start playing the sound in a loop, the `loop()` method is called for the sound. This occurs in the event handler when the Start button is pressed. When the Stop button is pressed, the `sound.stop()` method is called to make the sound stop playing.

COMPLEXITY
ADVANCED

9.3 How do I...
Play several sounds simultaneously?

Problem

I would like to create an applet that can play several guitar chords. I have the chords as AU files. I also have a drumbeat sound file I would like to play in the background, so I can play the chords over it. I know how to play sounds, but how do I play sounds simultaneously?

Technique

As shown in the previous example, sound clips are contained in an interface called AudioClip in the applet package. An AudioClip is loaded by invoking the `GetAudioClip` method with the name of the sound file as an argument. As stated previously, the loading takes place when the program refers to the sound clip. The AudioClip is played by invoking its **play** method. The AudioClip is played in a loop by invoking its **loop** method. Figure 9.3 shows an example of the output.

Figure 9.3 Several sounds can be played simultaneously simulating guitar chords.

Steps

1. Create the applet source file. Create a new file called `Guitar.java` and
enter the following source:

```java
import java.awt.*;
import java.awt.event.*;
import java.applet.*;

/*
 * the applet class
 */
public class Guitar extends Applet implements ActionListener {

/*
 * the guitar chords
 */
AudioClip chords[] = new AudioClip[7];

/*
 * the drum clip
 */
AudioClip drum;
String chordnames[] = {"a", "c", "d", "low_e",
➥"high_e", "g", "chaa"};
String drumbeat  = "drum";
Button chordbuttons[] = new Button[7];
Button btnStart;
Button btnStop;
/*
 * Called when the applet is loaded
 * Load all sounds and add user interface
 */
public void init () {

    String name;
    int i;
    Panel keyboard = new Panel();
    Panel controls = new Panel();

    this.setLayout(new BorderLayout());
    keyboard.setLayout(new FlowLayout());
    controls.setLayout(new FlowLayout());
    add ("Center", keyboard);
    add ("South", controls);

    for (i=0; i<7; i+=1) {
        name = chordnames[i]+".au";
        showStatus ("Getting " + name);
        chords[i] = getAudioClip (getCodeBase(), name);
        chordbuttons[i] = new Button (chordnames[i]);
            keyboard.add (chordbuttons[i]);
            chordbuttons[i].addActionListener(this);
    }
    showStatus ("Getting " + drumbeat + ".au");
    drum = getAudioClip (getCodeBase(), drumbeat + ".au");
```

```
        btnStart = new Button ("Start");
        controls.add (btnStart);
        btnStop = new Button ("Stop");
        controls.add (btnStop);
        btnStop.addActionListener(this);
        btnStart.addActionListener(this);
    }

    /*
     * Handle button presses
     * @param ev - event object
     * @param arg - target object
     */
    public void actionPerformed (ActionEvent ev)
    {
        Object object1 = ev.getSource();
        if (object1 == chordbuttons[0])
        {
            chords[0].play ();
        }
        else if (object1 == chordbuttons[1])
        {
            chords[1].play ();
        }
        else if (object1 == chordbuttons[2])
        {
            chords[2].play ();
        }
        else if (object1 == chordbuttons[3])
        {
            chords[3].play ();
        }
        else if (object1 == chordbuttons[4])
        {
            chords[4].play ();
        }
        else if (object1 == chordbuttons[5])
        {
            chords[5].play ();
        }
        else if (object1 == chordbuttons[6])
        {
            chords[6].play ();
        }
            else if (object1 == btnStart) {
                drum.loop ();
        }
        else if (object1 == btnStop)
        {
                drum.stop ();
        }
    }
}
```

2. Create an HTML document that contains the applet. Create a new file called **howto93.html** that contains the following code:

```
<html>
<head>
<title>Guitar</title>
</head>
<applet code="Guitar.class" width=200 height=200>
</applet>
<hr size=4>

</html>
```

3. Compile and test the applet. Compile the source by using `javac`. Test the applet by using the Appletviewer; enter the following command:

```
appletviewer howto93.html
```

This example requires several sound files that need to reside in the same directory as the applet. These files can be found on the CD and are named `a.au`, `c.au`, `d.au`, `low_e.au`, `high_e.au`, `g.au`, `chaa.au`, and `drum.au`.

4. When the applet is executed, a window opens, with seven buttons, each labeled with the name of the chord. Pressing the buttons plays the chord. At the bottom are two buttons labeled Start and Stop. The Start button starts the drumbeat playing in the background. The Stop button stops the playing of the drumbeat.

How It Works

An array of AudioClip (`chords`) is declared, and each chord sound file is loaded in turn with the `getAudioClip()` method. The `getAudioClip()` method needs the URL and filename as parameters. The URL is supplied with the `getCodeBase()` method that returns the URL of the applet. The chord filename is supplied as the file. To play the sound, the `play()` method is called for the sound. This occurs in the event handler when a chord button is pressed. To start playing the drumbeat in a loop, the `loop()` method is called for the drumbeat. This occurs in the event handler when the Start button is pressed. When the Stop button is pressed, the `drum.stop()` method is called to stop the drumbeat from playing. While the drumbeat is playing in the background, the chords can be played simultaneously.

9.4 How do I...
Coordinate animation and sound?

Problem

I want to write a video game that has sound in it. I want sounds to be played when a target or the player is hit. I know how to animate graphics and play sounds, but I need to know how to coordinate them. How do I coordinate animation and sound?

Technique

Sounds can be played asynchronously. This means that the audio clip can be invoked in response to a target or player being hit. When either of these events is detected, the `play()` method can be invoked to coordinate animation and sound. Figure 9.4 shows an example of the output.

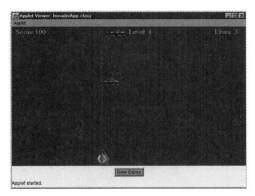

Figure 9.4 Sounds can be tied to events to create a sense of realism in a game.

Steps

1. Create the applet source file. Create a new file called `InvaderApp.java` and enter the following source:

```java
import java.awt.*;
import java.awt.event.*;
import java.applet.Applet;
import java.awt.image.*;

/**
 * A class that describes a target "invader"
```

```
 * This hold a single invader
 */
class Invader {

/*
 * this invader's position and velocity
 */
double x, y, dx, dy;

/*
 * this invader's missile position and velocity
 * only one missile allowed per invader
 */
int mx, my, mdy;

/*
 * The images for an invader
 */
Image img[] = new Image[4];

/*
 * inplay is true if this invader has not been killed
 */
boolean inplay;

/*
 * fired is set to true when this invader fires a missile
 */
boolean fired = false;

/*
 * state is used to cycle through the four images
 * of this invader
 */
double state;

/*
 * value is the score value; it depends on the speed
 */
int value;

/*
 * Initialize position and speed for this invader
 */
void random (int speed, int w, int h) {

    x = 10 + (w-20)*Math.random ();
    y = 10 + ((h>>1)-20)*Math.random ();
    dx = (speed>>1) - speed*Math.random ();
    dy = (speed>>1) - speed*Math.random ();
    inplay = true;
    state = 3 * Math.random ();
    fired = false;
    mdy = 20;
    value = speed * 10;
}
```

```
/*
 * Calculate new invader and missile position
 * Also fires a missile at random
 * @param w     panel width
 * @param h     panel height
 */
void compute (int w, int h) {

    if (x <= 0 || x > w) dx = -dx;
    if (y <= 0 || y > h>>1) dy = -dy;
    if (my > h-20) fired = false;
    if (fired) my += mdy;
    else my = 0;
    if (inplay && !fired && Math.random () > 0.99) {
        fired = true;
        mx = (int) x; my = (int) y+25;
    }
    x += dx; y += dy;
}


/*
 * paint invader and missile (if it has been fired)
 * @param g - destination graphics object
 * @param obs - imageobserver associated
 * with this graphics context
 */
public void paint (Graphics g, ImageObserver obs) {

    int whichImage;

    if (inplay) {
        whichImage = (int) state;
        g.drawImage (img[whichImage & 0x3], (int) x-25,
            (int) y-25, obs);
        state += .25;
    }
    if (fired) {
        g.setColor (Color.green);
        g.drawLine ((int) mx, (int) my, (int) mx, (int) my-10);
    }
}


/*
 * Tests whether the player's missile has hit this invader
 * Returns true if invader is hit
 * @param pmx - player's missile x position
 * @param pmy - player's missile y position
 */
boolean killer (int pmx, int pmy) {

    int deltaX, deltaY;

    if (!inplay) return false;
        deltaX = (int) Math.abs (x-pmx);
        deltaY = (int) Math.abs (y-pmy);
        if (deltaX < 20 && deltaY < 20) {
```

```
                inplay = false;
                return true;
            }
            return false;
    }
}

/**
 * A class to describe the player, very similar to Invader
 * except in reverse
 */
class Player {

/*
 * position of the player
 */
int x, y=-100;

/*
 * position of the player's missile
 */
int mx, my, mdy = -20;

/*
 * two different player images
 */
Image img1, img2;

/*
 * fired is true if player has fired a missile
 * inplay is true if the game is not over
 */
boolean fired = false, inplay=true;

/*
 * called when a player fires a missile
 */
void fire () {

    if (fired || !inplay) return;
    mx = x; my = y;
    fired = true;
}

/*
 * Calculate next missile position
 */
void compute () {

    if (my < 0) fired = false;
    if (fired) my += mdy;
    else my = y;
}

/**
 * Paint player and missile
```

```
 * @param g - destination graphics object
 * @param obs - image observer
 */
public void paint (Graphics g, ImageObserver obs) {

    if (fired) {
        if (inplay) g.drawImage (img2, x-25, y, obs);
        g.setColor (Color.white);
        g.drawLine (mx, my, mx, my+10);
    } else if (inplay) g.drawImage (img1, x-25, y, obs);
}

/**
 * Returns true if the player has been killed
 * @param bmx, bmy - position of enemy missile
 */
boolean killer (int bmx, int bmy) {

    int dx, dy;

    if (!inplay) return false;
    dx = (int) Math.abs (x-bmx);
    dy = (int) Math.abs (y-bmy);
    if (dx < 20 && dy < 20) {
        return true;
    }
    return false;
}
}

/*
 * much of the game logic is here
 */
class Playfield extends Panel implements Runnable,
➡MouseListener, MouseMotionListener
{

static final int PLAYER_HIT = 1;
static final int INVADER_HIT = 2;

InvaderApp invaderApp;

/*
 * the number of invaders in play
 */
int NInvaders=0;

/*
 * the maximum number of invaders possible
 */
final int MaxInvaders = 32;

/*
 * array of invaders
 */
Invader invaders[] = new Invader[MaxInvaders];
```

```
Player player;

/*
 * offscreen image for double-buffering
 */
Image offscreen;

/*
 * dimension of offscreen graphics image
 */
Dimension psize;

/*
 * graphics object associated with offscreen image
 */
Graphics offgraphics;

/*
 * game action thread
 */
Thread theThread;

/*
 * the playfield background color
 */
Color bgcolor = new Color (51, 0, 153);
int score, playerLives, playLevel;
Font font;

/**
 * constructor saves instance of the applet
 * @param invaderApp - instance of the applet
 */
public Playfield (InvaderApp invaderApp) {

    this.invaderApp = invaderApp;
    addMouseListener(this);
    addMouseMotionListener(this);

}

/*
 * game action thread
 */
public void run() {

    psize = getSize();
    offscreen = createImage (psize.width, psize.height);
    offgraphics = offscreen.getGraphics ();
    font = new Font ("TimesRoman", Font.BOLD, 18);
    offgraphics.setFont (font);

    while (true) {
        compute ();
        repaint ();
        try {
```

```
                Thread.sleep(25);
            } catch (InterruptedException e) { }
        }
}

/*
 * calculate new positions for all objects
 */
synchronized void compute () {

    for (int i=0; i<NInvaders; i+=1) {
        invaders[i].compute (psize.width, psize.height);
        if (invaders[i].killer (player.mx, player.my)) {
            invaderApp.hit (INVADER_HIT);
            player.fired = false;
            score += invaders[i].value;
        }
        if (player.killer (invaders[i].mx, invaders[i].my)) {
            invaderApp.hit (PLAYER_HIT);
            invaders[i].fired = false;
            playerLives -= 1;
            if (playerLives < 1) player.inplay = false;
        }
    }
    player.compute ();
}

/**
 * override default update
 * draw into offscreen image and then copy it to the screen
 * @param g - destination graphics object
 */
public synchronized void update(Graphics g) {

    offgraphics.setColor (bgcolor);
    offgraphics.fillRect (0, 0, psize.width, psize.height);

    for (int i = 0 ; i < NInvaders ; i++)
        if (invaders[i].inplay) invaders[i].paint
➡(offgraphics, this);
player.paint (offgraphics, this);

    offgraphics.setColor (Color.green);
    offgraphics.drawString ("Score", 10, 20);
    offgraphics.drawString (Integer.toString (score), 60, 20);
    offgraphics.drawString ("Level", psize.width>>1, 20);
    offgraphics.drawString (Integer.toString (playLevel),
        (psize.width>>1)+50, 20);
    offgraphics.drawString ("Lives", psize.width-80, 20);
    offgraphics.drawString (Integer.toString (playerLives),
        psize.width-30, 20);
    if (playerLives < 1) offgraphics.drawString ("Game Over",
        (psize.width>>1)-30, psize.height>>1);
    g.drawImage (offscreen, 0, 0, null);
}
```

```java
/*
 * Start the game thread
 */
public void start() {

    theThread = new Thread (this);
    theThread.start ();
}

/*
 * Stop the game thread
 */
public void stop() {

    if (theThread != null)
        theThread = null;
}
public void mouseClicked(MouseEvent e){}
public void mouseEntered(MouseEvent e){}
public void mouseExited(MouseEvent e){}

public void mouseReleased(MouseEvent e){}

public void mouseMoved(MouseEvent e)
{
    int x =e.getX();
    int y =e.getY();
    player.x = x;
    player.y = psize.height-45;
    if (player.x < 20) player.x = 20;
    if (player.x > psize.width-20) player.x = psize.width-20;
}

public void mousePressed(MouseEvent e)
{
    player.fire ();
}

public void mouseDragged(MouseEvent e)
{
}

}

/*
 * the applet class
 */
//////////////////////////////////////////////////////////////
//////////////////////////////////////////////////////////////
//////////////////////////////////////////////////////////////
public class InvaderApp extends Applet implements
➥ActionListener
{

/*
 * the playfield instance
```

```
    */
Playfield panel;

Button btnNewGame;

/*
 * temporary storage for images
 */
Image img[] = new Image[4];

/*
 * the speed of the game
 * the number of invaders in this round
 */
int speed, NInvadersInPlay;

/*
 * Called when the applet is loaded
 * Load the images
 */
public void init() {

    int i;
    MediaTracker tracker = new MediaTracker (this);

    setLayout(new BorderLayout());

    panel = new Playfield (this);
    add("Center", panel);
    Panel p = new Panel();
    add("South", p);
    btnNewGame = new Button("New Game");
    p.add(btnNewGame);
    btnNewGame.addActionListener(this);


    showStatus ("Getting Invader images...");
    for (i=0; i<4; i+=1) {
        img[i] = getImage (getDocumentBase(), "T"+(i+1)+".gif");
        tracker.addImage (img[i], 0);
    }

    try {
        tracker.waitForID(0);
    } catch (InterruptedException e) { }

        for (i=0; i<panel.MaxInvaders; i+=1) {
        panel.invaders[i] = new Invader ();
        panel.invaders[i].inplay = false;
        panel.invaders[i].img[0] = img[0];
        panel.invaders[i].img[1] = img[1];
        panel.invaders[i].img[2] = img[2];
        panel.invaders[i].img[3] = img[3];
    }
    panel.player = new Player ();
```

```
    showStatus ("Getting player images...");
    panel.player.img1 = getImage (getDocumentBase(),
➥"Player1.gif");
panel.player.img2 = getImage (getDocumentBase(),
➥"Player2.gif");

    tracker.addImage (panel.player.img1, 1);
    tracker.addImage (panel.player.img2, 1);
    try {
        tracker.waitForID (1);
    } catch (InterruptedException e) { }
    showStatus ("Ready to play!");
}

/*
 * Start the action thread
 */
public void start() {

    panel.start();
}

/*
 * Stop the action thread
 */
public void stop() {

    panel.stop();
}

public void actionPerformed(ActionEvent ev)
{
        speed = 10;
        panel.player.inplay = true;
        panel.playerLives = 3;
        panel.score = 0;
        panel.playLevel = 1;
        NInvadersInPlay = 2 * panel.playLevel + 1;
        panel.NInvaders = NInvadersInPlay;
        for (int i=0; i<panel.NInvaders; i+=1)
            panel.invaders[i].random (speed,
                panel.psize.width, panel.psize.height);

        play (getCodeBase(), "gong.au");
        if (NInvadersInPlay >= panel.MaxInvaders)
            NInvadersInPlay = panel.MaxInvaders;
}

/**
 * Play the appropriate sound when something is hit
 * @param which - which sound to play
 */
public void hit (int which) {

    switch (which) {
        case Playfield.INVADER_HIT:
```

```
                    NInvadersInPlay -= 1;
                    if (NInvadersInPlay < 1) {
                        play (getCodeBase(), "gong.au");
                        panel.playLevel += 1;
                        NInvadersInPlay = 2 * panel.playLevel + 1;
                        speed += 4;
                        panel.NInvaders = NInvadersInPlay;
                        for (int i=0; i<panel.NInvaders; i+=1)
                        panel.invaders[i].random (speed,
                            panel.psize.width, panel.psize.height);
                    } else {
                        play (getCodeBase(), "drip.au");
                    }
                    break;

                    case Playfield.PLAYER_HIT:
                    play (getCodeBase(), "doh2.au");
                    break;
            }
        }
    }
```

2. Create an HTML document that contains the applet. Create a new file called **howto94.html** that contains the following code:

```
<html>
<head>
<title>InvaderApp</title>
</head>
<applet code="InvaderApp.class" width=600 height=400>
</applet>
<hr size=4>

</html>
```

3. Compile and test the applet. Compile the source by using **javac**. InvaderApp requires several sound and image files. These files are included on the CD-ROM. Test the applet by using the Appletviewer; enter the following command:

```
appletviewer howto94.html
```

4. InvaderApp is a fully-functional videogame. Press the Start button to begin the game. The gunship can be moved left and right by just moving the mouse. To fire, press the mouse button.

How It Works

The InvaderApp program contains four classes: an **Invader** class, which describes a target invader; the **Player** class, which describes the player; the **PlayField** class, which is the main engine to the game; and the **InvaderApp** class, which manages the game.

The `Invader` class describes the single invader. It contains the invader position and velocity, along with a missile position and velocity. It also contains four images for the invader that are cycled to make the invader more interesting. The `inPlay` variable is set to `True` if the invader has not been killed. The `fired` variable is set to `True` if the invader has fired a missile. The `state` variable is used to determine which image is displayed for this invader. The variable `value` is the score value for this invader.

The `random()` method initializes the position and velocity of this invader to random values. The velocity of the invader is dependent on the `speed` argument. The `speed` argument is determined by the play level in the applet: Higher play levels cause higher speeds. This makes the game challenging at higher levels. The score value is also dependent on the speed.

The `compute()` method calculates the next position for the invader. It also computes the position of the missile if it has been fired. If the missile has not been fired, it will be fired randomly. The invader's position is incremented by its velocity. If the invader encounters the boundary of the panel specified by the `w` and `h`, then the velocity in the respective direction is inverted. This gives the illusion of bouncing off the walls.

The `paint()` method paints the invader image and the invader's missile if it has been fired. The `killer()` method determines whether the player's missile has hit this invader. The player's missile position is given by `pmx` and `pmy`. This is used to determine if the missile is within the rectangle bounding the invader. The method returns `True` if the invader has been hit.

The `Player` class is similar to the `Invader` class. It contains `paint()` and `killer()` methods, which are analogous to those of the `Invader` class. The `fire()` method fires a missile from the current player position if it has not been fired already. A different player image is drawn if the player has fired a missile. This gives more life to the game. The `compute()` method calculates the new missile position only if a missile has been fired.

The `PlayField` class is a separate thread that contains the game engine itself. An array of invaders is maintained, along with a single instance of `player`. An offscreen image and an offscreen image context are maintained to implement double-buffering.

The `run()` method first creates the offscreen image and graphics context. It also sets the font. It then continuously computes the new invader and missile positions by calling `compute()`. The screen is updated with calls to `repaint()`.

The `compute()` method invokes each invader's `compute()` method. It then tests whether an invader has been hit by a player missile by calling the `Invader.killer()` method. If an invader has been hit, the sound for an invader being hit is played, the player's missile is eliminated, and `score` is incremented. A similar test is performed for the player. In this case a different sound is played, and the number of player lives is decreased.

The update() method overrides the default update() method to avoid unnecessary flickering. The invaders are drawn by calling the Invader.paint() methods for all invaders. The player is drawn by calling the Player.paint() method. The score, play level, and number of player lives are drawn. All this drawing is done in the offscreen image via the offscreen graphics context. The offscreen image is drawn onscreen.

If a mousePressed() event occurs, the Player.fire() method is invoked. If a mouseMoved() method occurs, the player's position is set to the mouse x position. Care is taken to keep the player position within panel bounds.

The play field start() and stop() methods start and stop the play field thread, respectively.

The InvaderApp class manages the game. The init() method creates an instance of the play field panel and adds it to the center of the applet panel. A button is added at the bottom of the applet panel for starting a new game. The images for the invaders are loaded via the getImage() method. MediaTracker is used to wait for the images to load. The invaders are created and initialized. An instance of the player is created, and its images are loaded.

If the player presses the New Game button, the play field variables are initialized and the game is started.

Comments

The game can be improved in many ways. Different types of targets can be added, and multiple missiles can be managed. Another cool improvement is to change the hit sounds to explosions and to add sounds for firing.

COMPLEXITY
ADVANCED

9.5 How do I...
Use clipping to perform animation?

Problem

I know how to simulate animation by displaying a series of images. However, this can mean substantial loading time due to the number of images needed. I would like to apply the clipping technique from Example 7.6 to a single image to produce the effect of animation. How do I use clipping to perform animation?

Technique

As shown in Example 7.6, the easiest way to draw part of an image is to use clipping. A graphics object can be created with a clipping rectangle specified. To draw part of an image, the new graphics context must be created with the coordinates, width, and height of the section of the image that needs to be drawn. Figure 9.5 shows an example of the running applet.

> **NOTE**
>
> A general rule is as follows: To copy a section of image (x1,y1,w,h) to the screen at the coordinates (x2,y2), create a graphics context with a clipping region of (x2,y2,w,h) and draw the image at the coordinates (-x1,-y1).

Figure 9.5 Animation can be achieved by clipping an image several times.

Steps

1. Create the applet source file. Create a new file called **BallSpin.java** and enter the following source:

```java
import java.applet.*;
import java.awt.*;
import java.net.*;

/*
 * the applet class
 */
public class BallSpin extends Applet implements Runnable {

/*
 * the number of sub-images in the entire image
 */
int nImages;

/*
 * the full-size image
 */
Image theImage;

/*
 * the animation thread
 */
```

```
Thread thread;

/*
 * the position of the displayed image
 */
int xOffset;
int yOffset;

/*
 * offscreen image for double-buffering
 */
Image offImage;

/*
 * graphics object associated with the offscreen image
 */
Graphics offg;

/*
 * dimension of the offscreen image
 */
Dimension offSize;

/*
 * the sub-image to be drawn
 */
int whichImage;

/*
 * the dimension of each sub-image
 */
Dimension imageDim = new Dimension ();

/*
 * Initializes the applet
 * Loads the entire image
 */
public void init () {

    int i;

    thread = null;

    offSize = getSize ();
    offImage = createImage (offSize.width, offSize.height);
    offg = offImage.getGraphics ();

    nImages = 7;
    imageDim.width = 48;
    imageDim.height = 53;

    MediaTracker tracker = new MediaTracker (this);

        String name = "ballspin.gif";
    theImage = getImage (getDocumentBase (), name);
```

```java
        tracker.addImage (theImage, 100);
        showStatus ("Getting image: "+name);
        try {
            tracker.waitForID (100);
        } catch (InterruptedException e) { }

        xOffset = nImages * 30;
        yOffset = 3 + offSize.height - imageDim.height;
        whichImage = nImages;
        repaint ();
        thread = new Thread (this);
        thread.start ();
    }

    /*
     * Start the animation
     */
    public void start () {

        xOffset = nImages * 30;
        yOffset = 3 + offSize.height - imageDim.height;
        whichImage = nImages;
        if (thread != null)
            thread = null;
        thread = new Thread (this);
        thread.start ();
    }

    /*
     * Stop the animation
     */
    public void stop ()
    {
        if (thread != null)
            thread = null;
    }

    /**
     * call update for efficiency
     * @param g - destination graphics object
     */
    public void paint (Graphics g) {

        update (g);
    }

    /**
     * draw the sub-image at xOffset, yOffset
     * @param g - destination graphics object
     */
    public void update (Graphics g) {

        Graphics offgClip;

        offg.setColor (Color.white);
        offg.fillRect (0, 0, offSize.width, offSize.height);
```

```
        offgClip = offg.create (xOffset, yOffset, imageDim.width,
            imageDim.height);
        offgClip.drawImage (theImage, 0 - (whichImage
➡* imageDim.width),
0, this);
        g.drawImage (offImage, 0, 0, this);
}

/*
 * Animation thread forces repaint every 100ms
 */
public void run () {

    int i;

    for (i=0; i<nImages; i+=1) {
        xOffset -= 30;
        whichImage -= 1;
        repaint ();
        try {
            Thread.sleep (100);
        } catch (InterruptedException e) { }
    }
}
}
```

2. Create an HTML document that contains the applet. Create a new file called **howto95.html** that contains the following code:

```
<html>
<head>
<title>Single Image Animation</TITLE>
</head>
<applet code="BallSpin.class"  width=225 height=125>
</applet>
<hr size = 4)

</html>
```

3. Compile and test the applet. Compile the source by using **javac** or the makefile provided. Test the applet by using the Appletviewer; enter the following command:

```
appletviewer howto95.html
```

4. When BallSpin is executed, a window opens and a ball rolls from the right to the left.

How It Works

The BallSpin applet loads a single GIF image, which contains several sub-images of a rolling ball. Clipping is used to draw these individual images in an animated fashion such that the ball appears to roll across the screen.

The applet `init()` method creates an offscreen image for double-buffering. The complete image is loaded from the server by using the `Applet.getImage()` method. `MediaTracker` is used to wait for the image to load. A status message is displayed during image load.

The `start()` method initializes the image display location and starts a separate animation thread. The `stop()` method simply stops the animation thread. The `paint()` method calls the `update()` method to avoid unnecessary flickering. The `run()` method is the animation thread that calculates the new image position, forcing a `repaint()` every 100 milliseconds.

The `update()` method erases the offscreen image, `offg`, by filling it with the color white. A second graphics object, `offgClip`, is created as a copy of the offscreen image with a clipping rectangle defined as the dimensions of the sub-images. The sub-image is drawn into the clipped graphics object by invoking `Graphics.drawImage()`. The variable `whichImage` is used to specify which sub-image is drawn. Finally, the offscreen image, `offImage`, is drawn to the screen with a call to `Graphics.drawImage()`.

Comments

The original purpose for this technique was to reduce the number of files that had to be downloaded by the applet, and thus speed up the loading time. As it turns out, that was not its only advantage. The single image containing all the images turns out to be considerably smaller than the sum of all the smaller images. This means that the applet will download faster using this technique.

CHAPTER 10
NETWORKING

10

NETWORKING

How do I...

Networking is one of the strengths of the Java API. Classes and methods exist to access Internet sockets, create server sockets, get host names and addresses, and force Web browsers to show specified documents. Socket connections can be made to arbitrary ports, but there are specific classes for accessing data via the HTTP port. Many applets may want to exploit these classes for server-to-client data transfer for reasons of efficiency and simplicity.

Most of these classes are found in the `java.net` package. This package must be imported in order to use the classes.

Data transfer is normally performed using streams. Therefore, before we dive into the network too deeply, we need to understand the operation of streams.

Applications can perform all networking operations. Sometimes the client restricts applets for security reasons. However, users typically allow connections to the server from which they were downloaded, but may not allow connections to other hosts.

10.1   Write Byte Data to a Stream

This example shows how to write bytes to a stream. In earlier releases of Java, byte streams were used to process many different kinds of data. Type specific streams are now available, but byte streams are still useful for some applications.

10.2   Read Byte Data from a Stream

This example shows how to read bytes.

10.3   Perform Buffered Writes to a Stream

This example performs buffered writes to a stream.

10.4   Perform Buffered Reads from Streams

This example shows how to use buffers when reading to improve I/O performance.

10.5   Write Other Data Types to Streams

This example shows how to write double values to a stream.

10.6   Read Other Data Types from Streams

Not all data is of type character or byte. This example shows how to read double values from a stream.

10.7   Perform Buffered Writes of Characters

This example shows how to write characters to a file by using streams.

10.8   Perform Buffered Reads of Characters

This example shows how to use the correct streams and methods to read characters via a stream.

10.9   Use Streams to Move Data over the Internet

This example shows how to use a special type of stream, `InputStreamReader`, to move data over the Internet.

10.10 Access a URL

This example demonstrates the mechanism for forcing Web browsers to show specific documents. Both full-page and frame changes are supported.

The example extends the functionality of Example 6.6. In that example, advertiser banners are animated by using common transition effects. This example allows the user to click on a particular banner that will cause the browser to show the page corresponding to that advertisement.

10.11 Translate Host Names to Internet Addresses

This example uses methods in the `InetAddress` class, which is similar in function to the `nslookup` utility found on many UNIX platforms.

10.12 Create a Socket

In this example you determine whether a remote host is running by attempting to open a specific port. If the port can be opened successfully, the remote host must be running.

COMPLEXITY
BEGINNING

10.1 How do I ...
Write byte data to a stream?

Problem

I have heard that Java uses streams to communicate in Java. What are streams? How can I write to a stream?

Technique

Streams are named after real-world streams—the small rivers that cross the land. Like the water-carrying variety, Java streams are paths that data can flow across to get from one place to another.

Few activities in the computer are as complicated as input/output (I/O). The process of getting data off a piece of foreign hardware, often on a remote computer, is very complex. Java streams take all that complexity and hide it inside the simplicity of streams. In the olden days, two or three years ago, programmers considered it normal to use different programming statements and facilities to access data stored on different media. It seemed okay to learn one approach for reading from a network, another to read a disk file, and yet another to read from a CD drive. Java handles all these data types through the same analogy, the stream. There are small differences in the way streams are handled from one situation to the next, but the approach is identical.

Byte data is very common in programming. In fact, all data can be transferred as bytes if necessary. In fact, under Java 1.2, almost everything was treated as bytes. Although other streams have been created specially for other data types, byte streams remain important data structures. In this example, you will learn how to write to a byte stream.

Steps

1. Create the application source file. Create a new file called WriteStream.java and enter the following source:

```java
import java.io.*;

public class WriteStream
{
    // This program runs as an application
    public static void main(String[] arguments)
    {
        //Create an array of data to print
        int[] allBytes = {2,4,6,8,10,12,14,16,
18,20,22,24,26,28,30};
try
        {
            //declare a stream
            FileOutputStream ofile = new
FileOutputStream("bytes.dat");
for (int i=0; i < allBytes.length; i++)
                //write to the stream
                ofile.write(allBytes[i]);
            ofile.close();
        } catch (IOException e)// handle any errors
            {
                System.out.println("Error - " + e.toString());
            }//catch
    }//main
}//WriteStream
```

2. Compile and test the applet. Compile the source by using javac. Figure 10.1 shows a snapshot of the running application.

Figure 10.1 FileOutputStream creates a new file, if needed, and writes data to it.

How It Works

File streams are the simplest type of streams to program. All you have to do to use a file stream is to declare it as shown here:

```
FileOutputStream ofile = new FileOutputStream("bytes.dat");
```

This statement connects the variable **ofile** with the file **"bytes.dat"**. Behind the scenes, the Java Virtual Machine (JVM) is pedaling like crazy to create all the hardware and software calls necessary to make this code work. After the stream is created and connected to the file, the following statement tells the JVM to put the data in the file:

```
ofile.write(allBytes[i]);
```

Note that the data is written one byte at a time, literally. Each byte is being individually written to a file. This is kind of like walking to the copier with each page you want to copy, copying it, and then returning it to the desk before picking up a second page. (When we introduce buffered streams later in this chapter, we will see how to grab a handful of data each time.) When this program is run, a new file is created on your hard drive. If you use **ls -l** or **DIR**, you can see it and prove to yourself that it worked.

COMPLEXITY
BEGINNING

10.2 How do I...
Read byte data from a stream?

Problem

Now that I know how to write byte data to a stream, how do I read it back into a program?

Technique

If this were a college course, a professor would probably say that the reading of this data from the file is an exercise left to the student. Because you are now grown, and because you are our customer, we will provide an example of how to do this.

Steps

1. Create the application source file. Create a new file called
`ReadStream.java` and enter the following source:

```java
import java.io.*;

public class ReadStream
{
    // This program runs as an application
    public static void main(String[] arguments)
    {
        try
        {
            //declare a stream
            FileInputStream ifile = new
➥ FileInputStream("bytes.dat");
boolean eof = false;
            int cntBytes = 0;
            while (!eof)
            {
                int thisVal = ifile.read();
                System.out.print( thisVal + " " );
                if (thisVal == -1)
                    eof = true;
                else
                    cntBytes++;
            } //while
            ifile.close();
            System.out.print("\nBytes read: " + cntBytes);

        } catch (IOException e)// handle any errors
            {
                System.out.println("Error - " + e.toString());
            }//catch
    }//main
}//ReadStream
```

2. Compile and test the application. Compile the source by using `javac`.
Figure 10.2 shows a snapshot of the running application.

Figure 10.2 `FileInputStream` moves data from an
external source into a program's memory area.

How It Works

Like his brother `FileOutputStream`, `FileInputStream` moves data from one place to another. In this case, the source is a file on disk and the destination is the program address space in memory. The following line of code names the stream and attaches it to the file "`bytes.dat`", created in Example 10.1, as shown here:

```
FileInputStream ifile = new FileInputStream("bytes.dat");
```

If the program needs data from the stream, it acquires it via the `read()` method, as shown here:

```
boolean eof = false;
int cntBytes = 0;
while (!eof)
{
  int thisVal = ifile.read();
    System.out.print( thisVal + " ");
    if (thisVal == -1)
    eof = true;
  else
    cntBytes++;
```

Notice how carefully this program looks for an end of file. If the program fails to anticipate the end of file condition correctly, or if the file doesn't exist, an I/O exception is thrown. In order to avoid this, the program tests for the end of file character, `-1`, after every byte is read.

COMPLEXITY
INTERMEDIATE

10.3 How do I...
Perform buffered writes to a stream?

Problem

I have heard that a stream is slow if used without a buffer. What is a buffered stream and how do I write to one?

Technique

If the magic of the streams has not been obvious to you yet, it will be now. All that you have to do to buffer the reads and writes in your program is to declare a second stream, called `BufferedOutputStream`, and pass it your `FileOutputStream` as a parameter. The buffering of the data will take place automatically. In effect, by adding one line of code to your program, you have implemented a ton of new processing power, as anyone who has written a buffering scheme from scratch can attest.

Steps

1. Create the application source file. Create a new file called
`BufferedWriteStream.java` and enter the following source:

```java
import java.io.*;

public class BufferedWriteStream
{
    // This program runs as an application
    public static void main(String[] arguments)
    {
        //Create an array of data to print
        int[] allBytes = {1,3,5,7,9,11,13,15,
17,19,21,23,25,27,29};
try
        {
            //declare a stream
            FileOutputStream ofile = new
FileOutputStream("bufBytes.dat");
BufferedOutputStream bufStream = new
 BufferedOutputStream(ofile);
for (int i=0; i < allBytes.length; i++)
                //write to the stream
                bufStream.write(allBytes[i]);
            bufStream.close();
        } catch (IOException e)// handle any errors
            {
                System.out.println("Error - " + e.toString());
            }//catch
    }//main
}//BufferedWriteStream
```

2. Compile and test the application. Compile the source by using `javac`.
Figure 10.3 shows a snapshot of the running application.

Figure 10.3 Buffered writes are much more efficient
than ordinary writes.

How It Works

We started by creating `FileOutputStream` just as we did in the preceding section:

```
FileOutputStream ofile = new FileOutputStream("bufBytes.dat");
```

In this case, however, we declared a second stream to buffer the first. Notice that the name of `FileOutputStream` is passed to the constructor of `BufferedOutputStream` as a parameter. This forms the connection between the two:

```
BufferedOutputStream bufStream = new BufferedOutputStream(ofile);
```

Notice that from this point forth, your code doesn't deal with the `FileOutputStream` at all. The `write()` methods and even the `close()` methods are executed against `BufferedOutputStream`:

```
for (int i=0; i < allBytes.length; i++)
    //write to the stream
    bufStream.write(allBytes[i]);
bufStream.close();
```

COMPLEXITY
INTERMEDIATE

10.4 How do I...
Perform buffered reads from streams?

Problem

Does buffering apply to reading data also? How do I read data through a buffer?

Technique

Yes, buffering applies to reading data also. Buffering reads can greatly improve performance by allowing your program to perform physical reads on larger chunks of data in anticipation of your needs. Because this approach makes better use of the hardware, it can greatly improve performance. Let's again use the copying machine analogy: Buffering is like getting an armload of documents and carrying them to the machine, even if you aren't sure that you will want to copy them all.

Steps

1. Create the application source file. Create a new file called
`BufferedReadStream.java` and enter the following source:

```java
import java.io.*;

public class BufferedReadStream
{
    // This program runs as an application
    public static void main(String[] arguments)
    {
        try
        {
            //declare a stream
            FileInputStream ifile = new
➥FileInputStream("bufBytes.dat");
BufferedInputStream bufStream = new
➥ BufferedInputStream(ifile);
boolean eof = false;
            int cntBytes = 0;
            while (!eof)
            {
                int thisVal = bufStream.read();
                System.out.print( thisVal + " ");
                if (thisVal == -1)
                    eof = true;
                else
                    cntBytes++;
            } //while
            bufStream.close();
            System.out.print("\nBytes read: " + cntBytes);

        } catch (IOException e)// handle any errors
            {
                System.out.println("Error - " + e.toString());
            }//catch
    }//main
}//BufferedReadStream
```

2. Compile and test the application. Compile the source by using `javac`.
Figure 10.4 shows a snapshot of the running application.

Figure 10.4 Buffering has the same effect on input as it
has on output.

How It Works

The declaration of `BufferedInputStream` is almost identical to that of `BufferedOutputStream`:

```
BufferedInputStream bufStream = new BufferedInputStream(ifile);
```

Similarly, all the methods called by the program are those of `BufferedInputStream`, as shown here:

```
int thisVal = bufStream.read();
```

COMPLEXITY
INTERMEDIATE

10.5 How do I...
Write other data types to streams?

Problem

I have noticed that all the stream examples so far have used byte streams. Do I have to use byte streams, or are there other types of streams available? How do I write values of type double?

Technique

By declaring yet another stream type, **DataOutputStream**, and wrapping it around **BufferedOutputStream**, you can make the stream handle any type of data. At the lowest level, all data is stored as bits in 8-bit clumps called bytes. **DataOutputStream**s simply separate the data in your program into byte-sized portions and send it to the buffer and on to the file.

Steps

1. Create the application source file. Create a new file called `BufferedWriteDataStream.java` and enter the following source:

```
import java.io.*;

public class BufferedWriteDataStream
{
    // This program runs as an application
    public static void main(String[] arguments)
    {
        //Create an array of data to print
        double[] allDoubles = {1.1,3.1,5.1,7.1,9.1,11.1,
➥13.1,15.1,17.1,19.1,21.1,23.1,25.1,27.1,29.1};
```

```
try
    {
        //declare a stream and attach it to a file
        FileOutputStream ofile = new
➥FileOutputStream("bufDouble.dat");

        //declare a buffer and attach it to a stream
        BufferedOutputStream bufStream = new
➥BufferedOutputStream(ofile);

        //declare a data stream and assign it to a buffer
        DataOutputStream datStream = new
➥DataOutputStream(bufStream);

        for (int i=0; i < allDoubles.length; i++)
            //write to the datastream
            datStream.writeDouble(allDoubles[i]);
        datStream.close();
    } catch (IOException e)// handle any errors
        {
            System.out.println("Error - " + e.toString());
        }//catch
    }//main
}//BufferedWriteDataStream
```

2. Compile and test the application. Compile the source by using `javac`.
Figure 10.5 shows a snapshot of the running application.

Figure 10.5 Other data types can be handled by
declaring DataOutputStream.

How It Works

In a fairly elegant fashion, you declare `DataOutputStream` and wrap it around
the buffer. This gives you the functionality of the new stream without killing the
buffering:

```
DataOutputStream datStream = new DataOutputStream(bufStream);
```

Notice that `BufferedOutputStream` not `FileOutputStream` is passed as a parameter. If `FileOutputStream` were passed, the buffering effect would be lost. The `DataOutputStream` methods for handling the data are type specific. The following code shows the `writeDouble()` method. Other methods exist for the other data types.

```
for (int i=0; i < allDoubles.length; i++)
  //write to the datastream
  datStream.writeDouble(allDoubles[i]);
datStream.close();
```

10.6 How do I ...
Read other data types from streams?

Problem

Do I use the same type of streams to read in double data that I used to write it out? I want to read numbers of type double to a stream.

Technique

Good guess. The answer is that `DataInputStream` serves the same purpose for input that `DataOutputStream` does for output.

Steps

1. Create the application source file. Create a new file called `BufferedReadDataStream.java` and enter the following source:

```
import java.io.*;

public class BufferedReadDataStream
{
    // This program runs as an application
    public static void main(String[] arguments)
    {
        try
        {
            //declare a stream
            FileInputStream ifile = new
➥FileInputStream("bufDouble.dat");
BufferedInputStream bufStream = new
➥BufferedInputStream(ifile);
DataInputStream datStream = new
➥DataInputStream(bufStream);
```

```
int cntDoubles = 0;
        try
        {
            while (true)
            {
                double thisVal = datStream.readDouble();
                System.out.print( thisVal + " ");
                cntDoubles++;
            } //while
        } catch (EOFException eof)
            {
                datStream.close();
                System.out.print("\nDoubles read: " + [ccc]
cntDoubles);
} //catch

        } catch (IOException e)// handle any errors
            {
                System.out.println("Error - " + e.toString());
            }//catch
    }//main
}//BufferedReadDataStream
```

2. Compile and test the application. Compile the source by using `javac`.
Figure 10.6 shows a snapshot of the running application.

Figure 10.6 Some data types can be read
using DataInputStream.

How It Works

DataInputStream wraps around the buffer and processes the data after getting
it from the buffer as shown here:

```
DataInputStream datStream = new DataInputStream(bufStream);
```

Special methods exist to read each data type. For doubles, the method is
readDouble():

```
double thisVal = datStream.readDouble();
```

It is always possible, although not so straightforward, to convert the data
types to or from strings (characters) and then use character streams instead.

10.7 How do I...
Perform buffered writes of characters?

Problem

Are character streams different from byte streams? Do I treat characters as bytes or do I use special streams to write them? What is the best way?

Technique

You can treat characters as bytes as long as you don't need Unicode characters. Each of the characters in the ASCII character set can be represented by a byte value. Other character sets, such as Japanese and Chinese, have far too many characters to fit in a single byte. In order to accommodate these languages, operating system vendors have added support for Unicode character sets. This topic is called *localization* and includes not only character sets, but also date format, time display, and other ways of representing information. Java enables you to set the locale for an application, thereby allowing much of this to be handled by built-in Java code.

JavaSoft recommends that all character I/O be done using character streams that handle Unicode characters properly. The character streams are called *writers* (for output) and *readers* (for input), instead of streams. `BufferedWriter` and `FileWriter` are the first examples of these streams. By default, character streams convert characters between Unicode and the native operating system and locale encoding.

Steps

1. Create the application source file. Create a new file called `BufferedWriteCharStream.java` and enter the following source:

```java
import java.io.*;

public class BufferedWriteCharStream
{
    // This program runs as an application
    public static void main(String[] arguments)
    {
        //Create an array of data to print
        char[] allChars = {'H','e','l','l','o',' ',
'W','o','r','l','d','\n'};
```

```
        try
            {
                //declare a stream and attach it to a file
                FileWriter ofile = new FileWriter("bufChar.dat");

                //declare a BufferedWriter - attach it to a stream
                BufferedWriter bufStream = new
➥BufferedWriter(ofile);

                for (int i=0; i < allChars.length; i++)
                    //write to the char stream
                    bufStream.write(allChars[i]);
                bufStream.close();
            } catch (IOException e)// handle any errors
                {
                    System.out.println("Error - " + e.toString());
                }//catch
        }//main
}//BufferedWriteCharStream
```

2. Compile and test the application. Compile the source by using `javac`. Figure 10.7 shows the file generated by the program.

Figure 10.7 With `BufferedWriteCharStream.java` you write to the buffered stream instead of to the character stream.

How It Works

Notice how similar the declaration of these streams is to that of the byte and data streams we studied earlier in this chapter. To declare an instance of the character stream, you use the following syntax:

```
FileWriter ofile = new FileWriter("bufChar.dat");
```

Because we want to maintain the buffering, we need to place `FileWriter` inside `BufferedWriter`:

```
//declare a BufferedWriter and attach it to a stream
BufferedWriter bufStream = new BufferedWriter(ofile);
```

As we did earlier, we need to write to the buffered stream instead of to the character stream:

```
for (int i=0; i < allChars.length; i++)
  //write to the char stream
  bufStream.write(allChars[i]);
```

COMPLEXITY
INTERMEDIATE

10.8 How do I...
Perform buffered reads of characters?

Problem

How do I read character data from a stream? Do I use the character streams as I did in Example 10.7?

Technique

The design of all the streams is pretty consistent. Therefore, you will use a very similar approach to reading character streams as you would for reading any other streams.

Steps

1. Create the application source file. Create a new file called `BufferedReadCharStream.java` and enter the following source:

```java
import java.io.*;

public class BufferedReadCharStream
{
    // This program runs as an application
    public static void main(String[] arguments)
    {
        try
        {
            //declare a stream
            FileReader ifile = new FileReader("bufChar.dat");
            BufferedReader bufStream = new
➡BufferedReader(ifile);
boolean eof = false;
            while (!eof)
            {
                String line = bufStream.readLine();
                if (line == null)
```

```
                        eof = true;
                    else
                        System.out.println(line);
                }//while
                bufStream.close();

            } catch (IOException e)// handle any errors
                {
                    System.out.println("Error - " + e.toString());
                }//catch
        }//main
    }//BufferedReadStream
```

2. Compile and test the application. Compile the source by using `javac`.
Figure 10.8 shows a snapshot of the running application.

Figure 10.8 Reading from a character stream is
very simple.

How It Works

In order to create a buffered reader, you declare both `FileReader` and
`BufferedReader`:

```
FileReader ifile = new FileReader("bufChar.dat");
BufferedReader bufStream = new BufferedReader(ifile);
```

As is our custom, we now deal exclusively with the buffered stream
methods. Notice that the method we use here is `readLine()`:

```
boolean eof = false;
    while (!eof)
    {
        String line = bufStream.readLine();
        if (line = = null)
            eof = true;
```

This method reads the entire line instead of just one character. The test for
the end of file is different also. Instead of looking for a special character such as
-1, we test for a null result of a `readLine()` call.

COMPLEXITY
ADVANCED

10.9 How do I...
Use streams to move data over the Internet?

Problem

I want to write a program that will go out and get the HTML text of a Web page and display it in a window. I don't want it to display in a browser—I just want to see the text. Can I use a stream to do this?

Technique

This requires a connection to the server, locating the file, and reading it into a program that displays the source. A stream called **InputStreamReader** is used to accomplish this. The **BufferedReader** stream type from Example 10.8 is used to provide buffering.

Steps

1. Create the applet source file. Create a new file called `GetInetFile.java` and enter the following source:

```java
import java.awt.*;
import java.awt.event.*;
import java.net.*;
import java.io.*;

public class GetInetFile extends Frame implements Runnable
{
    Thread thread1;
    URL doc;
    TextArea body = new TextArea("Getting text...");

    public GetInetFile()
    {
        super("Get URL");
        add(body);
        try
        {
            doc = new URL("http://www.lads.com
    ➥/ads/launch.html");
}//try
        catch (MalformedURLException e)
        {
            System.out.println("Bad URL:  " + doc);
        }//catch
```

```
        }//GetInetFile


        public static void main(String[] arguments)
        {
            GetInetFile frame1 = new GetInetFile();

            WindowListener l = new WindowAdapter()
            {
                public void windowClosing(WindowEvent e)
                {
                    System.exit(0);
                }//windowClosing
            };//WindowListener

            frame1.addWindowListener(l);
            frame1.pack();
            frame1.setVisible(true);
            if (frame1.thread1 == null)
            {
                frame1.thread1 = new Thread(frame1);
                frame1.thread1.start();
            }//null
        }//main

        public void run()
        {
            URLConnection URLConn = null;
            InputStreamReader inStream;
            BufferedReader info;
            String line1;
            StringBuffer strBuffer = new StringBuffer();
            try
            {
                URLConn = this.doc.openConnection();
                URLConn.connect();
                body.setText("Connection opened ... ");
                inStream = new InputStreamReader(URLConn.
➥getInputStream());
info = new BufferedReader(inStream);
                body.setText("Reading data ...");
                while ((line1 = info.readLine()) != null)
                {
                    strBuffer.append(line1 + "\n");
                }//while
                body.setText(strBuffer.toString());
            }//try
            catch (IOException e)
            {
                System.out.println("IO Error:" + e.getMessage());
            }//catch
        }//run
}// class Getfile
```

2. Compile and test the applet. Compile the source by using javac. You must be connected to the Internet for this to work. Figure 10.9 shows a snapshot of the running application.

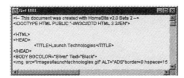

Figure 10.9 InputStreamReader is a stream that serves as a bridge from byte streams to character streams.

How It Works

The URL class contains methods that allow data movement from a file identified by a URL. First, declare an instance of the URL class and assign it to a specific URL that you are interested in:

```
doc = new URL("http://www.lads.com/ads/launch.html");
```

Next, make this connection to the remote server that contains the document:

```
URLConn = this.doc.openConnection();
        URLConn.connect();
```

Now you can use the connection to get the data. You initialize both **InputStreamReader** and **BufferedReader** to process the data. **InputStreamReader** is a stream that serves as a bridge from byte streams to character streams. Because TCP/IP returns bytes to the program through **URLConn**, your program must convert these bytes into characters to display in the frame. The easiest way to do this is by using **InputStreamReader**, which translates the bytes and encodes them as characters, saving you a lot of coding/debugging time:

```
inStream = new InputStreamReader(URLConn.getInputStream());
        info = new BufferedReader(inStream);
```

InputStreamReader has a counterpart called **OutputStreamWriter**. From this point forth, you simply execute **readLine()** calls against the buffer as in earlier examples to retrieve the data:

```
while ((line1 = info.readLine()) != null)
```

Comments

The URL class has a **getInputStream()** method that is a shortcut for opening a connection.

10.10 How do I...
Access a URL?

Problem

I found the Advertiser applet from Chapter 7, "Advanced Graphics," very useful. I want to make one improvement. I want to be able to force the Web browser to show a predefined location when the user clicks on any of the advertiser banners. I want to specify the universal resource locators (URLs) as applet parameters. I want to be able to specify unique URLs for each advertiser banner. I know how to access mouse down events, but I do not know how to force the Web browser to show a document. How do I force the browser to show a document?

Technique

The `showDocument()` method in the **appletContext** class forces Web browsers, such as Netscape Navigator, to show a document, given a URL. The `showDocument()` method takes the **URL** object as an argument. **URL** is a class that describes a URL; a URL is created by using one of the **URL** class's constructors. One of the constructors takes a string as an argument. This string is of the format commonly used by popular Web browsers.

The technique used by the Advertiser applet in Example 7.6 for specifying banner images and transition effects is extended here. We need to add one more field to the parameters: the URL associated with that banner. When a user clicks a particular banner, the `showDocument()` method is invoked, with the URL of the banner as an argument.

You must have a Java 1.1- or 1.2-compatible browser to run this application. As of this writing, no browsers are compliant. By the time you read this, at least one browser should be compliant.

Steps

1. Create the applet source file. Create a new file called `Advertiser.java` and enter the following source:

```
import java.util.*;
import java.awt.*;
import java.awt.event.*;
import java.applet.Applet;
import java.net.*;
```

```
/*
 * A class which performs the banner animation
 */
class Banner extends Panel implements Runnable{

/*
 * an instance of the applet for
 * invoking methods from Advertiser class
 */
Advertiser advertiser;

/*
 * instance of thread used for animation
 */
Thread thread;

/*
 * the next banner image to be displayed
 */
Image theImage;

/*
 * width and height of the new banner image
 */
int img_width, img_height;

/*
 * offscreen image for double-buffering
 */
Image offscreen;

/*
 * offg1 is the graphics object associated with
 * offscreen image. offg2 is the clipped version
 * of offg1
 */
Graphics offg1, offg2;

/*
 * xstart, ystart - x and y coordinate of clipping rectangle
 * width, height - width and height of clipping rectangle
 * effect_type - the effect type applied the next image
 */
int xstart, ystart, width, height, effect_type;

/**
 * constructor just saves instance of the applet
 * @param advertiser - instance of Advertiser applet
 */
Banner (Advertiser advertiser) {

    this.advertiser = advertiser;

}
```

```
/*
 * thread that calls repaint() every 25 ms
 * to effect animation
 */
public void run() {

    Dimension d = getSize();
    offscreen = createImage (d.width, d.height);
    offg1 = offscreen.getGraphics ();
    offg1.setFont (getFont ());
    offg1.setColor (Color.gray);
    offg1.fillRect (0, 0, d.width, d.height);
    while (true) {
        repaint ();
        try {
            Thread.sleep (25);
        } catch (InterruptedException e) {
            break;
        }
    }
}

/**
 * override update() method to avoid erase flicker
 * this is where the drawing is done
 * @param g - destination graphics object
 */
public synchronized void update(Graphics g) {

    int i, x, y, w, h;
    switch (effect_type) {
        case 0:
        offg1.drawImage (theImage, 0, 0, null);
        break;

        case 1:         // barn-door open
        if (xstart > 0) {
            xstart -= 5;
            width += 10;
            offg2 = offg1.create (xstart, 0, width, height);
            offg2.drawImage (theImage, -xstart, 0, null);
        } else offg1.drawImage (theImage, 0, 0, null);
        break;

        case 2:         // venetian blind
        if (height < 10) {
            height += 1;
            for (y=0; y<img_height; y+=10) {
                offg2 = offg1.create (0, y, width, height);
                offg2.drawImage (theImage, 0, -y, null);
            }
        } else offg1.drawImage (theImage, 0, 0, null);
        break;
```

```
                case 3:           // checker board
                if (width <= 20) {
                    if (width <= 10) {
                        i = 0;
                        for (y=0; y<img_height; y+=10) {
                            for (x=(i&1)*10; x<img_width; x+=20) {
                                offg2 = offg1.create (x, y, width, 10);
                                offg2.drawImage (theImage, -x, -y,
➥null);
}
                            i += 1;
                        }
                    } else {
                        i = 1;
                        for (y=0; y<img_height; y+=10) {
                            for (x=(i&1)*10; x<img_width; x+=20) {
                                offg2 = offg1.create (x, y,
➥width-10, 10);
offg2.drawImage (theImage, -x,
➥-y, null);
}
                            i += 1;
                        }
                    }
                    width += 5;
                } else offg1.drawImage (theImage, 0, 0, null);
                break;
        }
        g.drawImage (offscreen, 0, 0, null);
}

/**
 * Initialize variables for clipping rectangle
 * depending on effect type
 * @param which - the effect type for next image
 * @param img - the next image
 */
public void effect (int which, Image img) {

    img_width = img.getWidth (null);
    img_height = img.getHeight (null);
    theImage = img;
    switch (which) {
        case 0:
        break;

        case 1:           // barn door
        xstart = img_width >> 1;
        width = 0;
        height = img_height;
        break;
```

```
        case 2:
        width = img_width;
        height = 0;
        break;

        case 3:
        width = 0;
        break;
    }
    effect_type = which;
}

/*
 * Start the repaint thread
 */
public void start() {

    thread = new Thread(this);
    thread.start();
}

/*
 * Stop the repaint thread
 */
public void stop() {

    if (thread != null)
        thread = null;
}


}

/*
 * the Advertiser class proper
 */
public class Advertiser extends Applet implements Runnable,
➡MouseListener  {

/*
 * instance of Banner
 */
Banner panel;

/*
 * instance of thread for cycling effects
 * for each new image
 */
Thread thread;

/*
 * the total number of images
 */
int NBanners;
```

```
/*
 * the array of images
 */
Image img[] = new Image[10];

/*
 * the delay (dwell) time in milliseconds for each image
 */
int delay[] = new int[10];

/*
 * the effect type for each image
 */
int effect[] = new int[10];

/*
 * the URL to go to for each image
 */
URL url[] = new URL[10];

/*
 * the index variable pointing to the
 * current image, delay time, and associated URL
 */
int current = 0;

/*
 * called when applet is loaded
 * add the banner panel, load images, and parse applet
 * parameters
 */
public void init() {

    int i;
    setLayout(new BorderLayout());

    panel = new Banner (this);
    panel.addMouseListener(this);

    add("Center", panel);
    NBanners = 0;
    MediaTracker tracker = new MediaTracker (this);

    for (i=1; i<=10; i+=1) {
        String param, token;
        int j, next;

        param = getParameter ("T"+i);
        if (param == null) break;

        StringTokenizer st = new StringTokenizer (param, " ,");
```

```java
            token = st.nextToken ();
            img[NBanners] = getImage (getDocumentBase(), token);
            tracker.addImage (img[NBanners], i);
            showStatus ("Getting image: "+token);
            try {
                tracker.waitForID (i);
            } catch (InterruptedException e) { }

            token = st.nextToken ();
            delay[NBanners] = Integer.parseInt (token);

            token = st.nextToken ();
            effect[NBanners] = Integer.parseInt (token);

            token = st.nextToken ();
            try {
                url[NBanners] = new URL (token);
            } catch (MalformedURLException e) {
                url[NBanners] = null;
            }

            NBanners += 1;
        }
    }

    /*
     * thread that starts the next image transition
     */
    public void run () {

        while (true) {
            panel.effect (effect[current], img[current]);
            try {
                Thread.sleep (delay[current]);
            } catch (InterruptedException e) { }
            current += 1;
            current %= NBanners;
        }
    }

    /*
     * called when applet is started
     * start both threads
     */
    public void start() {

        panel.start();
        thread = new Thread(this);
        thread.start();
    }

    /*
     * called when applet is stopped
     * stops all threads
     */
    public void stop() {
```

```
        panel.stop();
        if (thread != null)
            thread = null;
}
/**
 * Called when user clicks in the applet
 * Force the browser to show the associated URL
 * MouseListener required methods*/
//////////////////////////////////////////////////////////
//////////////////////////////////////////////////////////
public void mouseClicked(MouseEvent e){}
public void mouseEntered(MouseEvent e){}
public void mouseExited(MouseEvent e){}

public void mouseReleased(MouseEvent e){}


public void mousePressed(MouseEvent e)
{

    if (url[current] != null)
    {
        System.out.println("current " + url[current]);
        getAppletContext().showDocument (url[current]);
    }
}


//////////////////////////////////////////////////////////
//////////////////////////////////////////////////////////

}
```

2. Create an HTML document that contains the applet. Create a new file called **howto1010.html** that contains the following code:

```
<head>
<title>Java Advertiser</title>
</head>
<applet code="Advertiser.class" width=262 height=50>
<param name=T1 value="T1.gif,1000,0,http://www.zdnet.com /">
<param name=T2 value="T2.gif,3000,1,http://home.netscape.com/ ">
<param name=T3 value="T3.gif,3000,2,http://www.shoppingplanet
➡.com/">
<param name=T4 value="T4.gif,3000,3,http://www.insight.com/">
</applet>
<hr size=4>
</body>
```

3. Compile and test the applet. Compile the source by using **javac**. The applet must be accessed by a Java 1.1- or 1.2-supported browser. When the applet is executed, an advertiser banner is running, similarly to that in

Example 7.6. Click on an ad when it is visible, and the browser goes to that Web page. In addition, the URL is displayed to `System.out` whenever the panel is clicked.

Figure 10.10 shows a snapshot of the running applet.

Figure 10.10 A banner contains links to the URL of a commercial site.

How It Works

The Advertiser applet is similar to that of Chapter 7. It contains two classes: the `Banner` class and the `Advertiser` class. The `Banner` class runs as a separate thread and implements the banner transition effects. As in Chapter 7, four transition effects are supported.

The `Advertiser` class is the applet itself and also runs as a separate thread. It manages the `Banner` class by directing it to perform transition effects defined by the user in the applet parameters. The `init()` method creates an instance of the `Banner` class and adds it to the center of the applet's panel. The `init()` method then parses up to 10 applet parameters. The number of applet parameters can be altered to suit the programmer. Each parameter is retrieved by using the `getParameter()` method.

Next, a `StringTokenizer` object is used to split the parameter into four fields. The first three fields are the same as in Example 7.6. The last field is a standard URL. The URL string in the parameter is used to create a `URL` object by invoking the `URL` constructor. The `URL` constructor throws `malformedURLException`, which must be caught and handled. The URLs are maintained in an array paralleling the arrays holding the images, effect types, and display times. The variable `NBanners` keeps the total number of banners.

The `run()` method constantly invokes the `Banner.effect()` method with the current effect type and the current image as arguments. The variable contains the index of the current banner displayed. The `start()` and `stop()` methods start and stop the threads used in the applet.

The `mousePressed()` method is called when the user clicks in the applet. When the user clicks a banner, the `showDocument()` method is invoked, with the current URL as an argument. This causes the Web browser to show the document specified by the URL.

Comments

showDocument() is a method in the AppletContext interface; it defines the services and information an applet can obtain from the browser in which it is running. The method Applet.getAppletContext() returns AppletContext for an applet.

There are two forms of showDocument(); they are listed in Table 10.1. The version of showDocument() used in this example causes destruction of the applet because the page containing it is replaced by the document displayed. The applet can display a page in a separate frame by using the version of showDocument() that takes a target frame as an argument. It is interesting to note that a hidden applet could be created in a frame of zero size. The applet can display a page in a separate frame or window, such as a navigation window separate from the browser window.

Table 10.1 showDocument Methods

METHOD	DESCRIPTION
showDocument(URL url)	Replaces the Web page currently being viewed with the given URL. This method may be ignored by applet contexts that are not browsers.
showDocument(URL url, String target)	Requests that the browser or Appletviewer show the Web page indicated by the URL argument. The target argument indicates where to display the frame. The target argument is interpreted as follows: "_self" : show in the current frame; "_parent" : show in the parent frame; "_top" : show in the topmost frame; "_blank" : show in a new unnamed top-level window; and name : show in a new top-level window named name. A new top-level window is created only if there isn't a window or frame with that name already; otherwise, the document is displayed there.

10.11 How do ...
Translate host names to Internet addresses?

Problem

I want to write an application, similar to the UNIX **nslookup** utility, that determines the Internet address associated with a host name. I know how to accept user input using an editable text field and displaying results in a non-editable text area. I want to use these techniques to implement the lookup application. To print the Internet addresses, I need to translate host names to Internet addresses. How do I translate host names to Internet addresses?

Technique

The class **InetAddress** contains several methods for dealing with Internet addresses. This class is declared final, so it cannot be extended. The static **getByName()** method returns an **InetAddress** object, given a string containing a host name. The **InetAddress.toString()** method can be used to create a string representation in the familiar dotted-decimal notation. User input is taken from an editable text field, and output is displayed in a noneditable text area by using techniques from Chapter 5, "Events and Parameters."

Steps

1. Create the application source file. Create a new file called **Lookup.java** and enter the following source:

```
import java.awt.*;
import java.awt.event.*;
import java.net.*;
import java.applet.*;

/*
 * Lookup application class
 */
public class Lookup extends Applet implements ActionListener  {

/*
 * text field for host name
 */
TextField nameField;

Button btnLookup;
```

```
/*
 * text area for displaying Internet addresses
 */
TextArea addrArea;

/*
 * instance of InetAddress needed for name-to-address
 * translation
 */
InetAddress inetAddr;

/*
 * insertion point in the Internet address
 * text area
 */
int insertIndex;

/*
 * constructor creates user interface
 */
public void init () {

    super.init ();

    setLayout (new BorderLayout ());

    Panel editPanel = new Panel ();
    editPanel.setLayout (new BorderLayout ());
    editPanel.add ("North", new Label ("Host name"));
    nameField = new TextField ("", 32);
    btnLookup = new Button("Lookup");
    editPanel.add ("Center", nameField);
    editPanel.add ("South", btnLookup);

    add ("North", editPanel);

    Panel areaPanel = new Panel ();
    areaPanel.setLayout (new BorderLayout ());
    addrArea = new TextArea ("", 24, 32);
    addrArea.setEditable (false);
    areaPanel.add ("North", new Label ("Internet address"));
    areaPanel.add ("Center", addrArea);

    add ("Center", areaPanel);
    btnLookup.addActionListener(this);

    insertIndex = 0;

    setSize (300, 200);
}

    public void actionPerformed(ActionEvent ev)
    {
        String name = nameField.getText ();
        try
```

```
    {
        inetAddr = InetAddress.getByName (name);
        String str = inetAddr.toString () + "\n";
        addrArea.insert (str, insertIndex);
        insertIndex += str.length ();
    } catch (UnknownHostException ex)
        {
            String str = name + "/ No such host\n";
            addrArea.insert (str, insertIndex);
            insertIndex += str.length ();
        }
}

} // end of Applet
```

2. Create an HTML document that contains the applet. Create a new file called `howto1011.html` that contains the following code:

```
<html>
<head>
<title>Lookup Internet Address</title>
</head>
<applet code="Lookup.class" width=300 height=200>
</applet>
<hr size=4>

</html>
```

3. Compile and test the application. Compile the source by using `javac`. You can also run `Lookup.java` as an applet by typing

```
appletviewer howto1011.html
```

When Lookup is executed, a window opens, with a text field and a text area. Type the host name desired and click the Lookup button. The IP address for the host name is determined and printed in the text area. Figure 10.11 shows a snapshot of the running application. If you get a security exception message when running this applet, it is because permission has not been given to run it. See Chapter 11, "Miscellaneous and Advanced Topics," for examples of how to control the permissions on your machine.

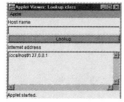

Figure 10.11 The `inetAddr` class provides functionality to deal with the IP addresses.

How It Works

The Lookup applet contains only one class, `Lookup` itself. The `Lookup` class extends the `Applet` class similarly to previous application examples.

Two panels are created, one containing `TextField` and one containing `TextArea`. The first panel contains a label at the top, a text field in the center, and a button at the bottom. The second panel contains a label at the top and a noneditable text area in the center. This second panel is added to the center of the frame. `BorderLayout` is used for both the frame and the panels.

The `actionPerformed()` method is called when the user enters a host name in the text field and clicks the Lookup button. The text in the text field is retrieved by using the `TextField.getText()` method and passed as an argument to `InetAddress.getByName()` method. This returns an instance of `InetAddress`. This instance of `InetAddress` is used to retrieve the Internet address as a string in decimal dot notation by using the `InetAddress.toString()` method. The Internet address is displayed in the text area by invoking the `insert()` method. An insert index is maintained to keep track of the insert position in the text area.

`InetAddress.getByName()` throws `UnknownHostException` if the host name given does not exist. This exception must be caught and handled. In this example, the message `no such host` is printed.

Comments

The `InetAddress` class is declared final so that it cannot be extended. This is done for security reasons.

COMPLEXITY

ADVANCED

10.12 How do I...
Create a socket?

Problem

I want to write an application that determines whether a remote host is running. If I can open an Internet socket on a known port, such as the Telnet port, that will tell me that the remote machine is running. I can use `TextField` to take the host name as input and `TextArea` to print the results. I don't know how to open a socket. How do I open a socket?

Technique

The java.net package contains a class—called Socket—for handling Internet sockets. A constructor is defined for creating a socket, given the host name and port number. The host name is of type **string**, and the port number is of type **int**. To open a socket, an instance of Socket must be declared and then created by using the Socket constructor.

Steps

1. Create the application source file. Create a new file called Ping.java and enter the following source:

```
import java.awt.*;
import java.awt.event.*;
import java.io.*;
import java.net.*;

/*
 * application class
 */
public class Ping extends Frame implements Runnable,
➡ActionListener {

/*
 * instance of Socket used for determining
 * whether remote host is alive
 */
Socket socket;

/*
 * hostname text entry field
 */
TextField addrField;

/*
 * the stop button
 */
Button stopButton;
Button startButton;

/*
 * the text area for printing remote
 * host status
 */
TextArea content;

/*
 * thread used to decouple user activity
 * from socket activity
 */
Thread thread;
```

```
/*
 * text area insert position
 */
int insertPos;

/*
 * constructor creates user interface
 */
public Ping () {

    int i;

    setTitle ("Ping");
    setLayout(new BorderLayout());

    addrField = new TextField ("", 20);
    startButton = new Button ("Start");
    stopButton = new Button ("Stop");
    content = new TextArea ("", 24, 80);
    content.setEditable (false);
    insertPos = 0;

    Panel p = new Panel ();
    p.setLayout (new FlowLayout ());
    p.add (addrField);
    p.add (startButton);
    p.add (stopButton);

    startButton.addActionListener(this);
    stopButton.addActionListener(this);
    addWindowListener(new WindowCloser());


    add ("North", p);
    add ("Center", content);

    thread = new Thread (this);

    setSize (400, 300);
    show ();
}

/**
 * handle action events
 * Enter keypress starts socket open thread
 * Stop button click stops socket thread
 * @param evt - event object
 * @param obj - object receiving this event
 */
public void actionPerformed (ActionEvent ev)
{
    Object object1 = ev.getSource();
    if (object1 == startButton)
    {
        if (thread != null)
            thread = null;
        thread = new Thread (this);
```

```
            thread.start ();
        }
        if (object1 == stopButton)
        {
            if (thread!= null)
                thread = null;
        }
}

/*
 * socket open thread
 * tries to open the telnet port (23)
 */
public void run () {

    String name;

    name = addrField.getText ();
        try {
                try {
                        socket = new Socket (name, 23);
                } catch (UnknownHostException e) {
                        insertString (name+" :unknown host\n");
                        return;
                }
        } catch (IOException e2) {
                insertString ("Unable to open socket\n");
                return;
        }

    insertString (name + " is alive\n");
    try {
        socket.close ();
        } catch (IOException e2) {
                insertString ("IOException closing socket\n");

                return;
        }
}

/**
 * helper method for adding text to the end
 * of the text area
 * @param s - text to add
 */
void insertString (String s) {

    content.insert (s, insertPos);
    insertPos += s.length ();
}

/**
 * application entry point
 * @param args - command-line arguments
 */
public static void main (String args[]) {
```

```
        new Ping ();
    }
}

class WindowCloser extends WindowAdapter
{
    public void windowClosing(WindowEvent e)
    {
        Window win = e.getWindow();
        win.setVisible(false);
        win.dispose();
        System.exit(0);
    }
}
```

2. Compile and test the application. Compile the source by using `javac`. Test the application by entering the following command:

```
java Ping
```

When Ping is executed, a window opens, with an editable text field. Enter a host name in the text field and click the Start button. A message should soon appear in the center text area, reporting the status of the remote host. Figure 10.12 shows an example of the running application. This program runs only as an application.

Figure 10.12 The Socket class enables a Java program to open a socket on another host.

How It Works

There is only one source file: `Ping.java`. It contains only one class: `Ping`. `Ping` extends `Frame` so that it creates a window frame for drawing. It also implements `Runnable` so that a separate thread can be used for opening the socket. This allows the user to stop the open attempt if a host does not respond.

An instance of class `Socket` is defined along with a text field, a text area, a Start button, a Stop button, and a thread. The variable `insertPos` maintains the current insert position for the text area.

The `Ping` constructor creates the user interface with a separate panel for the host name text field and the Start and Stop buttons. This panel is added to the top of the application frame. The text area is added to the center of the application frame. An instance of the thread is created for use later.

The `actionPerformed()` method handles action events. If the user enters a new host name and clicks the Start button, the thread currently running is stopped and a new thread is created and started.

The `run()` method contains the code for the thread. When it starts, it gets the host name from the text field by using `TextField.getText()` and attempts to open a socket with the given host name and port number 23. This version of the `Socket` constructor throws `UnknownHostException`, which must be caught. If this exception occurs, the host name along with `"unknown host"` is displayed. The `Socket` constructor also throws `IOException` in the event that a network-related error occurred. This must also be caught. An error message is displayed in this case.

If no exceptions are thrown, the socket was successfully opened, meaning that the remote host is running with a waiting telnet daemon. A `"host is alive"` message is printed, and the socket is closed by using the `Socket.close()` method. `Socket.close()` throws `IOException`, which must be caught. An error message is printed in this case for completeness.

The `insertString()` method inserts a given string at the end of the text area. It adds the length of the string to `insertPos` to maintain the end position of the text.

Comments

The UNIX `ping` utility performs more sophisticated communication tests to determine whether a host is running. This program is sufficient in many cases, but fails if a Telnet daemon is not running or not responding. The program could be extended to test for other ports such as `time`, `mail`, and `http`.

CHAPTER 11

MISCELLANEOUS AND ADVANCED TOPICS

11

MISCELLANEOUS AND ADVANCED TOPICS

How do I...

Java contains many rich features that make programming easier and more fun. The Java archive (JAR) files allow us to package applications and applets better. Security policy makes it possible to allow downloaded applets to do real work with minimal risk. Sets, maps, and lists make programming simpler and more reliable. Drawing cool graphics and printing them is easier and faster. In this chapter we will look at a whole set of varied but useful language features.

11.1 Place Programs in JAR Files

This example shows how to compress and store whole applets in a single file.

11.2 View the Contents of JAR Files

This example shows how to look inside compressed files.

11.3 Extract the Contents of JAR Files

Getting the code out of a JAR is at least as important as putting it in. In this example you will learn how to extract the code from a JAR file.

11.4 Modify the Contents of JAR Files

This is an example of changing metadata associated with a JAR.

11.5 Run Software in JAR Files

In this example you'll learn that you don't even have to extract programs from JARs to run them.

11.6 Allow Applets to Write to the Hard Drive

With this example you, too, can learn how to write to a hard drive the safe way.

11.7 Restrict the Permissions for Applications

This example shows how to restrict applications if you don't trust them.

11.8 Create Unique Lists of Items

Sets make it easy to create a unique collection or set.

11.9 Create a Collection That Allows Duplicates

Lists are collections that manage duplicates. They allow you to deal with duplicates easily.

11.10 Store Simple Pairs of Data for Quick Lookup

Maps connect a value to a unique key value. Maps make pairs of data, the key, and the value easy to create and manage.

11.11 Print Java Graphics

Printing graphics is not only possible, but easy.

11.12 Draw by Using Java2D

This example improves the looks of your application with powerful graphics classes.

11.1 How do I...
Place programs in JAR files?

Problem

What is a JAR file? I need to distribute my code to the users and I have heard that a JAR file is the way to do it. Why do I need a JAR file? How do I place my programs in one?

Technique

A JAR file is a file that can contain other files. It stores data in a compressed format. There are many benefits of storing your programs this way:

- *Security*—At times it is necessary to give applets permission to write to your hard drive, read from your hard drive, and so on. It would be unwise to open your computer and allow anyone on the Internet to have these privileges. What is needed is a way for you to verify that an applet was sent by someone you trust and not subsequently altered. Java provides a method called *code signing* to accomplish this.

  In order to sign your code, you must place it in a JAR file. If someone has set up his or her security to accept programs signed by you, your code can use facilities on that person's machine that are normally not allowed to downloaded programs.

- *Increased download speed*—The compression algorithms employed shrink your file and make it faster to download. In addition, if your application has sound and graphics files, they can be placed in the JAR and down-loaded together with the rest of the code.

- *Package versioning*—JAR files contain manifests. A manifest contains all the metadata about the JAR. Included in the manifest is a place for you to store the vendor and version information.

- *Portability*—A JAR file can be created on one platform and downloaded to another platform without modification or translation.

In this example we'll create a JAR file and place a set of files in it.

Steps

1. Copy the file `GetInetFile.class` from the CD-ROM (in the directory for material from Chapter 11) to your directory. Type the following command at the command line:

```
jar cvf  testjar.jar  GetInetFile.class
```

The meaning of the component parts of this command are

- jar—Invokes the JAR tool to process this file.

- c—Creates a new JAR file.

- v—Provides verbose feedback during the JAR file creation process.

- f—Indicates that the output of this process is a file. The default output of the c command is the standard output, the f command must be specified to direct the output to a file, whose name is given by the second argument.

Upon running this command, you will see feedback similar to that shown in Figure 11.1.

Figure 11.1 The JAR tool can compress your application and applet files into a package ready for downloading.

The **added manifest** message indicates that a file called the manifest has been created and stored in the JAR. The word *manifest* is used in the transportation industry to indicate the contents of a ship, as in ship's manifest. It describes the cargo in the hold of the ship. Similarly, the manifest of a JAR file describes the contents of the JAR.

Next we see the following line:

```
adding: GetInetFile.class <in=2364> <out=1307> <deflated 44%>
```

This line appears once for every file that is placed in the JAR. The input size is listed, as is the output size. The compression ration is expressed as (in–out)/in. In this case, it is (2364–1307)/2364=.447, or 44.7%.

2. Copy the file `Advertiser.class` from the CD-ROM (in the directory for material from Chapter 11) to your directory. Type the following command:

```
jar cvf  testjar2.jar Advertiser.class images
```

This command is the same as the preceding JAR command except for the addition of the word `images`. This is the name of a directory. If the JAR tool sees a directory name on the command line, it knows to include all the files in the directory using the same directory structure. Figure 11.2 shows the output from this process.

Figure 11.2 The JAR file may include a directory structure in addition to the actual files.

How It Works

Notice how the class file is added just as it was in the preceding example. Next, all the files from the images directory are added. The `images/` in front of the filename shows that this file is in a subdirectory.

COMPLEXITY
BEGINNING

11.2   How do I...
View the contents of JAR files?

Problem

I have created several JAR files on my hard drive. I have trouble keeping up with the contents of each of them. How do I find out what files are included in a JAR file?

Technique

Luckily, this is very straightforward. The same JAR tool that places files in JARs can also be used to peer inside them to inquire about the contents of the JAR.

Steps

1. Type the following at the command line:

```
jar tf  testjar.jar
```

The meaning of this command is as follows:

- jar—The JAR tool.

- t—Indicates that you want to examine the table of contents.

- f—Indicates that you want to see the file whose name is on the command line. Without the f option, the JAR tool will read the jar file from its standard input.

- testjar.jar—The name of the JAR.

This will cause the jar tool to look inside the JAR and tell us what is in there, as shown in Figure 11.3.

Figure 11.3 The tf option of the JAR tool allows you to inquire as to the contents of a JAR file.

The first line indicates that the directory META-INF has been created. It may seem strange that a file can contain a directory, but it is true nonetheless.

The second line is the file MANIFEST.MF. This is the manifest file spoken of earlier in this chapter.

Finally, you can see your file, GetInetFile.class, stored in the JAR.

2. Next, look the second JAR file that we created by typing the following at the command line:

```
jar tf  testjar2.jar
```

This JAR file contains more data than the previous one, as shown in Figure 11.4.

Figure 11.4 Files and directories are stored in the same JAR file.

After the now-familiar manifest information, the class file is listed. It is followed by a directory named **images**. Next, each of the images in this directory is listed.

How It Works

The jar tool contains many features. In this instance, we use the jar tool to peer inside a package to tell us about its contents.

COMPLEXITY

BEGINNING

11.3 How do I...
Extract the contents of JAR files?

Problem

Now I have all these great JAR files on my hard drive. I am really enjoying looking at their contents. What I would really like to do, though, is to get them out of this JAR file so that I can use them. How do I extract the contents of a JAR file?

Technique

It is not always necessary to extract the files from a JAR to use them. For now, though, we will assume that we have a need to turn them back into operating system files. Not surprisingly, the jar tool provides this functionality also.

Steps

1. Type the following command on the command line:

```
del GetInetFile.class
```

This deletes the class file from the directory.

2. Next, type the following command:

```
jar xf testjar.jar
```

Now, if you check for the **GetInetFile.class** file in the directory, you will find it there, as shown in Figure 11.5. You will also find that the directory **META-INF** containing the manifest file is also restored from the JAR file.

Figure 11.5 The JAR tool can be used to extract files from the JAR also.

How It Works

The jar tool can be used to convert jar files into operating system files for situations that require this. One such instance would be to move the file into another jar file.

11.4   How do I...
Modify the contents of JAR files?

Problem

Earlier you said that I can record vendor and version numbers in the JAR file. I don't know how to do that. Can you show me how?

Technique

If you had to make a wild guess which tool is used to add this meta-information to the JAR file, I bet you would guess the JAR tool. You would be correct. There are special commands that modify the manifest. The JAR tool automatically places the default manifest in the JAR when it is created.

Steps

1. Create a file using a text editor that contains the information you want to add to the manifest. Create a file that contains the following information, and call it **versInfo**:

```
Name: GetInetFile.class
Implementation-Title: "Get Inet File"
Implementation-Version: "build44"
Implementation-Vendor: "XYZ, Inc."
```

2. Enter the following at the command line:

```
jar umf versInfo testjar.jar
```

The command can be broken down as follows:

- u—Updates this JAR instead of creating a new one.

- m—Modifies the manifest file.

- f—Looks for a filename on the command line.

3. Now you are ready to see if it worked. To examine the contents of the manifest, type the following command:

```
jar xf testjar.jar
```

This extracts all the files in this JAR, including the manifest, which will be stored in the file named /META-INF/manifest.mf. The contents of this file can be seen by issuing a **type** or **cat** command, depending on your platform, as shown in Figure 11.6.

Figure 11.6 The manifest can be updated and viewed as a file if it is extracted from the JAR file.

How It Works

The general form of an entry in the manifest is *name:value*. For a detailed description of the manifest format, go to the Web site www.java.sun.com and do a search on the keyword manifest.

COMPLEXITY
INTERMEDIATE

11.5   How do I...
Run software in JAR files?

Problem

I have heard that it is possible to run software that is stored in a JAR file without ever extracting it. This would be great for my applications. How do I do that?

Technique

It is possible to allow the users to run your code from within a JAR file without ever requiring them to extract it. This only works, however, if you package it correctly. The purpose of this example is to show you how to package the JAR file and then to run it in order to prove that it works.

Steps

1. Create a text file with the following code, and call it `Lines.java`:

```java
import java.applet.Applet;
import java.awt.*;

/**
 * class LineColors holds 24 color values
 */
class LineColors {

/**
 * color[] array holds the colors to be used
 */
Color color[];

/**
 * class constructor
 * initializes the color array using an arbitrary algorithm
 */
public LineColors () {

    color = new Color[24];
    int i, rgb;

    rgb = 0xff;
    for (i=0; i<24; i+=1) {
        color[i] = new Color (rgb);
        rgb <<= 1;
        if ((rgb & 0x1000000) != 0) {
            rgb |= 1;
            rgb &= 0xffffff;
        }
    }
}
}

/**
 * class describing one line segment
 */
class Segment {

/*
 * x1, y1 - starting coordinates for this segment
 * x2, y2 - ending coordinates for this segment
 * dx1,...dy2 - velocities for the endpoints
 * whichcolor - the current index into color array
 * width, height - width and height of bounding panel
 * LC - instance of LineColors class
 */
double x1, y1, x2, y2;
double dx1, dy1, dx2, dy2;
int whichcolor, width, height;
LineColors LC;
```

```
/**
 * class constructor
 * initialize endpoints and velocities to random values
 * @param w - width of bounding panel
 * @param h - height of bounding panel
 * @param c - starting color index
 * @param lc - instance of LineColors class
 */
public Segment (int w, int h, int c, LineColors lc) {

    whichcolor = c;
    width = w;
    height = h;
    LC = lc;
    x1 = (double) w * Math.random ();
    y1 = (double) h * Math.random ();
    x2 = (double) w * Math.random ();
    y2 = (double) h * Math.random ();

    dx1 = 5 - 10 * Math.random ();
    dy1 = 5 - 10 * Math.random ();
    dx2 = 5 - 10 * Math.random ();
    dy2 = 5 - 10 * Math.random ();
}

/*
 * increment color index
 * calculate the next endpoint position for this segment
 */
void compute () {

    whichcolor += 1;
    whichcolor %= 24;

    x1 += dx1;
    y1 += dy1;
    x2 += dx2;
    y2 += dy2;

    if (x1 < 0 || x1 > width) dx1 = -dx1;
    if (y1 < 0 || y1 > height) dy1 = -dy1;
    if (x2 < 0 || x2 > width) dx2 = -dx2;
    if (y2 < 0 || y2 > height) dy2 = -dy2;
}

/**
 * draw the line segment using the current color
 * @param g - destination graphics object
 */
void paint (Graphics g) {

    g.setColor (LC.color [whichcolor]);
    g.drawLine ((int) x1, (int) y1, (int) x2, (int) y2);
}
}
```

```
/**
 * The applet/application proper
 */
public class Lines extends Applet {

/*
 * Nlines - number of line segments to be displayed
 * lines - array of instances of Segment class
 * LC - instance of LineColors class
 */
int width,height;
final int NLines = 4;
Segment lines[] = new Segment[NLines];
LineColors LC = new LineColors ();

/**
 * init is called when the applet is loaded
 * save the width and height
 * create instances of Segment class
 */
public void init () {

    setLayout(null);
    width = 300;
    height = 300;
    setSize(width, height);

    int i;
    for (i=0; i<NLines; i+=1)
        lines[i] = new Segment (width, height, (2*i) % 24, LC);
}

/**
 * recompute the next endpoint coordinates for each line
 * invoke paint() method for each line
 * call repaint() to force painting 50ms later
 * @param g - destination graphics object
 */
public void paint (Graphics g) {

    int i;
    for (i=0; i<NLines; i+=1) {
        lines[i].compute ();
        lines[i].paint (g);
    }
    repaint (50);
}

}
```

2. Create the following HTML file and call it HowTo115.html:

```
<head>
<title>Lines</title>
</head>
<applet code="Lines.class"
```

```
                    archive="Test2.jar"
                    width=262 height=250>
</applet>
<hr size=4>
</body>
```

3. Compile the file by using the following command:

```
Javac Lines.java
```

4. Create a file called **mainClass** and add the following line:

```
Main-Class: Lines
```

This file will be used to set a manifest property called **Main-Class**.

5. Type the following on the command line:

```
jar cmf mainClass test2.jar Lines.class
```

The breakdown of this command line is as follows:

- c—Creates the JAR file.

- m—Modifies the manifest also.

- f—Looks for a filename on the command line.

mainClass is the file you created to hold the property.

Test2.jar is the JAR filename.

Lines.class is the name of the class file to add to the JAR.

6. Delete the **Lines.class** file from the directory by typing the following:

```
del  Lines.class
```

This is so that you will know that the class file that is running is really in the JAR.

7. Type the following at the command line:

```
appletviewer HowTo115.html
```

The result is shown in Figure 11.7.

Figure 11.7
Programs can be
executed from
within JARs if the
JARs were created
properly.

Comments

The Main-Class manifest property is necessary only with the Java 1.2 interpreter when using the -jar switch.

COMPLEXITY
INTERMEDIATE

11.6 How do I...
Allow applets to write to the hard drive?

Problem

I want to be able to download an applet to my client's machine that will create a
file on his or her hard drive. I was told that this is now possible with Java 1.2.
How to I do this?

Technique

As of Java 1.2, it is now possible for an applet to write to the hard drive of a
client machine. This is tempered by the requirement that the owner of the
client machine give explicit permission for your applet to perform this task.
Java 1.2 contains a set of tools used to grant these permissions through the
policy file.

Prior to Java 1.2, the security policy was hard-coded in the security manager used by Java applications. The policy is now recorded in a file format in simple ASCII. It can be modified directly, or via any tool that is written to this format. It is recommended that you use the tools that are described here to alter this file.

Steps

1. The first thing we need to do is to run an applet that will prove to us that an applet will not be allowed to write to your hard drive without permission. To do this, type the following command at your command line:

```
appletviewer http://java.sun.com/docs/books/tutorial/
security1.2/tour1/example-1dot2/WriteFile.html
```

This file is provided by JavaSoft to write to your hard drive if your security file allows it. Running it causes the Appletviewer application to display the message shown in Figure 11.8.

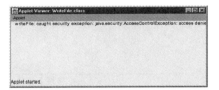

Figure 11.8 The Java Virtual Machine detects an unauthorized attempt to write to the disk and returns an error message.

This will always be the result of running an applet unless you give explicit permission for your platform to allow writes on your drive.

2. In order to give this permission, you invoke the **policytool** application by typing the following at the command line:

```
policytool
```

This will bring up the window shown in Figure 11.9.

When the policy tool is started, it looks for a policy file in your home directory. This file is called **java.policy**. If this file is not found, an error message appears and a blank interface appears on the screen. This is normal the first time you run the policy tool.

3. Create a new policy file by using the policy tool; click Add Policy Entry on the main Policy Tool window. Figure 11.10 shows the result.

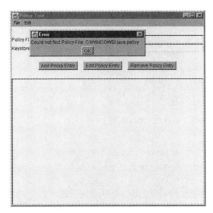

Figure 11.9 The policy tool will try to find an existing policy file. If it doesn't find it, an error message displays.

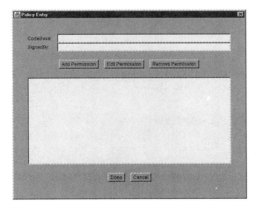

Figure 11.10 The policy file controls access to your machine through Java.

4. Type the following string in the text field labeled CodeBase:

```
http://java.sun.com/docs/books/tutorial/
➥security1.2/tour1/example-1dot2/
```

5. Leave the SignedBy box blank and press the Add Permission button. This brings up the dialog box shown in Figure 11.11.

There are six data entry areas in the Permissions dialog:

- The permission selection list box allows the user to select what kind of permission is to be granted.

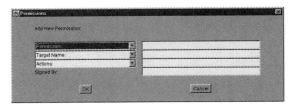

Figure 11.11 The Add Permission button brings up the Permissions dialog box.

- The permission text box shows what permission was chosen.

- Target Name is the name of the object that is being granted permission.

- The Target text box shows what target was chosen.

- The action is shown in the third text box. Write permission is being granted in this example.

- The Signed By box shows what code signer has this permission.

6. Pull down the Permission list box and select File Permission. Next to the Target Name list box, type **writetest**. Select Write from the Actions list box. Your dialog should look like the one shown in Figure 11.12.

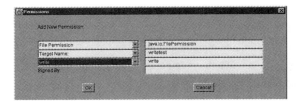

Figure 11.12 The file permission allows a write to the disk.

7. Click on the OK button. This brings up the policy entry tool, with the entries shown in Figure 11.13.

The Policy Entry dialog contains three data areas:

- The CodeBase text box shows what site is being given permission in this policy entry. It may be left blank.

- The SignedBy text box shows who is being given permission in this policy entry.

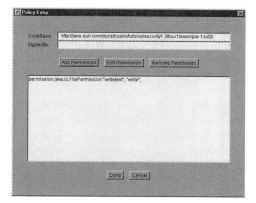

Figure 11.13 The policy entry tool
allows new permissions to be extended.

- The large unlabeled area at the bottom shows the existing policies
  in this policy file. After you add your entry, it will appear here.

8. Click the Done button and observe what has been written in the policy
tool's text fields. This is shown in Figure 11.14.

Figure 11.14 The text field shows
the privileges that have been
extended.

9. Choose Save As from the Policy Tool menu and save the file as
`C:\Test\mypolicy`.

10. Exit the policy tool.

Now we are ready to test our applications again and see whether the policy file allows the applet to write to the disk. There are two approaches to doing this: command file arguments and policy file modification. Let's look at the command-line option first:

1. Move to C:\Test.

2. Type the following command on the command line:

```
appletviewer -J-Djava.security.policy=mypolicy
http://java.sun.com/docs/books/tutorial/security1.2/tour1/
    example-1dot2/WriteFile.html
```

Type this all on one line and don't add any spaces. If you are using a DOS window, place it in a .BAT file and run that file.

-J tells Appletviewer that adjusting parameters are present.

-D tells Appletviewer that special security instructions follow.

The java.security.policy= entry tells which policy file is to be used.

The result is shown in Figure 11.15.

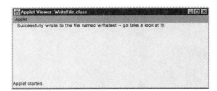

Figure 11.15 The file is written successfully if the policy is correctly created.

If you look at the file called writetest in that same directory, you will see that the write worked. You have just gotten out of the sandbox. Be frightened; be very frightened! Seriously, there is a need to be cautious when granting permissions. Obviously, if you let all applets from all sources have all permissions, then it will be only a matter of time before you contract a virus. Careful permission granting can be very useful though, especially in an intranet where you control both the client and the server.

The second way to allow an applet to have permissions is to place the policy in your java.security file located under your java.home directory.

CAUTION

Depending on what Java products you install on your system, you may find several java.security files. The correct one is under java.home. To do this follow these steps:

1. Open `java.security` in a text editor capable of editing a pure text file. WordPad and Notepad immediately come to mind.

2. Locate the following lines in this file:

```
policy.url.1=file:${java.home}/lib/security/java.policy
policy.url.2=file:${user.home}/.java.policy
```

3. Immediately below the second line, add this line:

```
policy.url.3=file:/C:/Test/mypolicy
```

Whenever you run an applet, or an application with a security manager, the policy files that are loaded and used by default are the ones specified in the security properties file. The mechanism for doing this is to add another `policy.url` entry. These entries cause policy files to be loaded and used with every attempt to run an application or applet.

Test the applet again. If the command-line version worked and this does not, you can bet dollars to doughnuts that you edited the wrong `java.security` file.

How It Works

The policy file serves as an instruction set for the java system. It looks in this file to determine if you want an application or applet to be able to operate in your system.

COMPLEXITY
INTERMEDIATE

11.7 How do I...
Restrict the permissions for applications?

Problem

In prior versions of Java, my applications had all permissions. They could inquire about the system, read and write files, and so on. I could not find a way to restrict this. Is it now possible to restrict the permissions of an application?

Technique

A security manager is not automatically working to restrict applications the way that it is for applets. You may, however, provide a security policy for applications if you choose. This example walks you through this process.

Steps

1. Type in the following code, and name the file **ReadProperties.java**:

```java
import java.lang.*;

class ReadProperties {

    public static void main(String[] args) {

        String str;

        try {

            str = System.getProperty("os.name",
➥"not specified");
System.out.println("  OS name: " + str);

            str = System.getProperty("java.version",
➥"not specified");
System.out.println("  JVM Version: " + str);

            str = System.getProperty("user.home",
➥"not specified");
System.out.println("  user.home: " + str);

            str = System.getProperty("java.home",
➥"not specified");
System.out.println("  java.home: " + str);

        } catch (Exception e) {
            System.err.println("Caught exception "
➥+ e.toString());
}
    }
}
```

2. Compile the **ReadProperties.java** file by using **javac**.

3. Run the program by typing the following:

```
java  ReadProperties
```

The following output, or something close to it, should appear:

```
OS name: Windows 95
JVM Version: 1.2
user.home: C:\WINDOWS
java.home: C:JDK1.2\JRE
```

4. Run the program again by using the default security manager, which you do by typing the following:

```
java -Djava.security.manager ReadProperties
```

Remember that the `java.security.policy=` entry tells which policy file is to be used.

Now the result looks different:

```
OS name: Windows 95
JVM Version: 1.2
Caught exception java.security.AccessControlException:
➡   access denied (java.util.PropertyPermission user.home read)
```

This indicates that the program asked for something that it wasn't supposed to, according to the security manager. This file is the default `java.policy` file for a Java 1.2 system.

```
// Standard extensions get all permissions by default

grant codeBase "file:${java.home}/lib/ext/" {
        permission java.security.AllPermission;
};

// default permissions granted to all domains

grant {
        // allows anyone to listen on un-privileged ports
        permission java.net.SocketPermission "localhost:
➡1024-", "listen";

        // "standard" properties that can be read by anyone

        permission java.util.PropertyPermission
➡"java.version", "read";
permission java.util.PropertyPermission
➡"java.vendor", "read";
permission java.util.PropertyPermission
➡"java.vendor.url", "read";
permission java.util.PropertyPermission
➡"java.class.version", "read";
permission java.util.PropertyPermission
➡"os.name", "read";
permission java.util.PropertyPermission
➡"os.version", "read";
permission java.util.PropertyPermission
➡"os.arch", "read";
permission java.util.PropertyPermission
➡"file.separator", "read";
permission java.util.PropertyPermission
➡"path.separator", "read";
permission java.util.PropertyPermission
➡"line.separator", "read";

        permission java.util.PropertyPermission
➡"java.specification.version", "read";
permission java.util.PropertyPermission
➡"java.specification.vendor", "read";
permission java.util.PropertyPermission
```

```
➥"java.specification.name", "read";

        permission java.util.PropertyPermission
➥"java.vm.specification.version", "read";
permission java.util.PropertyPermission
➥"java.vm.specification.vendor", "read";
permission java.util.PropertyPermission
➥"java.vm.specification.name", "read";
permission java.util.PropertyPermission
➥"java.vm.version", "read";
permission java.util.PropertyPermission
➥"java.vm.vendor", "read";
permission java.util.PropertyPermission
➥"java.vm.name", "read";
};
```

Notice that **java.home** and **user.home** do not appear in this file. We could hack this file to add these properties, but that would not be wise. The best way to give permissions is via the policy tool.

5. Start the policy tool by typing the following at the command line:

```
policytool
```

Then choose File and Open. Name the file **C:\Test\mypolicy**. That will bring up the window shown in Figure 11.16.

Figure 11.16 The same policy file can be used for restricting access.

6. Click on Add Policy entry and type the following in the CodeBase text field:

```
file:/C:/Test/
```

This will give you a dialog box that looks like the one shown in Figure 11.17

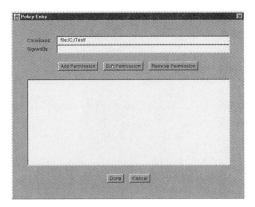

Figure 11.17 The CodeBase is the URL of the source of an applet or application.

7. Click the Add Permission button. Then add the values shown until the dialog looks like Figure 11.18.

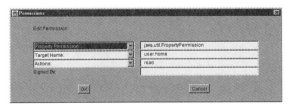

Figure 11.18 User.home is restricted by default.

8. Repeat this procedure for java.home, as shown in Figure 11.19.

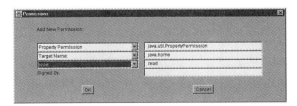

Figure 11.19 Java.home is another restricted system value.

9. Click Done to close the Add Permission dialog box. Save the policy file and exit.

10. Run the application again with the security manager on the command line. For this procedure to work, the application must be in the `C:\Test` directory:

```
java -Djava.security.manager -Djava.security.policy=
➥mypolicy ReadProperties
```

Note that the application can now read all the properties once again:

```
OS name: Windows 95
JVM Version: 1.2
user.home: C:\WINDOWS
java.home: C:JDK1.2\JRE
```

Next, remove the explicit reference to the security manager and run it again:

```
java  -Djava.security.manager ReadProperties
```

```
OS name: Windows 95
JVM Version: 1.2
user.home: C:\WINDOWS
java.home: C:JDK1.2\JRE
```

How It Works

The result is the same. This is because we already added `mypolicy` to the `java.security` file in Example 11.7. Now any permissions that we add to `mypolicy` will be reflected in the command-line calls.

Collections

The next several examples are concerned with the use of collections. Collections are the descendants of arrays; they are sets of items, but with rules of membership and methods to access and modify the contents. Table 11.1 lists the core collection interfaces.

Table 11.1   The Core Collection Interfaces

COLLECTION	DEFINITION
Collection	A group of objects.
Set	The familiar set abstraction. No duplicate elements are permitted.
List	An ordered collection.
Map	A mapping from keys to values.
SortedSet	A set whose elements are automatically sorted.
SortedMap	A map whose mappings are automatically sorted by key.

Table 11.2 lists concrete implementations of the core collections.

Table 11.2   Concrete Implementations of the Core Collections

IMPLEMENTATION	DEFINITION
HashSet	A set backed by a hash table. This class serves as a good general-purpose set implementation.
TreeSet	A balanced binary tree implementation of the SortedSet interface.
ArrayList	A resizable-array implementation of the List interface.
LinkedList	A doubly linked list.
HashMap	A hash table implementation of the Map interface.
TreeMap	A balanced binary tree implementation of the SortedMap interface.
Vector	A list with additional "legacy methods."
Hashtable	A synchronized hash table implementation of the Map interface.
WeakHashMap	A special-purpose implementation of the Map interface that stores only weak references to its keys. Weak references allow key-value pairs to be garbage-collected when the key is no longer referenced outside WeakHashMap.

In the examples that follow, you will see how to use collections to perform useful tasks.

COMPLEXITY

INTERMEDIATE

11.8   How do I...
Create unique lists of items?

Problem

I write a lot of applications where I must guarantee that the lists that I create have no duplicate methods. I know how to code this by hand, but isn't there some built-in mechanism to handle this situation?

Technique

There is indeed. As of version 1.2, Java now has several classes that are the rough equivalent of the Standard Template Library (STL) that C++ programmers have learned to love. One of the interfaces in this library is the **Set** interface. Classes that implement this interface can be used to guarantee that no duplicates are placed in a list.

Steps

1. Create the application source file. Create a new file called
WarningLetterSet.java and enter the following source:

```
import java.util.*;

public class WarningLetterSet
{
    public static void main(String args[])
    {
        // Create the lists of failing students
        String[] French = {"Amy", "Jose", "Jeremy",
➥"Alice", "Patrick"};

        String[] Algebra = {"Alan", "Amy", "Jeremy",
➥"Helen", "Alexi"};

        String[] History = {"Adel", "Aaron", "Amy",
➥"James", "Alice"};

        // Create the set to hold the failing students
        Set LettersHome = new HashSet();

        //Add the failing students from each class to the set
        for (int i=0; i< French.length; i++)
            LettersHome.add(French[i]);

        for (int j=0; j< Algebra.length; j++)
            LettersHome.add(Algebra[j]);

        for (int k=0; k< History.length; k++)
            LettersHome.add(History[k]);

        //Print out the number of letters to be sent and the
➥recipient list
        System.out.println(LettersHome.size()+" letters must be
➥sent to: "+LettersHome);

    }//Main
}//Warning Letters
```

2. Compile and test the application. Compile the source by using javac.

3. Run the application by typing the following:

```
Java  WarningLetterSet
```

This application might be used in a school where letters to parents go out
whenever a student is failing at least one course. If a student is failing
several courses, then only one letter should be sent. It is key to remove all
duplicates before sending letters. A set is ideal because sets don't allow
duplicates. If you try to add a duplicate, it will be rejected.

Figure 11.20 shows a snapshot of the running application.

Figure 11.20 Sets automatically reject duplicate entries.

How It Works

The first step is to create the lists of failing students:

```
String[] French = {"Amy", "Jose", "Jeremy", "Alice", "Patrick"};

String[] Algebra = {"Alan", "Amy", "Jeremy", "Helen", "Alexi"};

String[] History = {"Adel", "Aaron", "Amy", "James", "Alice"};
```

Next, we create a set to hold all of the names. We choose to create **HashSet** instead a **TreeSet** because of performance considerations:

```
Set LettersHome = new HashSet();
```

Next, we add the failing students from each class to the set. Notice that we add every element to the set and rely on it to discard the duplicates:

```
for (int i=0; i< French.length; i++)
    LettersHome.add(French[i]);

for (int j=0; j< Algebra.length; j++)
    LettersHome.add(Algebra[j]);

for (int k=0; k< History.length; k++)
    LettersHome.add(History[k]);
```

Next we print the number of letters to be sent and the recipient list. Notice that we don't manually iterate the set, but rather we refer to it by name, and it does its own iteration:

```
System.out.println(LettersHome.size()+" letters must be sent
➥to: "+LettersHome);
```

11.9 How do I...
Create a collection that allows duplicates?

Problem

I like the set example, but I need to be able to allow duplicates. The school that I work for wants to send a letter to the parents for each course that a student is failing. Thus, a single student could receive 2, 3,or even 4 letters (poor soul). Is there a neat and easy way to do this?

Technique

Yes there is. A list is just as convenient to use as a set, but it keeps all duplicates. It will be ideal for your purposes.

Steps

1. Create the application source file. Create a new file called WarningLetterList.java and enter the following source:

```
import java.util.*;

public class WarningLetterList
{
    public static void main(String args[])
    {
        // Create the lists of failing students
        String[] French = {"Amy", "Jose", "Jeremy",
"Alice", "Patrick"};

        String[] Algebra = {"Alan", "Amy", "Jeremy",
"Helen", "Alexi"};

        String[] History = {"Adel", "Aaron", "Amy",
"James", "Alice"};

        // Create the set to hold the failing students
        List LettersHome = new ArrayList();

        //Add the failing students from each class to the set
        for (int i=0; i< French.length; i++)
            LettersHome.add(French[i]);

        for (int j=0; j< Algebra.length; j++)
            LettersHome.add(Algebra[j]);

        for (int k=0; k< History.length; k++)
```

```
            LettersHome.add(History[k]);

        Collections.sort(LettersHome);

            //Print out the number of letters to be sent
    // and the recipient list
    System.out.println(LettersHome.size()+" letters must
    ➥be sent to: "+LettersHome);

        }//Main
    }//Warning Letters
```

2. Compile and run the application. Compile the source by using `javac`.

3. Type the following to run the application:

```
Java WarningLetterList
```

The list will preserve and print out the letters. Figure 11.21 shows a snapshot of the running application.

Figure 11.21 Lists allow duplicate entries.

How It Works

First, we declare a list to be `ArrayList()`:

```
List LettersHome = new ArrayList();
```

Next, we add the failing students from each class to the list just as we did for the set example, using the `add()` method:

```
for (int i=0; i< French.length; i++)
    LettersHome.add(French[i]);

for (int j=0; j< Algebra.length; j++)
    LettersHome.add(Algebra[j]);

for (int k=0; k< History.length; k++)
    LettersHome.add(History[k]);
```

For convenience in viewing, we will sort the `LettersHome` collection. This can be done in one single statement:

```
Collections.sort(LettersHome);
```

Once again, printing is trivial:

```
System.out.println(LettersHome.size()+" letters must be
➥sent to: "+LettersHome);
```

11.10 How do I...
Store simple pairs of data for quick lookup?

Problem

I want to build a quick system that tells me a student's name, given her Social Security number. I could create a database, but that seems like overkill. Is there any way to do a simple lookup list?

Technique

Yes there is. (If there weren't, you can be sure that this question would never have appeared in this book.) The `Map` interface was created for exactly such a purpose.

Steps

1. Create the application source file. Create a new file called `StudentIDMap.java` and enter the following source:

```java
import java.util.*;

public class StudentIDMap
{
    public static void main(String args[])
    {
        // Create the lists of failing students
        String[] SNames = {"Amy", "Jose", "Jeremy",
➥"Alice", "Patrick"};
        String[] ID = {"123456789", "259879864",
➥"988456997", "984876453", "9768696"};

        // Create the set to hold the failing students
        Map IDMap = new HashMap();

        //Add the failing students from each class to the set
        for (int i=0; i< SNames.length; i++)
            IDMap.put(ID[i],SNames[i]);
```

```
//Print out the student list
System.out.println(IDMap.size()+" Students entered: ");
System.out.println(IDMap);

}//Main
}//StudentIDMap
```

2. Compile and test the application. Compile the source by using `javac`.
Run the applications by typing the following at the command line:

```
java StudentIDMap
```

The result of the pairings is output to the screen. Figure 11.22 shows a
snapshot of the running application.

Figure 11.22 Maps create a pairing
between a key and another value.

How It Works

First, we will create two arrays: one for students and one for IDs. We depend
on the position in the list to associate the two elements:

```
String[] SNames = {"Amy", "Jose", "Jeremy", "Alice", "Patrick"};
String[] ID = {"123456789", "259879864", "988456997",
➥"984876453", "9768696"};
```

We will store them in `HashMap`, which is a map built on a hash table:

```
Map IDMap = new HashMap();
```

The `put()` function enters the pairs in the map:

```
for (int i=0; i< SNames.length; i++)
    IDMap.put(ID[i],SNames[i]);
```

Printing the results is trivial, as it is in the set and map examples:

```
System.out.println(IDMap.size()+" Students entered: ");
System.out.println(IDMap);
```

11.11 How do I...
Print Java graphics?

Problem

I have always wanted to print some of the graphics that I create. How can I create an application, put a button on it, and send a hard copy to the printer whenever I press the button?

Technique

A new set of printing classes has been added to Java as of version 1.2. The primary class, named `PrinterJob`, controls the printing. The other classes, `Book`, `PageFormat`, and `Paper`, are descriptive classes that provide instruction to `PrinterJob`.

Steps

1. Create the application source file. Create a new file called `PrintGraphics.java` and enter the following source:

```java
import java.awt.*;
import java.awt.event.*;

public class PrintGraphics extends Frame
➥implements ActionListener
{
    PrintCanvas canvas1;

    public PrintGraphics()
    {
        super("PrintGraphics");
        canvas1 = new PrintCanvas();
        add("Center", canvas1);

        Button b = new Button( "Print");
        b.setActionCommand("print");
        b.addActionListener(this);
        add("South",b);

        pack();

    }//constructor

    public void actionPerformed(ActionEvent e)
    {
        String cmd = e.getActionCommand();
        if (cmd.equals("print"))
        {
```

```
                PrintJob pjob = getToolkit().getPrintJob(this,
  ➥"PrintGraphics", null);
  if (pjob != null)
                {
                    Graphics pg = pjob.getGraphics();

                    if (pg != null)
                    {
                        canvas1.printAll(pg);
                        pg.dispose();
                    }//if
                    pjob.end();
                }//if

        }//if

    }//actionPerformed

    public static void main(String args[])
    {
        PrintGraphics test = new PrintGraphics();
        test.addWindowListener(new WindowCloser());
        test.show();

    }
}//class PrintGraphics

class PrintCanvas extends Canvas
{
    public Dimension getPreferredSize()
    {
        return new Dimension(200,200);
    }

    public void paint(Graphics g)
    {
        Rectangle r = getBounds();

        g.setColor(Color.yellow);
        g.fillRect(0,0, r.width, r.height);

        g.setColor(Color.blue);
        g.drawString("Hello, World", 100, 100);

        g.setColor(Color.red);
        g.drawLine(0,100,100,0);
        g.fillOval(135,140,15,15);
    }

}//class PrintCanvas

class WindowCloser extends WindowAdapter
{
    public void windowClosing(WindowEvent e)
    {
        Window win = e.getWindow();
```

```
                  win.setVisible(false);
                  win.dispose();
                  System.exit(0);
            }//windowClosing
      }//class WindowCloser
```

2. Compile and test the application. Compile the source by using `javac`.

You can run the file by typing the following at the command line:

```
java PrintGraphics
```

Figure 11.23 shows a snapshot of the running application.

Figure 11.23
Graphics may
be printed
from within a
Java applica-
tion.

How It Works

The first interesting declaration is the creation of a `PrintCanvas` object called
`canvas1`. This canvas holds the graphics that we want to print:

```
PrintCanvas canvas1;
```

The real action takes place in the event handler for the print button. When
this button is pressed, a `PrintJob` object is created and made to point to the
peer's printing facilities:

```
PrintJob pjob = getToolkit().getPrintJob(this, "PrintGraphics", null);
```

Next, a graphics object is created and made into a handle to the `PrintJob`
object:

```
Graphics pg = pjob.getGraphics();
```

If all that works well, the `printAll` method will be used to send the
graphics to the printer. The `printAll` method simply calls the `print` method of
all components, which in turn calls the `paint` method with the print graphics:

```
canvas1.printAll(pg);
```

It is now time to clean up by releasing both the `Graphics` the `PrintJob` objects. Each `PrintJob.getGraphics()` returns a handle to a new page, which is printed when the graphics object is disposed:

```
pg.dispose();
pjob.end();
```

The `PrintCanvas` class inherits from `Canvas`:

```
class PrintCanvas extends Canvas
```

Now, we add several graphics objects to the canvas to give it some color and make it interesting:

```
Rectangle r = getBounds();

    g.setColor(Color.yellow);
    g.fillRect(0,0, r.width, r.height);

    g.setColor(Color.blue);
    g.drawString("Hello, World", 100, 100);

    g.setColor(Color.red);
    g.drawLine(0,100,100,0);
    g.fillOval(135,140,15,15);
```

This simple example shows how the graphics displayed on a Java applet or application can be sent to a printer.

COMPLEXITY
ADVANCED

11.12 How do I...
Draw by using Java2D?

Problem

I draw a lot of graphics. I have heard about a graphics enhancement in Java 1.2 called Java2D. What does it offer above and beyond the existing `java.awt.*` classes? How do I write an application that uses these new classes?

Technique

Java2D is a set of classes that can be used to produce high-quality graphics, images, and text to your applications. They do not deprecate the existing **awt** classes, so you can still use them both if you wish. Java2D supports special fill patterns such as gradients and patterns. It also supports user-defined width and style for drawing strokes. Finally, it supports anti-aliasing to smooth out the edges of objects that are drawn on the screen. In addition, you can now specify your own coordinate space origin instead of the device coordinate space.

We are going to work a simple example that creates three kinds of filled polygons of different colors. We will cast the screen to be a `Graphics2D` screen type and then employ different methods to create the graphics.

Steps

1. Create the application source file. Create a new file called TwoDArcs2.java and enter the following source:

```java
import java.awt.*;
import java.awt.event.*;
import java.awt.geom.*;
import java.awt.image.BufferedImage;

public class TwoDArcs2 extends Canvas {

    private int w, h, x, y;
    //Declare the Arc objects
    private Arc2D.Float arc1 = new Arc2D.Float(Arc2D.CHORD);
    private Arc2D.Float arc2 = new Arc2D.Float(Arc2D.OPEN);
    private Arc2D.Float arc3 = new Arc2D.Float(Arc2D.PIE);

    //Buffering support
    private BufferedImage offImg;


    public TwoDArcs2() {
        setBackground(Color.white);
    }


    public void drawArcs(Graphics2D g2)
    {

    //Set the width of the outline

      g2.setStroke(new BasicStroke(5.0f));


      //Draw the chord
      arc1.setFrame(140,30, 67, 46);
      arc1.setAngleStart(45);
      arc1.setAngleExtent(270);
      g2.setColor(Color.blue);
      g2.draw(arc1);
      g2.setColor(Color.gray);
      g2.fill(arc1);
      g2.setColor(Color.black);
      g2.drawString("Arc2D.CHORD", 140, 20);

    //Draw the open arc
        arc2.setFrame(140,100, 67, 46);
        arc2.setAngleStart(45);
        arc2.setAngleExtent(270);
        g2.setColor(Color.gray);
```

```
        g2.draw(arc2);
        g2.setColor(Color.green);
        g2.fill(arc2);
        g2.setColor(Color.black);
        g2.drawString("Arc2D.OPEN", 140, 90);

//Draw the pie chart
        arc3.setFrame(140, 200, 67, 46);
        arc3.setAngleStart(45);
        arc3.setAngleExtent(270);
        g2.setColor(Color.gray);
        g2.draw(arc3);
        g2.setColor(Color.red);
        g2.fill(arc3);
        g2.setColor(Color.black);
        g2.drawString("Arc2D.PIE",140, 190);
    }


    public Graphics2D createDemoGraphics2D(Graphics g) {
        Graphics2D g2 = null;

        if (offImg == null ¦¦ offImg.getWidth() != w ¦¦
                        offImg.getHeight() != h) {
            offImg = (BufferedImage) createImage(w, h);
}

        if (offImg != null) {
            g2 = offImg.createGraphics();
            g2.setBackground(getBackground());
        }

        // .. set attributes ..
        g2.setRenderingHint(RenderingHints.KEY_ANTIALIASING,
                        RenderingHints.VALUE_ANTIALIAS_ON);

        // .. clear canvas ..
        g2.clearRect(0, 0, w, h);

        return g2;
    }


    public void paint(Graphics g) {

        Dimension d = getSize();
        w = d.width;
        h = d.height;
        //System.out.println(w * 2);
        //System.out.println(h);


        if (w <= 0 ¦¦ h <= 0)
            return;

        Graphics2D g2 = createDemoGraphics2D(g);
```

```
                    drawArcs(g2);
                    g2.dispose();

                    if (offImg != null && isShowing())  {
                        g.drawImage(offImg, 0, 0, this);
                    }

        }

        public static void main(String argv[]) {
            final TwoDArcs2 demo = new TwoDArcs2();
            WindowListener l = new WindowAdapter()
            {
                public void windowClosing(WindowEvent e)
➥{System.exit(0);}
};
            Frame f = new Frame("Java2D Arcs");
            f.addWindowListener(l);
            f.add("Center", demo);
            f.pack();
            f.setSize(400,300);
            f.show();
        }
    }
```

2. Compile and test the application. Compile the source by using `javac`.

When you run the application, a frame appears that contains three objects of different shape and color. Figure 11.24 shows a snapshot of the running application.

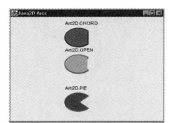

Figure 11.24 Java2D gives you the power to control your graphics applications more than ever before.

How It Works

The drawing takes place on a **Canvas** object called **TwoDArcs2**.(Actually, the drawing takes place on an offscreen image that is copied to the **Canvas**.) A canvas provides a visual container interface for the objects that will be placed on it:

```
public class TwoDArcs2 extends Canvas {
```

Next, we declare three arcs. Each of them is declared to be of type Arc2D.Float, the 2D arc class. Each of them is passed a different constant in the constructor. arc1 is passed a value making it a chord. arc2 is made into an open arc. arc3 is created as a pie:

```
private Arc2D.Float arc1 = new Arc2D.Float(Arc2D.CHORD);
private Arc2D.Float arc2 = new Arc2D.Float(Arc2D.OPEN);
private Arc2D.Float arc3 = new Arc2D.Float(Arc2D.PIE);
```

Before we draw the arcs, we set the pen to give us the line width. We set the stroke with the setStroke() method. This method takes a BasicStroke object as a parameter:

```
g2.setStroke(new BasicStroke(5.0f));
```

Having specified the stroke width and type, we are ready to draw the charts:

```
//Draw the pie chart

arc3.setFrame(140, 200, 67, 46);
arc3.setAngleStart(45);
arc3.setAngleExtent(270);
g2.setColor(Color.gray);
g2.draw(arc3);
g2.setColor(Color.red);
g2.fill(arc3);
g2.setColor(Color.black);
g2.drawString("Arc2D.PIE",140, 190);
    }
```

Notice that in these methods, we were using g2, which is the Graphics2D object:

```
public Graphics2D createDemoGraphics2D(Graphics g) {
    Graphics2D g2 = null;

    if (offImg == null || offImg.getWidth() != w ||
    // .. set attributes ..
```

A rendering hint is given here to set anti-aliasing on. This causes the edges of drawn images to be rendered smoothly:

```
g2.setRenderingHint(RenderingHints.KEY_ANTIALIASING,
                    RenderingHints.VALUE_ANTIALIAS_ON);

    // .. clear canvas ..
    g2.clearRect(0, 0, w, h);

    return g2;
    }
```

The object g2 is created by calling the createDemoGraphics2D() method:

```
Graphics2D g2 = createDemoGraphics2D(g);
drawArcs(g2);
g2.dispose();
```

Although this example merely scratches the surface of what can be done with Java2D, it gives you some feel for how you set up the environment for using these new classes.

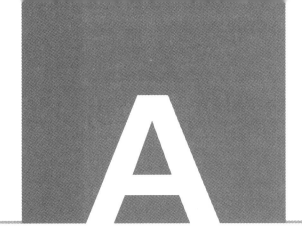

JAVA PLATFORM CORE PACKAGES

Java Platform Core Packages

PACKAGE	DESCRIPTION
com.sun.image.codec.jpeg	Provides classes for encoding and decoding JPEG images.
javax.accessibility	Provides support for persons with disabilities.
javax.swing.plaf	Provides one interface and many abstract classes that the Java Foundation Classes (JFC) uses to provide its pluggable look-and-feel capabilities.
javax.swing	Provides a set of "lightweight" (that is, all-Java) components.
javax.swing.border	Provides classes and interface for drawing specialized borders around a JFC component.
javax.swing.event	Provides for events fired by JFC components.
javax.swing.table	Provides classes and interfaces for dealing with javax.swing.JTable.
javax.swing.text	Provides classes and interfaces that deal with editable and noneditable text components.

continued on next page

continued from previous page

PACKAGE	DESCRIPTION
javax.swing.text.html	Provides the class (HTMLEditorKit) and supporting classes for creating HTML text editors.
javax.swing.text.rtf	Provides a class (RTFEditorKit) for creating Rich Text Format text editors.
javax.swing.tree	Provides classes and interfaces for dealing with javax.swing.JTree.
javax.swing.undo	Provides support for undo/redo capabilities in an application such as a text editor.
java.applet	Provides the classes necessary to create an applet and the classes an applet uses to communicate with its applet context.
java.awt	Contains all the classes for creating user inter faces and for painting graphics and images.
java.awt.color	Provides classes for color spaces.
java.awt.datatransfer	Provides interfaces and classes for transferring data between and within applications.
java.awt.dnd	Provides interfaces and classes for supporting drag-and-drop operations.
java.awt.event	Provides interfaces and classes for dealing with different types of events fired by Abstract Windowing Toolkit (AWT) components.
java.awt.font	Provides classes and interfaces relating to fonts.
java.awt.geom	Provides the Java 2D classes for defining and performing operations on objects related to two-dimensional geometry.
java.awt.im	Provides classes and an interface for the input method framework.
java.awt.image	Provides classes for creating and modifying images.
java.awt.image.renderable	Provides classes and interfaces for producing rendering-independent images.

PACKAGE	DESCRIPTION
java.awt.print	Provides classes and interfaces for a general printing API. The API includes such features as the ability to specify document types, mechanisms for control of page setup and page formats, and the ability to manage job control dialogs.
java.beans	Contains classes related to Java Beans development.
java.beans.beancontext	Provides classes and interfaces relating to Bean context.
java.io	Provides for system input and output through data streams, serialization, and the file system.
java.lang	Provides classes that are fundamental to the design of the Java programming language.
java.lang.ref	Provides reference object classes, which allow a program to interact with the garbage collector.
java.lang.reflect	Provides classes and interfaces for obtaining reflective information about classes and objects.
java.math	Provides classes for performing arbitrary-precision integer arithmetic (BigInteger) and arbitrary-precision decimal arithmetic (BigDecimal).
java.net	Provides the classes for implementing networking applications.
java.rmi	Provides the Remote Method Invocation (RMI) package.
java.rmi.activation	Provides support for RMI object activation.
java.rmi.dgc	Provides classes and interfaces for RMI distributed garbage collection (DGC).
java.rmi.registry	Provides a class and two interfaces for the RMI registry.
java.rmi.server	Provides classes and interfaces for supporting the server side of RMI. A group of classes is used by the stubs and skeletons generated by the rmic stub compiler.

continued on next page

continued from previous page

PACKAGE	DESCRIPTION
`java.security`	Provides the classes and interfaces for the security framework.
`java.security.acl`	The classes and interfaces in this package have been superseded by classes in the `java.security` package.
`java.security.cert`	Provides classes and interfaces for parsing and managing certificates.
`java.security.interfaces`	Provides interfaces for generating Rivest, Shamir, and Adleman AsymmetricCipher Algorithm (RSA) keys as defined in the RSA Laboratory Technical Note PKCS#1, and Digital Signature Algorithm (DSA) keys as defined in NIST's FIPS-186.
`java.security.spec`	Provides classes and interfaces for key specifications and algorithm parameter specifications.
`java.sql`	Provides the Java Database Connectivity (JDBC) package.
`java.text`	Provides classes and interfaces for handling text, dates, numbers, and messages in a manner independent of natural languages.
`java.util`	Provides useful utilities for data structures, date, time, internationalization, events (root interfaces), a simple string tokenizer, a random-number generator, observers, properties, and exceptions.
`java.util.jar`	Provides classes for creating and reading Java archive (JAR) files.
`java.util.mime`	Provides classes for dealing with Multipurpose Internet Mail Extension (MIME) types (RFC 2045, RFC 2046).
`java.util.zip`	Provides classes for computing checksums of data and for compressing and decompressing data using standard ZIP and GZIP formats.
`org.omg.CORBA`	CORBA support.
`org.omg.CORBA.ContainedPackage`	CORBA support.
`org.omg.CORBA.ContainerPackage`	CORBA support.

PACKAGE	DESCRIPTION
org.omg.CORBA.InterfaceDefPackage	CORBA support.
org.omg.CORBA.ORBPackage	CORBA support.
org.omg.CORBA.portable	CORBA support.
org.omg.CORBA.TypeCodePackage	CORBA support.
org.omg.CosNaming	CORBA support.
org.omg.CosNaming.NamingContextPackage	CORBA support.

DEPRECATED APIS

DEPRECATED CLASSES

com.sun.java.swing.text.DefaultTextUI

java.security.Identity

> This class is no longer used. Its functionality has been replaced by `java.security.KeyStore`, the `java.security.cert` package, and `java.security.Principal`.

java.security.IdentityScope

> This class is no longer used. Its functionality has been replaced by `java.security.KeyStore`, the `java.security.cert` package, and `java.security.Principal`.

java.io.LineNumberInputStream

> This class incorrectly assumes that bytes adequately represent characters. As of Java Development Kit (JDK) 1.1, the preferred way to operate on character streams is via the new character-stream classes, which include a class for counting line numbers.

java.security.Signer

> This class is no longer used. Its functionality has been replaced by `java.security.KeyStore`, the `java.security.cert` package, and `java.security.Principal`.

`java.io.StringBufferInputStream`

This class does not properly convert characters into bytes. As of JDK 1.1, the preferred way to create a stream from a string is via the **StringReader** class.

DEPRECATED INTERFACES

`java.security.Certificate`

A new certificate-handling package is created in JDK 1.2. This certificate interface is entirely deprecated and is here to allow for a smooth transition to the new package.

`java.rmi.server.LoaderHandler`

No replacement.

DEPRECATED FIELDS

`java.awt.Frame.CROSSHAIR_CURSOR`

Replaced by `Cursor.CROSSHAIR_CURSOR`.

`java.awt.Frame.DEFAULT_CURSOR`

Replaced by `Cursor.DEFAULT_CURSOR`.

`java.awt.Frame.E_RESIZE_CURSOR`

Replaced by `Cursor.E_RESIZE_CURSOR`.

`java.awt.Frame.HAND_CURSOR`

Replaced by `Cursor.HAND_CURSOR`.

`java.lang.SecurityManager.inCheck`

This type of security checking is not recommended. It is recommended that the `checkPermission` call be used instead.

`java.awt.Frame.MOVE_CURSOR`

Replaced by `Cursor.MOVE_CURSOR`.

`java.awt.Frame.N_RESIZE_CURSOR`

Replaced by `Cursor.N_RESIZE_CURSOR`.

`java.awt.Frame.NE_RESIZE_CURSOR`

Replaced by `Cursor.NE_RESIZE_CURSOR`.

`java.awt.Frame.NW_RESIZE_CURSOR`

Replaced by `Cursor.NW_RESIZE_CURSOR`.

`java.awt.Frame.S_RESIZE_CURSOR`

> Replaced by `Cursor.S_RESIZE_CURSOR`.

`java.awt.Frame.SE_RESIZE_CURSOR`

> Replaced by `Cursor.SE_RESIZE_CURSOR`.

`java.awt.Frame.SW_RESIZE_CURSOR`

> Replaced by `Cursor.SW_RESIZE_CURSOR`.

`java.awt.Frame.TEXT_CURSOR`

> Replaced by `Cursor.TEXT_CURSOR`.

`java.awt.Frame.W_RESIZE_CURSOR`

> Replaced by `Cursor.W_RESIZE_CURSOR`.

`java.awt.Frame.WAIT_CURSOR`

> Replaced by `Cursor.WAIT_CURSOR`.

DEPRECATED METHODS

`java.awt.Component.action(Event, Object)`

> As of JDK 1.1, should register this component as `ActionListener` on a component that fires action events.

`java.awt.List.addItem(String, int)`

> Replaced by `add(String, int)`.

`java.awt.List.addItem(String)`

> Replaced by `add(String)`.

`java.awt.CardLayout.addLayoutComponent(String, Component)`

> Replaced by `addLayoutComponent(Component, Object)`.

`java.awt.BorderLayout.addLayoutComponent(String, Component)`

> Replaced by `addLayoutComponent(Component, Object)`.

`java.awt.List.allowsMultipleSelections()`

> As of JDK 1.1, replaced by `isMultipleMode()`.

`java.lang.ThreadGroup.allowThreadSuspension(boolean)`

> The definition of this call depends on `ThreadGroup.suspend()`, which is deprecated. Further, the behavior of this call was never specified.

`java.awt.TextArea.appendText(String)`

> As of JDK 1.1, replaced by `append(String)`.

`java.security.AccessController.beginPrivileged()`

> This method will no longer exist after JDK 1.2 beta 4. Use the **doPrivileged** method instead.

`java.security.AccessController.beginPrivileged(AccessControlContext)`

> This method will no longer exist after JDK 1.2 beta 4. Use the **doPrivileged** method instead.

`java.awt.Component.bounds()`

> As of JDK 1.1, replaced by **getBounds()**.

`java.lang.SecurityManager.classDepth(String)`

> This type of security checking is not recommended. It is recommended that the **checkPermission** call be used instead.

`java.lang.SecurityManager.classLoaderDepth()`

> This type of security checking is not recommended. It is recommended that the **checkPermission** call be used instead.

`java.awt.List.clear()`

> As of JDK 1.1, replaced by **removeAll()**.

`java.awt.Container.countComponents()`

> As of JDK 1.1, replaced by **getComponentCount()**.

`java.awt.Choice.countItems()`

> As of JDK 1.1, replaced by **getItemCount()**.

`java.awt.Menu.countItems()`

> As of JDK 1.1, replaced by **getItemCount()**.

`java.awt.List.countItems()`

> As of JDK 1.1, replaced by **getItemCount()**.

`java.awt.MenuBar.countMenus()`

> As of JDK 1.1, replaced by **getMenuCount()**.

`java.lang.Thread.countStackFrames()`

> The definition of this call depends on **Thread.suspend()**, which is deprecated. Further, the results of this call were never well defined.

`com.sun.java.swing.JTable.createScrollPaneForTable(JTable)`

> As of the Java Foundation Classes (JFC) 1.0.2, replaced by **new JScrollPane(aTable)**.

java.lang.ClassLoader.defineClass(byte[], int, int)

> Replaced by defineClass(java.lang.String, byte[], int, int).

java.awt.List.delItem(int)

> Replaced by remove(String) and remove(int).

java.awt.List.delItems(int, int)

> As of JDK 1.1, not for public use. This method is expected to be retained only as a package private method.

java.awt.Component.deliverEvent(Event)

> As of JDK 1.1, replaced by dispatchEvent(AWTEvent e).

java.awt.Container.deliverEvent(Event)

> As of JDK 1.1, replaced by dispatchEvent(AWTEvent e).

java.awt.Component.disable()

> As of JDK 1.1, replaced by setEnabled(boolean).

java.awt.MenuItem.disable()

> As of JDK 1.1, replaced by setEnabled(boolean).

java.awt.Component.enable()

> As of JDK 1.1, replaced by setEnabled(boolean).

java.awt.MenuItem.enable()

> As of JDK 1.1, replaced by setEnabled(boolean).

java.awt.Component.enable(boolean)

> As of JDK 1.1, replaced by setEnabled(boolean).

java.awt.MenuItem.enable(boolean)

> As of JDK 1.1, replaced by setEnabled(boolean).

java.security.AccessController.endPrivileged()

> This method will no longer exist after JDK 1.2 beta 4. Use the doPrivileged method instead.

java.security.SignatureSpi.engineGetParameter(String)

java.security.SignatureSpi.engineSetParameter(String, Object)

> Replaced by engineSetParameter.

org.omg.CORBA.ServerRequest.except(Any)

> Use set_exception().

`org.omg.CORBA.ORB.get_current()`

Use `resolve_initial_references`.

`java.security.Security.getAlgorithmProperty(String, String)`

This method is used to return the value of a proprietary property in the master file of the Sun cryptographic service provider in order to determine how to parse algorithm-specific parameters. Use the new provider-based and algorithm-independent **AlgorithmParameters** and **KeyFactory** engine classes (introduced in JDK 1.2) instead.

`java.lang.ClassLoader.getBaseClassLoader()`

`java.sql.ResultSet.getBigDecimal(int, int)`

`java.sql.CallableStatement.getBigDecimal(int, int)`

`java.sql.ResultSet.getBigDecimal(String, int)`

`java.awt.Polygon.getBoundingBox()`

As of JDK 1.1, replaced by `getBounds()`.

`java.lang.String.getBytes(int, int, byte[], int)`

This method does not properly convert characters into bytes. As of JDK 1.1, the preferred way to do this is via the **getBytes(String enc)** method, which takes a character-encoding name, or the **getBytes()** method, which uses the platform's default encoding.

`java.awt.Graphics.getClipRect()`

As of JDK 1.1, replaced by `getClipBounds()`.

`java.awt.CheckboxGroup.getCurrent()`

As of JDK 1.1, replaced by `getSelectedCheckbox()`.

`java.awt.Frame.getCursorType()`

As of JDK 1.1, replaced by `Component.getCursor()`.

`java.sql.Time.getDate()`

`java.util.Date.getDate()`

As of JDK 1.1, replaced by `Calendar.get(Calendar.DAY_OF_MONTH)`.

`java.sql.Time.getDay()`

`java.util.Date.getDay()`

As of JDK 1.1, replaced by `Calendar.get(Calendar.DAY_OF_WEEK)`.

`java.lang.System.getenv(String)`

The preferred way to extract system-dependent information is by using the system properties of the **java.lang.System.getProperty** methods and the corresponding `getTypeName` methods of the `Boolean`, `Integer`, and `Long` primitive types, as in the following example:

```
String classPath = System.getProperty("java.class.path",".");

if (Boolean.getBoolean("myapp.exper.mode"))
    enableExpertCommands();
```

`java.awt.Toolkit.getFontList()`

> See `java.awt.GraphicsEnvironment#getFontFamilyNames`.

`java.awt.Toolkit.getFontMetrics(Font)`

> This returns integer metrics for the default screen.

`java.awt.Toolkit.getFontPeer(String, int)`

> See `java.awt.GraphicsEnvironment#getAllFonts`.

`java.sql.Date.getHours()`

`java.util.Date.getHours()`

> As of JDK 1.1, replaced by `Calendar.get(Calendar.HOUR_OF_DAY)`.

`java.lang.SecurityManager.getInCheck()`

> This type of security checking is not recommended. It is recommended that the `checkPermission` call be used instead.

`com.sun.java.swing.KeyStroke.getKeyStroke(char, boolean)`

> Use `getKeyStroke(char)`.

`com.sun.java.swing.AbstractButton.getLabel()`

> Replaced by `getText()`.

`java.awt.Scrollbar.getLineIncrement()`

> As of JDK 1.1, replaced by `getUnitIncrement()`.

`java.lang.Runtime.getLocalizedInputStream(InputStream)`

> As of JDK 1.1, the preferred way translate a byte stream in the local encoding into a character stream in Unicode is via the `InputStreamReader` and `BufferedReader` classes.

`java.lang.Runtime.getLocalizedOutputStream(OutputStream)`

> As of JDK 1.1, the preferred way to translate a Unicode character stream into a byte stream in the local encoding is via the `OutputStreamWriter`, `BufferedWriter`, and `PrintWriter` classes.

`java.sql.DriverManager.getLogStream()`

`java.awt.FontMetrics.getMaxDecent()`

> As of JDK 1.1.1, replaced by `getMaxDescent()`.

`com.sun.java.swing.JInternalFrame.getMenuBar()`

>As of JFC 1.0.3, replaced by **`getJMenuBar()`**.

`com.sun.java.swing.JRootPane.getMenuBar()`

>As of JFC 1.0.3 replaced by **`getJMenubar()`**.

`java.sql.Date.getMinutes()`

`java.util.Date.getMinutes()`

>As of JDK 1.1, replaced by **`Calendar.get(Calendar.MINUTE)`**.

`java.sql.Time.getMonth()`

`java.util.Date.getMonth()`

>As of JDK 1.1, replaced by **`Calendar.get(Calendar.MONTH)`**.

`java.awt.Scrollbar.getPageIncrement()`

>As of JDK 1.1, replaced by **`getBlockIncrement()`**.

`java.security.Signature.getParameter(String)`

`java.awt.Component.getPeer()`

>As of JDK 1.1, programs should not directly manipulate peers. Replaced by **`booleanisDisplayable()`**.

`java.awt.Font.getPeer()`

>Font rendering is now platform independent.

`java.awt.MenuComponent.getPeer()`

>As of JDK 1.1, programs should not directly manipulate peers.

`java.sql.Date.getSeconds()`

`java.util.Date.getSeconds()`

>As of JDK 1.1, replaced by **`Calendar.get(Calendar.SECOND)`**.

`java.rmi.server.RMIClassLoader.getSecurityContext(ClassLoader)`

`com.sun.java.swing.JPasswordField.getText()`

>As of JDK 1.2, replaced by **`getPassword()`**.

`com.sun.java.swing.JPasswordField.getText(int, int)`

>As of JDK 1.2, replaced by **`getPassword()`**.

`java.util.Date.getTimezoneOffset()`

>As of JDK 1.1, replaced by **`Calendar.get(Calendar.ZONE_OFFSET)`** and **`Calendar.get(Calendar.DST_OFFSET)`**.

`java.net.MulticastSocket.getTTL()`

>Use the **`getTimeToLive`** method instead, which allows you to get time-to-live values from 0 (excluded) to 255 (included).

`java.net.DatagramSocketImpl.getTTL()`

> Use `getTimeToLive` instead.

`java.sql.ResultSet.getUnicodeStream(int)`

`java.sql.ResultSet.getUnicodeStream(String)`

`com.sun.java.swing.ScrollPaneLayout.getViewportBorderBounds(JScrollPane)`

> As of JDK 1.1, replaced by `JScrollPane.getViewportBorderBounds()`.

`java.awt.Scrollbar.getVisible()`

> As of JDK 1.1, replaced by `getVisibleAmount()`.

`java.sql.Time.getYear()`

`java.util.Date.getYear()`

> As of JDK 1.1, replaced by `Calendar.get(Calendar.YEAR) - 1900`.

`java.awt.Component.gotFocus(Event, Object)`

> As of JDK 1.1, replaced by `processFocusEvent(FocusEvent)`.

`java.awt.Component.handleEvent(Event)`

> As of JDK 1.1, replaced by `processEvent(AWTEvent)`.

`java.awt.Component.hide()`

> As of JDK 1.1, replaced by `setVisible(boolean)`.

`java.lang.SecurityManager.inClass(String)`

> This type of security checking is not recommended. It is recommended that the `checkPermission` call be used instead.

`java.lang.SecurityManager.inClassLoader()`

> This type of security checking is not recommended. It is recommended that the `checkPermission` call be used instead.

`java.awt.TextArea.insertText(String, int)`

> As of JDK 1.1, replaced by `insert(String, int)`.

`java.awt.Container.insets()`

> As of JDK 1.1, replaced by `getInsets()`.

`java.awt.Component.inside(int, int)`

> As of JDK 1.1, replaced by `contains(int, int)`.

`java.awt.Polygon.inside(int, int)`

> As of JDK 1.1, replaced by `contains(int, int)`.

`java.awt.Rectangle.inside(int, int)`

> As of JDK 1.1, replaced by `contains(int, int)`.

`java.lang.Character.isJavaLetter(char)`

> Replaced by `isJavaIdentifierStart(char)`.

`java.lang.Character.isJavaLetterOrDigit(char)`

> Replaced by `isJavaIdentifierPart(char)`.

`java.awt.List.isSelected(int)`

> As of JDK 1.1, replaced by `isIndexSelected(int)`.

`java.lang.Character.isSpace(char)`

> Replaced by `isWhitespace(char)`.

`java.awt.Component.keyDown(Event, int)`

> As of JDK 1.1, replaced by `processKeyEvent(KeyEvent)`.

`java.awt.Component.keyUp(Event, int)`

> As of JDK 1.1, replaced by `processKeyEvent(KeyEvent)`.

`java.awt.Component.layout()`

> As of JDK 1.1, replaced by `doLayout()`.

`java.awt.Container.layout()`

> As of JDK 1.1, replaced by `doLayout()`.

`java.awt.ScrollPane.layout()`

> As of JDK 1.1, replaced by `doLayout()`.

`java.rmi.server.RMIClassLoader.loadClass(String)`

`java.awt.Component.locate(int, int)`

> As of JDK 1.1, replaced by `getComponentAt(int, int)`.

`java.awt.Container.locate(int, int)`

> As of JDK 1.1, replaced by `getComponentAt(int, int)`.

`java.awt.Component.location()`

> As of JDK 1.1, replaced by `getLocation()`.

`java.awt.Component.lostFocus(Event, Object)`

> As of JDK 1.1, replaced by `processFocusEvent(FocusEvent)`.

`java.awt.Component.minimumSize()`

> As of JDK 1.1, replaced by `getMinimumSize()`.

`java.awt.Container.minimumSize()`

> As of JDK 1.1, replaced by `getMinimumSize()`.

`java.awt.TextField.minimumSize()`

> As of JDK 1.1, replaced by `getMinimumSize()`.

`java.awt.TextArea.minimumSize()`

> As of JDK 1.1, replaced by `getMinimumSize()`.

`java.awt.List.minimumSize()`

> As of JDK 1.1, replaced by `getMinimumSize()`.

`java.awt.TextArea.minimumSize(int, int)`

> As of JDK 1.1, replaced by `getMinimumSize(int, int)`.

`java.awt.TextField.minimumSize(int)`

> As of JDK 1.1, replaced by `getMinimumSize(int)`.

`java.awt.List.minimumSize(int)`

> As of JDK 1.1, replaced by `getMinimumSize(int)`.

`com.sun.java.swing.text.View.modelToView(int, Shape)`

`java.awt.Component.mouseDown(Event, int, int)`

> As of JDK 1.1, replaced by `processMouseEvent(MouseEvent)`.

`java.awt.Component.mouseDrag(Event, int, int)`

> As of JDK 1.1, replaced by `processMouseMotionEvent(MouseEvent)`.

`java.awt.Component.mouseEnter(Event, int, int)`

> As of JDK 1.1, replaced by `processMouseEvent(MouseEvent)`.

`java.awt.Component.mouseExit(Event, int, int)`

> As of JDK 1.1, replaced by `processMouseEvent(MouseEvent)`.

`java.awt.Component.mouseMove(Event, int, int)`

> As of JDK 1.1, replaced by `processMouseMotionEvent(MouseEvent)`.

`java.awt.Component.mouseUp(Event, int, int)`

> As of JDK 1.1, replaced by `processMouseEvent(MouseEvent)`.

`java.awt.Component.move(int, int)`

> As of JDK 1.1, replaced by `setLocation(int, int)`.

`java.awt.Rectangle.move(int, int)`

> As of JDK 1.1, replaced by `setLocation(int, int)`.

`java.awt.Component.nextFocus()`

> As of JDK 1.1, replaced by `transferFocus()`.

`org.omg.CORBA.ServerRequest.op_name()`

> Use `operation()`.

`org.omg.CORBA.ServerRequest.params(NVList)`

arguments() provides the same functionality as params().

`java.util.Date.parse(String)`

As of JDK 1.1, replaced by DateFormat.parse(String s).

`java.awt.Component.postEvent(Event)`

As of JDK 1.1, replaced by dispatchEvent(AWTEvent).

`java.awt.Window.postEvent(Event)`

As of JDK 1.1, replaced by dispatchEvent(AWTEvent).

`java.awt.MenuComponent.postEvent(Event)`

As of JDK 1.1, replaced by dispatchEvent(AWTEvent).

`java.awt.MenuContainer.postEvent(Event)`

As of JDK 1.1, replaced by dispatchEvent(AWTEvent).

`java.awt.Component.preferredSize()`

As of JDK 1.1, replaced by getPreferredSize().

`java.awt.Container.preferredSize()`

As of JDK 1.1, replaced by getPreferredSize().

`java.awt.TextField.preferredSize()`

As of JDK 1.1, replaced by getPreferredSize().

`java.awt.TextArea.preferredSize()`

As of JDK 1.1, replaced by getPreferredSize().

`java.awt.List.preferredSize()`

As of JDK 1.1, replaced by getPreferredSize().

`java.awt.TextArea.preferredSize(int, int)`

As of JDK 1.1, replaced by getPreferredSize(int, int).

`java.awt.TextField.preferredSize(int)`

As of JDK 1.1, replaced by getPreferredSize(int).

`java.awt.List.preferredSize(int)`

As of JDK 1.1, replaced by getPreferredSize(int).

`java.io.DataInputStream.readLine()`

This method does not properly convert bytes to characters. As of JDK 1.1, the preferred way to read lines of text is via the BufferedReader.readLine() method. Programs that use the DataInputStream class to read lines can be converted to use the BufferedReader class by replacing code of the form

```
DataInputStream d = new DataInputStream(in);
```

with

```
BufferedReader d
    = new BufferedReader(new InputStreamReader(in));
```

`java.io.ObjectInputStream.readLine()`

This method does not properly convert bytes to characters. See `DataInputStream` for the details and alternatives.

`java.rmi.registry.RegistryHandler.registryImpl(int)`

As of JDK 1.2, Remote Method Invocation (RMI) no longer uses `RegistryHandler` to obtain the registry's implementation.

`java.rmi.registry.RegistryHandler.registryStub(String, int)`

As of JDK 1.2, RMI no longer uses `RegistryHandler` to obtain the registry's stub.

`java.awt.TextArea.replaceText(String, int, int)`

As of JDK 1.1, replaced by `replaceRange(String, int, int)`.

`java.awt.Component.reshape(int, int, int, int)`

As of JDK 1.1, replaced by `setBounds(int, int, int, int)`.

`java.awt.Rectangle.reshape(int, int, int, int)`

As of JDK 1.1, replaced by `setBounds(int, int, int, int)`.

`java.awt.Component.resize(Dimension)`

As of JDK 1.1, replaced by `setSize(Dimension)`.

`java.awt.Component.resize(int, int)`

As of JDK 1.1, replaced by `setSize(int, int)`.

`java.awt.Rectangle.resize(int, int)`

As of JDK 1.1, replaced by `setSize(int, int)`.

`org.omg.CORBA.ServerRequest.result(Any)`

Use `set_result()`.

`java.lang.Thread.resume()`

`java.lang.ThreadGroup.resume()`

`java.lang.System.runFinalizersOnExit(boolean)`

This method is inherently unsafe. It may result in finalizers being called on live objects while other threads are concurrently manipulating those objects, resulting in erratic behavior or deadlock.

`java.util.Properties.save(OutputStream, String)`

> This method does not throw **IOException** if an I/O error occurs while saving the property list. As of JDK 1.2, the preferred way to save a properties list is via the `store(OutputStream out, String header)` method.

`java.awt.CheckboxGroup.setCurrent(Checkbox)`

> As of JDK 1.1, replaced by `setSelectedCheckbox(Checkbox)`.

`java.awt.Frame.setCursor(int)`

> As of JDK 1.1, replaced by `Component.setCursor(Cursor)`.

`java.sql.Time.setDate(int)`

`java.util.Date.setDate(int)`

> As of JDK 1.1, replaced by `Calendar.set(Calendar.DAY_OF_MONTH, int date)`.

`java.awt.TextField.setEchoCharacter(char)`

> As of JDK 1.1, replaced by `setEchoChar(char)`.

`java.sql.Date.setHours(int)`

`java.util.Date.setHours(int)`

> As of JDK 1.1, replaced by `Calendar.set(Calendar.HOUR_OF_DAY, int hours)`.

`com.sun.java.swing.AbstractButton.setLabel(String)`

> Replaced by `setText(text)`.

`com.sun.java.swing.ToolTipManager.setLightWeightPopupEnabled(boolean)`

> As of JFC 1.1, replaced by `setToolTipWindowUsePolicy(int)`.

`java.awt.Scrollbar.setLineIncrement(int)`

> As of JDK 1.1, replaced by `setUnitIncrement(int)`.

`java.sql.DriverManager.setLogStream(PrintStream)`

`com.sun.java.swing.JInternalFrame.setMenuBar(JMenuBar)`

> As of JFC 1.0.3, replaced by `setJMenuBar(JMenuBar m)`.

`com.sun.java.swing.JRootPane.setMenuBar(JMenuBar)`

> As of JFC 1.0.3, replaced by `setJMenuBar(JMenuBar menu)`.

`java.sql.Date.setMinutes(int)`

`java.util.Date.setMinutes(int)`

> As of JDK 1.1, replaced by `Calendar.set(Calendar.MINUTE, int minutes)`.

`java.sql.Time.setMonth(int)`

`java.util.Date.setMonth(int)`

> As of JDK 1.1, replaced by `Calendar.set(Calendar.MONTH, int month)`.

`java.awt.List.setMultipleSelections(boolean)`

> As of JDK 1.1, replaced by `setMultipleMode(boolean)`.

`java.awt.Scrollbar.setPageIncrement(int)`

> As of JDK 1.1, replaced by `setBlockIncrement()`.

`java.security.Signature.setParameter(String, Object)`

> Use `setParameter`.

`java.sql.Date.setSeconds(int)`

`java.util.Date.setSeconds(int)`

> As of JDK 1.1, replaced by `Calendar.set(Calendar.SECOND, int seconds)`.

`java.net.MulticastSocket.setTTL(byte)`

> Use the `setTimeToLive` method instead, which allows you to set time-to-live values from 0 (excluded) to 255 (included).

`java.net.DatagramSocketImpl.setTTL(byte)`

> Use `setTimeToLive` instead.

`java.sql.PreparedStatement.setUnicodeStream(int, InputStream, int)`

`java.sql.Time.setYear(int)`

`java.util.Date.setYear(int)`

> As of JDK 1.1, replaced by `Calendar.set(Calendar.YEAR, year + 1900)`.

`java.awt.Component.show()`

> As of JDK 1.1, replaced by `setVisible(boolean)`.

`java.awt.Component.show(boolean)`

> As of JDK 1.1, replaced by `setVisible(boolean)`.

`java.awt.Component.size()`

> As of JDK 1.1, replaced by `getSize()`.

`com.sun.java.swing.JTable.sizeColumnsToFit(boolean)`

> As of JFC 1.0.3, replaced by `sizeColumnsToFit(int)`.

`java.lang.Thread.stop()`

`java.lang.ThreadGroup.stop()`

`java.lang.Thread.stop(Throwable)`

`java.lang.Thread.suspend()`

`java.lang.ThreadGroup.suspend()`

`java.util.Date.toGMTString()`

> As of JDK 1.1, replaced by `DateFormat.format(Date date)`, using a GMT `TimeZone`.

`java.util.Date.toLocaleString()`

> As of JDK 1.1, replaced by `DateFormat.format(Date date)`.

`java.io.ByteArrayOutputStream.toString(int)`

> This method does not properly convert bytes into characters. As of JDK 1.1, the preferred way to do this is via the `toString(String enc)` method, which takes an encoding-name argument, or the `toString()` method, which uses the platform's default character encoding.

`java.util.Date.UTC(int, int, int, int, int, int)`

> As of JDK 1.1, replaced by `Calendar.set(year + 1900, month, date, hrs, min, sec)` or `GregorianCalendar(year + 1900, month, date, hrs, min, sec)`, using `UTC TimeZone`, followed by `Calendar.getTime().getTime()`.

`com.sun.java.swing.text.View.viewToModel(float, float, Shape)`

DEPRECATED CONSTRUCTORS

These constructors are no longer supported. See the online help for a listing of legal constructors.

`java.util.Date(int, int, int, int, int, int)`

> As of JDK 1.1, replaced by `Calendar.set(year + 1900, month, date, hrs, min, sec)` or `GregorianCalendar(year + 1900, month, date, hrs, min, sec)`.

`java.util.Date(int, int, int, int, int)`

> As of JDK 1.1, replaced by `Calendar.set(year + 1900, month, date, hrs, min)` or `GregorianCalendar(year + 1900, month, date, hrs, min)`.

`java.sql.Date(int, int, int)`

`java.util.Date(int, int, int)`

> As of JDK 1.1, replaced by `Calendar.set(year + 1900, month, date)` or `GregorianCalendar(year + 1900, month, date)`.

`java.util.Date(String)`

> As of JDK 1.1, replaced by `DateFormat.parse(String s)`.

`java.net.Socket(InetAddress, int, boolean)`

> Use `DatagramSocket` instead for UDP transport.

`java.net.Socket(String, int, boolean)`

> Use **DatagramSocket** instead for UDP transport.

`java.io.StreamTokenizer(InputStream)`

> As of JDK 1.1, the preferred way to tokenize an input stream is to convert it into a character stream, as in the following example:

```
Reader r = new BufferedReader(new InputStreamReader(is));
StreamTokenizer st = new StreamTokenizer(r);
```

`java.lang.String(byte[], int, int, int)`

> This method does not properly convert bytes into characters. As of JDK 1.1, the preferred way to do this is via the **String** constructors that take a character-encoding name or that use the platform's default encoding.

`java.lang.String(byte[], int)`

> This method does not properly convert bytes into characters. As of JDK 1.1, the preferred way to do this is via the **String** constructors that take a character-encoding name or that use the platform's default encoding.

`java.sql.Timestamp(int, int, int, int, int, int, int)`

JDK 1.2 API DESCRIPTION

This appendix describes the packages of the JDK 1.2 API in terms of their interfaces, classes, exceptions, and errors. Also, hierarchical relationships between package elements are identified. This appendix is based on the API defined for JDK 1.2 release candidate 2 (RC2).

`java.applet`	`java.lang`
`java.awt`	`java.lang.ref`
`java.awt.color`	`java.lang.reflect`
`java.awt.datatransfer`	`java.math`
`java.awt.dnd`	`java.net`
`java.awt.event`	`java.rmi`
`java.awt.font`	`java.rmi.activation`
`java.awt.geom`	`java.rmi.dgc`
`java.awt.im`	`java.rmi.registry`
`java.awt.image`	`java.rmi.server`
`java.awt.image.renderable`	`java.security`
`java.awt.print`	`java.security.acl`
`java.beans`	`java.security.cert`
`java.beans.beancontext`	`java.security.interfaces`
`java.io`	`java.security.spec`

`java.sql`	`javax.swing.plaf.multi`
`java.text`	`javax.swing.table`
`java.util`	`javax.swing.text`
`java.util.jar`	`javax.swing.text.html`
`java.util.zip`	`javax.swing.tree`
`javax.accessibility`	`javax.swing.undo`
`javax.swing`	`org.omg.CORBA`
`javax.swing.border`	`org.omg.CORBA.DynAnyPackage`
`javax.swing.colorchooser`	`org.omg.CORBA.ORBPackage`
`javax.swing.event`	`org.omg.CORBA.portable`
`javax.swing.filechooser`	`org.omg.CORBA.TypeCodePackage`
`javax.swing.plaf`	`org.omg.CosNaming`
`javax.swing.plaf.basic`	`org.omg.CosNaming.NamingContextPackage`
`javax.swing.plaf.metal`	

PACKAGE `java.applet`

The `java.applet` package is one of the smallest packages in the Core API. It consists of one class and three interfaces that provide the basic functionality needed to implement applets.

Interfaces

AppletContext

The `AppletContext` interface defines methods that allow an applet to access the context in which it is being run.

AppletStub

The `AppletStub` interface supports communication between an applet and its browser environment, and is used to develop custom applet viewers.

AudioClip

The `AudioClip` interface provides methods that support the playing of audio clips.

Classes

Applet

The `Applet` class is the superclass of all applets. It provides methods to display images, play audio files, respond to events, and obtain information about an applet's execution environment. The `Applet` class is a subclass of `java.awt.panel`.

Exceptions and Errors

None.

PACKAGE java.awt

The java.awt package implements the core classes and interfaces of the Abstract Windowing Toolkit (AWT). It is a large package, containing 64 classes and 14 interfaces. These classes and interfaces provide the standard AWT GUI controls, as well as drawing, printing, and other capabilities.

Interfaces

ActiveEvent

The ActiveEvent interface defines methods that are implemented by event classes that are self-dispatching.

Adjustable

The Adjustable interface is implemented by classes, such as sliders and scrollbars, that allow a value to be selected from a range of values.

Composite

The Composite interface defines methods that are implemented by classes that allow drawing to be composed with an underlying graphics area.

CompositeContext

The CompositeContext interface defines methods for classes that provide a context for compositing drawing operations.

ItemSelectable

The ItemSelectable interface is implemented by classes whose objects, such as choices or lists, may contain selectable items.

LayoutManager

The LayoutManager interface is implemented by classes that can lay out Container objects.

LayoutManager2

The LayoutManager2 interface extends the LayoutManager interface to provide support for layout constraints.

MenuContainer

The MenuContainer interface defines methods for classes that may contain Menu objects.

Paint

The Paint interface extends the Transparency interface, providing support for defining color patterns for use in graphics operations.

PaintContext

The PaintContext interface provides methods that define the context for paint operations.

PrintGraphics

The `PrintGraphics` interface defines a graphics context for printing a single page.

Shape

The `Shape` interface defines methods that are implemented by classes that encapsulate geometric shapes.

Stroke

The `Stroke` interface provides methods that are implemented by classes that define pen strokes.

Transparency

The `Transparency` interface defines methods for classes that support transparency-related graphics operations.

Classes

AlphaComposite

The `AlphaComposite` class is a subclass of `Object` that implements alpha compositing rules for combining source and destination image pixels. It implements the `Composite` interface.

AWTEvent

The `AWTEvent` class is a subclass of `java.util.EventObject` that serves as the base class for all AWT-related events.

AWTEventMulticaster

The `AWTEventMulticaster` class is a subclass of `Object` that provides thread-safe multicast event dispatching capabilities. It implements the following interfaces of the `java.awt.event` package: `ActionListener`, `AdjustmentListener`, `ComponentListener`, `ContainerListener`, `FocusListener`, `InputMethodListener`, `ItemListener`, `KeyListener`, `MouseListener`, `MouseMotionListener`, `TextListener`, and `WindowListener`.

AWTPermission

The `AWTPermission` class is a subclass of `java.security.BasicPermission` that implements security permissions for a variety of AWT-related operations.

BasicStroke

The `BasicStroke` class is a subclass of `Object` that provides a set of properties for a basic implementation of the `Stroke` interface.

BorderLayout

The `BorderLayout` class is a subclass of `Object` that is used to lay out the components of a container along the container's border. It implements the `LayoutManager2` and `java.lang.Serializable` interfaces.

Button

The Button class is a subclass of Component that encapsulates a GUI text-labeled pushbutton.

Canvas

The Canvas class is a subclass of Component that provides a rectangular drawing area.

CardLayout

The CardLayout class is a subclass of Object that provides the capability to lay out a Container object in a card-like fashion. It implements the LayoutManager2 and java.io.Serializable interfaces.

Checkbox

The Checkbox class is a subclass of Container that provides the capability to display and work with checkbox and radio button GUI controls. It implements the ItemSelectable interface.

CheckboxGroup

The CheckboxGroup class is a subclass of Object that is used to group Checkbox objects together as a set of radio buttons. It implements the java.io.Serializable interface.

CheckboxMenuItem

The CheckboxMenuItem class is a subclass of MenuItem that is used to create a menu item that may be in an on or off state. It implements the ItemSelectable interface.

Choice

The Choice class is a subclass of Component that provides a pop-up menu of choices. It implements the ItemSelectable interface.

Color

The Color class is a subclass of Object that is used to define colors within a particular color space. It implements the Paint and java.io.Serializable interfaces.

Component

The Component class is a subclass of Object that provides the base class for the development of GUI components. It implements the MenuContainer, java.awt.imaga.ImageObserver, and java.io.Serializable interfaces.

ComponentOrientation

The ComponentOrientation class is a subclass of Object that implements the Serializable interface. It is used to specify the language-specific orientation of text.

Container

The `Container` class is a subclass of `Component` that acts as a container for other GUI components.

Cursor

The `Cursor` class is a subclass of `Object` that encapsulates a changeable cursor associated with a pointing device. It implements the `java.io.Serializable` interface.

Dialog

The `Dialog` class is a subclass of `Window` that provides a base class for the development of dialog boxes.

Dimension

The `Dimension` class is a subclass of `java.awt.geom.Dimension2D` that provides the capability to specify the height and width of an object. It implements the `java.io.Serializable` interface.

Event

The `Event` class is a subclass of `Object` that provides the base class for implementing events in the JDK 1.0 event model. It implements the `java.io.Serializable` interface.

EventQueue

The `EventQueue` class is a subclass of `Object` that implements the system event queue.

FileDialog

The `FileDialog` class is a subclass of `Dialog` that encapsulates a file system dialog box.

FlowLayout

The `FlowLayout` class is a subclass of `Object` that is used to lay out `Container` objects in a left-to-right and top-to-bottom fashion. It implements the `LayoutManager` and `java.io.Serializable` interfaces.

Font

The `Font` class is a subclass of `Object` that encapsulates text fonts. It implements the `java.io.Serializable` interface.

FontMetrics

The `FontMetrics` class is a subclass of `Object` that provides information about the properties of a font. It implements the `java.io.Serializable` interface.

Frame

The `Frame` class is a subclass of `Window` that provides a top-level application window. It implements the `MenuContainer` interface.

GradientPaint

The GradientPaint class is a subclass of Object that provides the capability to fill a drawing area with a linear gradient color fill. It implements the Paint interface.

Graphics

The Graphics class is a subclass of Object that is the base class for the development of graphics drawing contexts.

Graphics2D

The Graphics2D class is a subclass of Graphics that serves as the basic graphics context for the Java 2D API1.

GraphicsConfigTemplate

The GraphicsConfigTemplate class is a subclass of Object that is used as a template for the creation of GraphicsConfiguration objects. It implements the java.io.Serializable interface.

GraphicsConfiguration

The GraphicsConfiguration class is a subclass of Object that specifies the physical characteristics of a graphics display device.

GraphicsDevice

The GraphicsDevice class is a subclass of Object that describes the graphics display devices available to the system.

GraphicsEnvironment

The GraphicsEnvironment class is a subclass of Object that describes the entire graphics environment available to the system, including all of the accessible GraphicsDevice objects.

GridBagConstraints

The GridBagConstraints class is a subclass of Object that is used to specify how containers are to be laid out using GridBagLayout objects. It implements the java.lang.Cloneable and java.io.Serializable interfaces.

GridBagLayout

The GridBagLayout class is a subclass of Object that is used to lay out a container according to the properties of a GridBagConstraints object. It implements the LayoutManager2 and java.io.Serializable interfaces.

GridLayout

The GridLayout class is a subclass of Object that is used to lay out a container in a grid-like fashion. It implements the LayoutManager and java.io.Serializable interfaces.

Image

The `Image` class is a subclass of `Object` that encapsulates a displayable image.

Insets

The `Insets` class is a subclass of `Object` that specifies the border of a GUI component. It implements the `java.lang.Cloneable` and `java.io.Serializable` interfaces.

Label

The `Label` class is a subclass of `Component` that implements a GUI text label.

List

The `List` class is a subclass of `Component` that encapsulates a scrollable list GUI control. It implements the `ItemSelectable` interface.

MediaTracker

The `MediaTracker` class is a subclass of `Object` that is used to track the loading status of multimedia objects. It implements the `java.io.Serializable` interface.

Menu

The `Menu` class is a subclass of `MenuItem` that encapsulates a pull-down menu. It implements the `MenuContainer` interface.

MenuBar

The `MenuBar` class is a subclass of `MenuComponent` that provides the capability to attach a menu bar to a `Frame` object. It implements the `MenuContainer` interface.

MenuComponent

The `MenuComponent` class is a subclass of `Object` that is the base class for all other AWT menu-related classes. It implements the `java.io.Serializable` interface.

MenuItem

The `MenuItem` class is a subclass of `MenuComponent` that implements a menu item value that is selectable from a `Menu` object.

MenuShortcut

The `MenuShortcut` class is a subclass of `Object` that provides the capability to associate a keyboard accelerator with a `MenuItem` object. It implements the `java.io.Serializable` interface.

Panel

The `Panel` class is a subclass of `Container` that provides a rectangular container for other GUI components.

Point

The `Point` class is a subclass of `java.awt.geom.Point2D` that encapsulates a point in the xy-plane. It implements the `java.io.Serializable` interface.

Polygon

The `Polygon` class is a subclass of `Object` that is used to describe a mathematical polygon. It implements the `Shape` and `java.io.Serializable` interfaces.

PopupMenu

The `PopupMenu` class is a subclass of `Menu` that provides a menu that can be popped up at a specific location within a component.

PrintJob

The `PrintJob` class is a subclass of `Object` that is used to implement a system-specific printing request.

Rectangle

The `Rectangle` class is a subclass of `java.awt.geom.Rectangle2D` that encapsulates a mathematical rectangle. It implements the `Shape` and `java.io.Serializable` interfaces.

RenderingHints

The `RenderingHints` class is a subclass of `Object` that implements the `Map` and `Cloneable` interfaces. It is used to provide information for rendering objects for display.

RenderingHints.Key

The `RenderingHints.Key` class is an inner class of `RenderingHints` that provides a base class for specifying keys used in the rendering process.

Scrollbar

The `Scrollbar` class is a subclass of `Component` that provides a GUI scrollbar component. It implements the `Adjustable` interface.

ScrollPane

The `ScrollPane` class is a subclass of `Container` that provides a combiination of a panel and vertical and horizontal scrollbars.

SystemColor

The `SystemColor` class is a subclass of `Color` that is used to specify the color scheme used with GUI components. It implements the `java.io.Serializable` interface.

TextArea

The `TextArea` class is a subclass of `TextComponent` that provides a GUI text area control.

TextComponent

The TextComponent class is a subclass of Component that is the base class for TextField and TextArea.

TextField

The TextField class is a subclass of TextComponent that implements a GUI text input field.

TexturePaint

The TexturePaint class is a subclass of Object that provides the capability to fill a geometrical shape with a texture image. It implements the Paint interface.

Toolkit

The Toolkit class is a subclass of Object that provides access to implementation-specific AWT resources.

Window

The Window class is a subclass of Container that provides a basic window object.

Exceptions and Errors

AWTError

The AWTError class is a subclass of java.lang.Error that is thrown when a fundamental error occurs in the AWT operation.

AWTException

The AWTException class is a subclass of java.lang.Exception that signals the occurrence of an AWT-specific exception.

IllegalComponentStateException

The IllegalComponentStateException class is a subclass of java.lang.IllegalStateException that identifies that an AWT component is in the wrong state for a particular operation.

PACKAGE java.awt.color

The java.awt.color package is part of the Java 2D API. It provides five classes that support the capability to work with different color models.

Interfaces

None.

Classes

ColorSpace

The ColorSpace class is an abstract subclass of Object that specifies the color space used with other objects. It provides constants that define popular color spaces and methods for converting colors between color spaces.

ICC_ColorSpace

The ICC_ColorSpace class is a subclass of ColorSpace that provides a non-abstract implementation of the ColorSpace methods. It represents color spaces in accordance with the ICC Profile Format Specification, Version 3.4, August 15, 1997, from the International Color Consortium. For more information, refer to http://www.color.org.

ICC_Profile

The ICC_Profile class is a subclass of Object that provides a representation of color profile data for color spaces based on the ICC Profile Format Specification. Color profiles represent transformations from the color space of a device, such as a monitor, to a profile connection space, as defined by the ICC Profile Format Specification.

ICC_ProfileGray

The ICC_ProfileGray class is a subclass of ICC_Profile that supports color conversion to monochrome color spaces.

ICC_ProfileRGB

The ICC_ProfileRGB class is a subclass of ICC_Profile that supports color conversion between RGB and CIEXYZ color spaces.

Exceptions and Errors

CMMException

The CMMException class is a subclass of java.lang.RuntimeException that defines an exception that is thrown when the color model manager returns an error.

ProfileDataException

The ProfileDataException class is a subclass of java.lang.RuntimeException that defines an exception that is thrown when an error occurs in accessing or processing an ICC_Profile object.

PACKAGE java.awt.datatransfer

The java.awt.datatransfer package provides four classes and three interfaces that support clipboard operations.

Interfaces

ClipboardOwner

The ClipboardOwner interface defines the lostOwnership() method, which is invoked to notify an object that it has lost ownership of a clipboard. This interface is implemented by classes that copy data to a clipboard.

FlavorMap

The FlavorMap interface maps MIME types to Java data flavors.

Transferable

The `Transferable` interface defines methods that support the transfer of data via the clipboard or other mechanisms. It is implemented by classes that support clipboard-related data transfers.

Classes

Clipboard

The `Clipboard` class is a subclass of `Object` that provides access to system- and user-defined clipboards. It provides methods for getting and setting the contents of a clipboard and retrieving the name of a clipboard.

DataFlavor

The `DataFlavor` class is a subclass of `Object` that defines the types of data available for a transfer operation (such as those that take place via a clipboard). Flavors are implemented as MIME types. The `DataFlavor` class provides methods for reading and writing objects to be transferred and for accessing MIME type information. It implements the `java.io.Serializable` and `java.lang.Cloneable` interfaces.

StringSelection

The `StringSelection` class is a subclass of `Object` that supports the transfer of `String` objects as plain text. It provides methods for working with string-related data flavors. It implements the `Transferable` and `ClipboardOwner` interfaces.

SystemFlavorMap

The `SystemFlavorMap` class extends the `Object` class and provides a default implementation of the `FlavorMap` interface.

Exceptions and Errors

UnsupportedFlavorException

The `UnsupportedFlavorException` class is a subclass of `java.lang.Exception` that is used to signal that transferable data is not supported in a particular flavor.

PACKAGE `java.awt.dnd`

The `java.awt.dnd` package supports the new JDK 1.2 drag-and-drop capability. It contains 12 classes and four interfaces.

Interfaces

Autoscroll

The `Autoscroll` interface provides methods that support automatic scrolling through GUI components in support of drag-and-drop operations.

DragGestureListener

The DragGestureListener interface extends the EventListener interface to allow for the handling of the DragGestureEvent event.

DragSourceListener

The DragSourceListener interface extends the java.util.EventListener interface to define methods that are implemented by objects that originate drag-and-drop operations. These methods track the state of drag-and-drop operations and enable feedback to be provided to the user.

DropTargetListener

The DropTargetListener interface extends the java.util.EventListener interface to define methods that are implemented by objects that are the target of drag-and-drop operations.

Classes

DnDConstants

The DnDConstants class is a subclass of Object that defines constants that are used in drag-and-drop operations.

DragGestureEvent

The DragGestureEvent class extends the EventObject class to define an event to signal that a user has gestured that a drag-and-drop operation should be initiated.

DragGestureRecognizer

The DragGestureRecognizer class extends Object to provide an abstract class for the development of platform-dependent event listeners for drag-and-drop operations.

DragSource

The DragSource class is a subclass of Object that implements the source originator of a drag-and-drop operation. It defines several java.awt.Cursor objects that define the cursor state during drag-and-drop. Its startDrag() method is used to initiate drag-and-drop.

DragSourceContext

The DragSourceContext class is a subclass of Object that is used to manage the source-side of drag-and-drop operations. It manages events associated with the drag source and implements the DragSourceListener interface.

DragSourceDragEvent

The DragSourceDragEvent class is a subclass of DragSourceEvent. It implements the event that is handled by a DragSourceListener during the dragging stage of a drag-and-drop operation.

DragSourceDropEvent

The DragSourceDropEvent class is a subclass of DragSourceEvent. It implements the event that is handled by a DragSourceListener during the dropping stage of a drag-and-drop operation.

DragSourceEvent

The DragSourceEvent class is a subclass of java.util.EventObject that is used as the base class for DragSourceDragEvent and DragSourceDropEvent.

DropTarget

The DropTarget class is a subclass of Object that is used to implement the target of a drag-and-drop operation. Objects of DropTarget are associated with components that function as drop targets. These objects are typically GUI components. DropTarget implements the DropTargetListener and java.io.Serializable interfaces.

DropTarget.DropTargetAutoScroller

The DropTarget.DropTargetAutoScroller class is an inner class of DropTarget that supports scrolling operations.

DropTargetContext

The DropTargetContext class is a subclass of Object that is used to implement the context of a drop operation. Objects of this class are dynamically created when an object is dragged over a potential drop target. This class is used by the drop target to provide feedback to the user and to initiate the data transfer associated with the drag-and-drop operation.

DropTargetDragEvent

The DropTargetDragEvent class is a subclass of DropTargetEvent that informs DropTargetListener objects of the dragging state of a drag-and-drop operation.

DropTargetDropEvent

The DropTargetDropEvent class is a subclass of DropTargetEvent that informs DropTargetListener objects of the dropping state of a drag-and-drop operation.

DropTargetEvent

The DropTargetEvent class is a subclass of java.util.EventObject that serves as the base class for DropTargetDragEvent and DropTargetDropEvent.

MouseDragGestureRecognizer

The MouseDragGestureRecognizer class extends DragGestureRecognizer and implements the MouseListener and MouseMotionListener interfaces. This class provides support for mouse-based drag-and-drop listeners.

Exceptions and Errors

InvalidDnDOperationException

The `InvalidDnDOperationException` class is a subclass of `java.lang.IllegalStateException` that signals that a drag-and-drop operation cannot be carried out.

PACKAGE `java.awt.event`

The `java.awt.event` package provides the foundation for JDK 1.1-style event processing. It contains 21 classes and 13 interfaces.

Interfaces

ActionListener

The `ActionListener` interface extends the `java.util.EventListener` interface and defines methods that are implemented by classes that handle `ActionEvent` events.

AdjustmentListener

The `AdjustmentListener` interface extends the `java.util.EventListener` interface and defines methods that are implemented by classes that handle `AdjustmentEvent` events.

AWTEventListener

The `AWTEventListener` interface extends the `java.util.EventListener` interface and defines methods that are implemented by classes that handle the `AWTEvent`.

ComponentListener

The `ComponentListener` interface extends the `java.util.EventListener` interface and defines methods that are implemented by classes that handle `ComponentEvent` events.

ContainerListener

The `ContainerListener` interface extends the `java.util.EventListener` interface and defines methods that are implemented by classes that handle `ContainerEvent` events.

FocusListener

The `FocusListener` interface extends the `java.util.EventListener` interface and defines methods that are implemented by classes that handle `FocusEvent` events.

InputMethodListener

The `InputMethodListener` interface extends the `java.util.EventListener` interface and defines methods that are implemented by classes that handle `InputMethodEvent` events.

ItemListener

The `ItemListener` interface extends the `java.util.EventListener` interface and defines methods that are implemented by classes that handle `Item` events.

KeyListener

The `KeyListener` interface extends the `java.util.EventListener` interface and defines methods that are implemented by classes that handle `KeyEvent` events.

MouseListener

The `MouseListener` interface extends the `java.util.EventListener` interface and defines methods that are implemented by classes that handle `MouseEvent` events.

MouseMotionListener

The `MouseMotionListener` interface extends the `java.util.EventListener` interface and defines methods that are implemented by classes that handle `MouseEvent` events.

TextListener

The `TextListener` interface extends the `java.util.EventListener` interface and defines methods that are implemented by classes that handle `TextEvent` events.

WindowListener

The `WindowListener` interface extends the `java.util.EventListener` interface and defines methods that are implemented by classes that handle `WindowEvent` events.

Classes

ActionEvent

The `ActionEvent` class is a subclass of `java.awt.AWTEvent` that implements an event generated by user interface actions, such as clicking on a button or selecting a menu item.

AdjustmentEvent

The `AdjustmentEvent` class is a subclass of `java.awt.AWTEvent` that implements an event generated by scrolling actions.

ComponentAdapter

The `ComponentAdapter` class is a subclass of `Object` that provides a basic implementation of the `ComponentListener` interface.

ComponentEvent

The `ComponentEvent` class is a subclass of `java.awt.AWTEvent` that implements an event generated by changes to the position, focus, or sizing of a window component, or by a keyboard input or other mouse action.

ContainerAdapter

The ContainerAdapter class is a subclass of Object that provides a basic implementation of the ContainerListener interface.

ContainerEvent

The ContainerEvent class is a subclass of java.awt.ComponentEvent that implements an event generated by adding and removing components from a container.

FocusAdapter

The FocusAdapter class is a subclass of Object that provides a basic implementation of the FocusListener interface.

FocusEvent

The FocusEvent class is a subclass of ComponentEvent that implements an event generated by a change in the status of a component's input focus.

InputEvent

The InputEvent class is a subclass of ComponentEvent that is the base class for defining events generated by user keyboard and mouse actions.

InputMethodEvent

The InputMethodEvent class is a subclass of java.awt.AWTEvent that implements an event generated by changes to the text being entered via an input method.

InvocationEvent

The InvocationEvent class extends the java.awt.AWTEvent class and implements the java.awt.ActiveEvent interface. It signals the invocation of a Runnable object.

ItemEvent

The ItemEvent class is a subclass of AWTEvent that implements an event generated by a component state change, such as selecting an item from a list.

KeyAdapter

The KeyAdapter class is a subclass of Object that provides a basic implementation of the KeyListener interface.

KeyEvent

The KeyEvent class is a subclass of InputEvent that implements an event generated by user keyboard actions.

MouseAdapter

The MouseAdapter class is a subclass of Object that provides a basic implementation of the MouseListener interface.

MouseEvent

The `MouseEvent` class is a subclass of `InputEvent` that implements an event generated by low-level mouse actions.

MouseMotionAdapter

The `MouseMotionAdapter` class is a subclass of `Object` that provides a basic implementation of the `MouseMotionListener` interface.

PaintEvent

The `PaintEvent` class is a subclass of `ComponentEvent` that implements an event generated by the painting/repainting of a window.

TextEvent

The `TextEvent` class is a subclass of `java.awt.AWTEvent` that implements an event generated by text-related events, such as changing the value of a text field.

WindowAdapter

The `WindowAdapter` class is a subclass of `Object` that provides a basic implementation of the `WindowListener` interface.

WindowEvent

The `WindowEvent` class is a subclass of `ComponentEvent` that implements an event generated by events such as the opening, closing, and minimizing of a window.

Exceptions and Errors

None.

PACKAGE `java.awt.font`

The `java.awt.font` package is new to JDK 1.2. It provides 13 classes and two interfaces that support advanced font capabilities.

Interfaces

MultipleMaster

The `MultipleMaster` interface defines methods that are implemented by classes that support Type 1 Multiple Master fonts.

OpenType

The `OpenType` interface defines methods that are implemented by classes that support Open Type and True Type fonts.

Classes

FontRendererContext

The `FontRendererContext` class extends the Object class to provide a container for the information needed to correctly measure text.

GlyphJustificationInfo

The GlyphJustificationInfo class is a subclass of Object that provides information about the justification of a glyph.

GlyphMetrics

The GlyphMetrics class is a subclass of Object that defines the properties of a single glyph.

GlyphVector

The GlyphVector class is a subclass of Object that represents text as a sequence of integer glyph codes. It implements the java.lang.Cloneable interface.

GraphicAttribute

The GraphicAttribute class is a subclass of Object that is used to identify a graphic that is embedded in text.

ImageGraphicAttribute

The ImageGraphicAttribute class is a subclass of GraphicAttribute that is used to identify an image that is embedded in text.

LineBreakMeasurer

The LineBreakMeasurer class is a subclass of Object that organizes lines of text according to a wrapping width.

LineMetrics

The LineMetrics class extends the Object class to provide access to line-oriented text metrics.

ShapeGraphicAttribute

The ShapeGraphicAttribute class is a subclass of GraphicAttribute that is used to identify a Shape object that is embedded in text.

TextAttribute

The TextAttribute class is a subclass of java.text.AttributedCharacterIterator.Attribute that maintains a set of attributes for rendering text.

TextHitInfo

The TextHitInfo class is a subclass of Object that is used to specify a position within text.

TextLayout

The TextLayout class is a subclass of Object that provides support for laying out styled text. It implements the java.lang.Cloneable interface.

TextLayout.CaretPolicy

The TextLayout.CaretPolicy class is an inner class of TextLayout that specifies how the caret should be used with a TextLayout object. It is a subclass of Object.

TextLine.TextLineMetrics

The `TextLine.TextLineMetrics` class extends `Object` to provide basic metrics for working with text.

TransformAttribute

The `TransformAttribute` class extends `Object` and implements the `Serializable` interface. It allows transforms to be used as attributes.

Exceptions and Errors

None.

PACKAGE `java.awt.geom`

The `java.awt.geom` package is a new JDK 1.2 package that is part of the Java 2D API. It provides 30 classes and one interface that support standard geometrical objects and transformations.

Interfaces

PathIterator

The `PathIterator` interface provides constants and methods for iterating over the points in a path.

Classes

AffineTransform

The `AffineTransform` class is a subclass of `Object` that provides the capability to compute two-dimensional affine transformations. It implements the `java.lang.Cloneable` interface.

Arc2D

The `Arc2D` class is a subclass of `RectangularShape` that defines an arc within a bounding rectangle.

Arc2D.Double

The `Arc2D.Double` class is an inner class of `Arc2D` that specifies the arc in `double` precision.

Arc2D.Float

The `Arc2D.Float` class is an inner class of `Arc2D` that specifies the arc in `float` precision.

Area

The `Area` class is a subclass of `Object` that encapsulates an arbitrary 2D area. It implements the `java.awt.Shape` and `java.lang.Cloneable` interfaces.

CubicCurve2D

The `CubicCurve2D` class is a subclass of `Object` that encapsulates a cubic curve.

CubicCurve2D.Double

The CubicCurve2D.Double class is an inner class of CubicCurve2D that specifies the curve in double precision.

CubicCurve2D.Float

The CubicCurve2D.Float class is an inner class of CubicCurve2D that specifies the curve in float precision.

Dimension2D

The Dimension2D class is a subclass of Object that encapsulates width and height dimensions. It implements the java.lang.Cloneable interface.

Ellipse2D

The Ellipse2D class is a subclass of RectangularShape that represents an ellipse.

Ellipse2D.Double

The Ellipse2D.Double class is an inner class of Ellipse2D that specifies the ellipse in double precision.

Ellipse2D.Float

The Ellipse2D.Float class is an inner class of Ellipse2D that specifies the ellipse in float precision.

FlatteningPathIterator

The FlatteningPathIterator class is a subclass of Object that is used to flatten a path. It implements the PathIterator interface.

GeneralPath

The GeneralPath class is a subclass of Object that represents a general 2D path. It implements the java.awt.Shape and java.lang.Cloneable interfaces.

Line2D

The Line2D class is a subclass of Object that encapsulates a 2D line. It implements the java.awt.Shape and java.lang.Cloneable interfaces.

Line2D.Double

The Line2D.Double class is an inner class of Line2D that specifies the line in double precision.

Line2D.Float

The Line2D.Float class is an inner class of Line2D that specifies the line in float precision.

Point2D

The Point2D class is a subclass of Object that represents a 2D point. It implements the java.lang.Cloneable interface.

Point2D.Double

The `Point2D.Double` class is an inner class of `Point2D` that specifies the point in `double` precision.

Point2D.Float

The `Point2D.Float` class is an inner class of `Point2D` that specifies the point in `float` precision.

QuadCurve2D

The `QuadCurve2D` class is a subclass of `Object` that encapsulates a 2D quadratic curve. It implements the `java.awt.Shape` and `java.lang.Cloneable` interfaces.

QuadCurve2D.Double

The `QuadCurve2D.Double` class is an inner class of `QuadCurve2D` that specifies the curve using a `double` value.

QuadCurve2D.Float

The `QuadCurve2D.Float` class is an inner class of `QuadCurve2D` that specifies the curve using a `float` value.

Rectangle2D

The `Rectangle2D` class is a subclass of `RectangularShape` that encapsulates a 2D rectangle.

Rectangle2D.Double

The `Rectangle2D.Double` class is an inner class of `Rectangle2D` that specifies the rectangle using `double` values.

Rectangle2D.Float

The `Rectangle2D.Float` class is an inner class of `Rectangle2D` that specifies the rectangle using `float` values.

RectangularShape

The `RectangularShape` class is a subclass of `Object` that is the base class for other rectangular shapes. It implements the `java.awt.Shape` and `java.lang.Cloneable` interfaces.

RoundRectangle2D

The `RoundRectangle2D` class is a subclass of `RectangularShape` that defines a rectangle with rounded corners.

RoundRectangle2D.Double

The `RoundRectangle2D.Double` class is an inner class of `RoundRectangle2D` that specifies the rectangle using `double` values.

RoundRectangle2D.Float

The `RoundRectangle2D.Float` class is an inner class of `RoundRectangle2D` that specifies the rectangle using `float` values.

antoantaant282o8 act2

Exceptions and Errors

IllegalPathStateException
The IllegalPathStateException class is a subclass of java.lang.RuntimeException that signals an attempt to perform an operation on a path when it is in the incorrect state for that operation.

NoninvertibleTransformException
The NoninvertibleTransformException class is a subclass of java.lang.Exception indicating that an operation requiring an invertible transform was performed using a noninvertible transform.

PACKAGE java.awt.im

The java.awt.im package is a new package that supports the Input Method API. It contains three classes and one interface.

Interfaces

InputMethodRequests
The InputMethodRequests interface defines methods that must be implemented by an input handling class in order to function within the Input Method API. These methods are used to obtain information about the text being entered by the user.

Classes

InputContext
The InputContext class is a subclass of Object that is used to implement the connection between text editing components and input methods. It does this by generating events that are handled by the text editing components and input methods.

InputMethodHighlight
The InputMethodHighlight class is a subclass of Object that supports the highlighting and conversion of text that is input via an input method.

InputSubset
The InputSubset class extends java.lang.Character.Subset to provide Unicode support for input methods.

Exceptions and Errors
None.

PACKAGE java.awt.image

The java.awt.image package is a Java 2D API package that supports image processing. It provides 38 classes and 8 interfaces that support common image filters.

Interfaces

BufferedImageOp

The BufferedImageOp interface defines methods for classes that perform operations on BufferedImage objects.

ImageConsumer

The ImageConsumer interface defines methods for classes that receive image data from ImageProducer objects.

ImageObserver

The ImageObserver interface defines methods for classes that observe the loading/construction of Image objects.

ImageProducer

The ImageProducer interface defines methods for classes that produce image data for use by ImageConsumer objects.

RasterOp

The RasterOp interface is implemented by classes that support operations on Raster objects.

RenderedImage

The RenderedImage interface is implemented by classes that produce image data in the form of Raster objects.

TileObserver

The TileObserver interface defines methods for handling events generated by changes to tiles of an image.

WritableRenderedImage

The WritableRenderedImage interface defines methods for classes that implement images that can be overwritten.

Classes

AffineTransformOp

The AffineTransformOp class is a subclass of Object that performs a 2D affine transform between two images. It implements the BufferedImageOp and RasterOp interfaces.

AreaAveragingScaleFilter

The AreaAveragingScaleFilter class is a subclass of ReplicateScaleFilter that supports image resizing using an area-averaging algorithm.

BandCombineOp

The BandCombineOp class is a subclass of Object that performs operations that combine bands in a Raster object. It implements the RasterOp interface.

BandedSampleModel

The `BandedSampleModel` class is a subclass of `SampleModel` that provides advanced band control.

BufferedImage

The `BufferedImage` class is a subclass of `Image` that provides access to buffered image data. It implements the `WritableRenderedImage` interface.

BufferedImageFilter

The `BufferedImageFilter` class is a subclass of `ImageFilter` that supports `BufferedImage` objects. It implements the `RasterImageConsumer` and `java.lang.Cloneable` interfaces.

ByteLookupTable

The `ByteLookupTable` class is a subclass of `LookupTable` that supports byte data.

ColorConvertOp

The `ColorConvertOp` class is a subclass of `Object` that supports pixel-by-pixel color conversions. It implements the `BufferedImageOp` and `RasterOp` interfaces.

ColorModel

The `ColorModel` class is a subclass of `Object` that provides the base class for the development of a variety of color models. It implements the `Transparency` interface.

ComponentColorModel

The `ComponentColorModel` class is a subclass of `ColorModel` that provides support for a variety of color spaces.

ComponentSampleModel

The `ComponentSampleModel` class is a subclass of `SampleModel` that supports the separate storage of color component data.

ConvolveOp

The `ConvolveOp` class is a subclass of `Object` that supports convolution operations on image data. It implements the `BufferedImageOp` and `RasterOp` interfaces.

CropImageFilter

The `CropImageFilter` class is a subclass of `ImageFilter` that supports image cropping.

DataBuffer

The `DataBuffer` class is a subclass of `Object` that supports the buffering of image data.

DataBufferByte

The `DataBufferByte` class is a subclass of `DataBuffer` that supports `byte`-oriented image buffering.

DataBufferInt

The `DataBufferInt` class is a subclass of `DataBuffer` that supports `int`-oriented image buffering.

DataBufferShort

The `DataBufferShort` class is a subclass of `DataBuffer` that supports `short`-oriented image buffering.

DataBufferUShort

The `DataBufferUShort` class is a subclass of `DataBuffer` that supports unsigned `short`-oriented image buffering.

DirectColorModel

The `DirectColorModel` class is a subclass of `PackedColorModel` that supports direct RGB pixel colors.

FilteredImageSource

The `FilteredImageSource` class is a subclass of `Object` that combines an `ImageProducer` with an `ImageFilter`. It implements the `ImageProducer` interface.

ImageFilter

The `ImageFilter` class is a subclass of `Object` that supports general image filtering operations. It implements the `ImageConsumer` and `java.lang.Cloneable` interfaces.

IndexColorModel

The `IndexColorModel` class is a subclass of `ColorModel` that represents pixels as indices into a color map.

Kernel

The `Kernel` class is a subclass of `Object` that defines matrices for filtering operations.

LookupOp

The `LookupOp` class is a subclass of `Object` that supports image lookup operations. It implements the `BufferedImageOp` and `RasterOp` interfaces.

LookupTable

The `LookupTable` class is a subclass of `Object` that defines a lookup table for use in imaging operations.

MemoryImageSource

The `MemoryImageSource` class is a subclass of `Object` that provides image data from a memory source. It implements the `ImageProducer` interface.

MultiPixelPackedSampleModel

The MultiPixelPackedSampleModel class is a subclass of SampleModel that supports the processing of multiple one-sample pixels.

PackedColorModel

The PackedColorModel class is a subclass of ColorModel that represents color values directly within pixel data.

PixelGrabber

The PixelGrabber class is a subclass of Object that is used to retrieve a subset of the pixels of an image. It implements the ImageConsumer interface.

PixelInterleavedSampleModel

The PixelInterleavedSampleModel class extends ComponentSampleModel to provide the capability to store interleaved pixel image data.

RGBImageFilter

The RGBImageFilter class is a subclass of ImageFilter that supports the filtering of RGB color values.

Raster

The Raster class is a subclass of Object that implements a rectangular array of pixels.

ReplicateScaleFilter

The ReplicateScaleFilter class is a subclass of ImageFilter that implements a simple scaling algorithm.

RescaleOp

The RescaleOp class is a subclass of Object that supports image-rescaling operations. It implements the BufferedImageOp and RasterOp interfaces.

SampleModel

The SampleModel class is a subclass of Object that provides a base class for developing approaches to sampling image data.

ShortLookupTable

The ShortLookupTable class is a subclass of LookupTable that supports short-valued data.

SinglePixelPackedSampleModel

The SinglePixelPackedSampleModel class is a subclass of SampleModel that packs single-pixel samples in a single data element.

WritableRaster

The WritableRaster class is a subclass of Raster that provides support for image updating.

Exceptions and Errors

ImagingOpException

The `ImagingOpException` class is a subclass of `java.lang.RuntimeException` that indicates errors encountered during filtering operations.

RasterFormatException

The `RasterFormatException` class is a subclass of `java.lang.RuntimeException` that indicates format errors in `Raster` objects.

PACKAGE java.awt.image.renderable

The `java.awt.image.renderable` package provides four classes and three interfaces that support image rendering.

Interfaces

ContextualRenderedImageFactory

The `ContextualRenderedImageFactory` interface extends the `RenderedImageFactory` interface to provide methods that support rendering-independent operations. It is implemented by subclasses of `RenderableImageOp`.

RenderableImage

The `RenderableImage` interface provides a common set of methods for rendering-independent images. These methods support image operations that are independent of any specific image rendering.

RenderedImageFactory

The `RenderedImageFactory` interface defines the `create()` method for use by classes that provide different image renderings, depending on a particular set of rendering parameters.

Classes

ParameterBlock

The `ParameterBlock` class is a subclass of `Object` that provides a common set of parameters for use with `RenderableImageOp` objects. It implements the `java.lang.Cloneable` and `java.io.Serializable` interfaces.

RenderContext

The `RenderContext` class is a subclass of `Object` that specifies contextual information for rendering a `RenderableImage` object. This contextual information includes the area of interest, transforms, and rendering hints. It implements the `java.lang.Cloneable` interface.

RenderableImageOp

The `RenderableImageOp` class is a subclass of `Object` that supports context-specific image rendering. It implements the `RenderableImage` interface.

RenderableImageProducer

The `RenderableImageProducer` class is a subclass of `Object` that supports the asynchronous production of a `RenderableImage` object. It implements the `java.awt.image.ImageProducer` and `java.lang.Runnable` interfaces.

Exceptions and Errors

None.

PACKAGE `java.awt.print`

The `java.awt.print` package is a Java 2D API package that supports the printing of text and graphics. It contains eight classes and three interfaces.

Interfaces

PrinterGraphics

The `PrinterGraphics`interface provides access to a `PrinterJob` object.

Pageable

The `Pageable` interface specifies methods used for objects that represent a set of pages to be printed. These methods retrieve the number of pages to be printed and a specific page from within the page list.

Printable

The `Printable` interface defines the `print()` method for printing a page on a `Graphics` object.

Classes

Book

The `Book` class is a subclass of `Object` that maintains a list of pages to be printed. It provides methods for adding and managing pages. It implements the `Pageable` interface.

PageFormat

The `PageFormat` class is a subclass of `Object` that specifies the size and orientation of a page to be printed. It provides methods for setting the `Paper` object to be used and the page orientation. It also provides methods for switching the drawing space between portrait and landscape mode and for retrieving the characteristics of the drawing area. It implements the `java.lang.Cloneable` interface.

Paper

The `Paper` class is a subclass of `Object` that specifies the physical characteristics of the paper used for printing. It provides methods for getting and setting the paper size and the drawing area.

PrinterJob

The PrinterJob class is a subclass of Object that initiates, manages, and controls a printing request. Provides methods for printing Pageable objects and specifying print properties.

Exceptions and Errors

PrinterAbortException

The PrinterAbortException class is a subclass of PrinterException that indicates a print job has been aborted.

PrinterException

The PrinterException class extends java.lang.Exception to provide a base class for printing-related exceptions.

PrinterIOException

The PrinterIOException class extends PrinterException to indicate a printing I/O error.

PACKAGE java.beans

The java.beans package contains 15 classes and eight interfaces that provide the basic JavaBeans functionality. The java.beans package is covered in Part 7, "Creating JavaBeans."

Interfaces

AppletInitializer

The AppletInitializer interface provides support for initializing beans that are also applets.

BeanInfo

The BeanInfo interface is used to provide explicit information about a bean.

Customizer

The Customizer interface provides methods for customizing a bean's GUI.

DesignMode

The DesignMode interface is used to signal that a bean is in design (as opposed to execution) mode.

PropertyChangeListener

The PropertyChangeListener interface defines methods for handling events that result from changes to bound bean properties. It extends java.util.EventListener.

PropertyEditor

The PropertyEditor interface provides support for changing the properties of a bean.

VetoableChangeListener

The `VetoableChangeListener` interface extends `java.util.EventListener` to provide support for handing constrained property change events.

Visibility

The `Visibility` interface is used to signal whether a bean needs a GUI to perform its processing.

Classes

BeanDescriptor

The `BeanDescriptor` class is a subclass of `FeatureDescriptor` that provides global information about a bean.

Beans

The `Beans` class is a subclass of `Object` that provides general-purpose bean support.

EventSetDescriptor

The `EventSetDescriptor` class is a subclass of `FeatureDescriptor` that describes the events supported by a bean.

FeatureDescriptor

The `FeatureDescriptor` class is a subclass of `Object` that serves as a base class for explicit bean descriptions.

IndexedPropertyDescriptor

The `IndexedPropertyDescriptor` class is a subclass of `PropertyDescriptor` that supports indexed property descriptions.

Introspector

The `Introspector` class is a subclass of `Object` that provides `static` methods for obtaining information about a bean.

MethodDescriptor

The `MethodDescriptor` class is a subclass of `FeatureDescriptor` that provides information about a bean's methods.

ParameterDescriptor

The `ParameterDescriptor` class is a subclass of `FeatureDescriptor` that describes the parameters supported by a bean method.

PropertyChangeEvent

The `PropertyChangeEvent` class is a subclass of `java.util.EventObject` that signals a change in a bean's properties.

PropertyChangeSupport

The `PropertyChangeSupport` class is a subclass of `Object` that provides support for `PropertyChangeEvent` handling. It implements the `java.io.Serializable` interface.

PropertyDescriptor
The `PropertyDescriptor` class is a subclass of `FeatureDescriptor` that describes a bean property.

PropertyEditorManager
The `PropertyEditorManager` class is a subclass of `Object` that is used to access bean property editors.

PropertyEditorSupport
The `PropertyEditorSupport` class is a subclass of `Object` that provides a basic implementation of the `PropertyEditor` interface.

SimpleBeanInfo
The `SimpleBeanInfo` class is a subclass of `Object` that provides a basic implementation of the `BeanInfo` interface.

VetoableChangeSupport
The `VetoableChangeSupport` class is a subclass of `Object` that provides support for property change event handling. It implements the `java.io.Serializable` interface.

Exceptions and Errors
IntrospectionException
The `IntrospectionException` class is a subclass of `java.lang.Exception` that indicates that an exception occurred during introspection.

PropertyVetoException
The `PropertyVetoException` class is a subclass of `java.lang.Exception` that indicates an invalid property change.

PACKAGE java.beans.beancontext
The `java.beans.beancontext` package provides 9 classes and 11 interfaces that implement an execution context for beans.

Interfaces
BeanContext
The `BeanContext` interface is implemented by classes that act as containers for other beans. It extends the `BeanContextChild`, `java.util.Collection`, `java.beans.DesignMode`, and `java.beans.Visibility` interfaces.

BeanContextChild
The `BeanContextChild` interface defines methods that allow classes to access their execution environment.

BeanContextChildComponentProxy
The `BeanContextChildComponentProxy` interface provides access to the AWT component associated with a `BeanContextChildren` object.

BeanContextContainerProxy
The BeanContextContainerProxy interface provides access to the AWT container associated with a BeanContext object.

BeanContextMembershipListener
The BeanContextMembershipListener interface defines methods for handling events associated with changes in membership in a bean context. It extends the java.util.EventListener interface.

BeanContextProxy
The BeanContextProxy interface is implemented by beans that use the context of other beans.

BeanContextServiceProvider
The BeanContextServiceProvider interface defines methods that are used to provide services to a bean context.

BeanContextServiceProviderBeanInfo
The BeanContextServiceProviderBeanInfo interface extends the BeanInfo interface to provide explicit information about the services of an interface.

BeanContextServiceRevokedListener
The BeanContextServiceRevokedListener interface supports the handling of events associated with revocation of a service to a bean context. It extends the java.util.EventListener interface.

BeanContextServices
The BeanContextServices interface defines methods that allow a BeanContext object to make services available to its contained BeanContextChild objects. It extends the BeanContext and BeanContextServicesListener interfaces.

BeanContextServicesListener
The BeanContextServicesListener interface defines methods for handling events associated with a service becoming available to a bean context. It extends the BeanContextServiceRevokedListener interface.

Classes

BeanContextChildSupport
The BeanContextChildSupport class is a subclass of Object that provides a basic implementation of the BeanContextChild interface. It also implements the BeanContextServicesListener and java.io.Serializable interfaces.

BeanContextEvent
The BeanContextEvent class is a subclass of java.util.EventObject that serves as the base class for bean context-related events.

BeanContextMembershipEvent

The `BeanContextMembershipEvent` class is a subclass of `BeanContextEvent` that is used to signal a change in the set of beans that is contained in a bean context.

BeanContextServiceAvailableEvent

The `BeanContextServiceAvailableEvent` class is a subclass of `BeanContextEvent` that indicates that a service has been made available to a bean context.

BeanContextServiceRevokedEvent

The `BeanContextServiceRevokedEvent` class is a subclass of `BeanContextEvent` that indicates that a service is no longer available to a bean context.

BeanContextServicesSupport

The `BeanContextServicesSupport` class is a subclass of `BeanContextSupport` that provides a basic implementation of the `BeanContextServices` interface.

BeanContextServicesSupport.BCSSChild

The `BeanContextServicesSupport.BCSSChild` class is an inner class of `BeanContextServicesSupport` that is inherited from `BeanContextSupport`. It is a subclass of `BeanContextSupport.BCSChild`.

BeanContextSupport

The `BeanContextSupport` class is a subclass of `BeanContextChildSupport` that provides a basic implementation of the `BeanContext` interface. It also implements the `java.beans.PropertyChangeListener`, `java.beans.VetoableChangeListener`, and `java.io.Serializable` interfaces.

BeanContextSupport.BCSIterator

The `BeanContextSupport.BCSIterator` class is an inner class of `BeanContextSupport` that is used as an iterator within its parent. It is a subclass of `Object` that implements the `java.util.Iterator` interface.

Exceptions and Errors

None.

PACKAGE java.io

The `java.io` package provides 50 classes and 10 interfaces that implement stream-based input and output.

Interfaces

DataInput

The `DataInput` interface provides methods for reading primitive types from a byte stream.

DataOutput

The DataOutput interface provides methods for writing primitive types to a byte stream.

Externalizable

The Externalizable interface extends the Serializable interface to provide methods for writing objects to a stream and for reading them back from a stream.

FileFilter

The FileFilter interface provides the capability to filter path names.

FilenameFilter

The FilenameFilter interface provides the capability to filter file names during file name selection.

ObjectInput

The ObjectInput interface extends the DataInput interface to support the reading of objects from input streams.

ObjectInputValidation

The ObjectInputValidation interface supports the validation of objects within a graph.

ObjectOutput

The ObjectOutput interface extends the DataOutput interface to support the writing of objects to output streams.

ObjectStreamConstants

The ObjectStreamConstants interface provides constants that are used to perform object-based input and output.

Serializable

The Serializable interface identifies an object as being capable of being written to and read from a stream.

Classes

BufferedInputStream

The BufferedInputStream class is a subclass of FilterInputStream that supports input buffering.

BufferedOutputStream

The BufferedOutputStream class is a subclass of FilterOutputStream that supports output buffering.

BufferedReader

The BufferedReader class is a subclass of Reader that supports input buffering.

BufferedWriter

The `BufferedWriter` class is a subclass of `Writer` that supports output buffering.

ByteArrayInputStream

The `ByteArrayInputStream` class is a subclass of `InputStream` that supports input from a byte array.

ByteArrayOutputStream

The `ByteArrayOutputStream` class is a subclass of `OutputStream` that supports output to a byte array.

CharArrayReader

The `CharArrayReader` class is a subclass of `Reader` that supports input from a character array.

CharArrayWriter

The `CharArrayWriter` class is a subclass of `Writer` that supports output to a character array.

DataInputStream

The `DataInputStream` class is a subclass of `FilterInputStream` that allows primitive types to be read from an input stream. It implements the `DataInput` interface.

DataOutputStream

The `DataOutputStream` class is a subclass of `FilterOutputStream` that allows primitive types to be written to an output stream. It implements the `DataOutput` interface.

File

The `File` class is a subclass of `Object` that encapsulates a disk file. It implements the `Serializabe` and `java.lang.Comparable` interfaces.

FileDescriptor

The `FileDescriptor` class is a subclass of `Object` that encapsulates a file descriptor.

FileInputStream

The `FileInputStream` class is a subclass of `InputStream` that supports file-based input.

FileOutputStream

The `FileOutputStream` class is a subclass of `OutputStream` that supports file-based output.

FilePermission

The `FilePermission` class is a subclass of `java.security.Permission` that is used to control access to files. It implements the `Serializable` interface.

FileReader
The `FileReader` class is a subclass of `InputStreamReader` that supports file-based input.

FileWriter
The `FileWriter` class is a subclass of `OutputStreamWriter` that supports file-based output.

FilterInputStream
The `FilterInputStream` class is a subclass of `InputStream` that is used to filter data that is being read from a stream.

FilterOutputStream
The `FilterOutputStream` class is a subclass of `OutputStream` that is used to filter data that is being written to a stream.

FilterReader
The `FilterReader` class is a subclass of `Reader` that allows filtering of data that is being read.

FilterWriter
The `FilterWriter` class is a subclass of `Writer` that allows filtering of data that is being written.

InputStream
The `InputStream` class is a subclass of `Object` that provides the base class for all stream-based input.

InputStreamReader
The `InputStreamReader` class is a subclass of `Reader` that is used to read a stream using a `Reader` object.

LineNumberInputStream
The `LineNumberInputStream` class is a subclass of `FilterInputStream` that supports line number identification.

LineNumberReader
The `LineNumberReader` class is a subclass of `BufferedReader` that supports line number identification.

ObjectInputStream
The `ObjectInputStream` class is a subclass of `InputStream` that supports the reading of objects from streams. It implements the `ObjectInput` and `ObjectStreamConstants` interfaces.

ObjectInputStream.GetField
The `ObjectInputStream.GetField` class is an inner class of `ObjectInputStream` that provides support for the reading of individual object fields. It is a subclass of `Object`.

ObjectOutputStream

The `ObjectOutputStream` class is a subclass of `OutputStream` that supports the writing of objects to streams. It implements the `ObjectOutput` and `ObjectStreamConstants` interfaces.

ObjectOutputStream.PutField

The `ObjectOutputStream.PutField` class is an inner class of `ObjectOutputStream` that allows individual object fields to be accessed. It is a subclass of `Object`.

ObjectStreamClass

The `ObjectStreamClass` class is a subclass of `Object` that describes a serialized class. It implements the `Serializable` interface.

ObjectStreamField

The `ObjectStreamField` class is a subclass of `Object` that describes a field of a serialized class. It implements the `java.lang.Comparable` interface.

OutputStream

The `OutputStream` class is a subclass of `Object` that provides the basis for stream-based output.

OutputStreamWriter

The `OutputStreamWriter` class is a subclass of `Writer` that allows output streams to be accessed as `Writer` objects.

PipedInputStream

The `PipedInputStream` class is a subclass of `InputStream` that supports communication between threads.

PipedOutputStream

The `PipedOutputStream` class is a subclass of `OutputStream` that supports communication between threads.

PipedReader

The `PipedReader` class is a subclass of `Reader` that supports communication between threads.

PipedWriter

The `PipedWriter` class is a subclass of `Writer` that supports communication between threads.

PrintStream

The `PrintStream` class is a subclass of `FilterOutputStream` that supports printing to the standard output stream.

PrintWriter

The `PrintWriter` class is a subclass of `Writer` that supports printing to the standard output stream.

PushbackInputStream

The PushbackInputStream class is a subclass of FilterInputStream that allows data that is read in to be pushed back onto the input stream.

PushbackReader

The PushbackReader class is a subclass of FilterReader that allows data that is read in to be pushed back onto the input source.

RandomAccessFile

The RandomAccessFile class is a subclass of Object that supports random file input and output. It implements the DataInput and DataOutput interfaces.

Reader

The Reader class is a subclass of Object that provides the basis for Unicode character input.

SequenceInputStream

The SequenceInputStream class is a subclass of InputStream that supports the concatenation of two or more input streams.

SerializablePermission

The SerializablePermission class is a subclass of java.security.BasicPermission that controls access to object serialization.

StreamTokenizer

The StreamTokenizer class is a subclass of Object that supports input stream parsing.

StringBufferInputStream

The StringBufferInputStream class is a subclass of InputStream that supports input from String objects.

StringReader

The StringReader class is a subclass of Reader that supports input from String objects.

StringWriter

The StringWriter class is a subclass of Writer that supports output to String objects.

Writer

The Writer class is a subclass of Object that provides the basis for Unicode character-based output.

Exceptions and Errors

CharConversionException

The CharConversionException class is a subclass of IOException that signals that an error occurred during character conversion.

EOFException
The EOFException class is a subclass of IOException that signals that the end of a file has been encountered.

FileNotFoundException
The FileNotFoundException class is a subclass of IOException that signals that a file cannot be located.

IOException
The IOException class is a subclass of java.lang.Exception that serves as the base class for defining I/O-based exceptions.

InterruptedIOException
The InterruptedIOException class is a subclass of IOException signals that an I/O operation has been interrupted.

InvalidClassException
The InvalidClassException class is a subclass of ObjectStreamException that signals that an invalid class was encountered during object serialization.

InvalidObjectException
The InvalidObjectException class is a subclass of ObjectStreamException that signals that an invalid object was encountered during object serialization.

NotActiveException
The NotActiveException class is a subclass of ObjectStreamException that signals that serialization is not active.

NotSerializableException
The NotSerializableException class is a subclass of ObjectStreamException that signals that an object is not serializable.

ObjectStreamException
The ObjectStreamException class is a subclass of IOException that serves as a base class for defining exceptions that occur during object I/O.

OptionalDataException
The OptionalDataException class is a subclass of ObjectStreamException that signals that additional data was encountered when reading an object from an input stream.

StreamCorruptedException
The StreamCorruptedException class is a subclass of ObjectStreamException that an object stream contains errors.

SyncFailedException
The SyncFailedException class is a subclass of IOException that synchronization of I/O could not take place.

UTFDataFormatException

The `UTFDataFormatException` class is a subclass of `IOException` that an invalid UTF-8 string was read.

UnsupportedEncodingException

The `UnsupportedEncodingException` class is a subclass of `IOException` that identifies the use of unsupported data encoding.

WriteAbortedException

The `WriteAbortedException` class is a subclass of `ObjectStreamException` indicating that the writing of an object was aborted.

PACKAGE `java.lang`

The `java.lang` package provides 30 classes and three interfaces that implement fundamental Java objects. Because of its importance, the `java.lang` package is included with all Java platforms, ranging from EmbeddedJava to the full-blown JDK.

Interfaces

Cloneable

The `Cloneable` interface identifies a class as being cloneable by the `clone()` method of the `Object` class.

Comparable

The `Comparable` interface provides the `compareTo()` method for ordering the objects of a class.

Runnable

The `Runnable` interface identifies a class as being runnable as a separate thread.

Classes

Boolean

The `Boolean` class is a subclass of `Object` that wraps the primitive `boolean` type as a class. It implements the `java.io.Serializable` interface.

Byte

The `Byte` class is a subclass of `Number` that encapsulates a byte value. It implements the `Comparable` interface.

Character

The `Character` class is a subclass of `Object` that encapsulates a two-byte Unicode character value. It implements the `Comparable` and `java.io.Serializable` interfaces.

Character.Subset

The `Character.Subset` class is an inner class of `Character` that defines Unicode constants. It is a subclass of `Object`.

Character.UnicodeBlock
The `Character.UnicodeBlock` class extends `Character.Subset` to provide Unicode support.

Class
The `Class` class is a subclass of `Object` that is used to refer to classes as objects. It implements the `java.io.Serializable` interface.

ClassLoader
The `ClassLoader` class is a subclass of `Object` that is the base class for implementing custom class loaders for use with the runtime system.

Compiler
The `Compiler` class is a subclass of `Object` that is used to implement Just-In-Time (JIT) compilation.

Double
The `Double` class is a subclass of `Number` that encapsulates the `double` primitive type. It implements the `Comparable` interface.

Float
The `Float` class is a subclass of `Number` that encapsulates the `float` primitive type. It implements the `Comparable` interface.

InheritableThreadLocal
The `InheritableThreadLocal` class extends `ThreadLocal` to provide support for inheritance of thread values.

Integer
The `Integer` class is a subclass of `Number` that encapsulates the `int` primitive type. It implements the `Comparable` interface.

Long
The `Math` class is a subclass of `Number` that encapsulates the `long` primitive type. It implements the `Comparable` interface.

Math
The `Math` class is a subclass of `Object` that provides access to mathematical constants and functions.

Number
The `Number` class is a subclass of `Object` that is used as the base class for the wrapping of primitive numerical types. It implements the `java.io.Serializable` interface.

Object
The `Object` class is the highest class in the Java class hierarchy. It provides methods that are inherited by all Java classes.

Package

The Package class is a subclass of Object that is used to provide version information about a Java package.

Process

The Process class is a subclass of Object that is used to control external processes that are executed from within the Java runtime environment.

Runtime

The Runtime class is a subclass of Object that provides access to the Java runtime environment.

RuntimePermission

The RuntimePermission class is a subclass of java.security.BasicPermission that is used to control access to the runtime environment.

SecurityManager

The SecurityManager class is a subclass of Object that is used to implement a Java security policy.

Short

The Short class is a subclass of Number that encapsulates a short integer value. It implements the Comparable interface.

String

The String class is a subclass of Object that encapsulates a growable Unicode text string. It implements the Comparable and java.io.Serializable interfaces.

StringBuffer

The StringBuffer class is a subclass of Object that provides a buffer for the implementation of String objects. It implements the java.io.Serializable interface.

System

The System class is a subclass of Object that provides access to operating system-specific resources.

Thread

The Thread class is a subclass of Object that provides the capability to create objects that run as separate threads. It implements the Runnable interface.

ThreadGroup

The ThreadGroup class is a subclass of Object that represents a collection of Thread objects.

ThreadLocal
The ThreadLocal class is a subclass of Object that provides variables that are local to a specific thread instance.

Throwable
The Throwable class is a subclass of Object that is the base class for all Java errors and exceptions. It implements the **java.io.Serializable** interface.

Void
The ArithmeticException class is a subclass of Object that represents the class of the void primitive type.

Exceptions and Errors

AbstractMethodError
The AbstractMethodError class is a subclass of IncompatibleClassChangeError that indicates an attempt to invoke an abstract method.

ArithmeticException
The ArithmeticException class is a subclass of RuntimeException that is used to signal an arithmetic error, such as divide by zero.

ArrayIndexOutOfBoundsException
The ArrayIndexOutOfBoundsException class is a subclass of IndexOutOfBoundsException that indicates that an array index has exceeded its legal range.

ArrayStoreException
The ArrayStoreException class is a subclass of RuntimeException that indicates an attempt to store the wrong type of object in an array.

ClassCastException
The ClassCastException class is a subclass of RuntimeException that indicates an attempt to perform an illegal object cast.

ClassCircularityError
The ClassCircularityError class is a subclass of LinkageError that indicates a circularity in a class definition.

ClassFormatError
The ClassFormatError class is a subclass of LinkageError that indicates an error in the format of a class's bytecode file.

ClassNotFoundException
The ClassNotFoundException class is a subclass of Exception that signals that the class loader is unable to locate a particular class.

CloneNotSupportedException

The `CloneNotSupportedException` class is a subclass of `Exception` that signals an attempt to clone an object that does not implement the `Cloneable` interface.

Error

The `Error` class is a subclass of `Throwable` that is the base class of all Java error classes.

Exception

The `Exception` class is a subclass of `Throwable` that is the base class of all Java exception classes.

ExceptionInInitializerError

The `ExceptionInInitializerError` class is a subclass of `LinkageError` that indicates the occurrence of an unexpected exception.

IllegalAccessError

The `IllegalAccessError` class is a subclass of `IncompatibleClassChangeError` that indicates an attempt to access a field or method that violates the access modifier assigned to the field or method.

IllegalAccessException

The `IllegalAccessException` class is a subclass of `Exception` that signals an illegal attempt to load a class.

IllegalArgumentException

The `IllegalArgumentException` class is a subclass of `RuntimeException` that indicates an illegal attempt to pass an argument.

IllegalMonitorStateException

The `IllegalMonitorStateException` class is a subclass of `RuntimeException` that signals an attempt to use a monitor without owning it.

IllegalStateException

The `IllegalStateException` class is a subclass of `RuntimeException` that signals that a method invocation occurred while the runtime environment was not in an appropriate state for the method invocation.

IllegalThreadStateException

The `IllegalThreadStateException` class is a subclass of `IllegalArgumentException` that signals that a thread is not in an appropriate state for a requested operation.

IncompatibleClassChangeError

The `IncompatibleClassChangeError` class is a subclass of `LinkageError` that indicates an incompatible change to a class definition has occurred.

IndexOutOfBoundsException
The IndexOutOfBoundsException class is a subclass of RuntimeException that indicates an index has exceeded its range.

InstantiationError
The InstantiationError class is a subclass of IncompatibleClassChangeError indicating that an attempt to instantiate an abstract class or interface has occurred.

InstantiationException
The InstantiationException class is a subclass of Exception that indicates an attempt to instantiate an abstract class or interface.

InternalError
The InternalError class is a subclass of VirtualMachineError that indicates an unexpected internal error has occurred in the virtual machine.

InterruptedException
The InterruptedException class is a subclass of Exception that is thrown when a thread is interrupted.

LinkageError
The LinkageError class is a subclass of Error that indicates a class has changed in such a way that dependencies on that class are no longer valid.

NegativeArraySizeException
The NegativeArraySizeException class is a subclass of RuntimeException that is thrown as the result of attempting to allocate an array of negative size.

NoClassDefFoundError
The NoClassDefFoundError class is a subclass of LinkageError that indicates that a class definition cannot be found.

NoSuchFieldError
The NoSuchFieldError class is a subclass of IncompatibleClassChangeError that indicates an attempt to access a field that no longer exists.

NoSuchFieldException
The NoSuchFieldException class is a subclass of Exception that indicates that a referenced field name does not exist.

NoSuchMethodError
The NoSuchMethodError class is a subclass of IncompatibleClassChangeError that indicates an attempt to access a method that no longer exists.

NoSuchMethodException
The NoSuchMethodException class is a subclass of Exception indicating that a referenced method name does not exist.

NullPointerException

The NullPointerException class is a subclass of RuntimeException that is thrown by the use of a null reference.

NumberFormatException

The NumberFormatException class is a subclass of IllegalArgumentException that is thrown when an attempt is made to convert a String object to a number and the object does not have a valid numeric representation.

OutOfMemoryError

The OutOfMemoryError class is a subclass of VirtualMachineError that indicates that the JVM is out of memory and no memory could be made available.

RuntimeException

The RuntimeException class is a subclass of Exception that serves as the base class for defining exceptions that occur at runtime during normal JVM operation.

SecurityException

The SecurityException class is a subclass of RuntimeException that is thrown by a security policy violation.

StackOverflowError

The StackOverflowError class is a subclass of VirtualMachineError that indicates that a stack overflow has occurred.

StringIndexOutOfBoundsException

The StringIndexOutOfBoundsException class is a subclass of IndexOutOfBoundsException that indicates an attempt to access an element of a String object that is outside the string's bounds.

ThreadDeath

The ThreadDeath class is a subclass of Error that is thrown after a thread is stopped.

UnknownError

The UnknownError class is a subclass of VirtualMachineError that indicates that an unknown error occurred in the JVM.

UnsatisfiedLinkError

The UnsatisfiedLinkError class is a subclass of LinkageError that signals an attempt to access a nonexistent native method.

UnsupportedClassVersionError

The UnsupportedClassVersionError class extends ClassFormatError to identify situations where the JVM does not support the version of Java used by a class file.

UnsupportedOperationException

The UnsupportedOperationException class is a subclass of RuntimeException that is thrown by an object to indicate that it does not support a particular method.

VerifyError

The VerifyError class is a subclass of LinkageError that is thrown when the verifier encounters an inconsistency in a class file that it is verifying.

VirtualMachineError

The VirtualMachineError class is a subclass of Error that indicates that the virtual machine is incapable of further processing.

PACKAGE java.lang.ref

The java.lang.ref package provides five classes that implement the new JDK 1.2 reference object capability. Reference objects are objects that are used to refer to other objects. They are similar to C and C++ pointers.

Interfaces

None.

Classes

PhantomReference

The PhantomReference class is a subclass of Reference. When the referent of a registered PhantomReference object is no longer strongly, guardedly, or weakly reachable, the PhantomReference object is cleared and added to the ReferenceQueue to which it is registered.

Reference

The Reference class is a subclass of Object that implements a reference to another object.

ReferenceQueue

The ReferenceQueue class is a subclass of Object that is used to collect Reference objects whose reachability has changed.

SoftReference

The SoftReference class is a subclass of Reference. An instance of this class is automatically cleared when memory is low and its referent is reachable only via soft references.

WeakReference

The WeakReference class is a subclass of Reference. When the referent of a registered WeakReference object is no longer strongly or guardedly reachable, the WeakReference object is cleared and added to the ReferenceQueue to which it is registered. The referent is then subject to finalization.

Exceptions and Errors

None.

PACKAGE `java.lang.reflect`

The `java.lang.reflect` package contains seven classes and one interface that provide the capability to implement runtime discovery of information about an object's class.

Interfaces

Member

The `Member` interface is used to provide information that is reflected about a `Field`, `Constructor`, or `Method`.

Classes

AccessibleObject

The `AccessibleObject` class is a subclass of `Object` that is the superclass of the `Constructor`, `Field`, and `Method` classes. It was added to the class hierarchy in JDK 1.2 to provide the capability to specify whether an object suppresses reflection access control checks.

Array

The `Array` class is a subclass of `Object` that is used to obtain information about, create, and manipulate arrays.

Constructor

The `Constructor` class is a subclass of `AccessibleObject` that is used to obtain information about class constructors. It implements the `Member` interface.

Field

The `Field` class is a subclass of `AccessibleObject` that is used to obtain information about and access the field variables of a class. It implements the `Member` interface.

Method

The `Method` class is a subclass of `Object` that is used to obtain information about and access the methods of a class. It implements the `Member` interface.

Modifier

The `Modifier` class is a subclass of `Object` that is used to decode integers that represent the modifiers of classes, interfaces, field variables, constructors, and methods.

ReflectPermission

The `ReflectPermission` class is a subclass of `java.security.BasicPermission` that is used to specify whether the default language access checks should be suppressed for reflected objects.

Exceptions and Errors

InvocationTargetException

The `InvocationTargetException` class is a subclass of `java.lang.Exception` that wraps an exception thrown by an invoked method or constructor.

PACKAGE `java.math`

The `java.math` package provides two classes, `BigDecimal` and `BigInteger`, that provide the capability to perform arbitrary-precision arithmetic.

Interfaces

None.

Classes

BigDecimal

The `BigDecimal` class is a subclass of `java.lang.Number` that provides the capability to perform arbitrary-precision decimal arithmetic. It implements the `java.lang.Comparable` interface.

BigInteger

The `BigInteger` class is a subclass of `java.lang.Number` that provides the capability to perform arbitrary-length integer arithmetic. It implements the `java.lang.Comparable` interface.

Exceptions and Errors

None.

PACKAGE `java.net`

The `java.net` package provides 21 classes and five interfaces for TCP/IP network programming. Six new classes are introduced with JDK 1.2. The `java.net` package is covered in Part 8, "Network Programming."

Interfaces

ContentHandlerFactory

The `ContentHandlerFactory` interface is implemented by classes that create `ContentHandler` objects.

FileNameMap

The `FileNameMap` interface is implemented by classes that map file names to MIME types.

SocketImplFactory

The `SocketImplFactory` interface is implemented by classes that create `SocketImpl` objects.

SocketOptions

The SocketOptions interface defines constants that can be used to tailor a socket configuration.

URLStreamHandlerFactory

The URLStreamHandlerFactory interface is implemented by classes that create URLStreamHandler objects.

Classes

Authenticator

The Authenticator class is a subclass of Object that is used to authenticate a network connection.

ContentHandler

The ContentHandler class is a subclass of Object that is used to handle downloaded content based on its MIME type.

DatagramPacket

The DatagramPacket class is a subclass of Object that is used to implement UDP socket communication.

DatagramSocket

The DatagramSocket class is a subclass of Object that is used for UDP communication.

DatagramSocketImpl

The DatagramSocketImpl class is a subclass of Object that is a base class for implementing connectionless socket-based communication.

HttpURLConnection

The HttpURLConnection class is a subclass of URLConnection that supports the Hypertext Transfer Protocol (HTTP).

InetAddress

The InetAddress class is a subclass of Object that encapsulates an IP address.

JarURLConnection

The JarURLConnection class is a subclass of URLConnection that is used to access a JAR file via a network connection.

MulticastSocket

The MulticastSocket class is a subclass of DatagramSocket that supports multicast communication.

NetPermission

The NetPermission class is a subclass of java.security.BasicPermission that supports network security policy implementation.

PasswordAuthentication

The PasswordAuthentication class is a subclass of Object that supports network authentication by password.

ServerSocket

The ServerSocket class is a subclass of Object that is used to implement the server side of client-server applications.

Socket

The Socket class is a subclass of Object that provides an encapsulation of the client side of TCP and UDP sockets.

SocketImpl

The SocketImpl class is a subclass of Object that is used to create custom socket implementations.

SocketPermission

The SocketPermission class is a subclass of java.security.Permission that is used to define socket-level access controls. It implements the java.io.Serializable interface.

URL

The URL class is a subclass of Object that encapsulates a Universal Resource Locator. It implements the java.lang.Comparable and java.io.Serializable interfaces.

URLClassLoader

The URLClassLoader class is a subclass of java.security.SecureClassLoader that is used to load classes from a location specified by a URL.

URLConnection

The URLConnection class is a subclass of Object that is used as a base class for implementing TCP connections to a URL-referenced resource.

URLDecoder

The URLDecoder class extends Object to support x-www-form-urlencoded decoding.

URLEncoder

The URLEncoder class is a subclass of Object that supports x-www-form-urlencoded encoding.

URLStreamHandler

The URLStreamHandler class is a subclass of Object that is used to support the development of stream-based protocol handlers.

Exceptions and Errors

Exceptions

BindException

The BindException class is a subclass of SocketException that indicates that an error occurred during socket binding.

ConnectException

The ConnectException class is a subclass of SocketException that indicates that an error occurred during socket connection.

MalformedURLException

The MalformedURLException class is a subclass of java.io.IOException that identifies the use of an incorrectly formed URL.

NoRouteToHostException

The NoRouteToHostException class is a subclass of SocketException that indicates that the network was not able to establish a route to a remote host.

ProtocolException

The ProtocolException class is a subclass of java.io.IOException indicating that an error occurred in the protocol stack.

SocketException

The SocketException class is a subclass of java.io.IOException that indicates that an error occurred in the underlying socket implementation.

UnknownHostException

The UnknownHostException class is a subclass of java.io.IOException that is thrown by a reference to a host whose IP address could not be resolved.

UnknownServiceException

The UnknownServiceException class is a subclass of java.io.IOException that is thrown by an attempt to use a network service that is unknown to the requestor.

PACKAGE java.rmi

The java.rmi package provides three classes and one interface that support basic remote method invocation (RMI) capabilities.

Interfaces

Remote

The Remote interface is used to identify an object as being remotely accessible. It does not define any constants or methods.

Classes

MarshalledObject

The `MarshalledObject` class is a subclass of `Object` that supports object persistence for remote object activation by representing method arguments and return values as serialized byte streams. It implements the `java.io.Serializable` interface.

Naming

The `Naming` class is a subclass of `Object` that provides static methods for accessing remote objects via RMI URLs. It is used to bind object names to the remote objects they represent.

RMISecurityManager

The `RMISecurityManager` class is a subclass of `java.lang.SecurityManager` that defines the default security policy used with remote objects. This class can be extended to implement custom RMI security policies.

Exceptions and Errors

AccessException

The `AccessException` class is a subclass of `RemoteException` that is used to signal an access violation.

AlreadyBoundException

The `AlreadyBoundException` class is a subclass of `java.lang.Exception` that is used to signal that a name has already been bound.

ConnectException

The `ConnectException` class is a subclass of `RemoteException` that signals that a connection was refused by the remote host.

ConnectIOException

The `ConnectIOException` class is a subclass of `RemoteException` that signals that an I/O error occurred during connection establishment.

MarshalException

The `MarshalException` class is a subclass of `RemoteException` that identifies that an error in object marshalling occurred.

NoSuchObjectException

The `NoSuchObjectException` class is a subclass of `RemoteException` that identifies an attempt to invoke a method on an object that is no longer available.

NotBoundException

The `NotBoundException` class is a subclass of `java.lang.Exception` that identifies an attempt to look up a name that has not been bound.

RMISecurityException

The RMISecurityException class is a subclass of java.lang.SecurityException that identifies that a security exception has occurred during RMI.

RemoteException

The RemoteException class is a subclass of java.io.IOException that serves as a base class for RMI-related exceptions.

ServerError

The ServerError class is a subclass of RemoteException that identifies that an error occurred on a remote server as the result of processing a method invocation.

ServerException

The ServerException class is a subclass of RemoteException that identifies that an exception occurred on a remote server as the result of processing a method invocation.

ServerRuntimeException

The ServerRuntimeException class is a subclass of RemoteException that identifies that a runtime exception occurred on a remote server as the result of processing a method invocation.

StubNotFoundException

The StubNotFoundException class is a subclass of RemoteException that identifies that the stub of a requested remote object has not been exported.

UnexpectedException

The UnexpectedException class is a subclass of RemoteException that identifies that an exception occurred during a remote method invocation that was not specified in the method's signature.

UnknownHostException

The UnknownHostException class is a subclass of RemoteException that identifies an attempt to access the registry of an unknown host.

UnmarshalException

The UnmarshalException class is a subclass of RemoteException that identifies that an error occurred in the unmarshalling of a marshalled object.

PACKAGE java.rmi.activation

The java.rmi.activation package supports persistent object references and remote object activation. It contains seven classes and four interfaces.

Interfaces
ActivationInstantiator
The ActivationInstantiator interface is implemented by classes that create remotely activatable objects. It extends the Remote interface.

ActivationMonitor
The ActivationMonitor interface is implented by classes that monitor the activation status of an ActivationGroup object. The ActivationGroup object notifies its ActivationMonitor when objects in the group change their activation status or when the group as a whole becomes inactive. ActivationMonitor extends the Remote interface.

ActivationSystem
The ActivationSystem interface is implemented by classes that support the registration of activatable objects and ActivationGroup objects. It extends the Remote interface.

Activator
The Activator interface is implemented by a class that activates classes whose objects are remotely activatable. The system Activator object is invoked by a faulting remote reference. It then initiates the activation of the object needed to complete the remote reference. It extends the Remote interface.

Classes
Activatable
The Activatable class is a subclass of RemoteServer that is the base class for developing remotely activatable classes. It is extended by classes that require remote activation or object persistence.

ActivationDesc
The ActivationDesc class is a subclass of Object that encapsulates the information needed to activate a remotely activatable object. This information includes the object's class name, activation group, code location, and initialization data. The ActivationDesc class implements the java.io.Serializable interface.

ActivationGroup
The ActivationGroup class is a subclass of UnicastRemoteObject that is used to manage a group of activatable objects. It implements the ActivationInstantiator interface.

ActivationGroupDesc
The ActivationGroupDesc class is a subclass of Object that encapsulates the information needed to activate an ActivationGroup object. This information includes the object's class name, code location, and initialization data. The ActivationGroupDesc class implements the java.io.Serializable interface.

ActivationGroupDesc.CommandEnvironment

The `ActivationGroupDesc.CommandEnvironment` class is an inner class of `ActivationGroupDesc` that supports the implementation of startup options for `ActivationGroup` objects.

ActivationGroupID

The `ActivationGroupID` class is a subclass of `Object` that uniquely identifies an `ActivationGroup` object as well as its `ActivationSystem` object. It implements the `java.io.Serializable` interface.

ActivationID

The `ActivationID` class is a subclass of `Object` that uniquely identifies a remotely activatable object as well as its `Activator` object. It implements the `java.io.Serializable` interface.

Exceptions and Errors

ActivateFailedException

The `ActivateFailedException` class is a subclass of `java.rmi.RemoteException` that identifies the failure to activate a remotely activatable object.

ActivationException

The `ActivationException` class is a subclass of `java.lang.Exception` that is the superclass of `UnknownGroupException` and `UnknownObjectException`.

UnknownGroupException

The `UnknownGroupException` class is a subclass of `ActivationException` that is generated by an attempt to activate an object from an unknown `ActivationGroup` object.

UnknownObjectException

The `UnknownObjectException` class is a subclass of `ActivationException` that is generated by an attempt to activate an object that is unknown to an `Activator` object.

PACKAGE java.rmi.dgc

The `java.rmi.dgc` package supports distributed garbage collection. It contains two classes and one interface.

Interfaces

DGC

The `DGC` interface is implemented by the server side of the distributed garbage collector. It defines the `clean()` and `dirty()` methods for keeping track of which objects should be garbage-collected.

Classes

Lease
The Lease class is a subclass of Object that creates objects that are used to keep track of object references. It implements the java.io.Serializable interface.

VMID
The VMID class is a subclass of Object that implements an ID that uniquely identifies a Java virtual machine on a particular host. It implements the java.io.Serializable interface.

Exceptions and Errors
None.

PACKAGE java.rmi.registry
The java.rmi.registry package supports distributed registry operations. It contains one class and two interfaces.

Interfaces

Registry
The Registry interface provides methods for associating names with remotely accessible objects. It is implemented by classes that provide the RMI registry. It extends the Remote interface.

RegistryHandler
The RegistryHandler interface provides methods for accessing a Registry implementation. These methods have been deprecated in JDK 1.2.

Classes

LocateRegistry
The LocateRegistry class is a subclass of Object that provides methods for accessing the RMI registry on a particular host.

Exceptions and Errors
None.

PACKAGE java.rmi.server
The java.rmi.server package provides the low-level classes and interfaces that implement RMI. It contains 10 classes and nine interfaces.

Interfaces

LoaderHandler
The LoaderHandler interface provides methods for working with RMI class loaders.

RMIFailureHandler
The RMIFailureHandler interface defines methods for handling RMI failure events.

RMIClientSocketFactory
The RMIClientSocketFactory interface provides access to client sockets for RMI calls.

RMIServerSocketFactory
The RMIServerSocketFactory interface provides access to server sockets for RMI calls.

RemoteCall
The RemoteCall interface defines methods for supporting a remote method invocation.

RemoteRef
The RemoteRef interface extends the java.io.Externalizable interface and provides methods for implementing a reference to a remote object.

ServerRef
The ServerRef interface extends the RemoteRef interface to provide a server-side reference to a remote object.

Skeleton
The Skeleton interface provides methods that are implemented by server-side skeletons.

Unreferenced
The Unreferenced interface provides methods that are implemented by a remote object to determine when the object is no longer remotely referenced.

Classes

LogStream
The LogStream class is a subclass of java.io.PrintStream that supports the logging of RMI errors.

ObjID
The ObjID class is a subclass of Object that uniquely identifies a remote object. It implements the java.io.Serializable interface.

Operation
The Operation class is a subclass of Object that encapsulates a remote method.

RMIClassLoader
The RMIClassLoader class is a subclass of Object that supports class loading during RMI.

RMISocketFactory

The `RMISocketFactory` class is a subclass of `Object` that is used to load custom RMI socket implementations.

RemoteObject

The `RemoteObject` class is a subclass of `Object` that is the base class for developing remote objects. It implements the `Remote` and `java.io.Serializable` interfaces.

RemoteServer

The `RemoteServer` class is a subclass of `RemoteObject` that is the base class for implementing an RMI server.

RemoteStub

The `RemoteStub` class is a subclass of `RemoteObject` that is the base class of all RMI stubs.

UID

The `UID` class is a subclass of `Object` that uniquely identifies an object on a particular host. It implements the `java.io.Serializable` interface.

UnicastRemoteObject

The `UnicastRemoteObject` class is a subclass of `RemoteServer` that provides a default RMI server implementation.

Exceptions and Errors

ExportException

The `ExportException` class is a subclass of `java.rmi.RemoteException` indicating that an error occurred during object export.

ServerCloneException

The `ServerCloneException` class is a subclass of `java.rmi.RemoteException` that indicates an attempt to clone a non-cloneable remote object.

ServerNotActiveException

The `ServerNotActiveException` class is a subclass of `java.lang.Exception` that indicates that the remote server is not currently active.

SkeletonMismatchException

The `SkeletonMismatchException` class is a subclass of `java.rmi.RemoteException` indicating that the skeleton of a remote object is inappropriate for the object being referenced.

SkeletonNotFoundException

The `SkeletonNotFoundException` class is a subclass of `java.rmi.RemoteException` that signals that the skeleton of a remote object cannot be located.

SocketSecurityException

The SocketSecurityException class is a subclass of ExportException that signals a socket operation that violates the current security policy.

PACKAGE java.security

The java.security package provides 39 classes and eight interfaces that provide the foundation for the Security API.

Interfaces

Certificate

The Certificate interface is a deprecated interface that provides support for digital certificates.

Guard

The Guard interface defines methods for objects that protect other objects.

Key

The Key interface extends the java.io.Serializable interface to encapsulate a cryptographic key.

Principal

The Principal interface provides methods for a subject that may have an identity.

PrivateKey

The PrivateKey interface extends the Key interface to provide support for a private key.

PrivilegedAction

The PrivilegedAction interface is used to perform privileged actions that do not throw checked exceptions.

PrivilegedExceptionAction

The PrivilegedExceptionAction interface is used to perform privileged actions that do throw checked exceptions.

PublicKey

The PublicKey interface extends the Key interface to provide support for a public key.

Classes

AccessControlContext

The AccessControlContext class is a subclass of Object that is used to make access control decisions.

AccessController

The AccessController class is a subclass of Object that implements security access controls.

AlgorithmParameterGenerator

The `AlgorithmParameterGenerator` class is a subclass of `Object` that generates parameters for use with cryptographic algorithms.

AlgorithmParameterGeneratorSpi

The `AlgorithmParameterGeneratorSpi` class is a subclass of `Object` that defines a service provider interface for an `AlgorithmParameterGenerator` class.

AlgorithmParameters

The `AlgorithmParameters` class is a subclass of `Object` that encapsulates parameters used with cryptographic algorithms.

AlgorithmParametersSpi

The `AlgorithmParametersSpi` class is a subclass of `Object` that provides a service provider interface for an `AlgorithmParameters` class.

AllPermission

The `AllPermission` class is a subclass of `Permission` that implies all other permissions.

BasicPermission

The `BasicPermission` class is a subclass of `Permission` that provides a base class for implementing permissions that use the same naming approach. It implements the `java.io.Serializable` interface.

CodeSource

The `CodeSource` class is a subclass of `Object` that identifies the location from which code is loaded. It implements the `java.io.Serializable` interface.

DigestInputStream

The `DigestInputStream` class is a subclass of `java.io.FilterInputStream` that is used to read a message digest.

DigestOutputStream

The `DigestOutputStream` class is a subclass of `java.io.FilterOutputStream` that is used to write a message digest.

GuardedObject

The `GuardedObject` class is a subclass of `Object` that is used to protect other objects. It implements the `java.io.Serializable` interface.

Identity

The `Identity` class is a subclass of `Object` that implements an identity used for making access control decisions. It implements the `Principal` and `java.io.Serializable` interfaces.

IdentityScope

The `IdentityScope` class is a subclass of `Identity` that defines the scope of an identity.

KeyFactory
The KeyFactory class is a subclass of Object that is used to create Key objects.

KeyFactorySpi
The KeyFactorySpi class is a subclass of Object that provides a service provider interface to a KeyFactory class.

KeyPair
The KeyPair class is a subclass of Object that encapsulates a public-private key pair.

KeyPairGenerator
The KeyPairGenerator class is a subclass of KeyPairGeneratorSpi that is used to create key pairs.

KeyPairGeneratorSpi
The KeyPairGeneratorSpi class is a subclass of Object that provides a service provider interface to a KeyPairGenerator object.

KeyStore
The KeyStore class is a subclass of Object that supports the management of cryptographic keys.

KeyStoreSpi
The KeyStoreSpi class extends Object to provide a service provider interface for the KeyStore class.

MessageDigest
The MessageDigest class is a subclass of MessageDigestSpi that implements a message digest.

MessageDigestSpi
The MessageDigestSpi class is a subclass of Object that provides a service provider interface to a MessageDigest class.

Permission
The Permission class is a subclass of Object that defines a permission to a protected resource. It implements the Guard and java.io.Serializable interfaces.

PermissionCollection
The PermissionCollection class is a subclass of Object that implements a collection of Permission objects. It implements the java.io.Serializable interface.

Permissions
The Permissions class is a subclass of PermissionCollection that supports a mixed collection of Permission objects. It implements the java.io.Serializable interface.

Policy

The `Policy` class is a subclass of `Object` that implements a Java security policy.

ProtectionDomain

The `ProtectionDomain` class is a subclass of `Object` that identifies a set of classes with the same permissions.

Provider

The `Provider` class is a subclass of `java.util.Properties` that implements a service provider.

SecureClassLoader

The `SecureClassLoader` class is a subclass of `java.lang.ClassLoader` that supports secure class loading.

SecureRandom

The `SecureRandom` class is a subclass of `java.util.Random` that provides secure random-number-generation capabilities.

SecureRandomSpi

The `SecureRandomSpi` class extends `Object` and implements `Serializable` to provide a service provider interface for the `SecureRandom` class.

Security

The `Security` class is a subclass of `Object` that provides common access to security-related objects.

SecurityPermission

The `SecurityPermission` class is a subclass of `BasicPermission` that defines security-related permissions.

Signature

The `Signature` class is a subclass of `SignatureSpi` that provides digital signature support.

SignatureSpi

The `SignatureSpi` class is a subclass of `Object` that provides a service provider interface to a `Signature` class.

SignedObject

The `SignedObject` class is a subclass of `Object` that represents an object that has been signed. It implements the `java.io.Serializable` interface.

Signer

The `Signer` class is a subclass of `Identity` that is capable of signing a signature-related object.

UnresolvedPermission

The UnresolvedPermission class is a subclass of Permission that does not have an accessible permission class. It implements the java.io.Serializable interface.

Exceptions and Errors

AccessControlException

The AccessControlException class is a subclass of SecurityException that indicates a violation of security access controls.

DigestException

The DigestException class is a subclass of GeneralSecurityException that is thrown by errors in message digest calculation.

GeneralSecurityException

The GeneralSecurityException class is a subclass of java.lang.Exception that is used as the base class for defining the security-related exceptions.

InvalidAlgorithmParameterException

The InvalidAlgorithmParameterException class is a subclass of GeneralSecurityException that indicates that an invalid parameter was supplied to a cryptographic algorithm.

InvalidKeyException

The InvalidKeyException class is a subclass of KeyException that indicates that an invalid key was supplied to a cryptographic algorithm.

InvalidParameterException

The InvalidParameterException class is a subclass of IllegalArgumentException indicating that an invalid parameter was supplied to a cryptographic algorithm.

KeyException

The KeyException class is a subclass of GeneralSecurityException that identifies an exception related to a cryptographic key.

KeyManagementException

The KeyManagementException class is a subclass of KeyException that identifies an exception in the management of keys.

KeyStoreException

The KeyStoreException class is a subclass of GeneralSecurityException that identifies an exception in the storage of keys.

NoSuchAlgorithmException

The NoSuchAlgorithmException class is a subclass of GeneralSecurityException indicating that a requested algorithm does not exist.

NoSuchProviderException

The NoSuchProviderException class is a subclass of GeneralSecurityException indicating that a requested service provider does not exist.

PrivilegedActionException

The PrivilegedActionException class extends Exception to indicate that the performance of a privileged action resulted in a checked exception.

ProviderException

The ProviderException class is a subclass of java.lang.RuntimeException that is generated by a service provider.

SignatureException

The SignatureException class is a subclass of GeneralSecurityException that identifies an exception occurring during signature calculation.

UnrecoverableKeyException

The UnrecoverableKeyException class is a subclass of GeneralSecurityException that signals that a key cannot be recovered from a key store.

PACKAGE java.security.acl

The java.security.acl package provides five interfaces that provide the basic elements for implementing security access controls.

Interfaces

Acl

The Acl interface extends the Owner interface to define methods for classes that implement access control lists. An Acl object consists of zero or more AclEntry objects.

AclEntry

The AclEntry interface defines methods for an entry in an access control list. It identifies a set of permissions for a principal. It extends the java.lang.Cloneable interface.

Group

The Group interface extends the java.security.Principal interface to provide methods for working with a group of Principal objects. A Group object may also contain other Group objects.

Owner

The Owner interface defines methods for working with the owners of an access control list.

Permission

The Permission interface defines methods for implementing permissions to access-protected resources.

Classes

None.

Exceptions and Errors

AclNotFoundException

The AclNotFoundException class is a subclass of java.lang.Exception that signals a reference to a nonexistent access control list.

LastOwnerException

The LastOwnerException class is a subclass of java.lang.Exception that signals an attempt to delete the last owner of an access control list.

NotOwnerException

The NotOwnerException class is a subclass of java.lang.Exception that signals an attempt to modify an access control list by an object that is not its owner.

PACKAGE java.security.cert

The java.security.cert package provides seven classes and one interface that implement digital certificates.

Interfaces

X509Extension

The X509Extension interface provides methods that encapsulate extensions defined for X.509 v3 certificates and v2 certificate revocation lists.

Classes

Certificate

The Certificate class is a subclass of Object that provides an abstract base class for implementing identity certificates.

CertificateFactory

The CertificateFactory class extends Object to provide a factory for creating certificates and certificate revocation lists.

CertificateFactorySpi

The CertificateFactorySpi class extends Object to provide a security provider interface for the CertificateFactory class.

CRL

The CRL class extends Object to provide an abstract implementation of a certificate revocation list.

X509CRLEntry

The X509CRLEntry class extends Object and implements the X509Extension interface to provide an abstract class for a revoked certificate in a CRL.

X509CRL

The X509CRL class is a subclass of Object that implements an X.509 certificate revocation list. It implements the X509Extension interface.

X509Certificate

The X509Certificate class is a subclass of Certificate that provides an abstract base class for implementing X.509 digital certificates.

Exceptions and Errors

CRLException

The CRLException class is a subclass of java.security.GeneralSecurityException that identifies an exception occurring in the processing of a certificate revocation list.

CertificateEncodingException

The CertificateEncodingException class is a subclass of CertificateException that identifies that an exception occurred during the encoding of a certificate.

CertificateException

The CertificateException class is a subclass of java.security.GeneralSecurityException that acts as a base class for other certificate-related exceptions.

CertificateExpiredException

The CertificateExpiredException class is a subclass of CertificateException that identifies that an expired certificate has been encountered.

CertificateNotYetValidException

The CertificateNotYetValidException class is a subclass of CertificateException that identifies that a certificate has been processed before its valid date range.

CertificateParsingException

The CertificateParsingException class is a subclass of CertificateException that indicates that an error occurred in the parsing of a certificate.

PACKAGE java.security.interfaces

The java.security.interfaces package provides eight interfaces that support implementation of the NIST digital signature algorithm.

Interfaces

DSAKey

The DSAKey interface defines the getParams() method for accessing a Digital Signature Algorithm (DSA) public or private key.

DSAKeyPairGenerator

The DSAKeyPairGenerator interface is implemented by objects that can generate DSA key pairs.

DSAParams

The DSAParams interface defines methods for accessing a set of DSA key parameters.

DSAPrivateKey

The DSAPrivateKey interface extends the DSAKey and java.security.PrivateKey interfaces to provide access to a DSA private key.

DSAPublicKey

The DSAPublicKey interface extends the DSAKey and java.security.PublicKey interfaces to provide access to a DSA public key.

RSAPrivateCrtKey

The RSAPrivateCrtKey interface extends RSAPrivateKey with support for the Chinese Remainder Theorem.

RSAPrivateKey

The RSAPrivateKey interface extends PrivateKey to provide support for RSA private keys.

RSAPublicKey

The RSAPublicKey interface extends PublicKey to provide support for RSA public keys.

Classes

None.

Exceptions and Errors

None.

PACKAGE java.security.spec

The java.security.spec package provides nine classes and two interfaces that provide specifications for cryptographic keys.

Interfaces

AlgorithmParameterSpec

The AlgorithmParameterSpec interface provides no constants or methods. It is used to identify an object that provides cryptographic algorithm parameters.

KeySpec

The KeySpec interface provides no constants or methods. It is used to identify an object that is a key for a cryptographic algorithm.

Classes

DSAParameterSpec

The DSAParameterSpec class is a subclass of Object that provides parameters for a Digital Signature Algorithm (DSA) implementation. It implements the AlgorithmParameterSpec and java.security.interfaces.DSAParams interfaces.

DSAPrivateKeySpec

The DSAPrivateKeySpec class is a subclass of Object that implements a private DSA key. It implements the KeySpec interface.

DSAPublicKeySpec

The DSAPublicKeySpec class is a subclass of Object that implements a public DSA key. It implements the KeySpec interface.

EncodedKeySpec

The EncodedKeySpec class is a subclass of Object that implements an encoded public or private key. It implements the KeySpec interface.

PKCS8EncodedKeySpec

The PKCS8EncodedKeySpec class is a subclass of EncodedKeySpec that represents the PKCS #8 standard encoding of a private key.

RSAPrivateCrtKeySpec

The RSAPrivateCrtKeySpec class extends RSAPrivateKeySpec to specify an RSA private key using Chinese Remainder Theorem values.

RSAPrivateKeySpec

The RSAPrivateKeySpec class extends Object and implements KeySpec to provide support for RSA private keys.

RSAPublicKeySpec

The RSAPublicKeySpec class extends Object and implements KeySpec to provide support for RSA public keys.

X509EncodedKeySpec

The X509EncodedKeySpec class is a subclass of EncodedKeySpec that represents the X.509 standard encoding of a public or private key.

Exceptions and Errors

InvalidKeySpecException

The InvalidKeySpecException class is a subclass of java.security.GeneralSecurityException that identifies an invalid key specification.

InvalidParameterSpecException

The `InvalidParameterSpecException` class is a subclass of `java.security.GeneralSecurityException` that identifies an invalid parameter specification.

PACKAGE `java.sql`

The `java.sql` package provides six classes and 16 interfaces that provide Java database connectivity. This package is covered in Part 10, "Database Programming."

Interfaces

Array

The `Array` interface provides a reference to an array that is stored by the database server.

Blob

The `Blob` interface provides a reference to a binary large object that is stored by the database server.

CallableStatement

The `CallableStatement` interface extends the `PreparedStatement` interface to provide support for stored procedures.

Clob

The `Clob` interface provides a reference to a character large object that is stored by the database server.

Connection

The `Connection` interface encapsulates a database connection.

DatabaseMetaData

The `DatabaseMetaData` interface provides access to information about the database itself.

Driver

The `Driver` interface encapsulates a database driver.

PreparedStatement

The `PreparedStatement` interface provides access to precompiled, stored SQL statements.

Ref

The `Ref` interface provides a reference to a stored SQL value.

ResultSet

The `ResultSet` interface encapsulates the results of a database query.

ResultSetMetaData
The ResultSetMetaData interface provides information about a ResultSet object.

SQLData
The SQLData interface provides support for mapping SQL and Java data types.

SQLInput
The SQLInput interface represents an input stream of a SQL UDT instance.

SQLOutput
The SQLOutput interface represents a SQL UDT output stream.

Statement
The Statement interface provides support for executing SQL statements.

Struct
The Struct interface encapsulates a SQL structured type.

Classes

Date
The Date class is a subclass of java.util.Date that supports SQL date objects.

DriverManager
The DriverManager class is a subclass of Object that is used to manage database drivers.

DriverPropertyInfo
The DriverPropertyInfo class is a subclass of Object that provides information about a database driver.

Time
The Time class is a subclass of java.util.Time that supports SQL time objects.

Timestamp
The Timestamp class is a subclass of Object that encapsulates a SQL time stamp.

Types
The Types class is a subclass of Object that defines constants for use with SQL types.

Exceptions and Errors

BatchUpdateException
The BatchUpdateException class is a subclass of SQLException that signals the occurrence of errors during batch update operations.

DataTruncation

The DataTruncation class is a subclass of SQLWarning that indicates that a date value has been truncated.

SQLException

The SQLException class is a subclass of java.lang.Exception that serves as a base class for database exceptions.

SQLWarning

The SQLWarning class is a subclass of SQLException that signals warnings about database operations.

PACKAGE java.text

The java.text package provides 20 classes and two interfaces that support internationalization.

Interfaces

AttributedCharacterIterator

The AttributedCharacterIterator interface extends the CharacterIterator interface to provide support for iterating through text that is associated with style, internationalization, or other attributes.

CharacterIterator

The CharacterIterator interface provides internationalization support for bidirectional text iteration.

Classes

Annotation

The Annotation class is a subclass of Object that is used to work with text attribute values.

AttributedCharacterIterator.Attribute

The AttributedCharacterIterator.Attribute class extends Object and implements Serializable to define attribute keys that are used to identify text attributes.

AttributedString

The AttributedString class is a subclass of Object that encapsulates text and related attribute information.

BreakIterator

The BreakIterator class is a subclass of Object that provides support for identifying text-break boundaries. It implements the java.lang.Cloneable and java.io.Serializable interfaces.

ChoiceFormat

The ChoiceFormat class is a subclass of NumberFormat that allows number formatting to be associated with a range of numbers.

CollationElementIterator

The CollationElementIterator class is a subclass of Object that is used to iterate through international text strings.

CollationKey

The CollationKey class is a subclass of Object that is used to compare two Collator objects. It implements the java.lang.Comparable interface.

Collator

The Collator class is a subclass of Object that supports locale-specific string comparisons. It implements the java.lang.Comparable, java.lang.Cloneable, and java.io.Serializable interfaces.

DateFormat

The DateFormat class is a subclass of Format that provides international date formatting support.

DateFormatSymbols

The DateFormatSymbols class is a subclass of Object that provides support for locale-specific date formatting information. It implements the java.lang.Cloneable and java.io.Serializable interfaces.

DecimalFormat

The DecimalFormat class is a subclass of Object that provides international decimal point formatting support.

DecimalFormatSymbols

The DecimalFormatSymbols class is a subclass of Object that provides locale-specific decimal formatting information. It implements the java.lang.Cloneable and java.io.Serializable interfaces.

FieldPosition

The FieldPosition class is a subclass of Object that is used to identify fields in formatted output.

Format

The Format class is a subclass of Object that is the base class for international formatting support. It implements the java.lang.Cloneable and java.io.Serializable interfaces.

MessageFormat

The MessageFormat class is a subclass of Format that supports international message concatenation.

NumberFormat

The NumberFormat class is a subclass of Format that provides international number formatting support.

ParsePosition

The ParsePosition class is a subclass of Object that is used to keep track of the current parsing position.

RuleBasedCollator

The RuleBasedCollator class is a subclass of Collator that supports rule-based sorting.

SimpleDateFormat

The SimpleDateFormat class is a subclass of DateFormat that supports basic international date formatting.

StringCharacterIterator

The StringCharacterIterator class is a subclass of Object that provides a basic implementation of the CharacterIterator interface. It also implements the java.io.Serializable interface.

Exceptions and Errors

ParseException

The ParseException class is a subclass of java.lang.Exception that signals a parsing error.

PACKAGE java.util

The java.util package, like java.lang and java.io, is fundamental to any Java platform. It provides 34 classes and 13 interfaces that cover a wide variety of common programming needs. Most of the new classes and interfaces support the Collections API.

Interfaces

Collection

The Collection interface defines methods for working with arbitrary collections of objects.

Comparator

The Comparator interface defines methods for implementing a comparison function.

Enumeration

The Enumeration interface defines methods for working with an ordered collection of objects.

EventListener
The EventListener interface provides the basic interface to support Java event handling.

Iterator
The Iterator interface defines methods for iterating through an ordered collection.

List
The List interface extends the Collection interface to an ordered list of objects.

ListIterator
The ListIterator interface extends the Iterator interface to support iteration through a List object.

Map
The Map interface provides methods for mapping between two object sets.

Map.Entry
The Map.Entry interface defines methods for a single mapping element.

Observer
The Observer interface defines methods for observing the occurrence of an event, action, or processing.

Set
The Set interface extends the Collection interface to implement a collection in which each element occurs only once.

SortedMap
The SortedMap interface extends the Map interface to identify an ordering between the map elements.

SortedSet
The SortedSet interface extends the Set interface to order the collection of set elements.

Classes

AbstractCollection
The AbstractCollection class is a subclass of Object that provides an abstract implementation of the Collection interface.

AbstractList
The AbstractList class is a subclass of AbstractCollection that provides an abstract implementation of the List interface.

AbstractMap

The `AbstractMap` class is a subclass of `Object` that provides an abstract implementation of the `Map` interface.

AbstractSequentialList

The `AbstractSequentialList` class is a subclass of `AbstractList` that provides a sequential access data store.

AbstractSet

The `AbstractSet` class is a subclass of `AbstractCollection` that provides an abstract implementation of the `Set` interface.

ArrayList

The `ArrayList` class is a subclass of `AbstractList` that is implemented in terms of an array. It implements the `List`, `java.lang.Cloneable`, and `java.io.Serializable` interfaces.

Arrays

The `Arrays` class is a subclass of `Object` that provides support for array manipulation.

BitSet

The `BitSet` class is a subclass of `Object` that provides a growable vector of bits. It implements the `java.lang.Cloneable` and `java.io.Serializable` interfaces.

Calendar

The `Calendar` class is a subclass of `Object` that provides basic support for date, time, and calendar functions. It implements the `java.lang.Cloneable` and `java.io.Serializable` interfaces.

Collections

The `Collections` class is a subclass of `Object` that provides `static` methods for working with collections of objects.

Date

The `Date` class is a subclass of `Object` that provides basic date/time support. It implements the `java.lang.Comparable`, `java.lang.Cloneable`, and `java.io.Serializable` interfaces.

Dictionary

The `Dictionary` class is a subclass of `Object` that maps names to values.

EventObject

The `EventObject` class is a subclass of `Object` that provides the basic class from which most Java events are derived. It implements the `java.io.Serializable` interface.

GregorianCalendar

The GregorianCalendar class is a subclass of Calendar that implements a Gregorian calendar.

HashMap

The HashMap class is a subclass of AbstractMap that provides an implementation of the Map interface using a hash table. It implements the Map, java.lang.Cloneable, and java.io.Serializable interfaces.

HashSet

The HashSet class is a subclass of AbstractSet that implements the Set interface using a hash table. It implements the Set, java.lang.Cloneable, and java.io.Serializable interfaces.

Hashtable

The Hashtable class is a subclass of Dictionary that maps keys to their values. It implements the Map, java.lang.Cloneable, and java.io.Serializable interfaces.

LinkedList

The LinkedList class is a subclass of AbstractSequentialList that encapsulates a linked list data structure. It implements the List, java.lang.Cloneable, and java.io.Serializable interfaces.

ListResourceBundle

The ListResourceBundle class is a subclass of ResourceBundle that provides internationalization in the form of a list.

Locale

The Locale class is a subclass of Object that encapsulates a local region for internationalization purposes. It implements the java.lang.Cloneable and java.io.Serializable interfaces.

Observable

The Observable class is a subclass of Object that represents observable data in the model-view paradigm.

Properties

The Properties class is a subclass of Hashtable that represents a set of properties and property values.

PropertyPermission

The PropertyPermission class is a subclass of java.security.BasicPermission that implements access controls on system properties.

PropertyResourceBundle

The PropertyResourceBundle class is a subclass of ResourceBundle that manages internationalization resources using properties.

Random

The Random class is a subclass of Object that provides random-number generation capabilities. It implements the java.io.Serializable interface.

ResourceBundle

The ResourceBundle class is a subclass of Object that is used to manage internationalization resources.

SimpleTimeZone

The SimpleTimeZone class is a subclass of TimeZone that provides basic time zone information.

Stack

The Stack class is a subclass of Vector that implements a stack data structure.

StringTokenizer

The StringTokenizer class is a subclass of Object that supports the parsing of strings. It implements the Enumeration interface.

TimeZone

The TimeZone class is a subclass of Object that encapsulates the notion of a time zone. It implements the java.lang.Cloneable and java.io.Serializable interfaces.

TreeMap

The TreeMap class is a subclass of AbstractMap that provides a tree-based implementation of the Map interface. It implements the SortedMap, java.lang.Cloneable, and java.io.Serializable interfaces.

TreeSet

The TreeSet class is a subclass of AbstractSet that provides a tree-based implementation of the Set interface. It implements the SortedSet, java.lang.Cloneable, and java.io.Serializable interfaces.

Vector

The Vector class is a subclass of AbstractList that provides a growable array of objects. It implements the List, java.lang.Cloneable, and java.io.Serializable interfaces.

WeakHashMap

The WeakHashMap class extends AbstractMap and implements the Map interface to provide a hashtable-based Map implementation with weak keys.

Exceptions and Errors

ConcurrentModificationException

The ConcurrentModificationException class is a subclass of java.lang.RuntimeException that identifies invalid concurrent accesses to collections objects.

EmptyStackException

The EmptyStackException class is a subclass of java.lang.RuntimeException that signals an attempt to pop an object from an empty stack.

MissingResourceException

The MissingResourceException class is a subclass of java.lang.RuntimeException that signals an access to a missing resource.

NoSuchElementException

The NoSuchElementException class is a subclass of java.lang.RuntimeException that indicates an Enumeration contains no more elements.

TooManyListenersException

The TooManyListenersException class is a subclass of java.lang.Exception indicating that too many event listeners are associated with an event.

PACKAGE java.util.jar

The java.util.jar package provides seven classes for working with JAR files.

Interfaces

None.

Classes

Attributes

The Attributes class is a subclass of Object that maps Manifest attribute names to string values. It implements the java.util.Map and java.lang.Cloneable interfaces.

Attributes.Name

The Attributes.Name class is an inner class of Attributes that represents a specific attribute name of the Attributes map. It is a subclass of Object.

JarEntry

The JarEntry class is a subclass of java.util.zip.ZipEntry that represents an entry in a JAR file. It provides methods for reading the attributes and identities of JAR file entries.

JarFile

The JarFile class is a subclass of java.util.zip.ZipFile that is used to read JAR files. It supports reading of the manifest as well as individual JAR file entries.

JarInputStream

The JarInputStream class is a subclass of java.util.zip.ZipInputStream that is used to read a JAR file from an input stream.

JarOutputStream

The `JarOutputStream` class is a subclass of `java.util.zip.ZipOutputStream` that is used to write the contents of a JAR file to an output stream.

Manifest

The `Manifest` class is a subclass of `Object` that implements a JAR file manifest. It provides methods for accessing manifest names and their attributes. It implements the `java.lang.Cloneable` interface.

Exceptions and Errors

JarException

The `JarException` class is a subclass of `java.util.zip.ZipException` that is used to report errors that occur in the reading or writing of a JAR file.

PACKAGE `java.util.zip`

The `java.util.zip` package provides 14 classes and one interface for working with compressed files.

Interfaces

Checksum

The `Checksum` interface provides a common set of methods for classes that compute a checksum.

Classes

Adler32

The `Adler32` class is a subclass of `Object` that computes an Adler-32 checksum on an input stream. It implements the Checksum interface.

CRC32

The `CRC32` class is a subclass of `Object` that computes an CRC-32 checksum on an input stream. It implements the Checksum interface.

CheckedInputStream

The `CheckedInputStream` class is a subclass of `java.io.FilterInputStream` that computes a checksum of the data being read.

CheckedOutputStream

The `CheckedOutputStream` class is a subclass of `java.io.FilterOutputStream` that computes a checksum of the data being written.

Deflater

The `Deflater` class is a subclass of `Object` that supports compression using the ZLIB compression library.

DeflaterOutputStream

The `DeflaterOutputStream` class is a subclass of `java.io.FilterOutputStream` that compresses stream output using the deflate format of the ZLIB compression library.

GZIPInputStream

The `GZIPInputStream` class is a subclass of `InflatorInputStream` that supports the reading of GZIP-compressed data.

GZIPOutputStream

The `GZIPOutputStream` class is a subclass of `DeflatorOutputStream` that supports the writing of GZIP-compressed data.

Inflater

The `Inflater` class is a subclass of `Object` that supports decompression using the ZLIB compression library.

InflaterInputStream

The `InflaterInputStream` class is a subclass of `java.io.FilterIntputStream` that decompresses stream intput using the inflate format of the ZLIB compression library.

ZipEntry

The `ZipEntry` class is a subclass of `Object` that encapsulates a ZIP file entry. It implements the `java.lang.Cloneable` interface.

ZipFile

The `ZipFile` class is a subclass of `Object` that supports the reading of `ZipEntry` objects from ZIP files.

ZipInputStream

The `ZipInputStream` class is a subclass of `InflaterInputStream` that is used for reading streams that are in the compressed or uncompressed ZIP format.

ZipOutputStream

The `ZipOutputStream` class is a subclass of `DeflaterOutputStream` that is used to write compressed and uncompressed ZIP file entries to an output stream.

Exceptions and Errors

DataFormatException

The `DataFormatException` class is a subclass of `java.lang.Exception` that is used to identify the occurrence of a data format error during compression or decompression.

ZipException

The `ZipException` class is a subclass of `java.io.IOException` that signals an error in the reading or writing of a ZIP file or stream.

PACKAGE javax.accessibility

The javax. accessibility package provides seven classes and seven interfaces that support the use of assistive technologies for disabled users.

Interfaces

Accessible

The Accessible interface is implemented by all components that support accessibility. It defines the single getAccessibleContext() method to return an object that implements the AccessibleContext interface.

AccessibleAction

The AccessibleAction interface defines methods that can be used to determine which actions are supported by a component. It also provides methods for acccessing these actions.

AccessibleComponent

The AccessibleComponent interface defines methods for controlling the behavior and display of GUI components that support assistive technologies.

AccessibleHypertext

The AccessibleHypertext interface is implemented by GUI components that display hypertext. It supports assistive technologies for hypertext display.

AccessibleSelection

The AccessibleSelection interface provides support for determining which subcomponents of a GUI component have been selected, and for controlling the selection status of those components.

AccessibleText

The AccessibleText interface provides constants and methods for use with GUI components that display text. It allows assistive technologies to control the content, attributes, and layout of displayed text.

AccessibleValue

The AccessibleValue interface is implemented by GUI components that support the selection of a numerical value from a range of values, such as a scrollbar. This interface provides methods for getting and setting the numerical value and for determining the range of values.

Classes

AccessibleBundle

The AccessibleBundle class is a subclass of Object that provides access to resource bundles and supports string conversions.

AccessibleContext

The AccessibleContext class is a core accessibility API class and provides access to other assistive technology objects. It defines the information that is used by all accessible objects and is subclassed by objects that implement assistive technologies. It is a subclass of Object.

AccessibleHyperlink

The AccessibleHyperlink extends Object to provide accessibility support for a hyperlink or set of hyperlinks.

AccessibleResourceBundle

The AccessibleResourceBundle class is a subclass of java.util.ListResourceBundle that implements a resource bundle for assistive technology applications. It provides localized accessibility properties for a particular locale.

AccessibleRole

The AccessibleRole class is a subclass of AccessibleBundle that provides constants that describe the role of an accessibility GUI component, such as LIST, MENU, and CHECK_BOX.

AccessibleState

The AccessibleState class is a subclass of AccessibleBundle that describes the state of an accessibility object. AccessibleState objects are contained in AccessibleStateSet objects. The AccessibleState class provides constants that define common object states, such as BUSY, CHECKED, and ENABLED.

AccessibleStateSet

The AccessibleStateSet class is a subclass of Object that implements a collection of AccessibleState objects. AccessibleStateSet objects are used to define the overall state of an accessibility object.

Exceptions and Errors

None.

PACKAGE javax.swing

The javax.swing package is the core Swing package. It contains 90 classes and 22 interfaces that provide the foundation for the Swing API.

Interfaces

Action

The Action interface extends the java.awt.ActionListener interface defines methods for defining, enabling, and disabling a unit of program operation.

BoundedRangeModel

The BoundedRangeModel interface defines a data model used for range-bounded components, such as sliders and progress bars.

ButtonModel
The ButtonModel interface extends the java.awt.ItemSelectable interface to provide methods that define the state of a button.

CellEditor
The CellEditor interface defines methods that are used to edit the cell values of GUI components, such as tables.

ComboBoxEditor
The ComboBoxEditor interface defines methods for editing combo boxes.

ComboBoxModel
The ComboBoxModel interface extends the ListModel interface and defines methods for supporting the data model of a combo box.

DesktopManager
The DesktopManager interface provides methods that are implemented by classes that support a Java-based desktop.

Icon
The Icon interface defines methods that are implemented by classes that provide desktop and application icons.

JComboBox.KeySelectionManager
The JComboBox.KeySelectionManager interface defines a key for selecting items from a combo box.

ListCellRenderer
The ListCellRenderer interface defines methods for painting the cells in a JList object.

ListModel
The ListModel interface defines methods that support the data model for a list.

ListSelectionModel
The ListSelectionModel interface defines methods for selecting elements from a list.

MenuElement
The MenuElement interface defines methods that are implemented by items that are placed in a menu.

MutableComboBoxModel
The MutableComboBoxModel interface extends the ComboBoxModel interface to provide update support.

Renderer
The Renderer interface defines methods for obtaining access to and setting the value of GUI components.

RootPaneContainer
The RootPaneContainer interface defines methods that are implemented by top-level window components.

ScrollPaneConstants
The ScrollPaneConstants interface defines constants that are used by scrollable pane classes.

Scrollable
The Scrollable interface defines methods that are implemented by scrollable container classes.

SingleSelectionModel
The SingleSelectionModel interface defines methods for selecting a single item from a list of items.

SwingConstants
The SwingConstants interface defines constants for laying out GUI components.

UIDefaults.ActiveValue
The UIDefaults.ActiveValue interface supports an active (preset) approach to defining user interface default values.

UIDefaults.LazyValue
The UIDefaults.LazyValue interface supports a lazy (as-needed) approach to defining user interface default values.

WindowConstants
The WindowConstants interface defines constants that are used in window operations.

Classes
AbstractAction
The AbstractAction class is a subclass of Object that provides a default implementation of the Action interface. It also implements the java.lang.Cloneable and java.io.Serializable interfaces.

AbstractButton
The AbstractButton class is a subclass of JComponent that serves as a base class for developing other JFC buttons. It implements the SwingConstants and java.awt.ItemSelectable interfaces.

AbstractListModel
The AbstractListModel class is a subclass of Object that provides an abstract data model for list-related classes. It implements the ListModel and java.io.Serializable interfaces.

BorderFactory

The BorderFactory class is a subclass of Object that provides support for creating Border objects.

Box

The Box class is a subclass of java.awt.Container that lays out components in a BoxLayout. It implements the java.awt.accessibility.Accessible interface.

Box.Filler

The Box.Filler class is an inner class of Box that supports the layout of Box objects. It is a subclass of java.awt.Component.

BoxLayout

The BoxLayout class is a subclass of Object that supports the layout of containers in a box-like, top-to-bottom, left-to-right fashion. It implements the java.awt.LayoutManager2 and java.io.Serializable interfaces.

ButtonGroup

The ButtonGroup class is a subclass of Object that supports the development of radio button-like button groups in which only one button in the group can be selected at a time. It implements the java.io.Serializable interface.

CellRendererPane

The CellRendererPane class is a subclass of java.awt.Container that supports the organization of cell-oriented components, such as lists and tables. It implements the java.awt.accessibility.Accessible interface.

DebugGraphics

The DebugGraphics class is a subclass of java.awt.Graphics that provides debugging support.

DefaultBoundedRangeModel

The DefaultBoundedRangeModel class is a subclass of Object that provides a default implementation of the BoundedRangeModel interface. It also implements the java.io.Serializable interface.

DefaultButtonModel

The DefaultButtonModel class is a subclass of Object that provides a default implementation of the ButtonModel interface. It also implements the java.io.Serializable interface.

DefaultCellEditor

The DefaultCellEditor class is a subclass of Object that provides a default implementation of the javax.swing.table.TableCellEditor and javax.swing.tree.TreeCellEditor interfaces. It also implements the java.io.Serializable interface.

DefaultComboBoxModel

The `DefaultComboBoxModel` class is a subclass of `AbstractListModel` and implements the `MutableComboBoxModel` and `java.io.Serializable` interfaces. It provides a default model for combo boxes.

DefaultDesktopManager

The `DefaultDesktopManager` class is a subclass of `Object` that provides a default implementation of the `DesktopManager` interface.

DefaultFocusManager

The `DefaultFocusManager` class is a subclass of `FocusManager` that provides support for accessing the components governed by the focus manager.

DefaultListCellRenderer

The `DefaultListCellRenderer` class extends `JLabel` and implements the `ListCellRenderer` and `Serializable` interfaces to provide a default rendering for a list cell.

DefaultListCellRenderer.UIResource

The `DefaultListCellRenderer.UIResource` class is an inner class of `DefaultListCellRenderer` that implements the `UIResource` interface.

DefaultListModel

The `DefaultListModel` class is a subclass of `AbstractListModel` that provides support for managing the addition and deletion of list elements.

DefaultListSelectionModel

The `DefaultListSelectionModel` class is a subclass of `Object` that provides a default implementation of the `ListSelectionModel` interface. It also implements the `java.lang.Cloneable` and `java.io.Serializable` interfaces.

DefaultSingleSelectionModel

The `DefaultSingleSelectionModel` class is a subclass of `Object` that provides a default implementation of the `SingleSelectionModel` interface. It also implements the `java.io.Serializable` interface.

FocusManager

The `FocusManager` class is a subclass of `Object` that is used to manage the current input focus.

GrayFilter

The `GrayFilter` class is a subclass of `java.awt.image.RGBImageFilter` that provides a grayscale rendering of an image.

ImageIcon

The `ImageIcon` class is a subclass of `Object` that provides a default implementation of the `Icon` interface. It also implements the `java.io.Serializable` interface.

JApplet

The JApplet class is a subclass of `java.applet.Applet` that provides Swing support. It implements the `java.awt.accessibility.Accessible` and `RootPaneContainer` interfaces.

JButton

The JButton class is a subclass of `AbstractButton` that provides a Swing push-button. It implements the `java.awt.accessibility.Accessible` interface.

JCheckBox

The JCheckBox class is a subclass of `JToggleButton` that provides a Swing checkbox. It implements the `java.awt.accessibility.Accessible` interface.

JCheckBoxMenuItem

The JCheckBoxMenuItem class is a subclass of `JMenuItem` that implements a checkbox that can be used as a menu item. It implements the `SwingConstants` and `java.awt.accessibility.Accessible` interfaces.

JColorChooser

The JColorChooser class extends `JComponent` and implements the `Accessible` interface. It provides the capability for users to select a color from a color selection panel.

JComboBox

The JComboBox class is a subclass of `JComponent` that provides a combo box GUI component. It implements the `java.awt.ItemSelectable`, `java.awt.event.ActionListener`, `javax.swing.event.ListDataListener`, and `java.awt.accessibility.Accessible` interfaces.

JComponent

The JComponent class is a subclass of `java.awt.Container` that is the base class for all Swing components. It implements the `java.io.Serializable` interface.

JDesktopPane

The JDesktopPane class is a subclass of `JLayeredPane` that supports the implementation of a desktop manager. It implements the `java.awt.accessibility.Accessible` interface.

JDialog

The JDialog class is a subclass of `java.awt.Dialog` that provides a Swing dialog box. It implements the `RootPaneContainer`, `WindowConstants`, and `java.awt.accessibility.Accessible` interface.

JEditorPane

The JEditorPane class is a subclass of `JTextComponent` that supports text editing.

JFileChooser

The JFileChooser class extends JComponent and implements the Accessible interface. It allows a user to select a file from a file chooser panel.

JFrame

The JFrame class is a subclass of java.awt.Frame that adds Swing support. It implements the RootPaneContainer, WindowConstants, and java.awt. accessibility.Accessible interfaces.

JInternalFrame

The JInternalFrame class is a subclass of JComponent that provides a frame that can be used within a JDesktopPane object. It implements the RootPaneContainer, WindowConstants, java.awt.accessibility.Accessible, java.awt.event.ComponentListener, java.awt.event.MouseListener, and java.awt.event.MouseMotionListener interfaces.

JInternalFrame.JDesktopIcon

The JInternalFrame.JDesktopIcon class is an inner class of JInternalFrame that provides an icon for use with the JInternalFrame object. It is a subclass of JComponent and implements the java.awt.accessibility.Accessible interface.

JLabel

The JLabel class is a subclass of JComponent that provides a Swing label (text or image). It implements the SwingConstants and java.awt.accessibility.Accessible interfaces.

JLayeredPane

The JLayeredPane class is a subclass of JComponent that provides a multi-layered pane. It implements the java.awt.accessibility.Accessible interface.

JList

The JList class is a subclass of JComponent that provides a basic list component. It implements the Scrollable and java.awt.accessibility.Accessible interfaces.

JMenu

The JMenu class is a subclass of JMenuItem that provides a Swing menu. It implements the MenuElement and java.awt.accessibility.Accessible interfaces.

JMenuBar

The JMenuBar class is a subclass of JComponent that provides a Swing menu bar. It implements the MenuElement and java.awt.accessibility.Accessible interfaces.

JMenuItem

The JMenuItem class is a subclass of AbstractButton that provides a Swing menu item. It implements the MenuElement and java.awt.accessibility.Accessible interfaces.

JOptionPane

The JOptionPane class is a subclass of JComponent that provides support for option dialog boxes.

JPanel

The JPanel class is a subclass of JComponent that provides a generic Swing panel. It implements the java.awt.accessibility.Accessible interface.

JPasswordField

The JPasswordField class is a subclass of JTextField that provides the capability to enter a password without it being displayed.

JPopupMenu

The JPopupMenu class is a subclass of JComponent that provides a popup menu capability. It implements the java.awt.accessibility.Accessible and MenuElement interfaces.

JPopupMenu.Separator

The JPopupMenu.Separator class is an inner class of JPopupMenu that provides accessibility support. It implements a menu separator.

JProgressBar

The JProgressBar class is a subclass of JComponent that provides a vertical or horizontal progress bar. It implements the SwingConstants and java.awt.accessibility.Accessible interfaces.

JRadioButton

The JRadioButton class is a subclass of JToggleButton that provides a basic radio button. It implements the java.awt.accessibility.Accessible interface.

JRadioButtonMenuItem

The JRadioButtonMenuItem class is a subclass of JMenuItemu that can be used as a menu item. It implements the java.awt.accessibility.Accessible interface.

JRootPane

The JRootPane class is a subclass of JComponent that provides the root pane for window container operations. It implements the java.awt.accessibility.Accessible interface.

JScrollBar

The JScrollBar class is a subclass of JComponent that provides a basic scrollbar. It implements the java.awt.Adjustible and java.awt.accessibility.Accessible interfaces.

JScrollPane

The JScrollPane class is a subclass of JComponent that provides a scrollable panel. It implements the ScrollPaneConstants and java.awt.accessibility.Accessible interfaces.

JSeparator

The JSeparator class is a subclass of JComponent that provides a menu separator. It implements the java.awt.accessibility.Accessible interface.

JSlider

The JSlider class is a subclass of JComponent that provides a slider control. It implements the SwingConstants and java.awt.accessibility.Accessible interfaces.

JSplitPane

The JSplitPane class is a subclass of JComponent that is used to split exactly two components. It implements the java.awt.accessibility.Accessible interface.

JTabbedPane

The JTabbedPane class is a subclass of JComponent that provides a tabbed multi-layer pane. It implements the SwingConstants, java.io.Serializable, and java.awt.accessibility.Accessible interfaces.

JTable

The JTable class is a subclass of JComponent that provides a basic table implementation. It implements the Scrollable,
java.awt.accessibility.Accessible,
javax.swing.event.TableModelListener,
javax.swing.event.TableColumnModelListener,
javax.swing.event.ListSelectionListener, and
javax.swing.event.CellEditorListener interfaces.

JTextArea

The JTextArea class is a subclass of JTextComponent that provides a Swing text area component.

JTextField

The JTextField class is a subclass of JTextComponent that provides a Swing text field. It implements the SwingConstants interface.

JTextPane

The JTextPane class is a subclass of JEditorPane that supports styled text.

JToggleButton

The JToggleButton class is a subclass of AbstractButton that supports a two-state button. It implements the java.awt.accessibility.Accessible interface.

JToggleButton.ToggleButtonModel

The JToggleButton.ToggleButtonModel class is an inner class of JToggleButton that supports button configuration. It is a subclass of DefaultButtonModel.

JToolBar

The JToolBar class is a subclass of JComponent that provides a basic tool bar. It implements the java.awt.accessibility.Accessible interface.

JToolBar.Separator

The JToolBar.Separator class is an inner class of JToolBar that acts as a toolbar separator. It is a subclass of java.awt.Component.

JToolTip

The JToolTip class is a subclass of JComponent that provides a popup tool tip. It implements the java.awt.accessibility.Accessible interface.

JTree

The JTree class is a subclass of JComponent that provides a basic tree component. It implements the Scrollable and java.awt.accessibility.Accessible interfaces.

JTree.DynamicUtilTreeNode

The JTree.DynamicUtilTreeNode class is an inner class of JTree that supports dynamic tree node management. It is a subclass of DefaultMutableTreeNode.

JTree.EmptySelectionModel

The JTree.EmptySelectionModel class is an inner class of JTree that supports tree selection. It is a subclass of DefaultTreeSelectionModel.

JViewport

The JViewport class is a subclass of JComponent that acts as a porthole for viewing displayed information. It implements the java.awt.accessibility.Accessible interface.

JWindow

The JWindow class is a subclass of java.awt.Window that provides Swing support. It implements the RootPaneContainer and java.awt.accessibility.Accessible interfaces.

KeyStroke

The KeyStroke class is a subclass of Object that implements a user-typed keystroke. It implements the java.io.Serializable interface.

LookAndFeel

The `LookAndFeel` class is a subclass of `Object` that supports pluggable look and feel.

MenuSelectionManager

The `MenuSelectionManager` class is a subclass of `Object` that supports the management of menu selections.

OverlayLayout

The `OverlayLayout` class is a subclass of `Object` that supports overlay-type container layout. It implements the `java.awt.LayoutManager2` and `java.io.Serializable` interfaces.

ProgressMonitor

The `ProgressMonitor` class is a subclass of `Object` that supports the monitoring of an operation in progress.

ProgressMonitorInputStream

The `ProgressMonitorInputStream` class is a subclass of `java.io.FilterInputStream` that supports the monitoring of data that is read from an input stream.

RepaintManager

The `RepaintManager` class is a subclass of `Object` that supports the repainting of `JComponent` objects.

ScrollPaneLayout

The `ScrollPaneLayout` class is a subclass of `Object` that is used to lay out a `JScrollPane` object. It implements the `ScrollPaneConstants`, `java.awt.LayoutManager`, and `java.io.Serializable` interfaces.

ScrollPaneLayout.UIResource

The `ScrollPaneLayout.UIResource` class is an inner class of `ScrollPaneLayout` that provides access to a `UIResource`.

SizeRequirements

The `SizeRequirements` class is a subclass of `Object` that provides information used by layout managers. It implements the `java.io.Serializable` interface.

SwingUtilities

The `SwingUtilities` class is a subclass of `Object` that provides general `static` methods that are used by Swing components. It implements the `SwingConstants` interface.

Timer

The `Timer` class is a subclass of `Object` that provides a timer/event generator. It implements the `java.io.Serializable` interface.

ToolTipManager

The `ToolTipManager` class is a subclass of `java.awt.event.MouseAdapter` that is used to provide tool tip support. It implements the `java.awt.event.MouseMotionListener` interface.

UIDefaults

The `UIDefaults` class is a subclass of `java.util.Hashtable` that supports the storage of user interface parameter information.

UIManager

The `UIManager` class is a subclass of `Object` that supports look and feel management. It implements the `java.io.Serializable` interface.

UIManager.LookAndFeelInfo

The `UIManager.LookAndFeelInfo` class is an inner class of `UIManager` that supports the storage of look and feel information. It is a subclass of `Object`.

ViewportLayout

The `ViewportLayout` class is a subclass of `Object` that supports the layout of `JViewport` objects. It implements the `java.awt.LayoutManager` and `java.io.Serializable` interfaces.

Exceptions and Errors

UnsupportedLookAndFeelException

The `UnsupportedLookAndFeelException` class is a subclass of `java.lang.Exception` that signals that an unsupported look and feel has been selected.

PACKAGE `javax.swing.border`

The `javax.swing.border` package provides nine classes and one interface that implement borders and border styles.

Interfaces

Border

The `Border` interface provides methods for rendering a border around a Swing component.

Classes

AbstractBorder

The `AbstractBorder` class is a subclass of `Object` that provides an abstract base class used to implement other `javax.swing.border` classes. It implements the `Border` and `java.io.Serializable` interfaces.

BevelBorder

The `BevelBorder` class is a subclass of `AbstractBorder` that implements a two-line bevel border.

CompoundBorder

The CompoundBorder class is a subclass of AbstractBorder that combines two Border objects into a single border.

EmptyBorder

The EmptyBorder class is a subclass of AbstractBorder that implements an empty, spaceless border. It implements the java.io.Serializable interface.

EtchedBorder

The EtchedBorder class is a subclass of AbstractBorder that implements an etched border. The border can be etched either in or out.

LineBorder

The LineBorder class is a subclass of AbstractBorder that draws a line border around an object. The line thickness and color of the border may be specified.

MatteBorder

The MatteBorder class is a subclass of EmptyBorder that implements a matte-like border. The border can consist of a specified color or a javax.swing.Icon object.

SoftBevelBorder

The SoftBevelBorder class is a subclass of BevelBorder that implements a bevel border with softened (rounded) corners. The beveling may be raised or lowered.

TitledBorder

The TitledBorder class is a subclass of AbstractBorder that specifies a text tile at a specified position on the border.

Exceptions and Errors

None.

PACKAGE javax.swing.colorchooser

The javax.swing.colorchooser package provides three classes and one interface that support color selection.

Interfaces

ColorSelectionModel

The ColorSelectionModel interface defines methods that support the selection of colors.

Classes

AbstractColorChooserPanel

The AbstractColorChooserPanel class extends JPanel to provide an abstract class for the implementation of color choosers.

ColorChooserComponentFactory

The ColorChooserComponentFactory class extends Object to provide a factory for the generation of components used in color choosers.

DefaultColorSelectionModel

The DefaultColorSelectionModel class extends Object and implements the ColorSelectionModel and Serializable interfaces. It provides a base class for the implementation of color selection models.

Exceptions and Errors

None.

PACKAGE javax.swing.event

The javax.swing.event package provides 23 classes and 23 interfaces that implement Swing events and event listeners.

Interfaces

AncestorListener

The AncestorListener interface extends the java.util.EventListener interface to support handling of the AncestorEvent.

CaretListener

The CaretListener interface extends the java.util.EventListener interface to support handling of the CaretEvent.

CellEditorListener

The CellEditorListener interface extends the java.util.EventListener interface to support table cell editing by the handling of the ChangeEvent.

ChangeListener

The ChangeListener interface extends the java.util.EventListener interface to support general handling of the ChangeEvent.

DocumentEvent

The DocumentEvent interface provides methods for handling document change notifications.

DocumentEvent.ElementChange

The DocumentEvent.ElementChange interface provides methods for handling changes made to a document element.

DocumentListener

The DocumentListener interface extends the java.util.EventListener interface to support handling of the DocumentEvent.

HyperlinkListener

The HyperlinkListener interface extends the java.util.EventListener interface to support handling of the HyperlinkEvent.

InternalFrameListener
The `InternalFrameListener` interface extends the `java.util.EventListener` interface to support handling of the `InternalFrameEvent`.

ListDataListener
The `Listener` interface extends the `java.util.EventListener` interface to support handling of the `ListDataEvent`.

ListSelectionListener
The `ListSelectionListener` interface extends the `java.util.EventListener` interface to support handling of the `ListSelectionEvent`.

MenuDragMouseListener
The `MenuDragMouseListener` interface extends `EventListener` to provide support for the `MenuDragMouseEvent`.

MenuKeyListener
The `MenuKeyListener` interface extends `EventListener` to provide support for the `MenuKeyEvent`.

MenuListener
The `MenuListener` interface extends the `java.util.EventListener` interface to support handling of the `MenuEvent`.

MouseInputListener
The `MouseInputListener` interface extends `MouseListener` and `MouseMotionListener` to support a combined mouse event handler.

PopupMenuListener
The `PopupMenuListener` interface extends the `java.util.EventListener` interface to support handling of the `PopupMenuEvent`.

TableColumnModelListener
The `TableColumnModelListener` interface extends the `java.util.EventListener` interface to support handling of the `TableColumnModelEvent`.

TableModelListener
The `TableModelListener` interface extends the `java.util.EventListener` interface to support handling of the `TableModelEvent`.

TreeExpansionListener
The `TreeExpansionListener` interface extends the `java.util.EventListener` interface to support handling of the `TreeExpansionEvent`.

TreeModelListener
The `TreeModelListener` interface extends the `java.util.EventListener` interface to support handling of the `TreeModelEvent`.

TreeSelectionListener
The `TreeSelectionListener` interface extends the `java.util.EventListener` interface to support handling of the `TreeSelectionEvent`.

TreeWillExpandListener
The `TreeWillExpandListener` interface extends the `java.util.EventListener` interface to support handling of the `TreeExpansionEvent`.

UndoableEditListener
The `UndoableEditListener` interface extends the `java.util.EventListener` interface to support handling of the `UndoableEditEvent`.

Classes

AncestorEvent
The `AncestorEvent` class is a subclass of `java.AWT.AWTEvent` that indicates changes in a component's ancestor.

CaretEvent
The `CaretEvent` class is a subclass of `java.util.EventObject` that indicates a change in the text caret.

ChangeEvent
The `ChangeEvent` class is a subclass of `java.util.EventObject` that indicates a change in the state of a component.

DocumentEvent.EventType
The `DocumentEvent.EventType` class is a subclass of `Object` that is used to enumerate the types of document events.

EventListenerList
The `EventListenerList` class is a subclass of `Object` that provides a list of `EventListener` objects. It implements the `java.io.Serializable` interface.

HyperlinkEvent
The `HyperlinkEvent` class is a subclass of `java.util.EventObject` that indicates an action with respect to a hypertext link.

HyperlinkEvent.EventType
The `HyperlinkEvent.EventType` class is an inner class of `HyperlinkEvent` that enumerates the types of hyperlink events.

InternalFrameAdapter
The `InternalFrameAdapter` class is a subclass of `Object` that provides a default implementation of the `InternalFrameListener` interface.

InternalFrameEvent
The `InternalFrameEvent` class is a subclass of `java.awt.AWTEvent` that provides events related to `javax.swing.JInternalFrame` objects.

ListDataEvent

The ListDataEvent class is a subclass of `java.util.EventObject` that identifies changes in list-type components.

ListSelectionEvent

The ListSelectionEvent class is a subclass of `java.util.EventObject` that identifies changes in the current list selection.

MenuDragMouseEvent

The MenuDragMouseEvent class extends `MouseEvent` to provide support for menu-related drag-and-drop operations.

MenuEvent

The MenuEvent class is a subclass of `java.util.EventObject` that is used to signal menu-related events.

MenuKeyEvent

The MenuKeyEvent class is a subclass of `KeyEvent` that supports menu-related key actions.

MouseInputAdapter

The MouseInputAdapter class is a subclass of `Object` that provides a default implementation of the `MouseInputListener` interface.

PopupMenuEvent

The PopupMenuEvent class is a subclass of `java.util.EventObject` that is used to signal popup menu-related events.

SwingPropertyChangeSupport

The SwingPropertyChangeSupport class extends `java.beans.PropertyChangeSupport` to provide Swing support.

TableColumnModelEvent

The TableColumnModelEvent class is a subclass of `java.util.EventObject` that is used to identify changes in a table column model.

TableModelEvent

The TableModelEvent class is a subclass of `java.util.EventObject` that is used to identify changes in a table model.

TreeExpansionEvent

The TreeExpansionEvent class is a subclass of `java.util.EventObject` that indicates that a tree has been expanded.

TreeModelEvent

The TreeModelEvent class is a subclass of `java.util.EventObject` that is used to signal a change in a tree model.

TreeSelectionEvent

The TreeSelectionEvent class is a subclass of java.util.EventObject that is used to signal a change in the current tree selection. It implements the java.lang.Cloneable interface.

UndoableEditEvent

The UndoableEditEvent class is a subclass of java.util.EventObject indicating that an operation that can be undone has been performed.

Exceptions and Errors

None.

PACKAGE javax.swing.filechooser

The javax.swing.filechooser package provides three classes and no interfaces that support basic file system operations.

Interfaces

None.

Classes

FileFilter

The FileFilter class extends Object to provide an abstract class for file filtering operations.

FileSystemView

The FileSystemView class extends Object to provide a default file system view.

FileView

The FileView class extends Object to provide a default information about a file.

Exceptions and Errors

None.

PACKAGE javax.swing.plaf

The javax.swing. plaf package provides 42 classes and one interface that support pluggable look-and-feel.

Interfaces

UIResource

The UIResource interface is used to identify an object as supporting pluggable look-and-feel.

Classes

BorderUIResource

The `BorderUIResource` class extends `Object` and implements the `Border`, `UIResource`, and `Serializable` interfaces to define a `UIResource` for `Border` objects.

BorderUIResource.BevelBorderUIResource

The `BorderUIResource.BevelBorderUIResource` class extends `BevelBorder` and implements `UIResource` to support pluggable look-and-feel.

BorderUIResource.CompoundBorderUIResource

The `BorderUIResource.CompoundBorderUIResource` class extends `CompoundBorder` and implements `UIResource` to support pluggable look-and-feel.

BorderUIResource.EmptyBorderUIResource

The `BorderUIResource.EmptyBorderUIResource` class extends `EmptyBorder` and implements `UIResource` to support pluggable look-and-feel.

BorderUIResource.EtchedBorderUIResource

The `BorderUIResource.EtchedBorderUIResource` class extends `EtchedBorder` and implements `UIResource` to support pluggable look-and-feel.

BorderUIResource.LineBorderUIResource

The `BorderUIResource.LineBorderUIResource` class extends `LineBorder` and implements `UIResource` to support pluggable look-and-feel.

BorderUIResource.MatteBorderUIResource

The `BorderUIResource.MatteBorderUIResource` class extends `MatteBorder` and implements `UIResource` to support pluggable look-and-feel.

BorderUIResource.TitledBorderUIResource

The `BorderUIResource.TitledBorderUIResource` class extends `TitledBorder` and implements `UIResource` to support pluggable look-and-feel.

ButtonUI

The `ButtonUI` class extends `ComponentUI` to support pluggable look-and-feel for `JButtonUI` objects.

ColorChooserUI

The `ColorChooserUI` class extends `ComponentUI` to support pluggable look-and-feel for `JColorChooser` objects.

ColorUIResource

The `ColorUIResource` class extends `Color` and implements `UIResource` to support pluggable look-and-feel for `Color` objects.

ComboBoxUI
The ComboBoxUI class extends ComponentUI to support pluggable look-and-feel for JComboBoxUI objects.

ComponentUI
The ComponentUI class extends Object to support pluggable look-and-feel for Swing component objects.

DesktopIconUI
The DesktopIconUI class extends ComponentUI to support pluggable look-and-feel for JDesktopIcon objects.

DesktopPaneUI
The DesktopPaneUI class extends ComponentUI to support pluggable look-and-feel for JDesktopPane objects.

DimensionUIResource
The DimensionUIResource class extends Dimension and implements UIResource to support pluggable look-and-feel for Dimension objects.

FileChooserUI
The FileChooserUI class extends ComponentUI to support pluggable look-and-feel for JFileChooser objects.

FontUIResource
The FontUIResource class extends Font and implements UIResource to support pluggable look-and-feel for Font objects.

IconUIResource
The IconUIResource class extends Object and implements UIResource, Icon and Serializable to support pluggable look-and-feel for Icon objects.

InsetsUIResource
The InsetsUIResource class extends Insets and implements UIResource to support pluggable look-and-feel for Insets objects.

InternalFrameUI
The InternalFrameUI class extends ComponentUI to support pluggable look-and-feel for JInternalFrame objects.

LabelUI
The LabelUI class extends ComponentUI to support pluggable look-and-feel for JLabel objects.

ListUI
The ListUI class extends ComponentUI to support pluggable look-and-feel for JList objects.

MenuBarUI

The MenuBarUI class extends ComponentUI to support pluggable look-and-feel for JMenuBar objects.

MenuItemUI

The MenuItemUI class extends ButtonUI to support pluggable look-and-feel for JMenuItem objects

OptionPaneUI

The OptionPaneUI class extends ComponentUI to support pluggable look-and-feel for JOptionPane objects.

PanelUI

The PanelUI class extends ComponentUI to support pluggable look-and-feel for JPanel objects.

PopupMenuUI

The PopupMenuUI class extends ComponentUI to support pluggable look-and-feel for JPopupMenu objects.

ProgressBarUI

The ProgressBarUI class extends ComponentUI to support pluggable look-and-feel for JProgressBar objects.

ScrollBarUI

The ScrollBarUI class extends ComponentUI to support pluggable look-and-feel for JScrollBar objects.

ScrollPaneUI

The ScrollPaneUI class extends ComponentUI to support pluggable look-and-feel for JScrollPane objects.

SeparatorUI

The SeparatorUI class extends ComponentUI to support pluggable look-and-feel for JSeparator objects.

SliderUI

The SliderUI class extends ComponentUI to support pluggable look-and-feel for JSlider objects.

SplitPaneUI

The SplitPaneUI class extends ComponentUI to support pluggable look-and-feel for JSplitPane objects.

TabbedPaneUI

The TabbedPaneUI class extends ComponentUI to support pluggable look-and-feel for JTabbedPane objects.

TableHeaderUI

The `TableHeaderUI` class extends `ComponentUI` to support pluggable look-and-feel for `JTableHeader` objects.

TableUI

The `TableUI` class extends `ComponentUI` to support pluggable look-and-feel for `JTable` objects.

TextUI

The `TextUI` class extends `ComponentUI` to support pluggable look-and-feel for `JText` objects.

ToolBarUI

The `ToolBarUI` class extends `ComponentUI` to support pluggable look-and-feel for `JToolBar` objects.

ToolTipUI

The `ToolTipUI` class extends `ComponentUI` to support pluggable look-and-feel for `JToolTip` objects.

TreeUI

The `TreeUI` class extends `ComponentUI` to support pluggable look-and-feel for `JTree` objects.

ViewportUI

The `ViewportUI` class extends `ComponentUI` to support pluggable look-and-feel for `JViewport` objects.

Exceptions and Errors

None.

PACKAGE `javax.swing.plaf.basic`

The `javax.swing.plaf.basic` package provides 65 classes and one interface that support the basic look-and-feel.

Interfaces

ComboPopup

The `ComboPopup` interface defines methods required to implement a `BasicComboBoxUI`.

Classes

BasicArrowButton

The `BasicArrowButton` class extends `JButton` and implements the `SwingConstants` interface to support an arrow button with the basic look-and-feel.

BasicBorders

The BasicBorders class extends Object to provide a border factory for the basic look-and-feel.

BasicBorders.ButtonBorder

The BasicBorders.ButtonBorder class extends AbstractBorder and implements UIResource to provide a button border with the basic look-and-feel.

BasicBorders.FieldBorder

The BasicBorders.FieldBorder class extends AbstractBorder and implements UIResource to provide a field border with the basic look-and-feel.

BasicBorders.MarginBorder

The BasicBorders.MarginBorder class extends AbstractBorder and implements UIResource to provide a margin border with the basic look-and-feel.

BasicBorders.MenuBarBorder

The BasicBorders.MenuBarBorder class extends AbstractBorder and implements UIResource to provide a menu bar border with the basic look-and-feel.

BasicBorders.RadioButtonBorder

The BasicBorders.RadioButtonBorder class extends BasicBorders.ButtonBorder to provide a border with the basic look-and-feel.

BasicBorders.SplitPaneBorder

The BasicBorders.SplitPaneBorder class extends Object and implements the Border and UIResource interfaces to provide a split pane border with the basic look-and-feel.

BasicBorders.ToggleButtonBorder

The BasicBorders.ToggleButtonBorder class extends BasicBorders.ButtonBorder to provide a border with the basic look-and-feel.

BasicButtonListener

The BasicButtonListener class extends Object and implements the MouseListener, MouseMotionListener, FocusListener, ChangeListener, and PropertyChangeListener interfaces to handle button-related events for the basic look-and-feel.

BasicButtonUI

The BasicButtonUI class extends ButtonUI to support the basic look-and-feel.

BasicCheckBoxMenuItemUI

The BasicCheckBoxMenuItemUI class extends BasicMenuItemUI to support the basic look-and-feel for checkbox menu items.

BasicCheckBoxUI

The BasicCheckBoxUI class extends BasicRadioButtonUI to support the basic look-and-feel for checkboxes.

BasicColorChooserUI
The BasicColorChooserUI class extends ColorChooserUI to support the basic look-and-feel.

BasicComboBoxEditor
The BasicComboBoxEditor class extends Object and implements the ComboBoxEditor and FocusListener interfaces to provide a default editor for editable combo boxes.

BasicComboBoxEditor.UIResource
The BasicComboBoxEditor.UIResource class extends BasicComboBoxEditor and implements UIResource to provide a UIResource for the BasicComboBoxEditor class.

BasicComboBoxRenderer
The BasicComboBoxRenderer class extends JLabel and implements the ListCellRenderer and Serializable interfaces to support the rendering of combo boxes with the basic look-and-feel.

BasicComboBoxRenderer.UIResource
The BasicComboBoxRenderer.UIResource class extends BasicComboBoxRenderer and implements UIResource to provide a UIResource for the BasicComboBoxRenderer class.

BasicComboBoxUI
The BasicComboBoxUI class extends ComboBoxUI to support the basic look-and-feel.

BasicComboPopup
The BasicComboPopup class extends JPopupMenu and implements ComboPopup to provide a combo popup component for the basic look-and-feel.

BasicDesktopIconUI
The BasicDesktopIconUI class extends DesktopIconUI to support the basic look-and-feel.

BasicDesktopPaneUI
The BasicDesktopPaneUI class extends DesktopPaneUI to support the basic look-and-feel.

BasicDirectoryModel
The BasicDirectoryModel class extends AbstractListModel and implements the PropertyChangeListener interface to implement a file list with the basic look-and-feel.

BasicEditorPaneUI
The BasicEditorPaneUI class extends BasicTextUI to support the basic look-and-feel.

BasicFileChooserUI
The BasicFileChooserUI class extends FileChooserUI to support the basic look-and-feel.

BasicGraphicsUtils
The BasicGraphicsUtils class extends Object to provide graphic utilities used with the basic look-and-feel.

BasicIconFactory
The BasicIconFactory class extends Object and implements Serializable to provide a factory for the creation of icons with the basic look-and-feel.

BasicInternalFrameTitlePane
The BasicInternalFrameTitlePane class extends JComponent to provide a basic look-and-feel implementation of a title bar.

BasicInternalFrameUI
The BasicInternalFrameUI class extends InternalFrameUI to support the basic look-and-feel.

BasicLabelUI
The BasicLabelUI class extends LabelUI and implements the PropertyChangeListener interface to support the basic look-and-feel.

BasicListUI
The BasicListUI class extends ListUI to support the basic look-and-feel.

BasicLookAndFeel
The BasicLookAndFeel class extends Object and implements Serializable to provide the basic look-and-feel specification.

BasicMenuBarUI
The BasicMenuBarUI class extends MenuBarUI to support the basic look-and-feel.

BasicMenuItemUI
The BasicMenuItemUI class extends MenuItemUI to support the basic look-and-feel.

BasicMenuUI
The BasicMenuUI class extends BasicMenuItemUI to support the basic look-and-feel for menus.

BasicOptionPaneUI
The BasicOptionPaneUI class extends OptionPaneUI to support the basic look-and-feel.

BasicOptionPaneUI.ButtonAreaLayout

The BasicOptionPaneUI.ButtonAreaLayout class extends Object and implements LayoutManager to support the layout of option panes with the basic look-and-feel.

BasicPanelUI

The BasicPanelUI class extends PanelUI to support the basic look-and-feel.

BasicPasswordFieldUI

The BasicPasswordFieldUI class extends BasicTextFieldUI to support the basic look-and-feel for password fields.

BasicPopupMenuSeparatorUI

The BasicPopupMenuSeparatorUI class extends BasicSeparatorUI to support the basic look-and-feel for menu separators.

BasicPopupMenuUI

The BasicPopupMenuUI class extends PopupMenuUI to support the basic look-and-feel.

BasicProgressBarUI

The BasicProgressBarUI class extends ProgressBarUI to support the basic look-and-feel.

BasicRadioButtonMenuItemUI

The BasicRadioButtonMenuItemUI class extends BasicMenuItemUI to support the basic look-and-feel for radio button menu items.

BasicRadioButtonUI

The BasicRadioButtonUI class extends BasicToggleButtonUI to support the basic look-and-feel for radio buttons.

BasicScrollBarUI

The BasicScrollBarUI class extends ScrollBarUI and implements the LayoutManager and SwingConstants interfaces to support the basic look-and-feel.

BasicScrollPaneUI

The BasicScrollPaneUI class extends ScrollPaneUI and implements the ScrollPaneConstants interface to support the basic look-and-feel.

BasicSeparatorUI

The BasicSeparatorUI class extends SeparatorUI to support the basic look-and-feel.

BasicSliderUI

The BasicSliderUI class extends SliderUI to support the basic look-and-feel.

BasicSplitPaneDivider
The `BasicSplitPaneDivider` class extends `Container` and implements `PropertyChangeListener` to provide a divider used by `BasicSplitPaneUI`.

BasicSplitPaneUI
The `BasicSplitPaneUI` class extends `SplitPaneUI` to support the basic look-and-feel.

BasicTabbedPaneUI
The `BasicTabbedPaneUI` class extends `TabbedPaneUI` and implements the `SwingConstants` interface to support the basic look-and-feel.

BasicTableHeaderUI
The `BasicTableHeaderUI` class extends `TableHeaderUI` to support the basic look-and-feel.

BasicTableUI
The `BasicTableUI` class extends `TableUI` to support the basic look-and-feel.

BasicTextAreaUI
The `BasicTextAreaUI` class extends `BasicTextUI` to support the basic look-and-feel.

BasicTextFieldUI
The `BasicTextFieldUI` class extends `BasicTextUI` to support the basic look-and-feel.

BasicTextPaneUI
The `BasicTextPaneUI` class extends `BasicEditorPaneUI` to support the basic look-and-feel.

BasicTextUI
The `BasicTextUI` class extends `TextUI` and implements the `ViewFactory` interface to support the basic look-and-feel.

BasicTextUI.BasicCaret
The `BasicTextUI.BasicCaret` class extends `DefaultCaret` and implements `UIResource` to provide a text caret with the basic look-and-feel.

BasicTextUI.BasicHighlighter
The `BasicTextUI.BasicHighlighter` class extends `DefaultHighlighter` and implements `UIResource` to provide a text highlighter with the basic look-and-feel.

BasicToggleButtonUI
The `BasicToggleButtonUI` class extends `BasicButtonUI` to support the basic look-and-feel.

BasicToolBarSeparatorUI
The BasicToolBarSeparatorUI class extends BasicSeparatorUI to support the basic look-and-feel.

BasicToolBarUI
The BasicToolBarUI class extends ToolBarUI and implements SwingConstants to support the basic look-and-feel.

BasicToolTipUI
The BasicToolTipUI class extends ToolTipUI to support the basic look-and-feel.

BasicTreeUI
The BasicTreeUI class extends TreeUI to support the basic look-and-feel.

BasicViewportUI
The BasicViewportUI class extends ViewportUI to support the basic look-and-feel.

DefaultMenuLayout
The DefaultMenuLayout class extends BoxLayout and implements UIResource to provide a menu layout manager with the basic look-and-feel.

Exceptions and Errors
None.

PACKAGE javax.swing.plaf.metal
The javax.swing.plaf.metal package provides 47 classes and no interfaces that support the metal look-and-feel.

Interfaces
None.

Classes

DefaultMetalTheme
The DefaultMetalTheme class extends the Object class to provide a default implementation of the Metal look and feel.

MetalBorders
The MetalBorders class extends the Object class to provide a border with the Metal look and feel.

MetalBorders.ButtonBorder
The MetalBorders.ButtonBorder class extends the AbstractBorder class and implements the UIResource interface to create a border class with the Metal look and feel.

MetalBorders.Flush3DBorder

The `MetalBorders.Flush3DBorder` class extends the `AbstractBorder` class and implements the `UIResource` interface to create a border class with the Metal look and feel.

MetalBorders.InternalFrameBorder

The `MetalBorders.InternalFrameBorder` class extends the `AbstractBorder` class and implements the `UIResource` interface to create a border class with the Metal look and feel.

MetalBorders.MenuBarBorder

The `MetalBorders.MenuBarBorder` class extends the `AbstractBorder` class and implements the `UIResource` interface to create a border class with the Metal look and feel.

MetalBorders.MenuItemBorder

The `MetalBorders.MenuItemBorder` class extends the `AbstractBorder` class and implements the `UIResource` interface to create a border class with the Metal look and feel.

MetalBorders.PopupMenuBorder

The `MetalBorders.PopupMenuBorder` class extends the `AbstractBorder` class and implements the `UIResource` interface to create a border class with the Metal look and feel.

MetalBorders.RolloverButtonBorder

The `MetalBorders.RolloverButtonBorder` class extends the `AbstractBorder` class and implements the `UIResource` interface to create a border class with the Metal look and feel.

MetalBorders.ScrollPaneBorder

The `MetalBorders.ScrollPaneBorder` class extends the `AbstractBorder` class and implements the `UIResource` interface to create a border class with the Metal look and feel.

MetalBorders.TextFieldBorder

The `MetalBorders.TextFieldBorder` class extends the `AbstractBorder` class and implements the `UIResource` interface to create a border class with the Metal look and feel.

MetalBorders.ToolBarBorder

The `MetalBorders.ToolBarBorder` class extends the `AbstractBorder` class and implements the `UIResource` interface to create a border class with the Metal look and feel.

MetalButtonUI

The `MetalButtonUI` class extends the `BasicButtonUI` class with the Metal look and feel.

MetalCheckBoxIcon

The MetalCheckBoxIcon class extends the Object class and implements the Icon, UIResource, and Serializable interfaces to create a checkbox icon with the Metal look and feel.

MetalCheckBoxUI

The MetalCheckBoxUI class extends the MetalRadioButtonUI class to create a metal checbox.

MetalComboBoxButton

The MetalComboBoxButton class extends the JButton class with the Metal look and feel.

MetalComboBoxEditor

The MetalComboBoxEditor class extends the BasicComboBoxEditor class with the Metal look and feel.

MetalComboBoxEditor.UIResource

The MetalComboBoxEditor.UIResource class is an inner class of the MetalComboBoxEditor class that implements the UIResource interface to provide a UIResource for the MetalComboBoxEditor class.

MetalComboBoxIcon

The MetalComboBoxIcon class extends the Object class and implements the Icon and Serializable interfaces to create a combo box icon with the Metal look and feel.

MetalComboBoxUI

The MetalComboBoxUI class extends the BasicComboBoxUI class with the Metal look and feel.

MetalDesktopIconUI

The MetalDesktopIconUI class extends the BasicDesktopIconUI class with the Metal look and feel.

MetalFileChooserUI

The MetalFileChooserUI class extends the BasicFileChooserUI class with the Metal look and feel.

MetalIconFactory

The MetalIconFactory class extends the Object class and implements the Serializable interface to create an icon factory with the Metal look and feel.

MetalIconFactory.FileIcon16

The MetalIconFactory.FileIcon16 class extends the Object class and implements the Icon and Serializable interfaces to provide a file icon with the Metal look and feel.

MetalIconFactory.FolderIcon16

The MetalIconFactory.FolderIcon16 class extends the Object class and implements the Icon and Serializable interfaces to provide a folder icon with the Metal look and feel.

MetalIconFactory.TreeControlIcon

The MetalIconFactory.TreeControlIcon class extends the Object class and implements the Icon and Serializable interfaces to provide a tree control icon with the Metal look and feel.

MetalIconFactory.TreeFolderIcon

The MetalIconFactory.TreeFolderIcon class extends the MetalIconFactory.FolderIcon16 class to create a tree folder icon with the Metal look and feel.

MetalIconFactory.TreeLeafIcon

The MetalIconFactory.TreeLeafIcon class extends the MetalIconFactory.FileIcon16 class to create a tree file icon with the Metal look and feel.

MetalInternalFrameUI

The MetalInternalFrameUI class extends the BasicInternalFrameUI class with the Metal look and feel.

MetalLabelUI

The MetalLabelUI class extends the BasicLabelUI class with the Metal look and feel.

MetalLookAndFeel

The MetalLookAndFeel class extends the BasicLookAndFeel class with the Metal look and feel.

MetalPopupMenuSeparatorUI

The MetalPopupMenuSeparatorUI class extends the MenuSeparatorUI class to create a popup menu separator with the Metal look and feel.

MetalProgressBarUI

The MetalProgressBarUI class extends the BasicProgressBarUI class with the Metal look and feel.

MetalRadioButtonUI

The MetalRadioButtonUI class extends the BasicRadioButtonUI class with the Metal look and feel.

MetalScrollBarUI

The MetalScrollBarUI class extends the BasicScrollBarUI class with the Metal look and feel.

MetalScrollButton

The MetalScrollButton class extends the BasicArrowButton class with the Metal look and feel.

MetalScrollPaneUI

The MetalScrollPaneUI class extends the BasicScrollPaneUI class with the Metal look and feel.

MetalSeparatorUI

The MetalSeparatorUI class extends the BasicSeparatorUI class with the Metal look and feel.

MetalSliderUI

The MetalSliderUI class extends the BasicSliderUI class with the Metal look and feel.

MetalSplitPaneUI

The MetalSplitPaneUI class extends the BasicSplitPaneUI class with the Metal look and feel.

MetalTabbedPaneUI

The MetalTabbedPaneUI class extends the BasicTabbedPaneUI class with the Metal look and feel.

MetalTextFieldUI

The MetalTextFieldUI class extends the BasicTextFieldUI class with the Metal look and feel.

MetalTheme

The MetalTheme class extends the Object class to provide a general description of the Metal look and feel.

MetalToggleButtonUI

The MetalToggleButtonUI class extends the BasicToggleButtonUI class with the Metal look and feel.

MetalToolBarUI

The MetalToolBarUI class extends the BasicToolBarUI class with the Metal look and feel.

MetalToolTipUI

The MetalToolTipUI class extends the BasicToolTipUI class with the Metal look and feel.

MetalTreeUI

The MetalTreeUI class extends the BasicTreeUI class with the Metal look and feel.

Exceptions and Errors

None.

PACKAGE javax.swing.plaf.multi

The javax.swing.plaf.multi package provides 29 classes and no interfaces that supports the multiplexing look-and-feel.

Interfaces

None.

Classes

MultiButtonUI

The MultiButtonUI class extends the ButtonUI class with the multiplexing look and feel.

MultiColorChooserUI

The MultiColorChooserUI class extends the ColorChooserUI class with the multiplexing look and feel.

MultiComboBoxUI

The MultiComboBoxUI class extends the ComboBoxUI class with the multiplexing look and feel.

MultiDesktopIconUI

The MultiDesktopIconUI class extends the DesktopIconUI class with the multiplexing look and feel.

MultiDesktopPaneUI

The MultiDesktopPaneUI class extends the DesktopPaneUI class with the multiplexing look and feel.

MultiFileChooserUI

The MultiFileChooserUI class extends the FileChooserUI class with the multiplexing look and feel.

MultiInternalFrameUI

The MultiInternalFrameUI class extends the InternalFrameUI class with the multiplexing look and feel.

MultiLabelUI

The MultiLabelUI class extends the LabelUI class with the multiplexing look and feel.

MultiListUI

The MultiListUI class extends the ListUI class with the multiplexing look and feel.

MultiLookAndFeel

The MultiLookAndFeel class extends the LookAndFeel class with the multiplexing look and feel.

MultiMenuBarUI

The MultiMenuBarUI class extends the MenuBarUI class with the multiplexing look and feel.

MultiMenuItemUI

The MultiMenuItemUI class extends the MenuItemUI class with the multiplexing look and feel.

MultiOptionPaneUI

The MultiOptionPaneUI class extends the OptionPaneUI class with the multiplexing look and feel.

MultiPanelUI

The MultiPanelUI class extends the PanelUI class with the multiplexing look and feel.

MultiPopupMenuUI

The MultiPopupMenuUI class extends the PopupMenuUI class with the multiplexing look and feel.

MultiProgressBarUI

The MultiProgressBarUI class extends the ProgressBarUI class with the multiplexing look and feel.

MultiScrollBarUI

The MultiScrollBarUI class extends the ScrollBarUI class with the multiplexing look and feel.

MultiScrollPaneUI

The MultiScrollPaneUI class extends the ScrollPaneUI class with the multiplexing look and feel.

MultiSeparatorUI

The MultiSeparatorUI class extends the SeparatorUI class with the multiplexing look and feel.

MultiSliderUI

The MultiSliderUI class extends the SliderUI class with the multiplexing look and feel.

MultiSplitPaneUI

The MultiSplitPaneUI class extends the SplitPaneUI class with the multiplexing look and feel.

MultiTabbedPaneUI

The MultiTabbedPaneUI class extends the TabbedPaneUI class with the multiplexing look and feel.

MultiTableHeaderUI
The `MultiTableHeaderUI` class extends the `TableHeaderUI` class with the multiplexing look and feel.

MultiTableUI
The `MultiTableUI` class extends the `TableUI` class with the multiplexing look and feel.

MultiTextUI
The `MultiTextUI` class extends the `TextUI` class with the multiplexing look and feel.

MultiToolBarUI
The `MultiToolBarUI` class extends the `ToolBarUI` class with the multiplexing look and feel.

MultiToolTipUI
The `MultiToolTipUI` class extends the `ToolTipUI` class with the multiplexing look and feel.

MultiTreeUI
The `MultiTreeUI` class extends the `TreeUI` class with the multiplexing look and feel.

MultiViewportUI
The `MultiViewportUI` class extends the `ViewportUI` class with the multiplexing look and feel.

Exceptions and Errors
None.

PACKAGE `javax.swing.table`
The `javax.swing.table` package provides seven classes and four interfaces that implement the Swing table component.

Interfaces
TableCellEditor
The `TableCellEditor` interface extends the `javax.swing.CellEditor` interface to provide support for the text editing of table cells.

TableCellRenderer
The `TableCellRenderer` interface defines methods for rendering the cells of `JTable` objects.

TableColumnModel
The `TableColumnModel` interface defines methods for manipulating the rows of a table.

TableModel

The TableModel interface defines methods that are implemented by a data model that provides data for a JTable object.

Classes

AbstractTableModel

The AbstractTableModel class is a subclass of Object that provides an abstract implementation of the TableModel interface. It also implements the java.io.Serializable interface.

DefaultTableCellRenderer

The DefaultTableCellRenderer class is a subclass of javax.swing.JLabel that is used to render the individual cells of a table. It implements the TableCellRenderer and java.io.Serializable interfaces.

DefaultTableCellRenderer.UIResource

The DefaultTableCellRenderer.UIResource class is an inner class of DefaultTableCellRenderer that provides support for cell rendering.

DefaultTableColumnModel

The DefaultTableColumnModel class is a subclass of Object that provides a default implementation to the TableColumnModel interface. It also implements the java.beans.PropertyChangeListener, javax.swing.event.ListSelectionListener, and java.io.Serializable interfaces.

DefaultTableModel

The DefaultTableModel class is a subclass of AbstractTableModel that organizes its data using java.util.Vector objects. It implements the java.io.Serializable interface.

JTableHeader

The JTableHeader class is a subclass of javax.swing.JComponent that encapsulates the column header of a JTable object. It implements the TableColumnModelListener and java.awt.accessibility.Accessible interfaces.

TableColumn

The TableColumn class is a subclass of Object that defines the properties of a column in a JTable object. It implements the java.io.Serializable interface.

Exceptions and Errors

None.

PACKAGE javax.swing.text

The javax.swing.text package provides 63 classes and 21 interfaces that implement text-processing components.

Interfaces
AbstractDocument.AttributeContext
The `AbstractDocument.AttributeContext` interface supports attribute compression.

AbstractDocument.Content
The `AbstractDocument.Content` interface describes a sequence of editable content.

AttributeSet
The `AttributeSet` interface defines a read-only set of text attributes.

AttributeSet.CharacterAttribute
The `AttributeSet.CharacterAttribute` interface defines an attribute type signature.

AttributeSet.ColorAttribute
The `AttributeSet.ColorAttribute` interface defines a color type signature.

AttributeSet.FontAttribute
The `AttributeSet.FontAttribute` interface defines a font type signature.

AttributeSet.ParagraphAttribute
The `AttributeSet.ParagraphAttribute` interface defines a paragraph type signature.

Caret
The `Caret` interface defines a document insertion point caret.

Document
The `Document` interface defines a container for editable text.

Element
The `Element` interface defines a structural piece of a `Document` object.

Highlighter
The `Highlighter` interface provides support for highlighted text.

Highlighter.Highlight
The `Highlighter.Highlight` interface defines the location of highlighted text.

Highlighter.HighlightPainter
The `Highlighter.HighlightPainter` interface defines the manner in which highlighted text is to be painted.

Keymap
The `Keymap` interface binds keystrokes to actions.

MutableAttributeSet

The `MutableAttributeSet` interface extends the `AttributeSet` interface to provide methods for updating the set of attributes.

Position

The `Position` interface defines a location within a `Document` object.

Style

The `Style` interface defines text, paragraph, and other document-related styles.

StyledDocument

The `StyledDocument` interface extends the `Document` interface to provide style support.

TabExpander

The `TabExpander` interface provides support for tab settings.

TabableView

The `TabableView` interface provides support for viewing expanded tabs within a document.

ViewFactory

The `ViewFactory` interface provides support for creating different views of a document.

Classes

AbstractDocument

The `AbstractDocument` class is a subclass of `Object` that provides a basic implementation of the `Document` interface. It also implements the `java.io.Serializable` interface.

AbstractDocument.ElementEdit

The `AbstractDocument.ElementEdit` class is an inner class of `AbstractDocument` that provides undo/redo support. It is a subclass of `javax.swing.undo.AbstractUndoableEdit`.

AbstractWriter

The `AbstractWriter` class is an subclass of `Object` that supports the display of text.

BoxView

The `BoxView` class is a subclass of `CompositeView` that provides a box-like organization of document content.

ComponentView

The `ComponentView` class is a subclass of `View` that provides a view of a single document component.

CompositeView

The CompositeView class is a subclass of View that provides a view of multiple document components.

DefaultCaret

The DefaultCaret class is a subclass of Object that provides a default implementation of the Caret interface. It also implements the java.awt.event.FocusListener, java.awt.event.MouseListener, java.awt.event.MouseMotionListener, and java.io.Serializable interfaces.

DefaultEditorKit

The DefaultEditorKit class is a subclass of EditorKit that provides a basic text editing capability.

DefaultEditorKit.BeepAction

The DefaultEditorKit.BeepAction class is an inner class of DefaultEditorKit that creates a beep sound. It is a subclass of Object.

DefaultEditorKit.CopyAction

The DefaultEditorKit.CopyAction class is an inner class of DefaultEditorKit that copies data to the clipboard. It is a subclass of Object.

DefaultEditorKit.CutAction

The DefaultEditorKit.CutAction class is an inner class of DefaultEditorKit that cuts data to the clipboard. It is a subclass of Object.

DefaultEditorKit.DefaultKeyTypedAction

The DefaultEditorKit.DefaultKeyTypedAction class is an inner class of DefaultEditorKit that handles key presses. It is a subclass of Object.

DefaultEditorKit.InsertBreakAction

The DefaultEditorKit.InsertBreakAction class is an inner class of DefaultEditorKit that inserts a line break into a document. It is a subclass of Object.

DefaultEditorKit.InsertContentAction

The DefaultEditorKit.InsertContentAction class is an inner class of DefaultEditorKit that inserts content into a document. It is a subclass of Object.

DefaultEditorKit.InsertTabAction

The DefaultEditorKit.InsertTabAction class is an inner class of DefaultEditorKit that inserts a tab into a document. It is a subclass of Object.

DefaultEditorKit.PasteAction

The DefaultEditorKit.PasteAction class is an inner class of DefaultEditorKit that pastes content into a document from the clipboard. It is a subclass of Object.

DefaultHighlighter

The DefaultHighlighter class is a subclass of Object that provides a default implementation of the Highlighter interface.

DefaultHighlighter.DefaultHighlightPainter

The DefaultHighlighter.DefaultHighlightPainter class is an inner class of DefaultHighlighter that implements the Highlighter.HighlightPainter interface. It is a subclass of Object.

DefaultStyledDocument

The DefaultStyledDocument class is a subclass of AbstractDocument and implements the StyledDocument interface.

DefaultStyledDocument.AttributeUndoableEdit

The DefaultStyledDocument.AttributeUndoableEdit class is an inner class of DefaultStyledDocument that supports undoable edit operations.

DefaultStyledDocument.ElementSpec

The DefaultStyledDocument.ElementSpec class is an inner class of DefaultStyledDocument that supports the building of document elements. It is a subclass of Object.

DefaultTextUI

The DefaultTextUI class is a subclass of javax.swing.plaf.TextUI that provides a default implementation of the ViewFactory interface. It also implements the java.io.Serializable interface.

EditorKit

The EditorKit class is a subclass of Object that provides a base class for developing a text editor. It implements the java.lang.Cloneable and java.io.Serializable interfaces.

ElementIterator

The ElementIterator class extends Object and implements the Cloneable interface. It is used to iterate through the elements of a document.

FieldView

The FieldView class is a subclass of PlainView that supports a single-line editing view.

GapContent
The GapContent class extends Object and implements the
AbstractDocument.Content and Serializable interfaces to provide an encapsulation of a gap buffer.

IconView
The IconView class is a subclass of View that provides support for viewing an icon.

JTextComponent
The JTextComponent class is a subclass of javax.swing.JComponent that
provides the base class for Swing text components. It implements the
javax.swing.Scrollable and java.awt.accessibility.Accessible interfaces.

JTextComponent.KeyBinding
The JTextComponent.KeyBinding class is an inner class of JTextComponent
that provides key binding support. It is a subclass of Object.

LabelView
The LabelView class is a subclass of View that implements the TabableView interface.

LabelView2D
The LabelView2D class extends View to provide the capability to render a 2D label.

LayeredHighlighter
The LayeredHighlighter class is a subclass of object that implements the
Highlighter interface.

LayeredHighlighter.LayerPainter
The LayeredHighlighter.LayerPainter class is an inner class of
LayeredHighlighter that supports layered highlight rendering.

ParagraphView
The ParagraphView class is a subclass of BoxView that provides the capability
to display styled paragraphs. It implements the TabExpander interface.

PasswordView
The PasswordView class is a subclass of FieldView that provides password-hiding support.

PlainDocument
The PlainDocument class is a subclass of AbstractDocument that supports one
text font and color.

PlainView

The PlainView class is a subclass of View that supports the display of one font and one color. It implements the TabExpander interface.

Position.Bias

The Position.Bias class extends Object to provide the capability to specify a bias in a character position.

Segment

The Segment class is a subclass of Object that represents a text fragment.

SimpleAttributeSet

The SimpleAttributeSet class is a subclass of Object that provides a default implementation of the MutableAttributeSet interface. It also implements the java.io.Serializable interface.

StringContent

The StringContent class is a subclass of Object that provides a default implementation of the AbstractDocument.Content interface. It also implements the java.io.Serializable interface.

StyleConstants

The StyleConstants class is a subclass of Object that provides constants and methods for implementing text, paragraph, and document styles.

StyleConstants.CharacterConstants

The StyleConstants.CharacterConstants class is an inner class of StyleConstants that supports character styles. It is a subclass of Object and implements the AttributeSet.CharacterAttribute interface.

StyleConstants.ColorConstants

The StyleConstants.ColorConstants class is an inner class of StyleConstants that supports text colors. It is a subclass of Object and implements the AttributeSet.ColorAttribute and AttributeSet.CharacterAttribute interfaces.

StyleConstants.FontConstants

The StyleConstants.FontConstants class is an inner class of StyleConstants that supports fonts. It is a subclass of Object and implements the AttributeSet.FontAttribute and AttributeSet.CharacterAttribute interfaces.

StyleConstants.ParagraphConstants

The StyleConstants.ParagraphConstants class is an inner class of StyleConstants that supports paragraph styles. It is a subclass of Object and implements the AttributeSet.ParagraphAttribute interface.

StyleContext

The `StyleContext` class is a subclass of `Object` that provides style constants and resources. It implements the `java.io.Serializable` and `AbstractDocument.AttributeContext` interfaces.

StyledEditorKit

The `StyledEditorKit` class is a subclass of `DefaultEditorKit` that provides a text editor that supports text styles.

StyledEditorKit.AlignmentAction

The `StyledEditorKit.AlignmentAction` class is an inner class of `StyledEditorKit` that supports paragraph alignment. It is a subclass of `StyledEditorKit.StyledTextAction`.

StyledEditorKit.BoldAction

The `StyledEditorKit.BoldAction` class is an inner class of `StyledEditorKit` that supports text bolding. It is a subclass of `StyledEditorKit.StyledTextAction`.

StyledEditorKit.FontFamilyAction

The `StyledEditorKit.FontFamilyAction` class is an inner class of `StyledEditorKit` that supports the use of fonts. It is a subclass of `StyledEditorKit.StyledTextAction`.

StyledEditorKit.FontSizeAction

The `StyledEditorKit.FontSizeAction` class is an inner class of `StyledEditorKit` that supports the control of text font size. It is a subclass of `StyledEditorKit.StyledTextAction`.

StyledEditorKit.ForegroundAction

The `StyledEditorKit.ForegroundAction` class is an inner class of `StyledEditorKit` that supports the setting of text foreground color. It is a subclass of `StyledEditorKit.StyledTextAction`.

StyledEditorKit.ItalicAction

The `StyledEditorKit.ItalicAction` class is an inner class of `StyledEditorKit` that supports the use of italics. It is a subclass of `StyledEditorKit.StyledTextAction`.

StyledEditorKit.StyledTextAction

The `StyledEditorKit.StyledTextAction` class is an inner class of `StyledEditorKit` that supports text operations. It is a subclass of `TextAction`.

StyledEditorKit.UnderlineAction

The `StyledEditorKit.UnderlineAction` class is an inner class of `StyledEditorKit` that supports underlining. It is a subclass of `StyledEditorKit.StyledTextAction`.

TabSet
The TabSet class is a subclass of Object that defines a set of tab stops. It implements the java.io.Serializable interface.

TabStop
The TabStop class is a subclass of Object that encapsulates a single tab stop. It implements the java.io.Serializable interface.

TableView
The TableView class is a subclass of BoxView that provides table support.

TextAction
The TextAction class is a subclass of AbstractAction that is used to define key mappings for text operations.

Utilities
The Utilities class is a subclass of Object that provides utility methods for text operations.

View
The View class is a subclass of Object that defines a view of part of a document.

WrappedPlainView
The WrappedPlainView class is a subclass of BoxView that supports wrapped plain text. It implements the TabExpander interface.

Exceptions and Errors
BadLocationException
The BadLocationException class is a subclass of java.lang.Exception that identifies errors in Document objects.

ChangedCharSetException
The ChangedCharSetException class extends java.io.IOException to signal a change from one character set to another.

PACKAGE javax.swing.text.html
The javax.swing.text.html package consists of 28 classes that provide basic HTML editing capabilities.

Interfaces
None.

Classes
BlockView
The BlockView class extends BoxView to provide the capability to display and HTML block with CSS attributes.

CSS
The CSS class extends Object to define an enumeration of CSS attributes.

CSS.Attribute
The CSS.Attribute class extends Object to define keys for CSS-related attribute sets.

FormView
The FormView class extends ComponentView and implements the ActionListener interface to provide a view implementation for HTML form elements.

HTML
The HTML class extends Object to define constants used in HTML documents.

HTML.Attribute
The HTML.Attribute class extends Object to provide an enumeration of HTML attributes.

HTML.Tag
The HTML.Tag class extends Object to provide an enumeration of HTML tags.

HTML.UnknownTag
The HTML.UnknownTag class extends Object and implements the Serializable interface to identify an unknown HTML tag.

HTMLDocument
The HTMLDocument class extends DefaultStyledDocument to encapsulate an HTML document.

HTMLDocument.Iterator
The HTMLDocument.Iterator class extends Object to provide the capability to iterate over HTML tags.

HTMLEditorKit
The HTMLEditorKit class is a subclass of javax.swing.text.StyledEditorKit that provides a basic HTML editing capability.

HTMLEditorKit.HTMLFactory
The HTMLEditorKit.HTMLFactory class extends Object and implements the ViewFactory interface to provide the capability to build HTML views.

HTMLEditorKit.HTMLTextAction
The HTMLEditorKit.HTMLTextAction class extends StyledEditorKit.StyledTextAction to provide basic support for HTML text editing.

HTMLEditorKit.InsertHTMLTextAction

The HTMLEditorKit.InsertHTMLTextAction class extends Object to
HTMLEditorKit.HTMLTextAction.

HTMLEditorKit.LinkController

The HTMLEditorKit.LinkController class is an inner class of HTMLWriter that
provides basic mouse event-handling support. It is a subclass of
java.awt.event.MouseAdapter.

HTMLEditorKit.Parser

The HTMLEditorKit.Parser class extends HTMLEditorKit.HTMLTextAction to
provide the capability to insert HTML into an existing document.

HTMLEditorKit.ParserCallback

The HTMLEditorKit.ParserCallback class extends Object to support HTML
parsing.

HTMLFrameHyperlinkEvent

The HTMLFrameHyperlinkEvent class extends HyperlinkEvent to signal that an
HTML link is activated.

HTMLWriter

The HTMLWriter class extends AbstractWriter to provide a basic Writer
object for HTML documents.

InlineView

The InlineView class extends LabelView to display inline HTML elements with
CSS attributes.

ListView

The ListView class extends BlockView to provide the capability to display an
HTML list.

MinimalHTMLWriter

The MinimalHTMLWriter class extends AbstractWriter to provide an HTML
Writer that displays HTML that is not produced by the HTML editor kit API.

ObjectView

The ObjectView class extends ComponentView to support the <OBJECT> tag.

Option

The Option class extends Object to provide support for the <OPTION> tag.

ParagraphView

The ParagraphView class extends javax.swing.text.ParagraphView to
display an HTML paragraph with CSS attributes.

StyleSheet

The StyleSheet class extends StyleContext to provide CSS support.

StyleSheet.BoxPainter

The `StyleSheet.BoxPainter` class extends `Object` and implements the `Serializable` interface to support CSS box-like formatting.

StyleSheet.ListPainter

The `StyleSheet.ListPainter` class extends `Object` and implements the `Serializable` interface to support CSS list-like formatting.

Exceptions and Errors

None.

PACKAGE `javax.swing.tree`

The `javax.swing.tree` package provides ten classes and seven interfaces that provide the capability to work with `javax.swing.JTree` components. The `JTree` component is a GUI component that displays a set of hierarchical data as an outline.

Interfaces

MutableTreeNode

The `MutableTreeNode` interface extends the `TreeNode` interface to provide methods for modifying the properties of a `TreeNode` object.

RowMapper

The `RowMapper` interface is used to identify the row corresponding to a `TreeNode` object.

TreeCellEditor

The `TreeCellEditor` interface extends the `javax.swing.CellEditor` interface to support the editing of tree elements.

TreeCellRenderer

The `TreeCellRenderer` interface is used to render the nodes of a tree.

TreeModel

The `TreeModel` interface is used to model the data used to build a tree.

TreeNode

The `TreeNode` interface defines methods for classes that implement the nodes of a tree.

TreeSelectionModel

The `TreeSelectionModel` interface defines constants and methods for working with the current selection state of the nodes of a tree.

Classes

AbstractLayoutCache

The AbstractLayoutCache class extends Object and implements the RowMapper interface to support layout development.

AbstractLayoutCache.NodeDimensions

The AbstractLayoutCache.NodeDimensions class is an inner class of AbstractLayoutCache that provides support for size and positioning in support of layout development.

DefaultMutableTreeNode

The DefaultMutableTreeNode class is a subclass of Object that provides a default, modifiable tree node. It implements the MutableTreeNode, java.lang.Cloneable, and java.io.Serializable interfaces.

DefaultTreeCellEditor

The DefaultTreeCellEditor class extends Object and implements the ActionListener, TreeCellEditor, and TreeSelectionListener interfaces. It provides a basic capability to edit tree cells.

DefaultTreeCellRenderer

The DefaultTreeCellRenderer class extends JLabel and implements the TreeCellRenderer interface to provide the capability to render a tree cell.

DefaultTreeModel

The DefaultTreeModel class is a subclass of Object that provides a default TreeModel implementation. It also implements the java.io.Serializable interface.

DefaultTreeSelectionModel

The DefaultTreeSelectionModel class is a subclass of Object that provides a default TreeSelectionModel implementation. It also implements the java.lang.Cloneable and java.io.Serializable interfaces.

FixedHeightLayoutCache

The FixedHeightLayoutCache class extends AbstractLayoutCache to support fixed height layout.

TreePath

The TreePath class is a subclass of Object that identifies a path to a node of a tree. It implements the java.io.Serializable interface.

VariableHeightLayoutCache

The VariableHeightLayoutCache class extends AbstractLayoutCache to support variable height layout.

Exceptions and Errors

ExpandVetoException

The `ExpandVetoException` class extends `java.lang.Exception` to provide the capability to veto the expanding or collapsing of a tree.

PACKAGE `javax.swing.undo`

The `javax.swing.undo` package provides five classes and two interfaces that support the implementation of undo and redo capabilities.

Interfaces

StateEditable

The `StateEditable` interface is implemented by classes whose state can be undone or redone by the `StateEdit` class.

UndoableEdit

The `UndoableEdit` interface is implemented by classes that support the undoing or redoing of edit operations.

Classes

AbstractUndoableEdit

The `AbstractUndoableEdit` class is a subclass of `Object` that provides an abstract implementation of the `UndoableEdit` interface.

CompoundEdit

The `CompoundEdit` class is a subclass of `AbstractUndoableEdit` that provides the capability to implement compound undo/redo operations.

StateEdit

The `StateEdit` class is a subclass of `AbstractUndoableEdit` that supports undo/redo operations on objects that change state.

UndoManager

The `UndoManager` class is a subclass of `CompoundEdit` that provides for thread-safe undo/redo operations. It implements the `javax.swing.event.UndoableEditListener` interface.

UndoableEditSupport

The `UndoableEditSupport` class is a subclass of `Object` that supports the management of undoable editing operations.

Exceptions and Errors

CannotRedoException

The `CannotRedoException` class is a subclass of `RuntimeException` that indicates a redo operation cannot be performed.

CannotUndoException

The CannotUndoException class is a subclass of RuntimeException that indicates an undo operation cannot be performed.

PACKAGE org.omg.CORBA

The org.omg.CORBA package consists of 40 classes and 29 interfaces that implement the foundation for supporting Java-CORBA integration.

Interfaces

ARG_IN

The ARG_IN interface identifies a method input argument.

ARG_INOUT

The ARG_INOUT interface identifies an argument that may be used as both an input and an output in a method invocation.

ARG_OUT

The ARG_OUT interface identifies a method output argument.

BAD_POLICY

The BAD_POLICY interface is used to indicate a bad policy.

BAD_POLICY_TYPE

The BAD_POLICY_TYPE interface is used to indicate a bad policy type.

BAD_POLICY_VALUE

The BAD_POLICY_VALUE interface is used to indicate a bad policy value.

CTX_RESTRICT_SCOPE

The CTX_RESTRICT_SCOPE interface is used as a flag to restrict the search scope of the get_values() method.

Current

The Current interface extends the Object interface to provide the capability to access information associated with a particular thread of execution.

DomainManager

The Current interface extends the Object interface to provide the capability to manage the policy associated with a particular domain.

DynAny

The Current interface extends the Object interface to support the dynamic traversal of CORBA Any values.

DynArray

The Current interface extends the Object and DynAny interfaces to support arrays.

DynEnum

The Current interface extends the Object and DynAny interfaces to support IDL enum types.

DynFixed

The Current interface extends the Object and DynAny interfaces to support IDL fixed types.

DynSequence

The Current interface extends the Object and DynAny interfaces to support IDL sequence types.

DynStruct

The Current interface extends the Object and DynAny interfaces to support IDL structs.

DynUnion

The Current interface extends the Object and DynAny interfaces to support IDL union types.

DynValue

The Current interface extends the Object and DynAny interfaces to support name value pairs.

IDLType

The IDLType interface encapsulates an IDL IDLType. It extends the Object and IRObject interfaces.

IRObject

The IRObject interface encapsulates an interface repository object. It extends the Object interface.

Object

The Object interface represents a CORBA object reference.

Policy

The Policy interface extends the Object interface to provide a basic mechanism for policy implementation.

PRIVATE_MEMBER

The PRIVATE_MEMBER interface extends the Object interface to support the implementation of private members.

PUBLIC_MEMBER

The PUBLIC_MEMBER interface extends the Object interface to support the implementation of public members.

UNSUPPORTED_POLICY
The UNSUPPORTED_POLICY interface extends the Object interface to support the specification of unsupported policy.

UNSUPPORTED_POLICY_VALUE
The UNSUPPORTED_POLICY_VALUE interface extends the Object interface to support the specification of unsupported policy.

VM_ABSTRACT
The VM_ABSTRACT interface extends the Object interface to support the specification of an abstract virtual machine.

VM_CUSTOM
The VM_CUSTOM interface extends the Object interface to support the specification of a custom virtual machine.

VM_NONE
The VM_NONE interface extends the Object interface to support the specification of an non-existent virtual machine.

VM_TRUNCATABLE
The VM_TRUNCATABLE interface extends the Object interface to support the specification of a truncatable virtual machine.

Classes

Any
The Any class is a subclass of Object that acts as a container for data of any primitive IDL type.

AnyHolder
The AnyHolder class is a subclass of Object that acts as a holder for Any objects used as INOUT and OUT method parameters.

BooleanHolder
The BooleanHolder class is a subclass of Object that is used to hold boolean values for use as INOUT and OUT arguments.

ByteHolder
The ByteHolder class is a subclass of Object that is used to hold byte values for use as INOUT and OUT arguments.

CharHolder
The CharHolder class is a subclass of Object that is used to hold char values for use as INOUT and OUT arguments.

CompletionStatus
The CompletionStatus class is a subclass of Object that identifies the completion status of a method that throws a SystemException.

Context

The Context class is a subclass of Object that provides information about the context in which a method invocation request takes place.

ContextList

The ContextList class is a subclass of Object that specifies properties associated with a Context object.

DefinitionKind

The DefinitionKind class is a subclass of Object that is used to hold Boolean types for use as INOUT and OUT arguments.

DoubleHolder

The DoubleHolder class is a subclass of Object that is used to hold double values for use as INOUT and OUT arguments.

DynamicImplementation

The DynamicImplementation class is a subclass of org.omg.CORBA.portable.ObjectImpl that provides support for the dynamic servant interface.

Environment

The Environment class is a subclass of Object that is used to make exceptions available to the client that requested a method invocation.

ExceptionList

The ExceptionList class is a subclass of Object that lists the exceptions that can be thrown by a method.

FixedHolder

The FixedHolder class is a subclass of Object that is used to hold fixed IDL type values for use as INOUT and OUT arguments.

FloatHolder

The FloatHolder class is a subclass of Object that is used to hold float values for use as INOUT and OUT arguments.

IntHolder

The IntHolder class is a subclass of Object that is used to hold int values for use as INOUT and OUT arguments.

LongHolder

The LongHolder class is a subclass of Object that is used to hold long values for use as INOUT and OUT arguments.

NVList

The NVList class is a subclass of Object that provides a list of NamedValue objects.

NamedValue

The NamedValue class is a subclass of Object that is used to describe method arguments and return values.

NameValuePair

The NameValuePair class extends Object to hold names and values of IDL structs in the DynStruct API.

ORB

The ORB class is a subclass of Object that serves as the CORBA object request broker.

ObjectHolder

The ObjectHolder class is a subclass of Object that is used to hold object references for use as INOUT and OUT arguments.

Principal

The Principal class is a subclass of Object that identifies a client making a remote method invocation request.

PrincipalHolder

The PrincipalHolder class is a subclass of Object that is used to hold Principal objects for use as INOUT and OUT arguments.

Request

The Request class is a subclass of Object that encapsulates a client request to invoke a remote method.

ServerRequest

The ServerRequest class is a subclass of Object that encapsulates a dynamic skeleton interface request.

ServiceDetail

The ServiceDetail class extends Object that implements the IDLEntity interface. It is used to provide service information.

ServiceDetailHelper

The ServiceDetailHelper class extends Object to provide helper support for service detail information.

ServiceInformation

The ServiceInformation class extends Object to provide information to a service information IDL struct.

ServiceInformationHelper

The ServiceInformationHelper class extends Object to provide helper support for the service information IDL struct.

ServiceInformationHolder

The ServiceInformationHolder class extends Object to provide holder support for the service information IDL struct.

SetOverrideType

The SetOverrideType class extends Object and implements the IDLEntity interface to provide support for the override type.

ShortHolder

The ShortHolder class is a subclass of Object that is used to hold short values for use as INOUT and OUT arguments.

StringHolder

The StringHolder class is a subclass of Object that is used to hold String objects for use as INOUT and OUT arguments.

StructMember

The StructMember class is a subclass of Object that describes a member of a CORBA data structure.

TCKind

The TCKind class is a subclass of Object that encapsulates the IDL TCKind object.

TypeCode

The TypeCode class is a subclass of Object that is used to identify a primitive IDL value type.

TypeCodeHolder

The TypeCodeHolder class is a subclass of Object that is used to hold TypeCode objects for use as INOUT and OUT arguments.

UnionMember

The UnionMember class is a subclass of Object that provides support for IDL union constructs.

ValueMember

The ValueMember class extends Object and implements the IDLEntity interface to provide an interface repository description of the value object.

Exceptions and Errors

BAD_CONTEXT

The BAD_CONTEXT class is a subclass of SystemException that supports the CORBA BAD_CONTEXT exception.

BAD_INV_ORDER

The BAD_INV_ORDER class is a subclass of SystemException that supports the CORBA BAD_INV_ORDER exception.

BAD_OPERATION
The BAD_OPERATION class is a subclass of **SystemException** that supports the CORBA BAD_OPERATION exception.

BAD_PARAM
The BAD_PARAM class is a subclass of **SystemException** that supports the CORBA BAD_PARAM exception.

BAD_TYPECODE
The BAD_TYPECODE class is a subclass of **SystemException** that supports the CORBA BAD_TYPECODE exception.

Bounds
The Bounds class is a subclass of **UserException** that provides support for the user-defined bounds exception.

COMM_FAILURE
The COMM_FAILURE class is a subclass of **SystemException** that supports the CORBA COMM_FAILURE exception.

DATA_CONVERSION
The DATA_CONVERSION class is a subclass of **SystemException** that supports the CORBA DATA_CONVERSION exception.

FREE_MEM
The FREE_MEM class is a subclass of **SystemException** that supports the CORBA FREE_MEM exception.

IMP_LIMIT
The IMP_LIMIT class is a subclass of **SystemException** that supports the CORBA IMP_LIMIT exception.

INITIALIZE
The INITIALIZE class is a subclass of **SystemException** that supports the CORBA INITIALIZE exception.

INTERNAL
The INTERNAL class is a subclass of **SystemException** that supports the CORBA INTERNAL exception.

INTF_REPOS
The INTF_REPOS class is a subclass of **SystemException** that supports the CORBA INTF_REPOS exception.

INVALID_TRANSACTION
The INVALID_TRANSACTION class is a subclass of **SystemException** that supports the CORBA INVALID_TRANSACTION exception.

INV_FLAG
The INV_FLAG class is a subclass of **SystemException** that supports the CORBA INV_FLAG exception.

INV_IDENT
The INV_IDENT class is a subclass of **SystemException** that supports the CORBA INV_IDENT exception.

INV_OBJREF
The INV_OBJREF class is a subclass of **SystemException** that supports the CORBA INV_OBJREF exception.

INV_POLICY
The INV_POLICY class is a subclass of **SystemException** that supports the CORBA INV_POLICY exception.

MARSHAL
The MARSHAL class is a subclass of **SystemException** that supports the CORBA MARSHAL exception.

NO_IMPLEMENT
The NO_IMPLEMENT class is a subclass of **SystemException** that supports the CORBA NO_IMPLEMENT exception.

NO_MEMORY
The NO_MEMORY class is a subclass of **SystemException** that supports the CORBA NO_MEMORY exception.

NO_PERMISSION
The NO_PERMISSION class is a subclass of **SystemException** that supports the CORBA NO_PERMISSION exception.

NO_RESOURCES
The NO_RESOURCES class is a subclass of **SystemException** that supports the CORBA NO_RESOURCES exception.

NO_RESPONSE
The NO_RESPONSE class is a subclass of **SystemException** that supports the CORBA NO_RESPONSE exception.

OBJECT_NOT_EXIST
The OBJECT_NOT_EXIST class is a subclass of **SystemException** that supports the CORBA OBJECT_NOT_EXIST exception.

OBJ_ADAPTER
The OBJ_ADAPTER class is a subclass of **SystemException** that supports the CORBA OBJ_ADAPTER exception.

PERSIST_STORE

The PERSIST_STORE class is a subclass of SystemException that supports the CORBA PERSIST_STORE exception.

PolicyError

The PolicyError class extends UserException to provide support for identifying policy-related errors.

SystemException

The SystemException class is a subclass of java.lang.RuntimeException that serves as the base class for implementing CORBA exceptions.

TRANSACTION_REQUIRED

The TRANSACTION_REQUIRED class is a subclass of SystemException that supports the CORBA TRANSACTION_REQUIRED exception.

TRANSACTION_ROLLEDBACK

The TRANSACTION_ROLLEDBACK class is a subclass of SystemException that supports the CORBA TRANSACTION_ROLLEDBACK exception.

TRANSIENT

The TRANSIENT class is a subclass of SystemException that supports the CORBA TRANSIENT exception.

UNKNOWN

The UNKNOWN class is a subclass of SystemException that supports the CORBA UNKNOWN exception.

UnknownUserException

The UnknownUserException class is a subclass of UserException that identifies an unknown user exception returned by the remote server.

UserException

The UserException class is a subclass of java.lang.Exception that supports the implementation of IDL-defined user exceptions.

WrongTransaction

The WrongTransaction class is a subclass of UserException that identifies a requested transaction as being from an incorrect transaction scope.

PACKAGE org.omg.CORBA.DynAnyPackage

The org.omg.CORBA.DynAnyPackage package defines four exceptions, which are used to support the DynAny interface.

Interfaces

None.

Classes

None.

Exceptions and Errors

Invalid

The Invalid class extends UserException to indicate that a bad DynAny or Any
is passed as a parameter.

InvalidSeq

The InvalidSeq class extends UserException to indicate an invalid array
sequence.

InvalidValue

The InvalidValue class extends UserException to a bad DynAny value was
encountered.

TypeMismatch

The TypeMismatch class extends UserException to indicate that the type of an
object does not match the type being accessed.

PACKAGE org.omg.CORBA.ORBPackage

The org.omg.CORBA.ORBPackage package defines the InconsistentTypeCode
and InvalidName exceptions.

Interfaces

None.

Classes

None.

Exceptions and Errors

InconsistentTypeCode

The InconsistentTypeCode class is a subclass of
org.omg.CORBA.UserException that indicates an attempt to create a dynamic
any with a type code that does not match the particular subclass of DynAny.

InvalidName

The InvalidName class is a subclass of org.omg.CORBA.UserException that
indicates that the ORB was passed a name for which there is no initial reference.

PACKAGE org.omg.CORBA.TypeCodePackage

The org.omg.CORBA.TypeCodePackage package defines the BadKind and
Bounds exceptions, which are used to signal exceptions related to type usage
and constraints.

Interfaces

None.

Classes

None.

Exceptions and Errors

BadKind

The BadKind class is a subclass of org.omg.CORBA.UserException that indicates that an inappropriate operation was attempted on an org.omg.CORBA.TypeCode object.

Bounds

The Bounds class is a subclass of org.omg.CORBA.UserException that indicates that an out-of-bounds exception occurred as the result of an operation on an org.omg.CORBA.TypeCode object.

PACKAGE org.omg.CORBA.portable

The org.omg.CORBA.portable package consists of five classes and four interfaces that are used to support vendor-specific CORBA implementations.

Interfaces

IDLEntity

The IDLEntity interface extends the Serializable interface to indicate that an implementing class is a Java value type from IDL that has a corresponding helper class.

InvokeHandler

The InvokeHandler interface provides the capability to invoke a ResponseHandler object.

ResponseHandler

The ResponseHandler interface provides the capability to respond to a method invocation.

Streamable

The Streamable interface provides methods for marshalling and unmarshalling holders to and from streams.

Classes

Delegate

The Delegate class is a subclass of Object that specifies a portable API for ORB-vendor-specific implementation of the org.omg.CORBA.Object methods.

InputStream

The `InputStream` class is a subclass of `Object` that provides methods for reading IDL types from streams.

ObjectImpl

The `ObjectImpl` class is a subclass of `Object` that provides a default implementation of the `org.omg.CORBA.Object` interface.

OutputStream

The `OutputStream` class is a subclass of `Object` that provides methods for writing IDL types to streams.

ServantObject

The `ServantObject` class extends `Object` to encapsulate a CORBA servant.

Exceptions and Errors

ApplicationException

The `ApplicationException` class extends `java.lang.Exception` to indicate that an exception occurred in the current application.

RemarshalException

The `RemarshalException` class extends `java.lang.Exception` to indicate that an exception occurred while remarshalling a method invocation.

PACKAGE org.omg.CosNaming

The `org.omg.CosNaming` package consists of 22 classes and two interfaces that implement a tree-structured naming service.

Interfaces

BindingIterator

The `BindingIterator` interface extends the `org.omg.CORBA.Object` interface and provides the capability to iterate through a list of name-object bindings.

NamingContext

The `NamingContext` interface extends the `org.omg.CORBA.Object` interface and provides access to the naming service.

Classes

Binding

The `Binding` class is a subclass of `Object` that associates a name with an object.

BindingHelper

The `BindingHelper` class is a subclass of `Object` that provides static methods for manipulating bindings.

BindingHolder

The BindingHolder class is a subclass of Object that holds the value of a Binding object.

BindingIteratorHelper

The BindingIteratorHelper class is a subclass of Object that provides static methods for manipulating binding iterators.

BindingIteratorHolder

The BindingIteratorHolder class is a subclass of Object that holds the value of a binding iterator.

BindingListHelper

The BindingListHelper class is a subclass of Object that provides static methods for manipulating binding lists.

BindingListHolder

The BindingListHolder class is a subclass of Object that holds the value of a binding list.

BindingType

The BindingType class is a subclass of Object that identifies the type of a Binding object.

BindingTypeHelper

The BindingTypeHelper class is a subclass of Object that provides static methods for manipulating binding types.

BindingTypeHolder

The BindingTypeHolder class is a subclass of Object that holds the value of a binding type.

IstringHelper

The IstringHelper class is a subclass of Object that provides static methods for manipulating strings.

NameComponent

The NameComponent class is a subclass of Object that is used to build hierarchical names.

NameComponentHelper

The NameComponentHelper class is a subclass of Object that provides static methods for manipulating name components.

NameComponentHolder

The NameComponentHolder class is a subclass of Object that holds the value of a name component. It implements the **org.omg.CORBA.portable.Streamable** interface.

NameHelper

The NameHelper class is a subclass of Object that provides static methods for manipulating names.

NameHolder

The NameHolder class is a subclass of Object that holds the value of a name. It implements the org.omg.CORBA.portable.Streamable interface.

NamingContextHelper

The NamingContextHelper class is a subclass of Object that provides static methods for manipulating name contexts.

NamingContextHolder

The NamingContextHolder class is a subclass of Object that holds the value of a naming context. It implements the org.omg.CORBA.portable.Streamable interface.

_BindingIteratorImplBase

The _BindingIteratorImplBase class is a subclass of org.omg.CORBA.DynamicImplementation that supports the implementation of binding iterators. It implements the BindingIterator interface.

_BindingIteratorStub

The BindingIteratorStub class is a subclass of org.omg.CORBA.portable.ObjectImpl that supports the implementation of a binding iterator stub.

_NamingContextImplBase

The _NamingContextImplBase class is a subclass of org.omg.CORBA.DynamicImplementation that supports the implementation of naming contexts. It implements the NamingContext interface.

_NamingContextStub

The NamingContextStub class is a subclass of org.omg.CORBA.portable.ObjectImpl that supports the implementation of a naming context stub.

Exceptions and Errors

None.

PACKAGE
org.omg.CosNaming.NamingContextPackage

The org.omg.CosNaming.NamingContextPackage package consists of 13 classes that implement aspects of the naming service's name context. The name context implements nodes within the tree-structured naming scheme.

Interfaces

None.

Classes

AlreadyBoundHelper

The `AlreadyBoundHelper` class is a subclass of `Object` that provides support for the `AlreadyBound` exception.

AlreadyBoundHolder

The `AlreadyBoundHolder` class is a subclass of `Object` that provides support for the `AlreadyBound` exception. It implements the `org.omg.CORBA.portable.Streamable` interface.

CannotProceedHelper

The `CannotProceedHelper` class is a subclass of `Object` that provides support for the `CannotProceed` exception.

CannotProceedHolder

The `CannotProceedHolder` class is a subclass of `Object` that provides support for the `CannotProceed` exception. It implements the `org.omg.CORBA.portable.Streamable` interface.

InvalidNameHelper

The `InvalidNameHelper` class is a subclass of `Object` that provides support for the `InvalidName` exception.

InvalidNameHolder

The `InvalidNameHolder` class is a subclass of `Object` that provides support for the `InvalidName` exception. It implements the `org.omg.CORBA.portable.Streamable` interface.

NotEmptyHelper

The `NotEmptyHelper` class is a subclass of `Object` that provides support for the `NotEmpty` exception.

NotEmptyHolder

The `NotEmptyHolder` class is a subclass of `Object` that provides support for the `NotEmpty` exception. It implements the `org.omg.CORBA.portable.Streamable` interface.

NotFoundHelper

The `NotFoundHelper` class is a subclass of `Object` that provides support for the `NotFound` exception.

NotFoundHolder

The `NotFoundHolder` class is a subclass of `Object` that provides support for the `NotFound` exception.

NotFoundReason

The NotFoundReason class is a subclass of **Object** that provides support for the NotFound exception.

NotFoundReasonHelper

The NotFoundReasonHelper class is a subclass of **Object** that provides support for the NotFoundReason object.

NotFoundReasonHolder

The NotFoundReasonHolder class is a subclass of **Object** that provides storage for a NotFoundReason object. It implements the org.omg.CORBA.portable.Streamable interface.

Exceptions and Errors

AlreadyBound

The AlreadyBound class is a subclass of **org.omg.CORBA.UserException** that identifies a name as being already bound with an object.

CannotProceed

The CannotProceed class is a subclass of **org.omg.CORBA.UserException** that signals that the CORBA implementation has come to a standstill.

InvalidName

The InvalidName class is a subclass of **org.omg.CORBA.UserException** that indicates that an invalid name has been used.

NotEmpty

The NotEmpty class is a subclass of **org.omg.CORBA.UserException** that signals a non-empty reference was encountered when one was not expected.

NotFound

The NotFound class is a subclass of **org.omg.CORBA.UserException** that signals that a referenced name cannot be found.

INDEX

Symbols

The Authoritative Encyclopedia of Computing

Resource Centers
Books & Software
Personal Bookshelf
WWW Yellow Pages
Online Learning
Special Offers
Site Search
Industry News

▶ *Choose the online ebooks that you can view from your personal workspace on our site.*

About MCP   Site Map   Product Support

Turn to the *Authoritative* Encyclopedia of Computing

You'll find over 150 full text books online, hundreds of shareware/freeware applications, online computing classes and 10 computing resource centers full of expert advice from the editors and publishers of:

- Adobe Press
- BradyGAMES
- Cisco Press
- Hayden Books
- Lycos Press
- New Riders

- Que
- Que Education & Training
- Sams Publishing
- Waite Group Press
- Ziff-Davis Press

mcp.com
The Authoritative Encyclopedia of Computing

Get the best information and learn about latest developments in:

- Design
- Graphics and Multimedia
- Enterprise Computing and DBMS
- General Internet Information
- Operating Systems
- Networking and Hardware
- PC and Video Gaming
- Productivity Applications
- Programming
- Web Programming and Administration
- Web Publishing

When you're looking for computing information, consult the authority.
The Authoritative Encyclopedia of Computing at mcp.com.

Other Related Titles

Java 1.2 Unleashed
Jamie Jaworski
ISBN: 1-57521-389-3
$49.99

JFC Unleashed
Michael Foley and Mark McCulley
ISBN: 0-7897-1466-3
$39.99

Java Distributed Objects Unleashed
Bill McCarty
ISBN: 0-672-31537-8
$49.99

Pure JFC Swing
Satyaraj Pantham
ISBN: 0-672-31423-1
$19.99

Mitchel Waite Signature Series: Data Structures and Algorithms in Java
Robert LaFore
ISBN: 1-57169-095-6
$49.99

Mitchel Waite Signature Series: Object-Oriented Programming in Java
Bill McCarty and Stephen Gilbert
ISBN: 1-57169-086-7
$59.99

Using Visual J++ 6
Scott Mulloy
ISBN: 0-7897-1400-0
$29.99

Java 1.2 Class Libraries Unleashed
Krishna Sankar
ISBN: 0-7897-1292-X
$39.99

SAMS

www.samspublishing.com

All prices are subject to change.

50% OFF ONE-YEAR SUBSCRIPTION

Don't Miss a Single Issue!

- **Interactive Java**
- **Applet Development**
- **CORBACorner**
- **Java Class Libraries**
- **Interviews with Java Gurus**
- **Product Reviews with the JDJ World Class Award**
- **Tips & Techniques • Infinite Java • Book Reviews**
- **Java Animation • Games & Graphics... and Much More**

www.JavaDevelopersJournal.com

SYS-CON Publications, Inc.
39 East Central Ave Pearl River, NY 10965
Tel: 914-735-1900   Fax: 914-735-3922

JAVA DEVELOPER'S JOURNAL **JDJ** ★★★★★★★ WORLD CLASS AWARD

50% OFF CERTIFICATE

❑ **1 Year JDJ $39.99 50% (12 Issues)**

❑ **2 Years $79 (24 Issues)**

❑ **FREE Trial Subscription (Three Months)** With No Obligation

SAVE 50% on a 1 year subscription if you subscribe NOW! – ONLY $39.99

Name:	❑ M/C ❑ Visa ❑ Amex
Title:	Card#:
Company:	Expiration Date:
Address:	Signature:
City: St: Zip:	
Tel: Fax:	

Java Developer's Journal one year is 11 regular monthly issues plus 1 additional special issue for a total of 12 issues in all. JDJ basic annual subscription rate is $49.00 in American funds, and must be drawn on a U.S. Bank. NY, NJ, CT residents, please add sales tax. Canada/Mexico $69; all other countries $99. Subscription begins upon receipt of payment. Please allow 6-8 weeks for delivery of first issue. International subscriptions must be payable in U.S. dollars.

As an owner of this book, you're eligible for a special offer from Inprise and Macmillan Computer Press

Get the latest in Java™ technology with new Borland® JBuilder™ 2. JBuilder 2 includes JFC/Swing, JDK 1.2, JDK Switching, 200+ JavaBeans™ with source, BeansExpress,™ BeanInsight,™ CodeInsight, Pure JDBC, and support for CORBA, RMI, Enterprise JavaBeans, Servlets, and more.

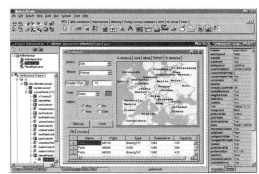

Visually create JDBC database applications with DataExpress. Full support for master-detail lookups, sorting, bi-directional cursors, transactions, and more.

JBuilder 2 Standard: $99.95. Includes 100 JavaBeans
JBuilder 2 Professional: $249.95 (Reg. $799). Includes 200+ JavaBeans with source + Pure JDBC integrated database tools.
JBuilder 2 Client/Server Suite: $1,999 (Reg. $2,499). Includes VisiBroker™ for Java, Deployment Server for Java, Native drivers to DBMS, Enterprise JavaBeans, Servlets, CORBA, RMI, etc.

JBuilder 2 Professional
Visual development for Java with integrated database tools

JBuilder 2 Professional is the most comprehensive set of visual development tools for creating Pure Java business and database applications. You get everything in JBuilder Standard, including JDK Switching, CodeInsight, BeansExpress, and BeanInsight, plus: Pure Java DataExpress components, complete JDBC connectivity, high-performance grid control with source, 200+ JBCL and JFC/Swing beans with source, data-aware dbSwing beans with source, Servlet Wizard, command-line tools, and Local InterBase® Server.

Additional Features

Only JBuilder 2 features 100% Pure Java Code creation: no markers, no proprietary code added, and no platform agenda.

Move up to JBuilder 2 and start writing 100% Pure Java code today! Call Inprise at 1-800-645-4559, offer code 1541. Or visit us at www.inprise.com/jbuilder/ now!

Instant access to the best minds in the business, and you get all the credit.

Get immediate access to thousands of pages of reference material on the technologies you need most. ❶ Develop intense applications using exclusive online pre-releases of major technical books. Click-search and you get real working ❷ answers — even source code that you paste directly into your program. Achieve serious status ❸ faster by flying through anything they throw at you. Just by ❹ subscribing to the most current working knowledge in the business, ❺ EarthWeb's ITKnowledgeSM.

Get your 2-week FREE trial* today at www.bk22.itksub.com
Do it before December 31, 1998 and get the introductory rate of only $95
(save $200 off the regular price).

*Browse table of contents and chapter 1 of all books free of charge. Further access requires credit card information, however fee will not be processed until the free trial period expires. Cancel up to 24 hours before billing date. Corporate volume discounts are available. ©1998 EarthWeb Inc. All rights reserved. EarthWeb's ITKnowledge is a service mark of EarthWeb, Inc. EarthWeb and the EarthWeb logo are registered trademarks of EarthWeb Inc.

EARTHWEB
Go further *faster*

What's on the CD

Code

Complete code listings from the book.

3rd Party Products

- JBuilder Publisher's Edition—The most comprehensive set of visual development tools for creating Pure Java business and database applications.

- KAWA—A powerful and intuitive environment for Java development.

- Bluette—Compile and run source programs and browse class hierarchy and members.

- The Gamelet Toolkit—A framework of classes and interfaces used for developing arcade style video games and entertainment applets

- Java Class Disassembler (JCD)—Win32 GUI program that allows you to view the contents of Java class files.

- CooCoo—Full java chat and communications program.

Read This Before Opening Software

By opening this package, you are agreeing to be bound by the following:

This software is copyrighted and all rights are reserved by the publisher and its licensers. You are licensed to use this software on a single computer. You may copy the software for backup or archival purposes only. Making copies of the software for any other purpose is a violation of United States copyright laws. THIS SOFTWARE IS SOLD AS IS, WITHOUT WARRANTY OF ANY KIND, EITHER EXPRESSED OR IMPLIED, INCLUDING BUT NOT LIMITED TO THE IMPLIED WARRANTIES OF MERCHANTABILITY AND FITNESS FOR A PARTICULAR PURPOSE. Neither the publisher nor its dealers and distributors nor its licensers assume any liability for any alleged or actual damages arising from the use of this software. (Some states do not allow exclusion of implied warranties, so the exclusion may not apply to you.)

The entire contents of this disc and the compilation of the software are copyrighted and protected by United States copyright laws. The individual programs on the disc are copyrighted by the authors or owners of each program. Each program has its own use permissions and limitations. To use each program, you must follow the individual requirements and restrictions detailed for each. Do not use a program if you do not agree to follow its licensing agreement.